Corporate Sustainability Leadership

Corporate sustainability, now regarded as a vitally important topic on the agenda for businesses, has in recent years not only become embedded in postgraduate study, but is now also widely taught at the undergraduate level in business schools. *Corporate Sustainability Leadership* reflects the growing need for an accessible text at all levels of study. The book brings the topic of corporate sustainability fully up to date by incorporating new directions in the areas of corporate responsibility and sustainability.

Written by the authors of the highly successful *Understanding Business Ethics*, this book provides a primary resource for any undergraduate or graduate corporate sustainability class. Unlike other textbooks in corporate sustainability, which are often edited collections from multiple authors, this book develops themes throughout each chapter using a consistent voice to ensure an integrative learning experience for both students and instructors. With ten chapters and ten cases, all of which are supplemented with online test banks, instructor guides, and PowerPoint slides, this textbook provides enough content for a complete class on corporate sustainability.

Using stakeholder theory as a foundation, *Corporate Sustainability Leadership* allows readers to develop a better understanding of how organizations can effectively satisfy the needs of their critical stakeholders. It addresses the issues of corporate sustainability from both a micro and macro perspective. Micro issues related to corporate sustainability include leadership, organizational change, management decision making, human resource organizational strategies, organizational ethics, organizational culture, corporate sustainability reporting, corporate sustainability performance, and corporate compliance. The macro issues addressed include suppliers, corporate sustainability communications, consumers, the natural environment, governments, NGOs, and the developing world. In addition, there are ten unique company cases from organizations that are household names, such as Bayer, Shell, Volkswagen, and Dow Chemical.

Peter A. Stanwick is an Associate Professor in the Department of Management at Auburn University. He is the co-author of *Understanding Business Ethics*, now in its third edition. He is also the co-author of *International Management: A Stakeholder Approach*.

Sarah D. Stanwick is an Associate Professor in the School of Accountancy at Auburn University. She is the co-author of *Understanding Business Ethics*, now in its third edition. She is also the co-author of *International Management: A Stakeholder Approach*.

"In their latest work, *Corporate Sustainability Leadership*, Drs. Peter and Sarah Stanwick have crafted an exceptionally well researched, well written and relatable guide that will be an enormous benefit for professors and their students. [They] have gone much deeper into concepts and topics such as corporate leadership, stakeholder relationship and ethical considerations than is typical for a more general business textbook. For any student, any professor, any scholar of corporate leadership, this textbook will provide a depth and breadth of information."

Scott Kenneth Campbell, PhD

Corporate Sustainability Leadership

Peter A. Stanwick and
Sarah D. Stanwick

Routledge
Taylor & Francis Group

LONDON AND NEW YORK

First published 2021
by Routledge
2 Park Square, Milton Park, Abingdon, Oxon OX14 4RN

and by Routledge
52 Vanderbilt Avenue, New York, NY 10017

Routledge is an imprint of the Taylor & Francis Group, an informa business

British Library Cataloguing-in-Publication Data
A catalogue record for this book is available from the British Library

Library of Congress Cataloging-in-Publication Data
Names: Stanwick, Peter Allen, author. | Stanwick, Sarah D. (Sarah Dunn) author.
Title: Corporate sustainability leadership / Peter A Stanwick and Sarah D Stanwick.
Description: First Edition. | New York : Routledge, 2020. | Includes bibliographical references and index. |
Identifiers: LCCN 2020002341 (print) | LCCN 2020002342 (ebook) |
ISBN 9781138494985 (hardback) | ISBN 9781138495005 (paperback) |
ISBN 9781351024983 (ebook)
Subjects: LCSH: Sustainable development–Economic aspects. | Organizational effectiveness. | Organizational change. | Leadership.
Classification: LCC HC79.E5 S71153 2020 (print) | LCC HC79.E5 (ebook) |
DDC 658.4/092–dc23
LC record available at https://lccn.loc.gov/2020002341
LC ebook record available at https://lccn.loc.gov/2020002342

ISBN: 978-1-138-49498-5 (hbk)
ISBN: 978-1-138-49500-5 (pbk)
ISBN: 978-1-351-02498-3 (ebk)

Typeset in Bembo
by Swales & Willis, Exeter, Devon, UK

Contents

1 The role of corporate sustainability in today's society

Introduction

Just as society has evolved over time, so have the responsibilities of corporations. The role of corporate sustainability in a firm is a dynamic one in which managers must constantly address the ever-changing needs of its stakeholders in order to ensure the firm's long-term sustainability. In this opening chapter, a number of fundamental concepts related to corporate sustainability are addressed. These concepts include: how business titans from the past addressed philanthropy and corporate sustainability; the evolution of corporate sustainability; why corporate sustainability is important for firms; the criticisms related to corporate sustainability; conscious capitalism; the corporate sustainability pyramid; the description of stakeholder theory; the identification of critical stakeholders; stakeholder engagement; stakeholder dialogues and corporate sustainability; and stakeholder theory and corporate sustainability. The chapter begins with an opening vignette discussing Merck's philanthropic actions related to curing river blindness. The chapter finishes with a description of Merck's unethical actions related to its painkiller Vioxx.

Opening vignette: Merck's effort to cure river blindness

Onchocerciasis, which is commonly referred to as river blindness, occurs in fast-flowing rivers that provide a breeding ground for blackflies. Blackfly bites can transmit worms into the human body. The worms grow into adults and cluster in nodules to produce large quantities of young worms. The young worms cause inflammation in the human body, leading to itching, blindness, epilepsy, and premature death.[1] River blindness historically has occurred in 36 countries in Africa, Latin America, and Yemen.[2]

A scientist for the Kitasato Institute in Tokyo, Dr. Satoshi Omura, discovered a bacterium called Streptomyces which was able to kill the parasites causing river blindness. Dr. Omura sent samples of the bacteria to Dr. William Campbell who worked for Merck pharmaceuticals. Dr. Campbell developed the drug Ivermectin from a compound in the bacteria culture sent by Dr. Omura which could be used to cure river blindness.[3] The drug was a variant of Avermectin, which was originally developed to kill parasites in dogs.

The development of the drug was championed by Roy Valgelos at Merck who had been promoted to Chief Executive Officer from his previous position as head of research.[4] In 1987, Merck announced that it had formed a partnership with the World Health Organization (WHO) to distribute the drug for no charge under the brand name of Mectizan for as long as the drug was needed to fight the disease. This was a critical decision for Merck to make since most of the people who needed the drug could not afford to purchase the drug.[5] The drug is taken in one dose and paralyzes and sterilizes the parasitic worms. The worms can survive in a human body for many years and can grow to the length of two feet while producing millions of larvae. The drug cannot reverse the disease of individuals who are already blind, but it can stop people from becoming blind due to the disease.[6]

In 1998, Merck expanded its Mectizan program to include the treatment of Lymphatic Filariasis (LF), which is also known as Elephantiasis. LF occurs through parasitic infection from mosquitoes and damages the body's lymphatic system. LF results in the swelling of the limbs and genitals. It is estimated that more than 1.3 billion people are at risk of being infected with LF with 30 percent of the projected cases occurring in Africa.[7]

The goal of the Merck program is to try to eliminate river blindness globally by 2025. An estimated 37 million people suffer from river blindness with a majority of the cases occurring in 29 countries in Africa.[8] By 2017, the WHO verified that in four Latin American countries, Colombia, Ecuador, Mexico, and Guatemala, river blindness has been eliminated in the country. The Mectizan program reaches 250 million people annually and over 2 billion treatments have been administered between 1987 and 2017.[9] In 2015, Dr. Satoshi Omura and Dr. William Campbell shared the Nobel Prize in medicine for their work on the development of Ivermectin.[10]

What is corporate sustainability?

Corporate sustainability can be defined as the ability of firms to integrate social and environmental issues into their operations through interaction with stakeholders on a voluntary basis.[11] As a result, the objective of corporate sustainability is the ability to address the needs of the firm's direct and indirect stakeholders without limiting the ability of the firm to address the needs of future stakeholders.[12]

The corporate sustainability model is based on the interconnectedness of the principles of social responsibility, the process of social responsiveness and the subsequent policies that are developed in order for the firm to address social and environmental issues. A corporate level strategy related to corporate sustainability allows firms to adapt to changing societal conditions. Firms have a social contract based on specific rights and obligations. It is through this social contract that the behavior of the firm conforms to the expectations and objectives of society and properly addresses the needs of all of its stakeholders.[13]

The foundations of contemporary philanthropy and corporate sustainability

Derived from the Greek word "philanthropic," meaning "to love people," contemporary philanthropy can be defined as any voluntary act in the giving to individuals and/or organizations to promote the common good.[14] The foundation of corporate sustainability can be traced back to the philanthropic commitments of wealthy individuals from the nineteenth century. The belief of these individuals was that they had a "duty" to use their accumulated wealth to aid those in need.

The philanthropy of two Robber Barons

It is the duty of the rich man to use "all (of his) surplus revenues ... in the manner which, in his judgment is best calculated to produce the most beneficial results for the community ... The man who dies rich, dies disgraced"[15] (Andrew Carnegie).

Andrew Carnegie

By the end of the 1800s, Andrew Carnegie had become the richest man in the world through his controlling interest in the steel industry, and his company, United States Steel. Carnegie was also involved in building bridges and railroad cars. He did not initially have extensive knowledge of the steelmaking process, but he was able to identify and hire men who were experts in the field. When he retired in 1901, he started to distribute his surplus wealth to those in need. His initial focus was on colleges and libraries. While Ivy League schools such as Cornell, Harvard and Princeton all wanted Carnegie to give money to their institutions, Carnegie favored small colleges and historically black colleges. Carnegie not only liked the curricula and the composition of the students in these colleges, but he also believed that these students were truly motivated to succeed since they made many sacrifices to obtain a college degree.

When Carnegie died in 1919, he left $23 million to his family and gave the rest of his wealth to various foundations and educational institutions he established from 1901 to 1911. He donated $125 million to the Carnegie Corporation of New York Foundation. The mission of this foundation was "to promote the advancement and diffusion of knowledge among people of the United States."[16] The Carnegie Corporation of New York was only one of many philanthropic projects of Carnegie. Other projects included the creation of the Carnegie

Institute of Technology, which would later become Carnegie Mellon University, as well as the establishment of programs supporting workers and the promotion of cultural activities. One of the more unique projects was the Simplified Spelling Board which promoted the simplified spellings of common words. Carnegie spent $350 million on philanthropic projects, which was estimated to be equivalent to $8.12 billion in 2009 dollars.[17]

His most famous contribution to the arts was Carnegie Hall in New York. While on his honeymoon on board a ship from New York to London, Carnegie met Walter Damrosch who was the conductor and musical director of the Symphony Society of New York. Damrosch told Carnegie of his dream to have a beautifully designed concert hall in New York. When Carnegie laid the cornerstone of the concert hall in 1890, he proclaimed that Carnegie Hall "is built to stand for ages, and during these ages it is probable that this hall will intertwine itself with the history of our country." Carnegie Hall's Opening Night was May 5, 1891.[18] It cost $1.1 million to build, which would be equivalent to $515 million in 2012.[19]

John D. Rockefeller

From early in his career, John Rockefeller was determined to control every step in the process connected with refining crude oil. His greatest ambition was to earn $100,000 and live for 100 years. He acquired numerous oil companies that would eventually become the Standard Oil Corporation and held monopoly control of the oil industry in the United States. In 1911, Standard Oil was forced to break up into several smaller companies due to the passage of the Sherman Anti-Trust Act in 1911. The foundations of oil companies that were formed after the federal government forced Standard Oil to be dissolved include the currently trading oil companies: ConocoPhillips, BP, Chevron and Exxon-Mobil. Rockefeller became the world's first billionaire in 1916 (which would be $30 billion in 2014). When Rockefeller died in 1937, his assets were equivalent to 1.5 percent of the total economic output of the United States. His estimated net worth when he died was equal to $340 billion in 2014.[20]

Rockefeller's philanthropic philosophy was based on his religious values. He donated $35 million to the Baptist seminary which would eventually become the University of Chicago. Rockefeller focused on what he called "wholesale philanthropy." Wholesale philanthropy would focus on contributing major donations to produce solutions to major societal problems. The establishment of the Rockefeller Sanitary Commission focused on solving public health issues. The first major initiative of the Commission was an attempt to eliminate hookworms affecting people living in the southern United States. At the time of the initiative, an estimated half of the population of North Carolina and another estimated 6 million people in eight other southern states had hookworms.

One of the symptoms of hookworms was being lethargic, creating the assumption that people from the south were lazy. The cause of the hookworms was poor hygiene and the only available cure at the time was for the infected people to use thymol capsules as a cure. The federal government was unwilling to pay to improve the hygiene conditions of the affected communities in order to eliminate the threat of hookworms. Through Rockefeller's financial commitment to medical research to reduce the cost of the thymol capsules, the capsules were developed for a reduced cost of 50 cents a dose. Rockefeller focused on medical research as a driving force for his wholesale philanthropy and used Johns Hopkins University as the starting point for his research strategy. Rockefeller would donate to universities whose faculty were involved in medical research.[21]

Victorian philanthropy of two business leaders

Victorian philanthropists were personally involved in the day to day lives of the poor to improve their standard of living. The philanthropic focus involved not only financial support but also dedicated unpaid volunteer workers who contributed their own time, energy, and money to improve the lives of the less fortunate. Additionally, the Victorian philanthropists believed that helping the poor was a moral issue in which the actions on their part helped satisfy the philanthropists' own moral needs.[22]

The Victorian philanthropic philosophy was in direct response to the impact the industrial revolution had on employees and local communities. As people moved from rural areas to growing towns and cities, they did not have enough resources to provide themselves with an adequate standard of living in their new locations. The pre-existing charities were overwhelmed by the demands of the new citizens of their local communities and additional charities were not being created to take care of the excess demands.[23]

Sir Titus Salt

Sir Titus Salt was an English industrialist who owned textile factories in the nineteenth century including in the Bradford area. The Bradford region in England was considered to be the largest textile production region in the world. Due to the air and water pollution generated by industrial development of the textile mills, Bradford was considered to be the most polluted town in England. The air was polluted with numerous chemicals, including sulfur, and the textile mills would dump the untreated effluent and sewage from the factories into the local river, which was used as the drinking water source for Bradford. The contamination of the river water led to people in the town developing cholera and typhoid. This resulted in the average life expectancy being only about 20 years. Sir Titus's company, Daniel Salt and Sons, was the largest employer in Bradford. Based on the environmental conditions in Bradford and the need to build a new factory, Sir Titus moved from Bradford and built a new industrial community called Saltaire in 1851. At the time of Sir Titus's death in 1876, Saltaire had 850 houses for his workers that had access to fresh water. In addition, the town had a hospital, library, park, church, and school. Sir Titus viewed Saltaire as not just a new community, but as an avenue to promote moral values among his workers. In a form of paternalistic capitalism, Sir Titus believed that Bradford was environmentally and morally polluted, and Saltaire provided a cleaner moral and environmental climate for his workers. Paternalistic capitalism occurs when the firm becomes like a "father figure" for the workers and protects them by offering them acceptable working and living conditions through the building of company funded homes. Furthermore, Sir Titus also realized that workers who had better living and working conditions would be more productive employees and would be more loyal to his company and less willing to strike over their working conditions.[24]

Saltaire was declared a World Heritage Site by the United Nations Educational, Scientific and Cultural Organization (UNESCO) in December 2001. UNESCO described Saltaire as a preserved industrial village which gives a vivid impression of how Victorian philanthropic paternalism operated. Saltaire had a profound influence on subsequent developments which focused on industrial social welfare and urban planning both in the UK and globally.[25] The Saltaire Mill stopped production in 1986 and was converted into a mixed retail center housing art galleries, restaurants, retail shopping, and micro-electronic production.[26]

Joseph Rowntree

Joseph Rowntree established Rowntree's & Co., which originally produced cocoa, chocolate, and gum pastilles, in 1869. From 1883 to 1894, the number of employees grew from 200 to 894 largely due to the growth in demand for its cocoa and gum pastilles. In 1901, Rowntree bought 123 acres at New Earswick, York to build his company-based community and supply low cost housing for his workers. Rowntree wanted to prove that workers earning 25 shillings a week could afford to live in well-built houses.

In 1904, Rowntree set up three trusts: (1) The Joseph Rowntree Village Trust, which was originally established for the development and maintenance of its New Earswick development, later focusing on broader housing issues and renamed in 1990 as the Joseph Rowntree Foundation; (2) The Joseph Rowntree Charitable Trust, focusing on social, charitable, and religious issues including adult education and Quaker activities; and (3) The Joseph Rowntree Trust, later renamed the Joseph Rowntree Reform Trust, focusing on social and political actions such as liberal initiatives and the acquisition of newspapers.[27]

New Earswick is currently under the direction of the Joseph Rowntree Housing Trust and is a mixed-income community. The village has numerous services including recreational centers, churches, and a primary and secondary school. The goal of the village is to provide an inclusive neighborhood and provide programs to address loneliness, dementia, poverty, and digital exclusion.[28]

In a Founder's Memorandum he wrote in 1904, Joseph Rowntree stated that:

In connection with Religious, Political and Social work, it is to be remembered that there may be no better way of advancing the objects one has at heart than to strengthen the hands of those who are effectively doing the work that needs to be done.[29]

The Joseph Rowntree Foundation continues currently as an independent social change organization whose mission is to solve poverty in the UK. Their mission is to inspire action and change, and to build and develop strong empowered communities without poverty or isolation. The outcomes of its mission include developing opportunities for people to leave poverty through work opportunities and through a better social security system. In addition, a goal is to have more people be able to afford to live in decent, affordable housing.[30]

Evolution of corporate sustainability

It was from the path of philanthropic commitments by wealthy individuals that the current concept of corporate sustainability has evolved. Individual philanthropic actions have continued throughout the early twentieth century to the present day in various forms.

In 1953, the New Jersey Supreme Court ruled that A.P. Smith Manufacturing Company was allowed to donate $1,500 to Princeton University. This action violated the explicit interests of the firm's shareholders. This decision allowed all publicly traded firms to establish a corporate philanthropy commitment without the threat of being sued by the shareholders. As a result, firms were allowed to make philanthropic contributions to improve local communities in the form of donations to universities, the performing arts and other social causes which enhanced the quality of life within the community.

In the early stages of corporate philanthropy, there was the belief that the philanthropic contributions should not generate financial gain for the firm. Therefore, the focus of the financial commitment was "from the heart" and not for "bottom line" purposes. This belief shifted when an article published in the *Harvard Business Review* in 2002 by Michael Porter and Mark Kramer[31] presented the argument that social and economic goals of the firm are not in conflict but are strongly connected. Porter and Kramer also argued that many economic investments yield social returns and many social investments yield economic returns. By integrating the focus of economic and social goals, Porter and Kramer argued that firms should use their capabilities related to their corporate strategy to be able to identify philanthropic initiatives that not only benefit society but also yield a financial benefit for the firms.[32]

Corporate sustainability can be categorized as either institutional or technical in nature. Institutional corporate sustainability focuses on initiatives that protect and improve social welfare conditions including community support, eco-friendly activities, and sustainable business practices. Technical corporate sustainability refers to initiatives that have a direct impact on the firm's primary stakeholders. Technical corporate sustainability usually focuses on issues related to its products such as safety, employee benefits and accountability for its corporate governance domain structure.[33]

Why is corporate sustainability important?

Corporate sustainability is important because of the positive impact on stakeholders. This impact is based on enlightened self-interests, corporate good citizenship, and the beneficial social role of business. The establishment of "company" towns is an example of enlightened self-interests. The use of paternalistic capitalism is beneficial to the workers since they have acceptable working and living conditions, which results in higher productivity and less turnover of the workers. An increase in productivity and reduction of turnover have positive financial benefits for the firm through the generation of high levels of profitability. In addition, firms that are proactive in the area of corporate sustainability can benefit by being ahead of government regulations that require future changes in the manufacturing process and/or output for shifting external factors such as environmental regulations.

For example, DuPont's proactive shift away from chlorofluorocarbons (CFCs) materials before government regulations banned CFCs allowed DuPont to be a pioneer in a new market segment. Another example is Starbucks, which has a much lower than average turnover in the retail food industry due, in part, to its sustainability initiatives and its comprehensive benefits package for its employees.[34]

Criticism of corporate sustainability

Critics of corporate sustainability, such as the economist Milton Friedman, argued that the only responsibility firms had was to maximize financial performance within the confines of the rule of law. Therefore, the only important stakeholder is the stockholder and the manager's mission is to solely focus on financial returns in any strategic decision. Friedman argued that investment in any type of social initiative would go against the manager's fiduciary duty to maximize the financial return on every investment decision. Therefore, embracing sustainability issues is viewed as a subversive action instead of a complementary action to maximizing financial performance of the firm. The argument continues by stating that individuals are free to use their own resources to support sustainability initiatives, but managers are "stealing" resources from the shareholders to make these investments at a firm level.

A rebuttal to this criticism is that maximizing short-term financial performance is too narrow a focus for firms in the twenty-first century. A short-term financial focus ignores the long-term impact and consequences of the short-term focus. As a result, the philosophy of a short-term focus is one in which firms view interactions with other firms and customers based on a transactional basis. Each transaction is separate and independent of past transactions. A long-term focus views the interaction of firms with other firms and customers as a long-term relationship in which past transactions impact the type of negotiations of future transactions.

The second point of the rebuttal is that the external environment is constantly changing and, therefore, the managers of the firm cannot predict future environmental conditions. For example, changes in government regulations may force an industry to adjust its environmental strategy to be compliant with new regulations. If the firm has already adopted those requirements due to its sustainability commitment, it can enhance the firm's competitive advantage since it has already made the investment and met the standards before its competitors. In addition, the establishment of a long-term positive relationship with stakeholders, such as local communities and society through philanthropy, community involvement, paternalism, and voluntary codes of ethics, creates a reciprocal positive relationship that is beneficial for the present and future operations of the firm.[35]

Another criticism is that corporate sustainability in the form of social responsibility is a vague concept which is difficult to measure. As a result, it is difficult to measure the success or failure of an investment related to social responsibility. The unpredictability of investments related to social responsibility are the result of three factors: the conscience of the managers making the investment decision; the costs associated with lost profitability based on the investment; and the voluntary discretion of the managers making the investment decisions.

This leads to a related criticism of "do-gooding" managers. The perception of a do-gooding manager is someone who is pursuing his/her own vision on improving society at the expense of shareholders' investment without proper due diligence of the results of social initiatives. An example of a potential "do-gooding" action is described in the opening vignette when Merck gave away a drug for free in order to cure river blindness. A potential consequence is the expectation that Merck and other pharmaceutical companies would follow suit and also offer drugs in developing countries for free or at a minimal price. As a result, a firm would be forced to move away from a purely strategic competitive decision-making process in order to fulfill the needs of these various stakeholders. A rebuttal to this criticism is that while every manager must be a good steward to the resources available to him/her in making strategic decisions, a holistic approach is needed in measuring the performance of a firm. As a result, it is impossible to completely separate a strategic investment related to its impact on financial performance relative to its impact on stakeholders other than the shareholders. While offering drugs free to those in need may not yield short-term financial results, this initiative can establish and enhance long-term reciprocal relationships with customers and other stakeholders.[36]

A common criticism is that a firm's investment in corporate sustainability is based on rhetoric and not action. Instead of being actually committed to sustainability initiatives, the firms make investments in sustainability so they can promote the public relations value of the investment.[37] A rebuttal to this criticism is that there will be firms that are not fully committed to the sustainability initiative and use it only as a marketing tool. However, those firms that are fully committed to the initiative receive the benefit of promoting their sustainability strategy as a way of enhancing their competitive advantage. As management guru Henry Mintzberg states, "the strategic decisions of large organizations inevitably involve social as well as economic consequences, inextricably intertwined ... there is no such thing as a purely economic strategic decision."[38]

Conscious capitalism

> Business needs to become holistic and integral with deeper comprehensive purposes. Corporations must rethink why they exist. If business owners/entrepreneurs begin to view business as a complex and evolving interdependent system and manage their business more consciously for the well-being of all their major stakeholders, while fulfilling their highest business purposes, then I believe that we would begin to see the hostility towards capitalism and business disappear.[39]
>
> John Mackey, CEO of Whole Foods

Conscious capitalism can be defined as the ability of a firm to align the purpose of the firm, the practice of capitalism and the interests of the stakeholders to generate virtuous actions.[40]

Conscious capitalism views the relationship between the firm and its stakeholders from a different perspective as compared with firms that do not embrace conscious capitalism. Conscious capitalistic firms have a holistic, ecosystem viewpoint of the world. These firms incorporate a higher purpose than financial performance in its belief system and are able to reconcile social commitment and caring with profitability via the development of synergistic operations.[41]

There are some common themes of firms that embrace conscious capitalism including: higher purpose, stakeholder orientation, integrated strategies, healthy cultures, and value-based leaders.

Higher purpose

Firms that embrace conscious capitalism view the profits of the firm as providing the means to a greater good instead of being the primary objective of the firm. Conscious capitalism firms take a long-term perspective in their decision-making process. As a result, these firms will not pursue short-term financial gains at the expense of long-term negative ethical and environmental impacts.

Stakeholder orientation

Conscious capitalistic firms are committed to focusing on the needs of all their multiple constituencies or stakeholders. These critical stakeholders include employees, customers, shareholders, suppliers, local communities, and the natural environment. As a result, the firms establish both financial- and stakeholder-based goals as part of their strategic focus.[42] A conscious capitalistic firm realizes that while all its stakeholders have a vested interest in the operations of the firm, all the stakeholders can be independent, and a primary goal of the firm is to optimize value creation for all of the stakeholders. While there can be conflicts among the interests of various stakeholders, it is expected that these conflicts are usually rare, and the firm is able to resolve the conflicts, which further enhances its relationship with its stakeholders. John Mackey of Whole Foods Market states that it is far more common to find a harmony of interests instead of conflicts among the stakeholders. As a result, this harmony creates a win–win–win–win business relationship among the firm and its stakeholders.[43]

Integrated strategies

Since firms embracing conscious capitalism establish both financial and social goals, they must integrate these goals into the strategic focus of their core business strategies. This integration process will ensure the firms are consistent with their overall strategic focus in order to satisfy the needs of all its stakeholders.

Healthy cultures

Conscious capitalistic firms establish and subsequently entrench a cultural belief system in their employees, which supports a strong sense of "community." These belief systems must be supported by high levels of employee participation in the decision-making process related to the strategic and operational focus of the firm. The results of a healthy culture include buy-in and commitment of the employees as well as the firm rewarding the employees through the sharing of ownership and profits.

Values-based leaders

How the Chief Executives of conscious capitalistic firms view the values of their firms should be in the spotlight instead of the CEO. The CEOs are perceived to be "servant leaders" of the firm instead of being celebrities. The compensation is typically lower than other CEOs in the industry and the structure of the compensation is primarily based on rewarding long-term ownership of the firm.

Examples of firms that have a conscious capitalism philosophy include Whole Foods, Trader Joe's, Southwest Airlines, Starbucks, and Patagonia.[44]

Robert Owen

Robert Owen is considered to be one of the first "conscious capitalists." He owned a textile mill at the beginning of the nineteenth century in New Lanark, Scotland. During the dawn of the industrial revolution from 1800 to 1825, Owen introduced shorter working weeks for his workers and established a grievance procedure for the workers to communicate their complaints to management. He guaranteed that there would not be any layoffs in bad economic times and established health, disability, and retirement plans for his workers. Owen built clean subsidized housing for his workers located in a safe neighborhood. He built a school where he moved the children who had been working in the mill. He also established a preschool, day care facility, and a night school for the workers and their families. As a result of his holistic view of understanding the needs of his workers, Owen's mill became the most productive and profitable textile mill in the world. However, his co-owners complained that despite the level of profitability of the mill being high, he wasn't maximizing potential profitability and that Owen should stop giving his employees all these benefits and instead increase the dividend to the shareholders. As a result, by 1825, the mill was shut down and Owen emigrated to the United States.[45]

The lesson learned is that it is difficult and eventually impossible to implement a conscious capitalistic system for a firm unless there is agreement by all owners of the firm. Therefore, it is much easier to implement a conscious capitalistic philosophy when the firm is first established as compared to when a firm has already been in business for many years.

Components of the corporate sustainability pyramid

Corporate sustainability can be viewed as the establishment of different responsibilities of the firm which are economic, legal, ethical, and philanthropic. Archie Carroll presented a framework in which the levels of corporate sustainability build upon each other in the shape of a pyramid. The pyramid is presented in Figure 1.1.[46]

Economic responsibilities

At the foundation of the pyramid are the firm's economic responsibilities. Firms must be profitable to be able to survive and they must be profitable in order to exercise their commitment to corporate sustainability. A firm's economic responsibilities also include the firm using resources in order to produce needed goods and services for society. Some specific economic responsibilities could include maximizing the earnings per share of the firm, generating a high level of profitability, having a strong competitive position in the marketplace and performing the operations of the firm in an efficient manner.

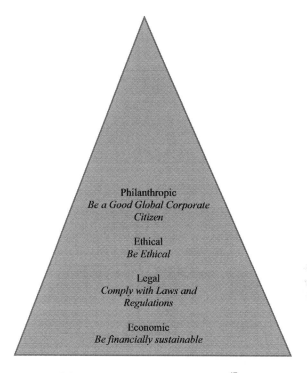

Philanthropic
Be a Good Global Corporate
Citizen

Ethical
Be Ethical

Legal
Comply with Laws and
Regulations

Economic
Be financially sustainable

Figure 1.1 Components of the corporate sustainability pyramid[47]

Legal responsibilities

The level above the economic responsibilities is the firm's legal responsibilities. The legal responsibilities of the firm are based on the firm complying will all the relevant laws and regulations that impact the firm. It is expected that while addressing its economic responsibilities, the firm abides by its legal responsibilities and achieves its financial objectives without violating the legal requirements that have been established by society.

In addition to complying with all local, state, federal, and international regulations, it is expected that the firm will be a good, law abiding global corporate citizen. It is critical for the firm to be legally responsible for its actions so that the revenue and profits generated by the firm through its goods and services meet the minimum legal and governmental standards.

Ethical responsibilities

Based on the expectations of society, the firm has an obligation to ensure its actions are ethical. However, this can be a constant challenge for firms since the expectations of what is considered ethical change over time based on societal norms. Ethical responsibilities are critical in the corporate sustainability pyramid because they separates firms within and across industries. Every firm is required to fulfill its economic and legal responsibilities for long-term survival. However, firms can be ethically neutral in their strategic focus. From an ethical neutral firm perspective, their legal responsibilities are also their ethical responsibilities. Therefore, firms that are proactive in their ethical commitment can add in their differentiation strategy since firms that have a strong ethical commitment are more likely to have strong positive interactions with their stakeholders. A firm's proactive focus on ethical commitment can include: ensuring the operations of the firm meet or exceed the stakeholders' expectations based on social and ethical norms; being able to effectively adapt to new and/or evolving ethical and moral norms within society; being able to ensure that ethical norms are not compromised or ignored in the operations of the firm; and being able to realize that stakeholders expect the firm's ethical behavior to be beyond the legal standards established by governments.

Philanthropic responsibilities

At the top of the pyramid is the firm's philanthropic responsibilities. These are considered discretionary responsibilities since these actions by the firm may not have a direct connection with the operations of the firm. Actions such as donating to charities and providing programs to help people in the local communities represent a philanthropic commitment which may or may not be directly related to the customers and markets of the firm. Furthermore, supporting cultural activities such as the performing arts is an avenue in which the firm enhances the benefits of society through discretionary contributions. In addition, philanthropic focused firms also can design programs in which their employees are able to volunteer for community service as well as providing financial support for community-based volunteer initiatives.[48]

What is stakeholder theory?

A stakeholder can be defined as any group that has a vested interest in the operations of the firm. Traditional stakeholders include shareholders, customers, employees, communities, government, suppliers, trade associations, and non-governmental organizations (NGOs) who represent special interests (e.g. human rights groups, environmental groups, labor rights groups) that are related to the operations of the firm.

The origins of contemporary stakeholder theory can be traced back to the 1930s. In 1931, A. A Berle had an article published in *Harvard Law Review*[49] which argued that all of the power given to a firm will be used to create benefits to the firm's shareholders. As guardians of the investments made by the shareholders, the firm has a fiduciary responsibility to maximize the level of profitability of the firm. In response to Berle's article, Merrick Dodd in the following year also had an article published by *Harvard Law Review*[50] which argued for the expansion of the scope of the firm. In addition to focusing on the needs of the shareholders, the responsibility of the firm also includes fulfilling obligations to the local communities, to its employees, and to the firm's customers. Dodd argued that firms are allowed to become legal entities by not only serving the shareholders but by also serving the other critical stakeholders.

Almost 40 years later, Milton Friedman revived the discussion of the role of stakeholders by writing an article published in the *New York Times Magazine* in 1970 titled "The Social Responsibility of Business Is to Increase Its Profits."[51] Friedman emphasized Berle's arguments that managers of a firm have a responsibility to focus solely on profit maximization. In a free market system, the owners of the firm "employ" the managers to run the operations of the firms with the expectation that the decisions made by the managers agree with the objectives of the owners. As a result, Friedman believed that social responsibility was a fundamentally subversive ideal which conflicts with the beliefs and wishes of the owners.

In 1984, Edward Freeman championed the opposing view first presented by Merrick Dodd by arguing that all stakeholders should be recognized, and their needs and expectations should be addressed by the firm as part of its responsibility as a legal entity. Freedman argued that serving the needs of all the critical stakeholders supports the interests of the shareholders.[52] For example, by serving the needs of the customer, the firm is able to sell more products in the marketplace, which increases the profitability of the firm. By serving the needs of the employees, the productivity rate and level of retention of employees increases, which increases the level of profitability. By serving the needs of the local community, people living in that community would have a positive image of the firm resulting in community members buying more products, which increase the level of profitability. By serving the needs of the government, the firm does not have to address negative consequences of failing to abide by legal requirements and regulations which could result in penalties and fines, and even managers being convicted of crimes.

As a result, following the government's expectation eliminates the loss of financial resources that would be needed to address these negative consequences. By serving the needs of the suppliers, the firm can establish strong positive long-term relationships with its suppliers which could yield a competitive advantage. This enhancement of competitive advantage would increase the level of profitability of the firm.

Identification of critical stakeholders

While all stakeholders play a role in guiding the actions of the firm, there can be situational adjustments as to which stakeholders will receive priority in addressing their needs. The three factors that determine the relative importance of the firm's critical stakeholders are: power, legitimacy, and urgency. Power can be defined as the extent to which a stakeholder has the ability to influence and impose its will on the operations of the firm. Legitimacy can be defined as the degree to which the demands of the stakeholder are appropriate within the operations of the firm. Urgency is defined as the degree to which the issues raised by the stakeholder group must be addressed within a short time frame. As a result, if all three factors are present for the stakeholder, the firm must perceive the needs and demands of the stakeholder to be of high-priority.[53]

Therefore, stakeholders can be classified based on the interconnection of their relationships with the firm based on their level of power, their level of legitimacy and the urgency of satisfying their needs. These interrelationships are shown in Figure 1.2.

Dominant stakeholders

The critical component for dominant stakeholders is power. Dominant stakeholders have the power to impose their demands on the firm. Dominant

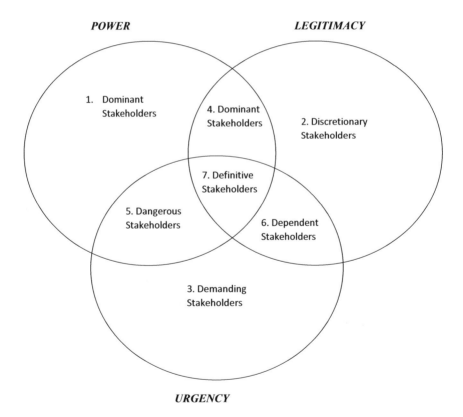

Figure 1.2 Classes of stakeholders[54]

stakeholders increase their power if they have the ability to coerce the actions of the firm, if they have financial resources to gain power in the relationship with the firm, or if they can command the attention of the news media.

Discretionary stakeholders

Discretionary stakeholders have the claim of legitimacy but not the power related to their interactions with the firm. Since these stakeholders provide neither power nor urgency, there is no pressure for the firm to react to the demands of these stakeholders. Discretionary stakeholders are usually viewed by the firm as philanthropic in nature. Although the firms are not pressured into serving the needs of these stakeholders, firms will still voluntarily address the needs when opportunities arise.

Demanding stakeholders

Demanding stakeholders have a sense of urgency but do not have either the power or the legitimacy to support their demands. These stakeholders are perceived to be "irritating" to the firm but do not pose a threat. As a result, these stakeholders are usually ignored by the firm since there is a minimal threat of negative consequences if these stakeholders' demands are not acted upon by the firm.

Dominant stakeholders

Dominant stakeholders are both powerful and legitimate and are critical stakeholders for the firm. These stakeholders can leverage their power and legitimacy in making sure their demands are heard and acted upon. Their interactions with the firm create a dominant coalition in which the stakeholders have the ability to influence the decisions made by the firm. The significance of these stakeholders can be seen in the structural orientation of the firm. Dominant stakeholders such as stockholders who have a significant financial investment in the firm may be included in the firm's Board of Directors. Employees are traditionally dominant stakeholders who are represented in the establishment of the firm's human resources department. Firms will also have a compliance function or department which addresses the demands of governmental stakeholders. Firms will also have a customer service function or department to address the needs of their customers. Dominant stakeholders will usually receive most of the focus of the managers of the firm. However, this does not mean that the firm should ignore its other stakeholders.

Dangerous stakeholders

Dangerous stakeholders have both power and urgency but lack legitimacy. These stakeholders will be coercive and potentially violent in order to have their demands met by the firms. Acts by dangerous stakeholders can include employees who call wildcat strikes and encourage employee sabotage. Environmental groups can be dangerous stakeholders when they disrupt and/or sabotage the operations of the firms in order to create a public forum for their demands.

Dependent stakeholders

Dependent stakeholders have both urgency and legitimacy, but not the power, to have their needs heard and acted upon by the firm. As a result, these stakeholders must rely on the actions of stakeholders who have power in order to have their concerns incorporated in the decision-making process of the firm. For example, all the non-human living organisms and their environment rely on government agencies and environmental groups to protect their interests. Local communities who are also impacted by the negative environmental consequences of the actions of a firm must also rely on the government and environmental NGOs to protect their interests.

Definitive stakeholders

Definitive stakeholders have the triumvirate of power, legitimacy, and urgency. As a result, these stakeholders will always have the highest level of priority for the firm. The needs of definitive stakeholders must be both quickly identified and actions taken in order to satisfy their needs. The definitive classification can be a temporary position for the stakeholders. Stakeholders could be in another position, but due to circumstances they become definitive. For example, customers could be dangerous stakeholders by having power and urgency in boycotting the firm due to the firm's working conditions of its outsourced production. These customers can shift to definitive stakeholders when the boycotting results in a public backlash and a subsequent significant financial impact on the firm, which gives their complaints legitimacy.

Stakeholder engagement

There are numerous ways in which the engagement of the firm and stakeholders can be evaluated. One approach is to examine firm responsiveness to its stakeholders based on values and beliefs. This approach would examine stakeholder engagement from normative and instrumental dimensions. A normative dimension is based on the principle of fairness by the firm. If a firm has a normative perspective related to stakeholders, the firm will treat and interact with all stakeholders equally without considering the relative importance of one stakeholder as compared with another. As a result, firms with a normative perspective related to stakeholders would treat all stakeholders based on respect, dignity, and fair consideration. In addition, a firm with a normative belief perspective would also ensure that each decision related to one stakeholder is consistent and fair in addressing the needs of all the stakeholders.

	Low Normative	High Normative
High Instrumental	Pragmatic Firms	Engaged Firms
Low Instrumental	Skeptical Firms	Idealistic Firms

Figure 1.3 Framework for stakeholder engagement[55]

A firm with a low normative belief perspective views interactions with stakeholders as an obligation that must be fulfilled by the firm. Furthermore, a low normative belief firm views the shareholders as always the most important stakeholder, which results in always ensuring the shareholders needs are met first before the firm addresses the needs of the other stakeholders.

The instrumental dimension refers to the relationship between the stakeholders and the firm. Instrumental stakeholders are those stakeholders whose support is critical in order for the firm to accomplish all of its goals. Therefore, a high level of engagement of stakeholders with the firm is not based on equity or fairness, but rather on the practical needs of having to interact with the stakeholders in order for the firm to accomplish its goals. As a result, high instrumental stakeholders' firms are those firms where an ongoing engagement with its stakeholders is critical for the firm to be able to perform its corporate responsibilities. Based on the dimensions of normative and instrumental, a framework can be developed to understand how firms engage with their stakeholders (Figure 1.3).

Skeptical firms

The firm with low normative and low instrumental dimensions is considered to be a skeptical firm. These firms are skeptical since they do not perceive or value moving beyond serving the needs of the stakeholders other than the shareholders. This is because these firms do not need stakeholder engagement in order to achieve their financial goals. The firms are doubtful about any value added by engaging with its stakeholders. However, it will engage with its stakeholders when it is required to by law. Skeptical firms traditionally occur in industries such as tobacco, gaming and petroleum.

Pragmatic firms

Firms which have a low normative dimension and a high instrumental dimension are considered to be pragmatic firms. These firms are pragmatic because they realize that engagement with stakeholders is critical for the long-term success of the firm. Having a strong relationship with the stakeholders facilitates the firm's ability to enhance its competitive positioning in the marketplace. However, pragmatic firms still view the shareholders as the stakeholder with the highest priority. Therefore, to be able to try to maximize their financial performance, pragmatic firms will engage with stakeholders if it directly results in enhancing the financial performance of the firm. An example of a pragmatic firm is Coca-Cola. Coca-Cola focuses on its financial performance and engages with its stakeholders on an ad hoc basis. For example, Coca-Cola will engage with relevant stakeholders who are impacted by environmental issues such as water depletion and pollution generation in developing countries in which Coca-Cola has operations.

Engaged firms

Firms with a high normative dimension and a high instrumental dimension are engaged firms. Engaged firms believe there is value in addressing the needs of all the stakeholders equally and understand that this creates benefits as they are dependent on the stakeholders for current and future financial success. It is the focus on long-term sustainability which allows engaged firms the ability to adjust strategic focus with support for all stakeholders. Engaged firms believe that serving the needs of the stakeholders and the shareholders are not mutually exclusive goals.

Idealistic firms

Idealistic firms have a high normative dimension and low instrumental dimension in engagement with their stakeholders, Idealistic firms believe that serving the needs of their stakeholders and society are their primary goals. The ability to generate positive financial results allows the firm to address the social needs of its stakeholders. Firms such as Ben and Jerry's and The Body Shop represent the intertwining of the social and financial missions of the firm.[56]

Stakeholder dialogue and corporate sustainability

For firms to effectively manage engagement with stakeholders, they must establish an interconnected dialogue with stakeholders. It is from the maintaining of this dialogue that firms are able to consistently understand the needs of the stakeholders as they integrate the stakeholder's needs in their decision-making processes. There are four factors that can impact the operationalization of a firm's dialogue with its stakeholders. Those four factors are: consciousness, capacity, commitment, and consensus.

Consciousness

The managers of the firm must have both knowledge and awareness of the needs of its stakeholders. This consciousness is critical for the successful interaction of dialogue for the stakeholders and the firm. It is through this consciousness that the firm understands the process and context needed to implement its corporate sustainability strategy, which is supported by the stakeholders. In addition, the consciousness of the employees related to social and environmental sustainability issues is critical since the employees are responsible for converting the firm's corporate sustainability philosophy into practice.

Capacity

Capacity refers to the type of resources that are available to the firm. These resources include physical, financial, organizational, and human resources. Firms with higher level capacity have the advantage of higher levels of flexibility in adopting their corporate sustainability philosophy as compared with firms that have a lower level of resources. This additional capacity allows firms to be able to make corporate sustainability investments, analyze societal demands and trends, and be able to develop specialized skills and competencies in building and maintaining strong relationships with stakeholders. Higher levels of capacity allow firms to entrench a long-term corporate sustainability commitment with their stakeholders.

Commitment

Commitment refers to the ability of the firm to give priority and allocate resources to corporate sustainability issues. Commitment is a critical linchpin in the firm's ability to establish and maintain stakeholder dialogue. Without commitment from both the managers and the employees of the firm, corporate sustainability initiatives cannot be developed and executed effectively. Commitment includes both financial and non-financial resources so the managers need to understand that there must be "buy-in" by all the employees of the firm in order to be able to fulfill its commitment to execute its corporate sustainability philosophy.

Consensus

An extension of the firm's commitment is the development and maintenance of a consensus between the firm and its stakeholders' agreement on the issues related to the corporate sustainability initiatives, as well as agreement as to the type of dialogue acceptable to both the firm and its stakeholders. Consensus is needed to try to avoid conflict between the firm and its stakeholders and should result in a harmonious relationship. The challenge with establishing a consensus is if the stakeholder dialogue involves multiple stakeholders who have diverging values and preferences. Therefore, the firm must establish goal congruence which allows the firms to be able to develop shared perspectives on common problems, questions, and issues.[57]

Stakeholder theory and corporate sustainability

Stakeholder theory is connected to corporate sustainability based on the relationship of the firm's actions for the expectations and needs of the stakeholders. Stakeholders are any group that has a vested interest in the operations of the firm. Stakeholder theory is based on the belief that stakeholders have legitimate interests in the operations of the firm.[58] As a result, stakeholder engagement must be a foundational component of corporate sustainability. Corporate sustainability is based on a fundamental obligation to fulfill the needs and expectations of stakeholders, which results in a two-way communication between the firm and its stakeholders. Therefore, managers must have the proper skill set to identify and understand the needs of the stakeholders.[59]

Chapter in action: Merck's unethical actions related to its painkiller, Vioxx

In the high growth area of drugs relieving pain in the 1990s, Merck developed a drug with the brand name of Vioxx which was believed to be better for the patient than existing pain reduction medication at the time. The advantage of Vioxx was that it would cause fewer gastrointestinal problems than traditional over the counter pain medications. In January 1999, Merck started a research study, called VIGOR, of more than 8,000 patients to examine the effectiveness of Vioxx. Half of the patients in the study were given Vioxx and the other half were given the over the counter medication naproxen. Merck was attempting to determine whether Vioxx was safer for the digestive system than naproxen.

In May 1999, the Federal Drug Administration (FDA) approved Vioxx to be available to the public through a prescription in the United States. In October 1999, the results of the VIGOR study showed that Vioxx patients had fewer ulcers and less gastrointestinal bleeding than those patients in the study who took naproxen. However, in November 1999, additional analysis of the study showed that 79 of the 4,000 patients who took Vioxx had serious heart problems or had died, while only 41 patients who had taken naproxen in the study had heart problems or died.

In December 1999, the safety panel at Merck, who was aware of the heart problems, was told that additional examination of the data resulted in the conclusion that the risks associated with heart problems and death among Vioxx patients were twice as high as in the controlled naproxen group. The recommendation of the safety panel was for Merck to continue to sell Vioxx with the rationale being that the safety panel could not tell whether Vioxx was causing the heart problems or naproxen was acting as an agent to reduce heart problems in the patients of the study. The results of the VIGOR study were published in the *New England Journal of Medicine* in which the authors of the study omitted related data pertaining to the incidences of heart attacks and other cardiovascular events occurring in the Vioxx patients in the study.

In addition, the research paper only identified 17 deaths for the Vioxx patients when the actual number was 20.[60]

Despite knowing the potentially fatal risks of using the drug, Merck continued to market the drug to doctors. The Merck sales representatives were told to "dodge" any potentially difficult questions raised by concerned doctors related to the serious potential side effects of Vioxx. The sales representatives were given an "obstacle handling guide." If the doctor asked a question related to cardiovascular problems, the sales representatives were told not to acknowledge the problem but instead state that Vioxx would not reduce the level of cardiovascular problems and that Vioxx should not be considered to be a substitute for a patient that needed to use aspirin for heart problems.

In October 2003, Merck presented a research study which demonstrated that Vioxx could be used to help children with juvenile rheumatoid arthritis. As a result, Merck was moving forward in positioning Vioxx as a pain medication for not only adults but also children. Additional external trials showed that Vioxx posed a potentially significant risk for the patient as compared with other types of pain medications.

On September 30, 2004, Merck announced that the company was going to withdraw Vioxx from the market because of the evidence presented in a number of studies which showed that Vioxx was linked to a higher level of heart problems among the patients who used Vioxx. From 1999 to 2004, over 100 million prescriptions of Vioxx had been issued by doctors to 2 million patients and Merck's global sales of Vioxx in 2003 was $2.5 billion and had contributed to an estimated 20 percent of Merck's overall level of profitability. The first trial from a lawsuit related to Vioxx took place in 2005. By 2011, Merck had paid approximately $6 billion to settle lawsuits for Vioxx, which had total sales of $11 billion from 1999 to 2004.[61] In November 2011, Merck pled guilty to illegally introducing a drug into interstate commerce and agreed to pay the United States Justice Department a fine of $950 million. The charges were based on Merck providing misleading marketing and sales techniques for the promotion of Vioxx. The specific charge Merck pled guilty to was Merck promoting Vioxx to treat rheumatoid arthritis before Merck had received approval by the FDA.[62]

Questions for thought

1. Can you reconcile the actions of Merck related to curing river blindness and the unethical behavior of its marketing of Vioxx? Explain.
2. Do you think most people know of the philanthropic actions of the robber barons of the nineteenth century?
3. How do the actions of Andrew Carnegie and John D. Rockefeller compare with those of Sir Titus Salt and Joseph Rowntree?
4. Do you perceive conscious capitalism as a "fad" or a permanent trend?
5. On which level of the pyramid do you think most Fortune 500 firms are positioned? Explain your answer.
6. Which stakeholders should always be considered "critical" for a firm?

Notes

1   Andrew Jack. 2016. Africa Eye War Waged on River Blindness. *The Financial Times*. October 12.
2   www.merck.com/about/featured-stories/mectizan.html
3   Luke Whelan. 2015. This Company Gave Away a Drug That Just Won the Nobel Prize and Helped Millions. *Mother Jones*. October 5.
4   Andrew Jack. 2016. Africa Eye War Waged on River Blindness. *The Financial Times*. October 12.
5   Luke Whelan. 2015. This Company Gave Away a Drug That Just Won the Nobel Prize and Helped Millions. *Mother Jones*. October 5.
6   Anonymous. 1987. Merck Offers Free Distribution of New River Blindness Drug. *The New York Times*. October 22.
7   www.merck.com/about/featured-stories/mectizan.html
8   Andrew Jack. 2016. Africa Eye War Waged on River Blindness. *The Financial Times*. October 12.
9   www.merck.com/about/featured-stories/mectizan.html
10 Luke Whelan. 2015. This Company Gave Away a Drug That Just Won the Nobel Prize and Helped Millions. *Mother Jones*. October 5.
11 Alexander Dahlsrud. 2008. How Corporate Social Responsibility is Defined: An Analysis of 37 Definitions. *Corporate Social Responsibility and Environmental Management*. 15: 1–13.
12 Thomas Dyllick and Kai Hockerts. 2002. Beyond the Business Case For Corporate Sustainability. *Business Strategy and the Environment*. 11: 130–141.
13 Steven L. Wartick and Philip L. Cochran. 1985. The Evolution of the Corporate Social Performance Model. *The Academy of Management Review*. 10(4): 758–769.
14 https://philanthropynewyork.org/sites/default/files/resources/History%20of% 20Philanthropy.pdf
15 Milton Goldin. 1988. The Founding Fathers of Modern Philanthropy. *Fund Raising Management*. 19(4): 48–51, 99.
16 Milton Goldin. 1988. The Founding Fathers of Modern Philanthropy. *Fund Raising Management*. 19(4): 48–51, 99.
17 Charles Harvey, Mairi Maclean, Jillian Gordon and Eleanor Shaw. 2011. Andrew Carnegie and the Foundations of Contemporary Entrepreneurial Philanthropy. *Business History*. 53(3): 425–450.
18 www.carnegiehall.org/-/media/CarnegieHall/Files/PDFs/About/History/Then_and_ Now_2018-2019.pdf?la=en&hash=617272B25DD5CD0E7470105B0F36C990 D95072FC
19 Morgan Brenan. 2012. How Much Would It Cost to Build Carnegie Hall Today? *Fortune*. September 19.
20 Carl O'Donnell. 2014. The Rockefellers: The Legacy of History's Richest man. *Forbes*. July 11.
21 Milton Goldin. 1988. The Founding Fathers of Modern Philanthropy. *Fund Raising Management*. 19(4): 48–51, 99.
22 Gertrude Himmelfarb. 1997. The Age of Philanthropy. *WQ*. Spring. 48–55.
23 Mark Freeman. 2003. Victorian Philanthropy and the Rowntree's: The Joseph Rowntree Charitable Trust. *Quaker Studies*. 7(2): 193–213.
24 N. Craig Smith. 2003. Corporate Social Responsibility: Whether or How? *California Management Review*. 45(4): 52–76.
25 https://whc.unesco.org/en/list/1028
26 www.saltairevillage.info/Saltaire_World_Heritage_Site_Nomination_Docu ment_1028.pdf
27 http://archive.rowntreesociety.org.uk/joseph-rowntree-1836-1925/

28 www.jrht.org.uk/community/new-earswick-york
29 www.jrf.org.uk/about-us/our-heritage/lasting-vision-change
30 *Our Strategic Plan 2018–2021.* Joseph Rowntree Foundation and Joseph Rowntree Housing Trust.
31 Porter, Michael E., and Mark R. Kramer. The Competitive Advantage of Corporate Philanthropy. *Harvard Business Review* 80, no. 12 (December 2002): 56–69.
32 Philip L. Cochran. 2007. The Evolution of Corporate Social Responsibility. *Business Horizons.* 56: 449–454.
33 Shuili Du, Valerie Swaen and Adam Lindgreen. 2013. The Roles of Leadership Styles in Corporate Responsibility. *Journal of Business Ethics.* 114: 155–169.
34 N. Craig Smith. 2003. Corporate Social Responsibility: Whether or How? *California Management Review.* 45(4): 52–76.
35 Steven L. Wartick and Philip L. Cochran. 1985. The Evolution of the Corporate Social Performance Model. *The Academy of Management Review.* 10(4): 758–769.
36 N. Craig Smith. 2003. Corporate Social Responsibility: Whether or How? *California Management Review.* 45(4): 52–76.
37 Henry Mintzberg. 1983. The Case for Corporate Social Responsibility. *The Journal of Business Strategy.* 4(2): 3–15.
38 Henry Mintzberg. 1983. The Case for Corporate Social Responsibility. *The Journal of Business Strategy.* 4(2): 3–15.
39 Michael Strong (Ed). 2009. *Be the Solution: How Entrepreneurs and Conscious Capitalists Can Solve All the World's Problems.* John Wiley & Sons: Hoboken, NJ.
40 Doug Rauch. 2011. Conscious Capitalism: A Better Road Map. *California Management Review.* 53(3): 91–97.
41 John Mackey. 2011. What Conscious Capitalism Really Is. *California Management Review.* 53(3): 83–90.
42 James O'Toole and David Vogel. 2011. Two and a Half Cheers for Conscious Capitalism. *California Management Review.* 53(3) Spring: 60–76.
43 John Mackey. 2011. What Conscious Capitalism Really Is. *California Management Review.* 53(3): 83–90.
44 James O'Toole and David Vogel. 2011. Two and a Half Cheers for Conscious Capitalism. *California Management Review.* 53(3) Spring: 60–76.
45 James O'Toole and David Vogel. 2011. Two and a Half Cheers for Conscious Capitalism. *California Management Review.* 53(3) Spring: 60–76.
46 Archie B. Carroll. 1991. The Pyramid of Corporate Social Responsibility: Toward the Moral Management of Organizational Stakeholders. *Business Horizon.* July-August: 39–48.
47 Archie B. Carroll. 1991. The Pyramid of Corporate Social Responsibility: Toward the Moral Management of Organizational Stakeholders. *Business Horizon.* July-August: 42.
48 Peter A. Stanwick and Sarah D. Stanwick. 2016. *Understanding Business Ethics.* Sage Publications: Thousand Oaks, CA.
49 Berle, Jr, A.A.. 1931. Corporate Powers as Powers in Trust. *Harvard Law Review* 44:7 May. 1049–1074.
50 Dodd, E.Merrick. 1932. For Whom are Corporate Managers Trustees. *Harvard Law Review.* 45:7. May. 1145–1163.
51 Friedman, Milton. 1970. The Social Responsibility of Business Is to Increase Its Profits. *New York Times Magazine* Septmeber 13. 122–126.
52 Peter A. Stanwick and Sarah D. Stanwick. 2016. *Understanding Business Ethics.* Sage Publications: Thousand Oaks, CA.
53 Peter A. Stanwick and Sarah D. Stanwick. 2016. *Understanding Business Ethics.* Sage Publications: Thousand Oaks, CA.

54 Peter A. Stanwick and Sarah D. Stanwick. 2016. *Understanding Business Ethics.* Sage Publications: Thousand Oaks, CA.
55 Peter A. Stanwick and Sarah D. Stanwick. 2016. *Understanding Business Ethics.* Sage Publications: Thousand Oaks, CA. 59.
56 Peter A. Stanwick and Sarah D. Stanwick. 2016. *Understanding Business Ethics.* Sage Publications: Thousand Oaks, CA.
57 Esben Rahbek Pedersen. 2008. Making Corporate Social Responsibility (CSR) Operable: How Companies Translate Stakeholder Dialogue Into Practice. *Business and Society Review.* 111(2): 137–163.
58 John L. Campbell. 2007. Why Would Corporations Behave in Socially Responsible Ways? An Institutional Theory of corporate Social Responsibility. *The Academy of Management Review.* 32(3): 946–967.
59 N. Craig Smith. 2003. Corporate Social Responsibility: Whether or How? *California Management Review.* 45(4): 52–76.
60 Anonymous. 2007. Timeline: The Rise and Fall of Vioxx. Npr.org. November 10.
61 Peter A. Stanwick and Sarah D. Stanwick. 2016. *Understanding Business Ethics.* Sage Publications: Thousand Oaks, CA.
62 Duff Wilson. 2011. Merck to Pay $950 Million Over Vioxx. *The New York Times.* November 22.

2 Leadership and organizational change and corporate sustainability

Introduction

In order for any firm to embrace corporate sustainability, it must have leaders who will champion the cause and be able to create a working environment that would be willing to accept change when it is necessary to ensure the long-term corporate sustainability vision of the firm. In this chapter, both concepts are discussed in depth for any manager to understand that implementing corporate sustainability strategies can be both challenging and rewarding. The concepts presented in this chapter include characteristics of corporate sustainability leadership; transformational and transactional leadership; the values-based model of transformational leadership; corporate sustainability and power; organizational politics and corporate sustainability; organizational change and corporate sustainability; and organizational change leadership and corporate sustainability. The chapter begins with a discussion of the role of transformational leadership at Unilever related to corporate sustainability. The chapter finishes with Pablo Isla's, the CEO of Inditex, commitment to corporate sustainability.

Transformational leadership at Unilever

Unilever is a global consumer products company with 161,000 employees and over 400 brands used by 2.5 billion people on any given day. Unilever had sales in 2018 of 51 billion euros and had 12 brands which had sales of more than 1 billion euros annually.[1]

From soaps and shampoos to ice cream and teas, Unilever is truly a global leader with global critical stakeholders. Unilever is committed to making transformational change by focusing on significant global issues beyond financial objectives. Unilever's transformational change is based on making fundamental changes globally to issues that not only impact its businesses but also people around the world. Transformational issues such as climate change, inequality, hunger, and health are areas in which Unilever establishes partnerships with external stakeholders, including advocacy groups, in order to address these issues in a systematic manner. Because of its size and influence, Unilever has the ability to alter current institutional systems by making positive transformational changes related to issues like combating climate change and promoting human development.[2]

Within its strategic framework, Unilever has adopted a sustainable living plan which is incorporated into the foundation to its business model. The three major goals of the sustainable living plan are to: help more than a billion people improve their health and well-being by 2020, reduce the environmental footprint of its products by 50 percent and enhance livelihoods for millions.[3]

Improving health and hygiene

Millions of people die globally because they do not have access to safe drinking water or they live in conditions of poor sanitation and hygiene. The World Health Organization (WHO) estimates that 9 percent of all global diseases and 6 percent of all deaths are due to poor health and hygiene conditions. Unilever products such as soap, toothpaste, hand sanitizers, and Vaseline can improve the health conditions of people globally. In addition, toilet cleaners and water purifiers can also help prevent disease and improve people's health and well-being.

Through its Lifebuoy brand, Unilever has established handwashing programs around the world in order to stop the spread of disease. For example, a child dies from either pneumonia or diarrhea every 23 seconds globally. Handwashing can reduce the spread of pneumonia by 23 percent and diarrhea by up to 45 percent. Lifebuoy is the global market leader in germ protection soap and is sold in nearly 50 countries and is the only soap that is accredited by the Royal Society of Public Health, London. As a result, Unilever sells soap for 0.12 euros to ensure that those who may not be able to afford to buy soap are given the opportunity to buy and use soap. Unilever established a 'Lifebuoy's School of 5' program in which it encourages people to change their behaviors about washing their hands.[4] The five principles are: making it understood, making it easy, making it desirable, making it rewarding, and making it a habit. Making it understood refers to the importance of using soap when washing your hands. Many people believe that washing your hands with only water is enough to kill the bacteria on your skin. Making it easy refers to the ability to change people's daily routines to include hand washing by having reminders about when it is necessary to wash your hands. Making it desirable is targeted toward making it fun for children through the use of comic books, stickers and no-touch foaming hand dispensers. Making it rewarding is giving positive reinforcement for children who wash their hands daily. Making it a habit refers to the ability to make handwashing part of the daily routine. If handwashing is done consistently for over 21 days, it is considered to be a permanent habit. As a result, Unilever gives children and mothers 21-day diaries and rewards if the children consistently wash their hands for the three week record in the diary.[5]

By 2018, the health and hygiene programs at Unilever had reached 1.24 billion people, of which 635 million had participated in local programs and 587 million in Lifebuoy's handwashing programs. From 2010 to 2018, the handwashing programs reached 1 billion people. In addition, from 2012 to 2017, 16.5 million people have gained improved access to a toilet through Unilever programs. From 2005 to 2018, 55 million people have received safe drinking water through Unilever's water purification system, which has reached 106 billion liters. Over 4 million people were helped through Unilever's Vaseline healing program from 2015 to 2018. Furthermore, from 2010 to 2018, 83.5 million people participated in Unilever's oral health programs.[6]

Reducing environmental impact in half

Another area of transformational leadership by Unilever is its corporate sustainability commitment to reduce its environmental footprint. Unilever has set a goal of cutting its environmental impact in half by 2030. Unilever is taking action to address issues related to climate change and the depletion of natural resources. Not only does this initiative focus on environmentally based stakeholders, Unilever presents the strategic argument of increased financial performance due to the reduction of risk by securing sustainable sources of supply of raw materials, the reduction of costs due to the reduction of packaging materials, as well as higher levels of manufacturing efficiencies. The details of the environmental initiative include focusing on sustainable agriculture, efficient land use, food security, reduction of water and energy usage, eco-efficient focus on manufacturing and distribution, and the support of public policy related to the presentation of issues related to climate change.

As of 2018, the results of the environmental sustainability initiatives included a 31 percent reduction of waste associated with the disposal of Unilever products for consumer use, 56 percent of agricultural raw materials sourced in a sustainable manner, 52 percent reduction of CO_2 emissions from energy per ton of production, 44 percent reduction of water abstraction per ton of production, 97 percent reduction of total waste sent for disposal per ton of production, and over 600 million euros of energy costs saved through eco-efficiency since 2008.[7]

Enhancing livelihoods for millions

Unilever's corporate sustainability initiative is related to the ability to have a positive impact on millions of people as it grows its business. Unilever acknowledges that it has a significant impact on millions of people in many communities across its global value chain. Unilever suppliers and distribution networks are composed of millions of small-scale farmers, distributors, and retailers. As a result, Unilever has established three pillars to enhance the livelihoods of millions of people.

The first pillar is ensuring fairness in the workplace. Unilever's guidance for fairness is based on the United Nations Guiding Principles on Business and Human Rights in order to ensure every person connected to Unilever has their human rights protected. The second pillar is creating advancement opportunities for women. Unilever empowers women by providing advancing opportunities in its operations, by promoting a safe work environment, by providing training to enhance their skill levels, by expanding opportunities in its retail value chain and by challenging negative gender beliefs that restrict career advancement for women. The third pillar is the development of business relationships that are inclusive. The focus of inclusion includes encouraging innovation and entrepreneurship to improve the livelihoods of the 500,000 small-scale farmers and the incomes of 5 million small-scale retailers that sell Unilever products.

In 2018, the results of this sustainability initiative included: Unilever having 61 percent of its procurement expenditures from suppliers who meet the requirements of Unilever's responsible sourcing policy; having only 0.69 accidents per 1 millions hours worked by Unilever employees; having 1.85 million women who are enabled to have access to initiatives of promoting safety; new skills development and the expansion of new career opportunities; having 49 percent of Unilever managers being women; supporting 746,000 small-scale farmers to improve their livelihoods; and supporting 1.73 million small-scale retailers.[8]

Characteristics of corporate sustainability leadership

There are a number of characteristics related to corporate sustainability leadership. These characteristics include distributed, emergent, and hosting.

Distributed

Sustainability leadership is distributive in nature. Truly sustainability leaders believe that their leadership actions are more important to the firm than themselves. If the firm has the ability to implement sustainability leadership activities across managers and followers, then the firm benefits by the dispersion of power to multiple decision makers. This bottom-up approach to leadership allows interconnectedness in the commitment to succeed in implementing the corporate sustainability initiatives. By empowering the followers to be able to make leadership decisions, the leaders facilitate the support of the followers by having them engaged, challenged and committed to their roles as both leaders and followers. Therefore, corporate sustainability leaders create opportunities for the employees to come together and be able to create their own sustainability solutions with the ability to explore, learn, and implement a viable course of action addressing the corporate sustainability issue.

Emergent

Due to the dynamic and constantly shifting internal and external environments, sustainability leaders must be aware that conditions are constantly changing from both a financial and non-financial perspective. As a result, due to the distributive nature discussed previously, sustainability leadership emerges due to unanticipated changes. Therefore, sustainability leadership develops or emerges to adapt to changes in the interactions and interdependencies that the firm has with external environmental factors. Adaptability through emerging leadership is needed since sustainability requires a new type of leadership, new innovation, and adjustment of the behavior of the employees.

Hosting

Sustainability leaders use hosting, which involves creating organizational conditions which will support employees with the necessary resources to establish and maintain sustainability leadership throughout the firm. Sustainability leaders recognize that hosting is needed since sustainability can be a complex problem to solve and, therefore, all the parts of the interconnected system need to be involved in the decision-making process to address corporate sustainability issues. A component of hosting is for the sustainability leaders to reduce or eliminate the negative impact of a bureaucratic structure of the firm, which limits the ability of the employees to develop relevant, viable sustainability solutions.[9]

Transformational and transactional leadership

Transformational leadership and corporate sustainability

A transformational leader is one who focuses on the development of a long-term vision for the firm. The establishment of the vision is the foundation for his/her perspective related to corporate sustainability. A transformational leader is charismatic and has the ability to project both strategic and non-strategic visions to the firm's employees. As a result, a transformational leader has the opportunity to champion the corporate sustainability commitment of the firm. The transformational leadership style allows the employees to freely develop new ideas and be able to make decisions in an autonomous setting. As "believers" of the vision of the transformational leader, the employees understand the importance of corporate sustainability and are able to effortlessly incorporate the values of corporate sustainability in their own decision-making processes. Transformational leadership is also altruistic in its style, which supports the values of corporate sustainability throughout the firm and is projected to the firm's stakeholders.

Transformational leaders have a much more effective style than transactional leaders by not only presenting a long-term vision but also inspiring and fostering a commitment of the employees in their focus toward achieving corporate sustainability goals. Authentic transformational leaders are those who lead by example in corporate sustainability issues. An authentic transformational leader can empower the employees to make their own decisions. The transformational leader will have confidence in the ability of the employees to be motivated to develop and executive decisions which incorporate corporate sustainability.[10]

Transactional leadership and corporate sustainability

Transactional leadership is based on the belief that leaders can accomplish goals by establishing transactions between the leader and the employees that are mutually beneficial. Transactional leaders focus on operational and routine activities within a firm. Under this leadership style, the leader allocates resources, monitors the activities of the employee and directly guides the employee in order to achieve the objectives of the firm. Since the focus is on compliance, this leadership style is more difficult in embracing the different components of corporate sustainability.

Since employees are motivated by agreeing to transactions with the leader, the employees are less likely to think and act outside the established parameters of their job description. As a result, their commitment to corporate sustainability will be based on the type of transactional "reward" that will be given for their actions. Transactional leaders control the behavior by the type of incentives given to the employees. Yet, transformational leaders can move beyond a control mechanism in allowing the employees to think and act beyond the established guidelines as the employees believe in the corporate sustainability vision of the leader.[11]

Therefore, transformational leaders are more likely to be able to lead the firm in being proactive in the design and implementation of effective corporate sustainability initiatives. Transformational leaders are more likely to encourage and support organizational change that is needed to embrace new corporate sustainability initiatives. In addition, by inspiring followers with his/her vision and creating excitement in the accomplishment of goals beyond the status quo, transformational leaders can convert their long-term vision into the long-term financial sustainability of the firm. Transformational leaders are able to reframe the future direction of the firm, which would integrate the firm's corporate sustainability actions into the future vision for the firm.[12]

Values–based model of transformational leadership

The enhanced value of the transformational leadership style as compared with the transactional leadership style can be shown in the values–based model of transformational leadership (Figure 2.1). The values–based model of transformational leadership comprises of the leadership values and styles

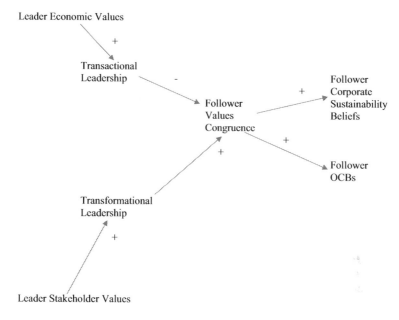

Figure 2.1 Value-based model of transformational leadership[13]

(transformational and transactional) of the manager, follower values congruence, and outcomes related to corporate sustainability beliefs and organizational citizenship behaviors (OCBs).

Leader values and leadership styles

The values of the leader are critical in the establishment of the criteria and rules for decision making, the development of the style of leadership, and the direct influence on the beliefs, attitudes, and behaviors of the followers. Leadership values can be separated based on the shareholders or focusing on the needs of all the critical stakeholders.

Leader economic values / transactional leader

Leader economic values is based on the belief that leaders are obligated to focus on the shareholders through profit maximization, sales growth, cost control, and shareholder returns. This singular approach to addressing only the needs of the shareholders restricts the availability of the leader to manage the actions of the employees beyond a formal transactional relationship.

Leaders who follow economic values focus on personal gain and follower rewards in order to achieve the goals of the firm. Transactional leaders focus on offering contingent rewards based on the actions and results of the employees and have a philosophy of management-by-exception where they are not actively involved in the decision-making processes of their subordinates. The basis of following economic values results in the leader ensuring the employees follow established rules and procedures which are incorporated in the employee's contingent rewards. Therefore, transactional leaders manage employees through the firm's existing structure, systems, and culture.

Leader stakeholder values/transformational leader

Leader stakeholder values is based on the belief that leaders are obligated to focus on the firm's stakeholders instead of just on the shareholders of the firm. The leader stakeholder's values identify the needs of each of the stakeholder groups and integrate those needs in the leader's decision-making process and actions. The stakeholder values of the leader align with the belief systems and actions of a transformational leader.

Since transformational leaders look beyond profit and self-achievement in pursuit of a greater good, transformational leaders embrace stakeholder values as an effective component of their leadership capabilities. In addition, stakeholder values support the leader's visionary message related to values, moral justifications, and installing a sense of collective purpose for the employees to facilitate their own motivation, which ensures the firm's overall goals are achieved.

Follower values congruence

Values congruence refers to the agreed shared values between the leaders and their employees. Because of their visionary beliefs and their charismatic personality, transformational leaders are able to achieve values congruence with their employees. Values congruence is a vital component of transformational leadership and is critical in integrating stakeholder values in the leader's decision-making process.

Alternatively, transactional leadership has a potentially negative association with follower values congruence. Transactional leaders depend on contingent rewards to motivate their followers. As a result, transactional leaders need to have regular monitoring of performance outcomes in order to establish goals resulting in a lower emphasis on relationship building and the lack of opportunity to develop a collective vision with their followers. As a result, the transactional leaders focus on their formal authority to issue directives and manage based on a short-term perspective since it can be directly linked to transactional-based rewards offered by the leaders. Therefore, transactional leaders have neither the desire nor the opportunity to develop value congruence with their followers.

Values-based leadership outcomes

Follower corporate sustainability beliefs

In order for employees to engage in socially responsible behavior and make decisions that are beneficial to the firm's stakeholders, they must believe that their actions are critical to the firm's overall effectiveness. As a result, transformational leaders who are grounded in values needed to serve the needs of the stakeholders have the ability to influence the behavior of the employees so that they appreciate their added value in focusing on corporate sustainability initiatives. Transformational leaders have the ability to develop the employees' understanding of the connection between their collective engagement in corporate sustainability activities and the overall effectiveness of the firm. The commitment of the employees is not only based on the effective transfer of the transformational leader's vision but also on serving as a role model in how the leader addresses issues related to corporate sustainability.

Follower organizational citizenship behaviors

Organizational citizenship behavior (OCB) is defined as the discretionary behavior of employees who are not recognized through a formal reward process, but instead support the overall goals of the firm. Examples of OCB behaviors include employees volunteering for special tasks that are not included in their job descriptions, helping the orientation process for new employees, helping coworkers when needed and participating in community activities. The transformational leader is able to encourage and reinforce the OCBs of his/her followers based on the vision presented by the leader. Alternatively, a transactional leader would not be able to instill OCBs because employees are motivated to only successfully complete the "transaction" with the leader.[14]

Responsible leadership

The evolution of transformational leadership has led to the development of responsible leadership. Traditionally, while leadership focuses on the ability to influence others and to facilitate the actions needed in order to achieve the goals of the firm, responsible leadership incorporates the pursuit of social goals as part of the leadership process. Responsible leadership can be defined as the decisions and actions made by the firm's leaders in addressing not only the interests of the stakeholders of the firm but also the promotion of positive social change for local communities and society.[15]

Responsible leaders are ones who focus the needs of all the stakeholders, which results in not only developing mutually beneficial stakeholder relationships but also secures the legitimacy of the firm to society. As a result, responsible leaders can use their influence to resolve conflicts among the stakeholders and the firm to encourage the stakeholders to be included in the dialogue pertaining to the firm's

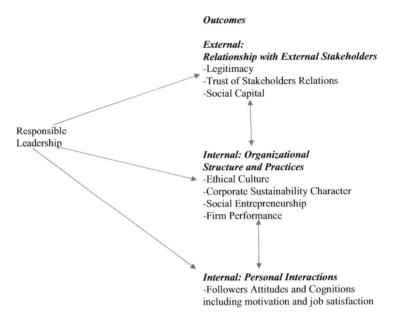

Figure 2.2 The multiple firm impacts of responsible leadership[16]

corporate sustainability commitment. The effectiveness of the responsible leader as a liaison between the firm and the stakeholders is based on the ability to reach a consensus related to the various stakeholders and their relationship with the firm. This consensus allows firms with responsible leaders to be able to develop significant benefits both internally and externally for the firm. The impact of responsible leadership at both a macro and micro level is shown in Figure 2.2.

External level: relationship with external stakeholders

Legitimacy

As was mentioned previously, responsible leadership fosters legitimacy among its stakeholders. Legitimacy is the ability of the firm to give the perception to its stakeholders that its actions are desirable and appropriate, and its values and beliefs are supported by social norms. Legitimacy can be categorized into three types: pragmatic, cognitive, and moral. Pragmatic legitimacy is the ability to satisfy the self-interested expectations by its main stakeholders. Cognitive legitimacy is based on the role and behavior of the firm in society. Moral legitimacy is based on the moral judgment and the evaluation of the firm's activities based on moral norms and values. Therefore, legitimacy is critical for a successful integration of corporate sustainability initiatives since the firm's actions are consistent with the expectations of the stakeholders and society.

Trustful stakeholder relations

Trust can be intensified based on character and relationships. Character-based trust focuses on the relationship between the responsible leader and his/her employees. This type of trust is developed through the demonstration of positive attributes of the leader such as integrity, fairness, and ability. Relationships based on trust focus on the social exchange process between the firm and its stakeholders with the goal of developing long-term relationships and goodwill. The relationship based on trust allows the responsible leader to develop the vision and implementation of the firm's commitment to corporate sustainability initiatives. The establishment of these trusted long-term relationships allows the firm to understand and develop corporate sustainability programs that serve the needs of all stakeholders.

Stakeholder social capital

The development of long-term trusted relationships between the firm and its stakeholders creates the development of social capital through goodwill. The creation of stakeholder social capital gives the firm the ability to use this capital in order to facilitate a collective action. Social capital allows for an open dialogue and can be "spent" to resolve disagreements among stakeholders and the firm. Since the firm has established a trust with the stakeholders, the firm is given an opportunity to resolve potential complaints from the stakeholders before the disagreement escalates publicly and legally.

Internal: organizational structure and practices

Ethical culture

The ethical culture refers to the type of work environment that is created and supported by responsible leaders of the firm. The presence of an ethical culture and the emphasis of corporate sustainability are driving forces in entrenching the overall firm beliefs of its commitment to continuing development of corporate sustainability initiatives. By being able to shape the formal and informal behavioral control systems of the employees of the firm, responsible leaders can transfer this positive commitment to the employees' ability to successfully implement corporate sustainability actions.

Corporate sustainability character

It is from this supportive ethical culture that the firm develops a perceived importance of corporate sustainability in its strategic vision. The corporate sustainability character is based on the sensemaking process of the employees. Sensemaking is the ability to understand external factors based on the perceptions of the employees. If the responsible leader can convince his/her employees that corporate sustainability is an important component of the firm's strategic focus, the employees will be more likely to be engaged in stakeholder dialogues based on social and environmental issues. As a result, the combined sensemaking of the firm's employees enhances the ability for the employees to understand the values which result in the firm being able to effectively implement its corporate sustainability programs.

Social entrepreneurship

Responsible leaders have the ability to foster social innovation through supporting creative ideas from its employees. This entrepreneurial spirit is shown in the creation, acceptance, and implementation of new processes and products which will be profitable as well as serving a social mission. Through the establishment of long-term relationships with stakeholders, the firm is able to use the social entrepreneurship drive of its employees to identify corporate sustainability initiatives which had not been considered a traditional entrepreneurship model through feedback from stakeholders, such as governments and NGOs.

Firm performance

A critical goal of responsible leaders is to be able to accomplish financial performance goals in a highly ethical manner. Due to the development of strong trustful relationships and the building of social capital with their stakeholders, firms can differentiate themselves from their competitors and, subsequently, enhance their financial performance.

Internal: personal interactions

Followers' attitudes and cognitions

Responsible leaders are positive role models for the employees of the firm. As a role model, responsible leaders are able to engage employees in corporate sustainability initiatives. In addition, responsible leaders can enhance the corporate citizenship behavior of the employees, further embracing the firm's commitment to corporate sustainability. Corporate citizenship behavior occurs when employees go beyond their job responsibilities to facilitate the achievement of the firm's goals.[17]

Corporate sustainability and power

Firms with a strong corporate sustainability commitment can generate a high level of power in relationships with their stakeholders. By effectively managing the needs of the stakeholders, they can externally influence the decisions made by the stakeholders which impact the local community.[18] Firms can establish inter-organizational stakeholder allies which create reciprocity relationships between the firm and its stakeholders. As a result, the establishment of powerful organizational networks that are connected with communities and individuals can result in the development of shared goals of corporate community involvement between the firm and its stakeholders. Therefore, as a firm is able to build a coalition of support with its stakeholders based on trust and loyalty, it will be able to use its informal power in implementing its corporate sustainability initiatives.[19]

Organizational politics and corporate sustainability

Organizational politics can be defined as the unsanctioned influence used by individuals to seek to promote the individual's self-interests at the expense of organizational goals. The manipulative and self-serving behavior of employees who use political leverage to reach their own goals can be a direct threat against the corporate sustainability initiatives established by the firm. Furthermore, political actions by the employees support a transactional leadership style. The actions to address the self-interests of the employee are based on a contingent reward for the use of manipulation to obtain individual goals.[20]

Organizational politics can be categorized based on whether the influence is related to the means or the ends to get a certain action accomplished. Within this framework, the other factor is whether the organization has sanctioned the influential behavior. Table 2.1 shows the different types of behavior related to types of influence and whether the organization approves of the action. The four quadrants are: non–political job behavior, organizationally dysfunctional political behavior, charismatic political behavior, and organizationally undesirable political behavior.

Table 2.1 Organizational political behavior[21]

Influence Means	Influence ends	
	Sanctioned by organization	**Non-sanctioned by organization**
Sanctioned by organization	Non–political job behavior	Organizationally dysfunctional political behavior
Not sanctioned by organization	Charismatic political behavior	Organizationally undesirable political behavior

Quadrant 1: non-political job behavior

Quadrant 1 behavior occurs when the leader's influence is organizationally sanctioned. This is considered non-political behavior because the firm approves of the leader using influence in both the means and the ends to accomplish a task. As a result, the leader has a legitimate formal authority to use influence in both the process and the outcomes of the action.

Quadrant 2: organizationally dysfunctional political behavior

Quadrant 2 behavior occurs when the leader's influence is organizationally sanctioned for the means but not for the ends. Since the firm has not approved the outcomes that the leader has achieved, this type of behavior can be considered an abuse of the leader's formal power based on his/her position. This behavior is considered to be dysfunctional since the resources that the leader had legitimate access to are being used for outcomes without the firm's approval.

Quadrant 3: charismatic political behavior

Quadrant 3 behavior occurs when the influenced means have not been sanctioned by the organization, but the influenced ends have been. The leader can accomplish legitimate organizational objectives through actions that have not been formally approved by the firm. As a result, a leader in this quadrant uses informal authority through charisma to accomplish the desired goals. A leader who is charismatic can influence his/her followers into corresponding behavior so that the goals of the firm can be achieved. As a result, charismatic political behavior is a common remedy for leaders who do not have the required formal authority to influence followers for the firm to achieve its desired results.

Quadrant 4: organizationally undesirable political behavior

Quadrant 4 behavior occurs when neither the means nor the ends are approved by the firm. As a result, this is considered to be organizationally undesirable political behavior. It is expected that the firm will not tolerate this type of "rogue" behavior. When a leader uses his/her charismatic personality to accomplish the objectives of the firm, it is not acceptable for a leader to use charisma to achieve his/her own self-interests that are not consistent with the objectives of the firm. As a result, this behavior is considered to not only be highly unethical, but it could also be in violation of not only the norms of the firm but also the laws and regulations governing the actions of the firm.[22]

The role of political tactics

There are eight categories of political tactics that can be used to try to influence the behavior of another person. These tactics include blaming or attacking others; use of information; creating and maintaining a favorable image; developing a base of support; ingratiation; power coalitions; associating with influential people; and creating obligations.

Blaming or attacking others

Blaming or attacking others can be both reactive and proactive by the individual to influence others. Scapegoating is used to reactively blame someone else for the failure of a project or initiative. Using the adage "when something goes wrong, the first thing to be fixed is the blame," scapegoating deflects blame from the individual and directs it at another person.

Proactive blaming occurs when the individual is competing against other employees for financial rewards, promotion or increased recognition of achievements. As a result, an individual will attempt to present the rival in unfavorable terms in the view of influential decision makers of the firm. These unfavorable terms include blaming the rival for failures or dismissing the contribution of the rival as unimportant, poorly timed, self-serving or just plain luck.

Use of information

Information can be used as either proactive, reactive or both depending on the circumstances. As a political tactic, information can be withheld from individuals, it can be distorted to favor certain individuals, or it could be used to overwhelm other individuals. Individuals will politically withhold information if the information requires an explanation which would reflect negatively on the individual. Information that is distorted does not mean the information has been falsified, which would be a serious violation within the code of conduct of the firm. Distortion of the facts is presenting the facts in a favorable format for the individuals. Distorted information could include only data which is favorable to the individual and omit unfavorable data. This type of selective disclosure allows the individual to control the message of the information as it is presented to other individuals.

The other extreme of the continuum is to overwhelm the individual with information. By presenting too much information, it becomes a burden on the individual receiving the information to determine which information is relevant and which information is not relevant for the decision-making process. This overkill of information is based on the belief that relevant information which would have a negative impact on the individual presenting the information is buried and will not be discovered by the individual receiving the information.

Creating and maintaining a favorable image

Creating and maintaining a favorable image is a proactive political behavior which is designed to promote self-interests. A favorable image can be in the form of general physical appearance but it is also based on the actions of the individuals. Behaviors like being sensitive to organizational norms as well as having the individual's successes highlighted foster a favorable image. The promotion of self-interests can include taking credit for the ideas and/or accomplishment of others through omission of the true party responsible for the achievement. This promotion of self-interests can also occur when the individual takes credit for being part of the "team" while, the individual did not contribute to the success of the team. In addition, personality traits such as likeability, enthusiasm, thoughtfulness, and honesty create a strong positive favorable image of the individual.

Developing a base of support

A critical political tactic is the ability to proactively build support within the firm. Regardless of the issue, if the individual has a strong support base, s/he will have less difficulty implementing his/her ideas throughout the firm. Building support can include ensuring other individuals understand the person's idea before a decision is made. Another method of building support is to get other decision makers involved in the decision-making process to ensure they will support the proposal since they are committed to the idea by contributing to the decision.

Ingratiation

Ingratiation is the political tactic of being more personable and likeable in the perception of other individuals. Giving praise to others, especially one's superiors, allows the individuals to be perceived in a favorable manner by others. This positive feedback gives the individual the political leverage to use these favorable relationships to his/her advantage when they are needed.

Power coalitions

Individuals who are associated with and have a personal relationship with those who have a high level of power within the firm are able to use this power coalition to his/her advantage. Intertwined in previous characteristics such as having a power base and building a strong positive relationship through image and ingratiation, the individual can rely on power coalitions to support the ideas presented by that individual.

Associating with influential people

Related to power coalitions, an individual who has close relationships with influential people can use these relationships to achieve his or her goals. The more powerful the individual's external network of influential people, the more flexibility the individual has of using internal and external influential people to achieve the desired goals of the individual.

Creating obligations

A critical political tactic is the ability to create obligations from other individuals. If the individual helps another individual in the firm accomplish his/her goal, it is expected that the other individual will also help when called upon by the first individual. This unspoken reciprocity agreement between the two parties is a very effective technique to accomplishing the goals of each individual. Using the adage of "if you scratch my back, I'll scratch yours" gives the security for both parties that each party will support the other when the need arises.[23]

Organizational change and corporate sustainability

The purpose of organizational change is to move the firm from its current position to a more desirable position. The type of change spans the spectrum from minor evolutionary changes to more radical changes. Firms need to perceive change as an opportunity that must be anticipated and managed. If a firm fails to change, the previous opportunities may become threats as its competitors have implemented the necessary changes in order to match the current industry conditions.

Three types of change can be used by the firm in order to effectively implement its corporate sustainability initiatives: developmental, transitional, and transformational. Developmental change occurs when a firm improves an existing skill, method or condition. Transitional change occurs when the firm moves its foundation from its current state to a future state. Transformational change occurs when the firm makes a quantum adjustment and fundamentally changes the composition of the firm.

In order for the firm to interconnect organizational change and corporate sustainability in its decision-making process, the firm must embrace a solutions-based model which focuses on providing values instead of just goods or services. The solutions-based model integrates social costs, environmental externalities, and resource information in its financial calculations. In addition, the solutions-based model embraces the development of stakeholder networks, changes the attitudes of its employees, and changes the perception of how the firm views its business.

Organizational change will always be challenged by the resistance of some employees. Some employees embrace the status quo and will resist any change, and other employees do not like the uncertainty that is related to organizational change. These employees fear that change could impact their status, pay or comfort within the firm. Furthermore, employees may find it difficult to accommodate any changes in their current job positions. The level of resistance will increase with the complexity of the proposed change. Resistance can be either

Table 2.2 Resistance to change factors and strategies to reduce them[25]

Individual level	
Barriers to change	*Strategy*
– Misunderstanding or lack of communication	– Negotiation
– Lack of trust	– Manipulation
– Threat of job status and/or security	– Participation
Group level	
Barriers to change	*Strategy*
– Group culture	– Group participation in change
– Ignoring institutions in the group	– Individual–group interactions
– Individual–group conflict	– Changing group values
Organizational level	
Barriers to change	*Strategy*
– Lack of strategy and/or long-term plans	– Developing new strategies, policies and frameworks
– High level of bureaucracy	– Identifying managerial champions
– Lack of top management commitment	– Firm-wide collaboration

explicit or covert in nature by the employees. Actions which demonstrate a resistance to change include disputes over resources, a voicing of doubt about the benefits of the changes, and the unwillingness to commit to implementing the changes. Table 2.2 highlights the different barriers to change and the strategies that can be used to reduce those barriers.[24]

Drivers of change and corporate sustainability

External drivers of change

Globalization

Globalization has opened up markets around the world and has dispersed capital and direct foreign investment to developing and developed countries. However, global activity, based on trade and financial flows, disproportionally benefits more affluent countries. In addition, environmental costs are also distributed unevenly so that developing countries receive a disproportionate level of issues which have a negative impact on the environment.

Alliances

The formation of alliances of various stakeholders in social and environmental groups, firms, local governments, and communities creates influential partnerships. The linkage between NGOs and various stakeholders allows for more effective dissemination of information and gives firms another communication channel with critical stakeholders. Therefore, NGOS have emerged as a powerful force for corporate change related to corporate sustainability. For example, the NGO, Global Forest Watch, identities old growth forests to protect and gives information about sustainable forests to firms such as Ikea in selling wood products whose origin is from sustainable forests. The World Wide Fund for Nature (WWF) provides Unilever with information related to sustainable fishing which is used by Unilever for its fish-based products.

Internal drivers of change

Costs of non-compliance

The cost of non-compliance with government laws and regulations could have a significant financial impact on the firm. Depending on the scope and number of violations, firms can be fined millions of dollars for violation of compliance standards. Therefore, having a stakeholder focus includes serving the needs of the community and government not only in the implementation of corporate sustainability initiatives but also for ensuring full compliance with all laws and government regulations.

Employee awareness

Employee awareness of issues such as environmental and occupational health and safety conditions increases the employees' demands for firm compliance. For transformational leaders, this driver is not a concern because these issues have already been incorporated in the development and execution in the leader's vision toward corporate sustainability. However, these issues can be a concern for transactional leaders who may not have a direct transaction between all the operations of the firm and the activities of the employees.

Leadership and risk management

The leader must identify and address potential areas of risk for the firm. Embracing the philosophy of the transformational leader, the leader must understand the importance of public opinion in the evaluation of firm risk. It is the responsibility of the leader to ensure that there is a high level of public trust with the firm. In addition the leader must ensure that partnerships are formed with stakeholders to aid in the reduction of risk. The leader also must encourage employees to identify and resolve potential areas of risk for the firm.

The leader must also be aware that its stakeholders expect that they live in a "risk free" world based on the actions of the firm. For example, a pulp and paper mill in Canada was using chlorine bleaching in its manufacturing process which created high environmental risks. Concerns were raised by stakeholders including local farmers, aboriginal residents, and environmental activists. The mill modified its production process to reduce the pollution level at minimal cost, yet it increased the long-term viability of production of the mill.

Natural capitalism

Natural capitalism is based on increasing the profitability of the firm by reducing the environmental "footprint" made by the firm. Areas of natural capitalism include increased productivity of natural resources, increased recyclability of product components, and the elimination of waste materials. Therefore, corporate sustainability initiatives which include natural capitalism serve the dual purpose of serving the needs of the stakeholders and increasing the financial returns for the shareholders.

Innovative culture

A critical driver for organizational change directly impacting corporate sustainability is the firm's innovative culture. Transformational leaders who inspire employees to be innovative and creative can yield significant positive returns for the firms. An innovative culture recognizes that society and stakeholders need change over time. Therefore, continuous innovation is needed for the firm to continuously adjust its corporate sustainability initiatives to address the evolving needs of the stakeholders. In addition, an innovative culture also yields avenues in which the firm can differentiate its competitive advantage, increasing the financial performance of the firm.[26]

Organizational change leadership and corporate sustainability

For a firm to effectively design and implement successful corporate sustainability initiatives, it must ensure that there is strong employee commitment for the initiatives. As a result, firms must ensure that the employees understand the rationale for the corporate sustainability initiative and be able to adapt their behavior, if necessary, in order to implement the initiative. There are three phases firm must implement in order to align the commitment and behavior of the employees with the vision and focus of the corporate sustainability initiatives. The three phases are making the case for change, translating vision into action and expanding boundaries. Figure 2.3 highlights the different dimensions in the three phase model of a corporate sustainability initiative.

Phase 1: making the case for change

If the firm has not had past experience in addressing corporate sustainability issues, there must be a clear and compelling case presented to the employees for embracing change. If the firm is not familiar with the potential complexities of formulating and implementing solutions for corporate sustainability

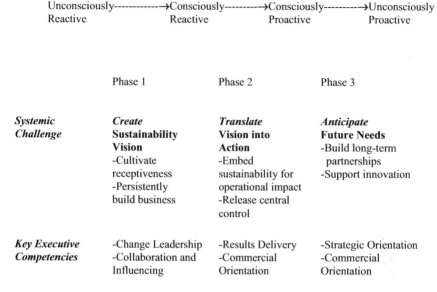

Figure 2.3 Three phase model of a corporate sustainability initiative[27]

issues, the firm needs to use collaboration and influence in the development and commitment of its employees, highlighting the benefits of properly addressing these issues.

This influence shifts the firm from a position of unconscious to conscious reactivity. It is common for firms to initially be reactive to corporate sustainability issues due to the lack of familiarity with the potential complexities. Threats and opportunities for the firm can change over time and could be "under the radar" for the firm until some action comes to light and forces the leaders to react to changes in the status quo.

When firms are forced to make changes to address corporate sustainability issues, they are reactive since the firm lacks the shared and consistent understanding of what constitutes the causes and potential solutions of the corporate sustainability issues. After the issue has been identified, it is the responsibility of the leaders to not only influence the employees but also be leaders of change. The leaders must be able to communicate a compelling vision and ensure a commitment by informing the employees.

In order to establish this commitment, the leaders must understand the specific motivations of the firm's critical stakeholders and partner with other managers within the firm to integrate the corporate sustainability commitment throughout the firm. Leaders must be able to identify and develop specific sets of business processes to manage the risks and capture new opportunities related to corporate sustainability. At the end of phase 1, corporate sustainability emerges as a strong mandate among the employees as the firm moves from consciously reactive to consciously proactive.

Phase 2: translating vision into action

As firms shift from phase 1 to phase 2, the firm's commercial orientation becomes the driving force to align the corporate sustainability initiative with the value creation for the firm. This is a significant change from phase 1 in which the firm was reacting to corporate sustainability issues that needed to be addressed by the firm. The focus shifts from "putting out the fires" related to corporate sustainability issues to building a fire wall by proactively developing corporate sustainability initiatives.

The role of the leader is to convert the employee commitments into a comprehensive change program which has established, clearly defined initiatives with firm commercial targets. For the commitment to become entrenched in the beliefs of the employees, the corporate sustainability initiative must also deliver financial and other firm-based results to support the viability of the corporate sustainability initiative.

As a result, integrated in the corporate sustainability initiative is the tracking of clear metrics to measure the success of the initiative. The leaders must be able to measure the financial, environmental, and social impact of the corporate sustainability initiative to see what adjustments, if any, are needed for the execution of future initiatives. Therefore, in phase 2, the focus on being a better corporate citizen through increased corporate sustainability must be coupled with positive financial results for the firm. As the firm shifts from phase 2 to phase 3, the focus of the firm changes in relation to corporate sustainability toward future actions.

Phase 3: expanding boundaries

In phase 3, the leaders use the firm's corporate sustainability strategy as leverage to enhance its competitive advantage. The firm now views corporate sustainability as a strategic opportunity and focuses on developing a long-term corporate sustainability strategy. In phase 3, the goal is to infuse corporate sustainability beliefs in the DNA of the firm. To reinforce the firm's long-term commitment, the leaders will pursue long-term investments and potential partnerships to help guide the future corporate sustainability vision of the firm. A component of this long-term focus is to identify the future needs of the firm's stakeholders and attempt to anticipate, influence, and benefit from potential future government regulations related to sustainability. In phase 3, the firm shifts from consciously proactive to unconsciously proactive since corporate sustainability is interwoven within the firm and is considered part of the firm's DNA. The firm integrates corporate sustainability in its decision-making process like a pilot putting an airplane on autopilot.[28]

Pablo Isla: the best-performing CEO in the world's view of corporate sustainability

Established in 1963, Inditex is one of the largest fashion retailers in the world with eight brands (Zara, Pull&Bear, Massimo Dutti, Bershka, Stradivarious, Oysho, Zara Home, and Uterque) and over 7,400 stores in 96 markets globally. With over 170,000 employees, Inditex is a global vertically integrated company that performs all the fashion production functions, including design, manufacturing, distribution, and retail.[29]

Born in Spain in 1964, Pablo Isla became CEO of Inditex in 2005 and added the position of Chairman in 2011.[30] In 2017, *Harvard Business Review* ranked Pablo Isla as the "Best Performing CEO in the World." Pablo Isla's management style encourages a culture that supports corporate sustainability. All the firm's decisions have corporate sustainability impact integrated into the decision-making process. This includes environmental-based issues such as recycling materials, reutilization of garments, eco-efficiency issues, 40 percent reduction in water consumption, and 20 percent reduction in energy consumption.

Pablo Isla's commitment to corporate sustainability also addresses the needs of all Inditex's stakeholders, including ensuring a corporate culture supporting its employees, providing a positive values system for its stakeholders and continuous community investments.

In an intersection of stakeholder involvement and corporate sustainability, Pablo Isla states:

> We need to get used to this world in which we operate. We need to be very transparent, very serious as a company, in all the countries in which we have activities, be very focused in what we do, and finally we come back to what I was saying before, trying to execute our business model to satisfy the demands of our customers in all the different geographies in which we operate.[31]

As a transformational CEO, Pablo Isla believes in the four pillars of the retail industry. The first pillar is Inditex's employees. It is critical that the employees are motivated and are encouraged to be creative and take the initiative in order to bring about the most effective development and execution of Inditex's objectives. The second pillar is to always ensure the customers get the best products including the best value related to price and quality. The third pillar is the use of global technology solutions to continuously develop new opportunities for Inditex. The fourth pillar is long-term sustainability, which is the foundation of any business model. Corporate sustainability initiatives include the sustainable origin of raw materials, the reusing or recycling of textile products that are at the end of its life cycle, designing eco-efficient stores, rational and fair use of water, and the elimination of waste in a smart manner.[32]

Sustainable growth strategy

Pablo Isla believes in a circular economy that maximizes the use of the firm's resources through the recovery of the firm's products after they have been used in order to recycle the materials for use within the next generation of products. A critical component of a circular economy is for the firm to have a high level of corporate transparency.

Isla's belief in transparency is the cornerstone in ensuring Inditex's stakeholders understand how the actions of the firm are attempting to satisfy the needs of its global stakeholders. Transparency and corporate sustainability commitment are demonstrated in Inditex's actions including supply chain management, adequate working conditions, ensuring occupational health and safety compliance, dignified salaries, the use of collective bargaining for factories, female empowerment, and the protection of migrants.[33]

Questions for thought

1. Do you think it is common for Fortune 500 firms such as Unilever to have transformational leaders related to corporate sustainability? Why or why not?
2. Why would Fortune 500 firms have transactional leaders if this leadership style is not as effective as a transformational leadership style related to corporate sustainability?
3. What would be some of the differences in how transformational and transactional leaders interact with their stakeholders related to corporate sustainability?
4. Can leaders of a firm implement corporate sustainability initiatives without using their power?
5. How important are organizational politics in a firm which is succeeding at achieving its goals related to corporate sustainability?
6. How common do you think employee resistance to change is in Fortune 500 firms? Does this resistance change over time for the employees and the firm overall?
7. Were you familiar with Inditex? How does a relatively unknown firm have the best performing CEO in the world according to *Harvard Business Review*?

Notes

1 www.unilever.com/about/who-we-are/about-Unilever/
2 www.unilever.com/sustainable-living/transformational-change/index.html
3 www.unilever.com/about/who-we-are/about-Unilever/
4 www.unilever.com/sustainable-living/improving-health-and-well-being/health-and-hygiene/healthy-handwashing-habits-for-life/
5 www.unilever.com/sustainable-living/improving-health-and-well-being/health-and-hygiene/healthy-handwashing-habits-for-life/helping-people-get-into-healthy-hygiene-habits/

6 www.unilever.com/sustainable-living/improving-health-and-well-being/
7 www.unilever.com/sustainable-living/reducing-environmental-impact/
8 www.unilever.com/sustainable-living/enhancing-livelihoods/
9 Peter McGhee and Patricia Grant. 2017. Sustainability Leadership: It's Not about Heroes. In eds. Gabriel Eweje and Ralph J. Bathurst. *CSR, Sustainability, and Leadership*. Routledge: New York. 11–30.
10 Peter A. Stanwick and Sarah D. Stanwick. 2016. *Understanding Business Ethics*. Sage Publications: Thousand Oaks, CA.
11 Peter A. Stanwick and Sarah D. Stanwick. 2016. *Understanding Business Ethics*. Sage Publications: Thousand Oaks, CA.
12 Shuili Du, Valerie Swaen, Adam Lindgreen and Sankar Sen. 2013. The Roles of Leadership Styles in Corporate Responsibility. *Journal of Business Ethics*. 114: 155–169.
13 Kevin S. Groves and Michael A. LaRocca. 2011. Responsible Leadership Outcomes Via Stakeholder CSR Values: Testing a Values-Centered Model of Transformational Leadership. *Journal of Business Ethics*. 98: 37–55.
14 Kevin S. Groves and Michael A. LaRocca. 2011. Responsible Leadership Outcomes Via Stakeholder CSR Values: Testing a Values-Centered Model of Transformational Leadership. *Journal of Business Ethics*. 98: 37–55.
15 Gabriel Eweje and Ralph J. Bathurst. 2017. *CSR, Sustainability, and Leadership*. Routledge: New York.
16 Christian Voegtlin, Moritz Patzer and Andreas Georg Scherer. 2012. Responsible Leadership in Global Business: A New Approach to Leadership and Its Multi-Level Outcomes. *Journal of Business Ethics*. 105(1): 1–16.
17 Christian Voegtlin, Moritz Patzer and Andreas Georg Scherer. 2012. Responsible Leadership in Global Business: A New Approach to Leadership and Its Multi-Level Outcomes. *Journal of Business Ethics*. 105(1): 1–16.
18 Jean-Pascal Gond and Daniel Nyberg. 2017. Materializing Power to Recover Corporate Social Responsibility. *Organizational Studies*. 38(3): 1127–1148.
19 Denise Kleinrichert. 2008. Ethics, Power and Communities: Corporate Social Responsibility Revisited. *Journal of Business Ethics*. 78: 475–485.
20 Marjorie L. Randall, Russell Cropanzano, Carol A. Bormann and Andrej Birjulin. 1999. Organizational Politics and Organizational Support as Predictors of Work Attitudes, Job Performance, and Organizational Citizenship Behavior. *Journal of Organizational Behavior*. 20: 159–174.
21 Bronston T. Mayes and Robert W. Allen. 1977. Toward a Definition of Organizational Politics. *Academy of Management Review*. 2(4): 675.
22 Bronston T. Mayes and Robert W. Allen. 1977. Toward a Definition of Organizational Politics. *Academy of Management Review*. 2(4): 672–678.
23 Robert W. Allen, Dan L. Madison, Lyman W. Porter, Patricia A. Renwick and Bronston T. Mayes. 1979. Organizational Politics: Tactics and Characteristics of Its Actors. *California Management Review*. 22(1): 77–83.
24 Rodrigo Lozano. 2013. Are Companies Planning Their Organisational Changes for Corporate Sustainability? An Analysis of Three Case Studies on Resistance to Change and Their Strategies to Overcome It. *Corporate Social Responsibility and Environmental Management*. 20(5): 275–295.
25 Rodrigo Lozano. 2013. Are Companies Planning Their Organisational Changes for Corporate Sustainability? An Analysis of Three Case Studies on Resistance to Change and Their Strategies to Overcome It. *Corporate Social Responsibility and Environmental Management*. 20(5): 280.
26 Dexter Dunphy, Andrew Griffiths and Suzanne Benn. 2003. *Organizational Change for Corporate Sustainability: A Guide for Leaders and Change Agents of the Future*. Routledge: New York.

27 Christoph Lueneburger and Daniel Goleman. 2010. The Change Leadership Sustainability Demands. *Sloan Management Review*. 51(4) Summer: 52.
28 Christoph Lueneburger and Daniel Goleman. 2010. The Change Leadership Sustainability Demands. *Sloan Management Review*. 51(4) Summer: 49–55.
29 www.inditex.com/en/about-us/who-we-are
30 www.nestle.com/asset-library/documents/media/press-release/2018-january/cv-pablo-isla.pdf
31 https://hbr.org/ideacast/2017/10/2017s-top-performing-ceo-on-getting-product-right
32 Pablo Isla. 2018. Pablo Isla on Four Pillars of the Retail Industry. *The Wall Street Journal*. January 17.
33 https://uk.fashionnetwork.com/news/Inditex-s-president-Pablo-Isla-highlights-the-important-of-sustainable-growth-and-circular-economy,851729.html

3 Corporate sustainability and management decision making

Introduction

Regardless of the focus of the firm's corporate sustainability strategy, all components of the firm's commitment to corporate sustainability are based on the decisions made by the firm's managers. This chapter highlights the complex interactions that can occur when managers develop and implement their corporate sustainability decisions. While it is expected that managers will always make "rational" decisions, it is not always the case and it may not be the best approach to take in certain circumstances when the firm needs to quickly address corporate sustainability issues which could have a negative impact on the firm if a solution is not properly developed and executed. Concepts that are presented in this chapter include: rational decision making; avoidance decision making; logical incrementalism; decision biases; sensemaking; systems development; and management control systems. The chapter opens with a description on how Goodera Information Technologies facilitates the corporate sustainability process for its clients. The chapter ends with a description of how the company Valutus incorporates corporate sustainability values in the decision-making process.

Goodera's ability to facilitate corporate sustainability decision making

Goodera Information Technologies (GIT) started in 2003 in Bengaluru, India. The strategic focus of the company is to provide a technology platform used by firms, foundations, governments, and non-governmental organizations in the development and implementation of corporate sustainability initiatives. Goodera's technology platform is used by its clients to collect and analyze data in local languages to help in the manager's decision-making process. The firm also establishes technology dashboards in order to report the corporate sustainability information to the firm's critical stakeholders.[1]

Goodera's co-founder, Richa Bajpai, stated that:

> Our mission as a company is to actually power this entire world with good. When we're competing with the likes of Amazon and Flipkart with regards to talent, we say that this is a company where you can do good and at the same time, do good business. So, our heart and the mind is the right place and we've been lucky enough to get investors who want to back something like this ... People are now ready to see technology as something which can benefit this whole ecosystem. So, if it doesn't go out to the masses, and if it doesn't solve problems, or lead to transparency or better accountability, then the technology is not doing its work.[2]

The origins of what was to become GIT started when co-founders Richa Bajpai and Abhishek Humbad were working on a renewable energy startup firm and realized that there were transparency and accountability issues related to firm's commitment to corporate sustainability. They found that what was actually being implemented was not the information that was being communicated by the firm to its stakeholders. Goodera's technology platform was developed in order to transfer real-time information of the actual actions related to the firm's commitment to corporate sustainability.

As a result, this transparent information was critical to the stakeholders in order to ensure their needs were acknowledged and addressed. In addition, this real-time information allowed Goodera's clients to effectively adapt and adjust the actions of its corporate sustainability programs to ensure that what the organization had promised to stakeholders was consistent with the actual actions of the client. The benefit of a data-based platform is that it allows more seamless communication between the client and the stakeholders, which enhances the ability of the stakeholders to collaborate with the client to make more informed managerial decisions related to corporate sustainability issues.

The Goodera platform allows for data to be submitted and analyzed in real time from different technology devices including smart phones, iPads, and traditional desktop computers. As a result, the client can review shifting trends related to its corporate sustainability programs instantaneously. One of Goodera's clients working on a corporate sustainability project in Africa adjusted its focus and financial commitment by shifting resources from one area to another area within the project based on the data analytics provided by Goodera.

Goodera's data base standardizes the data which allows the clients a more effective way to analyze the data and the impact of the managers' decisions. Employees also have the convenience of a centralized data base in order to identify corporate sustainability opportunities within the firm such as volunteer programs.

Goodera emphasizes that corporate sustainability should not be viewed as a cost to the firm but should be considered as part of a long-term financial sustainability strategy. Corporate sustainability initiatives that provide welfare to stakeholders such as the local communities and the natural environment are necessary for the long-term sustainability of society, including the consumers of the firm.[3]

Decision-making process

A manager must make numerous decisions on a daily basis. As a result, it is imperative for the manager to be aware of the factors that can impact his/her decisions. The decision-making process can be categorized into five major dimensions: rational, avoidance, logical incrementalism, political, and garbage can.[4]

Rational decision making and sustainability

Rationality can be defined as behavior that is logical in the pursuance of the firm's goals and objectives. However, within the individual's rational decision-making process are the constraints of bounded rationality. Bounded rationality can be defined as the limits in the effectiveness of the decision-making process based on cognitive and political realities. As a result, individuals may have to "satisfice" their decisions by making not only optimal decisions but also decisions that are "good enough" to satisfy the critical components of the objective.

In addition, rational decisions are usually incremental in nature because the previous decisions and actions "anchor" and, therefore, influence the future decisions of the individual. This "logical incrementalism" incorporates not only objective information but also factors in the individual's intuition and how the decisions will be accepted politically within the firm. Rational decision making incorporates three major components: decision-specific factors, environmental factors, and firm factors. An integrated model of the rational decision-making process is shown in Figure 3.1.

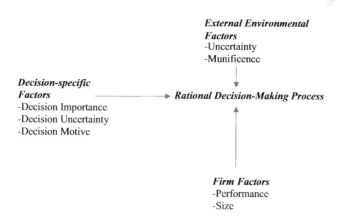

Figure 3.1 Integrated model of rational decision making[5]

Decision-specific factors

Decision importance

The importance of the decision impacts how the individual makes the decision. It is expected that the higher the level of importance, the higher probability the decision maker will ensure that the decision is made in a rational manner. This determination of rationality is based on the belief that the importance of the decision will lead to important outcomes and consequences which may need to be justified in a rational manner after the decision has been made.

Decision uncertainty

The level of uncertainty the individual has related to the decision can impact the rationality of the decision. It is expected that the individual will try to reduce the level of uncertainty and ensure that the decision is based on a highly rational decision-making process.

Decision motive

The motive of the decision refers to the conditions in which the decision needs to be made to develop an appropriate level of action. For example, whether the decision is based on seizing an opportunity or resolving a crisis generates very different motives for the individual to structure his/her decision-making process.

Based on bounded rationality, it is acceptable to "satisfice" a decision for a firm's opportunity which may not be the desirable optimal outcome. However, satisficing may not be acceptable or appropriate if the firm must address a crisis. Under a crisis scenario, it is imperative that the decision maker develop a high level of rationality which can be converted into an optimal solution to the problem facing the firm. Therefore, if the decision related to seizing a future opportunity fails, there are negative consequences, but those consequences are not fatal. If the decision related to resolving a crisis fails, it could result in the firm no longer being a viable business.

External environmental factors

Environmental uncertainty

Environmental uncertainty refers to the unpredictable shifting of external factors related to the environment. As a result, the higher the level of environmental dynamism or change, the higher the levels of rational decision making that are necessary to address the shifting conditions facing the firm. Changing environmental conditions which can increase the level of environmental uncertainty include factors such as political changes, macroeconomic shifts, technology shifts, government regulation changes, competitive changes, and demographic changes.

Environmental munificence

Environmental munificence can be defined as the abundance or scarcity of critical resources needed for the firm to manage its operations. The scarcer the resources available to the firm, the higher the demands on the decision maker to optimize the decisions to capture and use efficiently the scarce resources needed by the firm. The more abundant the resources, the less pressure on the decision maker to try to optimize the decision since the resources are not scarce and, therefore, the decision maker can make a "satisficing" based decision to capture the necessary resources.

Firm factors

Firm performance

One viewpoint is that it is expected that firm performance has a positive relationship with rational decision making. As the firm financial performance increases, it has better access to resources and, therefore, has the opportunity to develop comprehensive rational decisions. Alternatively, it can also be argued that firms that have decreasing levels of financial performance are more likely to be in a crisis mode where they must have a highly rational decision-making process to address the crisis issues. Therefore, it could be concluded that, regardless of the trend in the firm's performance, the decision makers must establish a highly rational decision-making process.

Firm size

As firms become larger, it is expected that firms will implement more formal and rational decision-making processes as a method to help co-ordinate the complex functions of the firm. The formality of the decision-making process and the increasing number of management levels within the firm will entrench the rational decision-making process within the firm.[6]

Rational decision making is based on the belief that managers will make decisions based on known objectives where the managers are able to analyze the external environment and the internal operations. Therefore, rational decision making is a comprehensive, normative process in which the managers gather information, develop alternative courses of action, and then objectively identify and implement the optimal alternative.

From a corporate sustainability perspective, rational decision making can be a two-edged sword related to the firm's ongoing commitment to corporate sustainability. While rational decision making should be embraced when managers focus on corporate sustainability issues, rational decision making can also limit the managers to considering non-traditional solutions to corporate sustainability problems. The managers and their superiors must realize that issues related to corporate sustainability can be as predictable or unpredictable as any other type of issues which the firm must address to ensure its long-term viability. As a result, managers should not abandon non-rational thinking, even if it is more difficult to justify after the decision has been implemented related to corporate sustainability issues.

Avoidance decision making and sustainability

Avoidance is the decision-making process which is most commonly linked to employees' resistance to change. A core component of resistance to change is the corresponding uncertainty based on the unknown results of the change process. Therefore, due to this inherent resistance, firms will embrace the status quo as a desirable objective since it will reduce uncertainty in the outcomes of the decisions implemented by the firm. As a result, managers who embrace an avoidance decision-making process do not seek out alternative courses of action which would disrupt the status quo. This can create potentially irrational decision making where defending the status quo supersedes the development of an optimal solution for the firm.

As was mentioned in the previous section related to rational decision making, avoidance to properly address issues related to corporate sustainability can lead to sub-optimal courses of action for the firm. Managers must be aware that following the status quo does not solve crisis issues related to corporate sustainability.

Logical incrementalism and sustainability

Logical incrementalism involves a step-by-step incremental decision-making process. The underlying assumption of logical incrementalism is that since the external environment is unstable and the cognitive capabilities of the managers are limited, the best course of action to take is to make small, incremental adjustments to the strategic focus of the firm. Justifications for logical incrementalism include making small adjustments in order to make sense of the external environment and be flexible enough to make additional adjustments when necessary. Therefore, logical incrementalism has three characteristics which are: (1) incremental and not dramatic decisions are made at any given time; (2) the decision-making process is slow and steady toward a broad or global goal; and (3) the incremental process allows the managers to gather more information and feedback from their initial decisions.

Logical incrementalism moves up a step further than the firm following the status quo. However, logical incrementalism will not result in an effective solution if quicker and more radical actions are needed by the firm to address the corporate sustainability issues.

Political mode and sustainability

Managers in a political mode of decision making have significant challenges in the establishment of a broad consensus on the objectives of the firm. In a political climate, full information is never available since each manager wants to control information to ensure the information is favorable to the manager's own decisions. The underlying assumption of a political-based culture is that the employees will have competing interests and will fight and defend decisions and actions that are in their own self-interests. Therefore, employees that are able to form the most powerful coalition will have their decisions implemented by the firm.

As a result, a political mode of decision making can yield sub-optimal results for the firm since the political process and not achieving the optimal result drive the decision-making process related to corporate sustainability issues. In addition, if the political influence of the decision makers also yields serving the self-interests of the decision makers, the solutions proposed by the decision makers are not transparent and can have a negative impact on the firm's relationships with its stakeholders.

Garbage can mode and sustainability

Garbage can mode of decision making is based on the inherent inconsistencies in the decision-making process. The firms are viewed as "organized anarchies" with no specific rationale for how decisions are made. Garbage can mode uses the reverse order of the decision-making process as compared with rational decision making. While rational decision making identifies a problem and then seeks a solution, garbage can theory is based on the belief that the decision maker has a solution and then tries to find a problem to match. Therefore, garbage can theory can be connected with political decision making in the sense that if a decision maker wants a certain outcome or solution, the decision maker will seek a problem that can be identified in order to achieve that solution.[7]

Garbage can mode decision making can lead to sub-optimal decision making related to corporate sustainability since the managers have a preconceived notion of what the solution should be before the decision-making process starts. As a result, the decision makers will guide the decision-making process to ensure that the desired solution becomes the accepted solution. Of course, the desired solution may not be the optimal solution and the managers may have completely ignored alternative courses of action which have a much higher probability of yielding the optimal course of action for the firm's corporate sustainability issues.

Decision bias and sustainability

Decision bias occurs when the individual's perception is distorted based on the subjective interpretation of the facts of the situation. Decision biases can either be cognitive or motivational based. A cognitive bias occurs when there is a systematic discrepancy between the "correct" answer in a task based on the individual's judgement and the actual answer given by the individual.

Motivation biases occur when the judgment of the individual is influenced by the desirability or undesirability of events, consequences, and outcomes. For example, individuals with a vested interest in a project will give overly optimistic evaluations of the components of the projects to influence other decision makers to approve the development of the project.

Types of biases

There are three different types of biases: strategy based, association based, and psychophysically based.

Strategy-based biases

Strategy-based biases occur when the individual develops a strategy which is sub-optimal due to the bias.

GAMBLER'S FALLACY

This bias is based on the belief that independent events are not independent. For example, every time a coin is tossed the odds are 50 percent either heads or tails. However, for example, if the first eight tosses resulted in heads, an individual's belief is that the next toss must be tails due to probability. It is called a gambler's fallacy since a gambler will reduce the calculated probability of the event occurring in the future based on the past performance. The fallacy occurs since the events are independent and there is no relationship connecting the probability of the events.

Association-based biases

Association-based biases occur when there is automatic mental association of an event based on past events.

EASE OF RECALL

This bias occurs when the individual overstates the probability of an event based on ease in which the individual can remember the event.

MYOPIC PROBLEM REPRESENTATION

This bias occurs when the individual does not have the complete mental model needed to develop a solution and, therefore, adopts an oversimplification of the problem.

OVERCONFIDENCE

This bias occurs when the individual gives estimates of completion of a task that are above what would be considered acceptable for the completion of the action.

AFFECT-INFLUENCED

This bias occurs when the individual has an emotional predisposition for or against a specific outcome that taints the individual's judgment.

CONFIRMATION

This bias occurs when there is a desire for the individual to confirm the individual's belief which leads to selectivity of information where favorable information for the action is included in the decision-making process and unfavorable information is ignored.

DESIRABILITY OF A POSITIVE EVENT

This bias, also called "wishful thinking" or the "optimism bias," occurs when the probability of an event occurring increases because the individual "wishes" that the event would occur.

Psychophysically based biases

Psychophysically based biases occur when there is a disconnect between the physical stimuli and the psychological responses.

ANCHORING

Anchoring occurs when the estimation of numerical values is based on the initial or anchor value. As a result, subsequent estimation of numerical values may be inaccurate since the individual has anchored on the numerical value from the first number presented in the discussion.

CERTAINTY BIAS

Individuals are usually risk adverse and would prefer sure actions and results rather than gambling with similar expected outcomes.

EQUALIZING BIAS

Equalizing bias occurs when the individual incorrectly gives the same weight to all objectives or similar probabilities to all potential outcomes.

Of the three types of biases, the strategy-based biases are the easiest to correct since the use of analytical models can help identify and correct this type of bias.[8]

How to overcome biases which impact a corporate sustainability initiative

The impact of climate change is a major corporate sustainability issue both in the present and in the future from a global perspective. As climate shifts occur, society and other stakeholders of firms must be heard for firms to be able to adapt their strategic focus addressing these issues. However, a significant challenge is that there are numerous cognitive biases which can distort the message and the recommended solutions to climate change issues. Figure 3.2 shows the impact of cognitive biases on the decision-making process related to climate change initiatives.

Perception biases

The first stage of cognitive biases is perception-based biases. These biases have a direct impact on the identification of the problem since, if the perception is that climate change is not an issue to address, there is no value in developing a decision-making process which results in the development of climate change solutions. There are three major types of cognitive biases based on perceptions issue framing, availability bias, and affect heuristics.

Issue framing

The framing of the severity of climate change is critical in how managers and employees view any initiative related to addressing the issues. Since the magnitude of the consequences of climate change are unknown and its effects are challenged, climate change is often framed from a technical viewpoint which

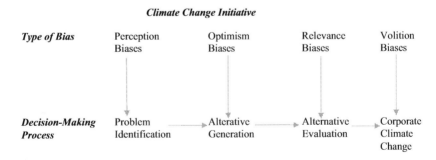

Figure 3.2 Cognitive biases which impact climate change initiative decision-making process[9]

does not have a direct connection to the general public. A solution to this type of bias is to change the framing of climate change to present more "layman" terms concerning the current and future consequences of climate change.

Availability bias

Availability bias refers to the ability of managers to easily remember events that are recent and close together. This is a challenge related to climate change issues since they are less frequent, hard to specifically identify, and evidence is dispersed geographically. A solution to this bias is to use simulations and experimental exercises in order to demonstrate the impact of climate change and try to "connect" the dots of the evidence of climate change in different countries.

Affect heuristics

Affect heuristics refers to managers evaluating a course of action and exaggerating the benefits of a desired action and downplaying the risks of the favorable action. From a climate change perspective, affect heuristics will support the perspective by convincing oneself that there have always been changes in weather (which is different than climate change), so the reported evidence of climate change is, in reality, just the normal course of changing weather conditions. A solution to this heuristic is to present different climate change scenarios in which the decision makers are forced to quantify the risk or benefits of the decision based on the potential consequences.

Optimism biases

Optimism biases occur when the manager has a distorted perspective on the ability to realistically evaluate the potential options for a solution related to the corporate sustainability initiative. The overconfidence in the manager clouds the ability of the decision maker to objectively evaluate the viability of the different potential courses of action. The two types of optimism biases are overoptimism/overconfidence and self-serving bias.

Overoptimism/overconfidence

Overoptimism occurs when the managers making the decisions related to climate change believe the risks of climate change will not impact the firm in their lifetime and at some point in the future new technology will be developed to reduce the impact of climate change. A solution to this bias is to present worst-case scenarios highlighting the consequences if the managers are not correct with their level of overconfidence. In addition, the managers could be given examples of how other firms are reacting to climate change initiatives to emphasize the potential danger of being overly optimistic.

Self-serving bias

Self-serving bias occurs when managers place their own objectives above the common good and the best interests of the firm. As a result, the managers believe that they have effectively addressed the issues related to climate change and have developed optimal solutions related to their alternative courses of action. A solution to this bias is for the firm to join industry-level sustainability coalitions to understand how other firms are addressing climate change. In addition, managers should embrace both positive and negative feedback based on the previous actions implemented by the firm.

Relevance biases

Relevance biases are based on the managers using biases to discount the relevance and impact of the decisions on future consequences. For example, common predictions pertaining to climate change is that the earth average temperature will increase 2 degrees by 2050. For the managers, this forecast could potentially have little impact on the type of decisions that are made related to climate change issues. As a result, relevance biases can impact the evaluation of the alternative courses of action being considered by the manager. There are three types of relevance biases, which are: anchoring, hyperbolic discounting, and query theory.

Anchoring

Anchoring bias is based on managers using current short-term forecasts as the basis of making decisions related to climate change. Therefore, the forecast of a temperature increase of two degrees is too small a change and by 2050 is too far in the distance for managers to make decisions that can impact this long-range forecast. Therefore, managers use their current knowledge as the starting point for any decisions related to climate change. A solution to using anchors is to challenge the manager to change his/her decision anchoring by using current knowledge to extrapolate how those decisions will be interconnected in the future to demonstrate the potential consequences of forecast over 30 years in the future.

Hyperbolic discounting

Hyperbolic discounting biases occur when managers focus on small immediate rewards instead of larger long-term-based rewards. For a publicly traded company, hyperbolic discounting occurs because the managers are evaluated based on the quarterly performance of the firm instead of results that are generated decades in the future. The solution to hyperbolic discounting is to acknowledge and reward both short-term and longer-term actions related to climate change.

Query theory

Query theory is based on the belief that managers will assess evidence that will result in immediate gratification and then focus on evidence which delays gratification of the manager. A solution to this bias is to ensure that both financial and social/environmental gains and losses are presented simultaneously so that multiple avenues of performance are evaluated by the managers.

Volition biases

Volition biases occur when the managers are not motivated to address climate change issues since their perception is that the issues are not the manager's responsibility. Since it is not the manager's "problem," the manager does not need to be involved in the decision-making process to develop a solution to the climate change issue. As a result, volition biases impact the perceived value of implementing a course of action which addresses climate change issues. There are three types of volition biases, which are: diffusion of responsibility, obedience to authority, and professional bias.

Diffusion of responsibility

Diffusion of responsibility bias occurs when managers view climate change not as a business-related problem, but as the responsibility of government to address the issues. Firms do not have the ability to solve all the problems related to climate change. The solution to this bias is to focus on specific components related to climate change which can be addressed by managers.

Obedience to authority

Obedience to authority bias occurs when managers perceive that they are just following the rules and regulations established by industry-based organizations and government agencies. If the firm moves beyond compliance related to climate change, the firm may be at a competitive disadvantage compared to other firms in the same industry. The solution to this bias is to reconfigure the issue not as a threat to the firm, but as an opportunity. Therefore, addressing issues related to climate change can yield a competitive advantage and not a disadvantage by differentiating the firm in the market place.

Professional bias

Professional bias occurs when managers view all decisions based on shareholder maximization which pits the short-term financial objectives of the firm against social and environmental impacts. The solution to this bias is to refocus the mind-set of the managers to view their responsibility to address the needs of all the stakeholders instead of just the shareholders. Similar to the short-term focus of other biases, the managers must understand that addressing the needs of corporate sustainability and the natural environment is not mutually exclusive to achieving long-term financial goals.[10]

Addressing the complexity of sustainability in the decision-making process

Strategies related to corporate sustainability must potentially address multiple variables in multiple conditions in multiple locations. The interconnectedness of the decision-making process ensures that firms must be able to develop a systems approach in the identification and actions related to corporate sustainability. In order to address the issues related to corporate sustainability, the managers of the firm must recognize that firms operate in vast, complex, adaptive systems. The adaptive systems incorporate the complex and interconnected dynamic environmental, economic, and social system addressing the needs of the critical stakeholders of the firm.

Managers must be able to interpret the adaptability of the systems and utilize their knowledge to incorporate the firm's corporate sustainability commitment into the integrated decision-making process to address the complex issues related to corporate sustainability. A model demonstrating how managers address corporate sustainability in the decision-making process in presented in Figure 3.3.

Once the corporate sustainability issue has been identified, the next step is for the decision maker to interpret the issue based on his/her own cognitive process. It is at this step that potential decision biases may be integrated in

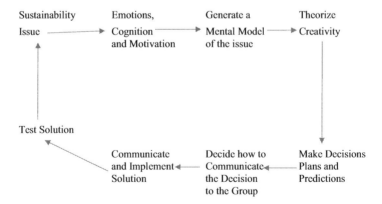

Figure 3.3 Addressing corporate sustainability in the decision-making process[11]

the decision process. Therefore, in addition to using heuristics, the decision maker incorporates his/her emotions and motivations in the decision-making process. The next step in the development of the manager's mental model is for the manager to be able to identify how to address the issue. The mental model refers to the development of the thought process in order to incorporate information in the decision-making process.

The next step is the development of creative and innovative ideas in order to create viable, realistic courses of action to be implemented to resolve the corporate sustainability issue. It is at this step that the manager must ensure that the critical stakeholders who will be impacted by this decision have been identified and that the decision is consistent with the needs of these stakeholders.

The fourth step is to decide on a specific course of action to address the sustainability issue based on various alternative options. In order to make the decision on the course of action, the manager must also make predictions about the outcomes of the actions based on his/her mental model. These predictions are critical in order to effectively implement the decision through the actions of the firm. The next step in the process is to decide how to communicate the decision to the interested parties both internally and externally. As was mentioned previously, the manager must be aware about how this decision impacts both internal and external stakeholders. The message of the communications must align with the expectations of the firm's stakeholders to ensure that the stakeholders will support the recommended course of action.

The sixth step is the implementation of the course of action and communication of that course of action to the firm's stakeholders. It is imperative that the rationale of the decision and course of action must be communicated effectively to the firm's stakeholders. The final step is the testing of the solution which refers to ensuring that there are metrics related to the expected outcomes to determine if the course of action was successful in addressing the sustainability issue. If the optimal solution was not implemented, the decision makers can learn from the feedback related to the outcomes in order to adjust their cognitive mental model to be able to increase the probability of optimal success in addressing future sustainability issues of the firm.[12]

Sensemaking in the corporate sustainability process

Sensemaking is the ability of the managers to make sense of their experiences and be able to apply that knowledge in the decision-making process. Sensemaking is composed of three components: cognitive, linguistic, and conative.

Cognitive sensemaking occurs when the manager considers the firm's relationships with its stakeholders and determines how the decisions related to corporate sustainability are able to help the common good. Linguistic sensemaking is the manager's ability to explain why the corporate sustainability initiatives were developed and to be able to engage with stakeholders on the

Cognitive What Managers Think	*Identify* *Orientation*	Individualistic Relational Collectivistic
	Legitimacy	Pragmatic Cognitive Moral
Linguistic What Managers Say	*Justification*	Legal Scientific Economic Ethical
	Transparency	Balanced Biased
Conative How Managers Tend To Behave	*Posture*	Defense Tentative Open
	Consistency	Strategically consistent Strategically inconsistent ------------------------------- Internally consistent Internally inconsistent
	Commitment	Instrumental Normative

Figure 3.4 Dimensions of the sensemaking process and corporate sustainability[13]

implementation of the initiatives. Cognitive sensemaking is the behavior and actions of the manager in the development and implementation of the corporate sustainability initiatives in order to demonstrate the firm's commitment and consistency in the identification of its stakeholders' needs. The dimensions of the sensemaking process related to corporate sustainability are shown in Figure 3.4.

Cognitive corporate sustainability dimensions

Identity orientation

The identity orientation of the firm related to corporate sustainability has three components: individualistic, relational, and collectivistic. An individualistic orientation means firms focus on individual liberty and self-interests and have separated themselves from other firms based on superior performance in the industry.

Firms with a relational orientation focus on the establishment and maintenance of strong relational partnerships with stakeholders, including public declarations of commitment to their stakeholders. A collectivistic orientation is based on the perspective that the firm views itself as part of a larger collective that moves beyond its critical stakeholders to forge relationship-based linkages with other organizations. The motto of these firms would be to address global issues such as poverty or climate change.

Therefore, from a corporate sustainability perspective, individualistic orientation firms would focus on initiatives that are based on a competitive nature and highlight superior abilities in order to accomplish the initiative. A relational orientation firm would emphasize corporate sustainability initiatives that strengthen the networks between the firm and other organizations. For example, a relational firm which highlights its sustainability commitment related to contributions made by the firm are favored by the employees. A collectivistic firm would focus on social and/or environmental issues such as global warming where the firm is linked with other organizations that support the same initiative.

Legitimacy

The legitimacy of the firm is based on the firm's need to gain acceptance in society and its stakeholders. The three approaches to legitimacy are: pragmatic, cognitive, and moral. Pragmatic legitimacy refers to the firm's ability to convince its stakeholders of the value of the firm based on its decisions, products, or processes. A firm's cognitive legitimacy is based on the firm being able to align its actions with perceived expectations from society. The focus of cognitive legitimacy is legitimatizing the actions of the firm based on the firm's ability to adapt to changing external environmental factors. The firm's moral legitimacy is based on the firm's ability to act with an acceptable behavior based on social norms with the stakeholder under conditions of extreme uncertainty due to fundamental social change.

Linguistic corporate sustainability dimensions

Justification

Firms can justify their actions through four dimensions: legal, scientific, economic, and ethical. Legal justification is stating the firm's actions are officially permitted based on current laws and regulations. This response by the firm occurs when stakeholders raise questions related to the firm's obligations, compliance, penalties, and settlements.

Scientific justification is used by the firm when the firm claims expertise-based scientific data collection and analysis. A firm will present economic justification when it can highlight tangible contributions to stakeholders for its actions. This contribution has had a positive financial impact on the firm's stakeholders.

Ethical justification occurs when the firm explains its reasons for its actions based on serving the global stakeholders related to universal goals such as the protection of human rights and the elimination of diseases and poverty.

Transparency

A firm's transparency refers to the firm's ability to present the rationale for the actions made by the firm. Therefore, the firm can either choose to present a balanced or biased perspective related to the description of its actions. A balanced perspective presents both favorable and unfavorable information related to the decision-making process and the outcomes of the decisions. A biased perspective presents information that is favorable and omits information presented to its stakeholders which is unfavorable.

Cognitive corporate sustainability dimensions

Posture

Posture refers to how the firm's response to the sustainability issue is develop based on the interactions with its stakeholders. There are three type of responses related to the posturing of the firm: defense, tentative, and open. A firm has a defensive posture when the firm does not accept any feedback from its stakeholders and assumes that its decisions and courses of action are both correct and optimal based on the circumstances facing the firm at the time of the decision-making process. This defensive posture would continue for the firm even if, in hindsight, the actions were proven to be inappropriate or ineffective.

A firm has a tentative posture related to its interaction with stakeholders based on the firm's inexperience with the issue or the firm does not have the necessary skills and resources needed to develop viable solutions to address the sustainability issue. The danger with the tentative posture is that it could give a signal to the stakeholders that the firm is not serious in resolving the sustainability issue and is using its sustainability commitment as window-dressing to satisfy the demands of the stakeholders.

A firm has an open posture when the firm is willing to listen and respond to the requests of its stakeholders. By having an open posture, firms can share not only the solutions related to corporate sustainability issues, but the firms also can get input from stakeholders on how to adapt to changing external environmental conditions.

Consistency

The firm's consistency related to corporate sustainability is based on the firm's being able to develop consistency in the overall sustainability strategy and consistency in the type of corporate sustainability activities at any given point in time. A firm can be either strategically consistent or strategically inconsistent. A firm which is strategically consistent has corporate sustainability embedded directly in the firm's strategic discussions and processes. Alternatively, if the firm is strategically inconsistent, the firm does not make any preparation guiding its selection of corporate sustainability activities and simply reacts spontaneously to the demands of internal and external stakeholders.

Internally, the firm can also be consistent and inconsistent. Internal consistency occurs when the firm is willing to integrate proposed corporate sustainability within the holistic set of decisions and actions made the firm. Internal inconsistency occurs when the firm addresses corporate sustainability issues arbitrarily without a systematic framework to help guide the decision-making process.

Commitment

The firm's commitment to corporate sustainability is based on the ability to incorporate the activities related to corporate sustainability within the culture of the firm. It is critical for corporate sustainability issues to receive unwavering support from top managers within the firm to facilitate the entrenchment of the corporate sustainability commitment in the belief structure of the employees.

The firm's commitment can be either instrumental or normative. Instrumental commitment is based on the type of incentives the firm would be able to capture externally for its actions related to corporate sustainability. For example, a government may give tax relief or other incentives for a firm to shift from fossil fuels to alternative fuels in its manufacturing facilities. Instrumental commitment also relates to the external pressure on the firm by stakeholders to be committed to corporate sustainability issues or be faced with potential punishment from stakeholders. For example, customers may demand that the firm shift its outsourcing operations to those with more favorable working conditions.

Normative commitment refers to the firm's ability to understand and respond to internal moral considerations for the firm's actions. This moral commitment is reflected in the integration of responsible corporate processes into the firm's everyday activities.[14]

Systems development and corporate sustainability

As was mentioned in the previous section, managers must view their decisions related to corporate sustainability based on a systems approach where there is a network of overlapping and interrelated elements. Firms can be viewed as open social systems which must address environmental and organizational uncertainty and need to be accountable to stakeholders.

Therefore, it is important for managers to view firms as stakeholders' systems. The open system related to stakeholders results in the firm having a moral duty to take stakeholders' needs into consideration in the decision-making process. The managers must understand that from a systems approach, they must develop multiple interconnecting sustainability initiatives that will be beneficial to all stakeholders congruently.

Firms can also be viewed as interpretative systems. In order to identify and incorporate the interrelated networking that occurs within a firm, the managers must develop information processing mechanisms that can be used to identify events, trends, and developments that are relevant to stakeholders and sustainability initiatives. By scanning the external environment for relevant information, managers are able to identify emerging issues, solutions, and potential pitfalls which can impact the sustainability commitment.[15]

Management control systems and corporate sustainability

A management control system is a system in which a firm gathers and uses information in order to be able to evaluate the performance level of different resources within the firm. Therefore, a management control system can be defined as a formal information-based process where routines and procedures are developed to monitor the activities within the firm.

Management control systems can be used to evaluate firm practices related to corporate sustainability and if the management control system is used effectively, it could actually push the firm in the direction of adopting a proactive corporate sustainability focus. The management control system could play an important role in ensuring environmental and social activities are integrated into the firm's strategic plans and objectives.

Management control systems can be used by managers to facilitate decisions related to corporate sustainability when the issue is related to competitive advantage, stakeholder legitimacy, corporate reputation management, legal compliance, external pressures from the firm's industry, or development of more efficient processes within the firm.

Management control systems enable managers to make decisions pertaining to relative risks of external factors such as new government regulations and potential opportunities such as improvements in the waste management processes or the reduction in the use of resources. The levers of control framework identify the manager's ability to develop and renew the firm's corporate sustainability strategy. The levers of control framework has four components which include: beliefs, boundaries, diagnostic, and interactive as methods used to analyze how firms leverage their management control systems to implement the firm's corporate sustainability strategies.

Beliefs

The firm's belief system is based on the explicit and formal set of statements that the managers use in order for top-level managers to communicate the firm's values to its stakeholders. These statements are created and communicated through documents such as the firm's credo, mission statement, or vision statement. The purpose of the beliefs-based statement is to develop and secure the commitment of the employees toward the common goals related to corporate sustainability. Belief systems are expected to incorporate a broad set of values. They not only entrench the employees' commitment but also present the firm's values to the other stakeholders of the firm related to the long-term corporate sustainability objectives.

Boundaries

The boundary level of control refers to the specific definitions and parameters established by the firm to guide the behavior of the employees. These parameters usually identify the risks and negative consequences of unacceptable behavior which don't support the corporate sustainability strategy. Managers use strategic boundaries to ensure the most efficient use of the firm's resources. For example, the firm can identify potential environmental risks and potential liabilities by ignoring corporate sustainability issues. The identification can be through the use of internal audits which evaluate how the employees have used the firm's resources related to the development and implementation of the firm's corporate sustainability strategy.

An additional boundary the firm can use is the development of voluntary guidelines, codes of conduct, and legal standards related to corporate sustainability. These boundary systems are critical when there is environmental uncertainty, high cost of non-compliance, and a potential negative impact on the firm's reputation. The boundary systems are critical since the firm cannot rely solely on government regulations and legislation to guide the behavior of their employees.

Diagnostic

Diagnostic use of the management control system occurs when the managers evaluate the performance of the firm's objectives with the firm's expected objectives. Diagnostics include both financial and non-financial objectives as well as both short-term and long-term objectives. The feedback based on the evaluation of the firm's objectives allows the managers to adjust their actions if they do not obtain the desired objectives. Therefore, diagnostics can be used to monitor compliance with external regulations and standards which facilitate corporate sustainability-based decision making. This measurement system also generates relevant information for the firm's stakeholders on how well the firm has been able to accomplish its corporate sustainability objectives.

Interactive

Interactive controls are the formal processes that managers use to facilitate the management of strategic uncertainties as well as help identify future opportunities. Strategic uncertainties are contingencies which were not anticipated by managers when they were developing their strategic focus. Interactive processes give the managers the ability to identify challenges to their strategic agenda. The firm's interactive use of controls is based on intensive use by superiors, subordinates, and the personal communication between the two groups.

Interactive processes to support the firm's corporate sustainability strategy incorporate the view of external stakeholders such as NGOs, local communities, and shareholders. This interactive system allows for a two-way communication between the mangers and the stakeholders which can be beneficial to the firm through the identification of unrealized strategies that had not been considered by managers as well as feedback received from the stakeholders of their perception of the firm's performance related to corporate sustainability. Therefore, this interactive process can be used to develop new corporate sustainability initiatives that can lead to future strategic change and renewal.[16]

Converting management control systems to sustainability control systems

Sustainability control systems use the same framework as management control systems by focusing on management accounting and control systems. As a result, managers use the foundation of the firm's management control system and convert it into sustainability control systems through the use of: strategic planning, budgeting, financial measurement systems, non-financial measurement systems, hybrid measurement systems, project management, and evaluation and reward systems.

Strategic planning

Strategic planning occurs when managers focus on long-range planning decisions that typically cover between five and ten years in the future. Managers develop short-term plans which guide the firm in the direction to achieve its longer-range goals. From a sustainability control system perspective, strategic planning would establish short-term sustainability goals which move the firm toward the achievement of its long-term sustainability goals.

Budgeting

Budgeting refers to the allocation of resources that are integrated into the strategic planning for both short-term and long-term goals. The budgeting includes not only new projects but also resource revisions of on-going projects. Budgeting also takes place in the sustainability control systems based on the allocation of resources for short-term and long-term corporate sustainability projects.

Financial measurement systems

Financial measurement systems include factors such as sales, profitability, and return on investment (ROI). Sustainability control systems would include financial measurements such as environmental and sustainability cash flow analysis.

Non-financial measurement systems

Non-financial measurement systems would include factors such as the introduction of new products and the firm's market share in the industry. Sustainability control systems would include factors such as the firm's environmental performance evaluation, and material and energy flow accounting systems.

Hybrid measurement systems

Hybrid measurement systems include a set of financial and non-financial indicators which measure whether or not the firm has achieved its desired objectives. Sustainability control systems would include sustainability performance measurement and sustainability balanced scorecard evaluation of the firm.

Project management

Project management evaluates the firm's activities to ensure projects are delivered on time and within the assigned budget. Sustainability control systems focus on factors such as social and eco-efficiency analysis.

Evaluation and reward

Evaluation and reward systems are used to evaluate and guide the efforts of the employees and the groups within the firm. Sustainability control systems would focus on the establishment of a reward system based on multidimensional performance systems. An example of a multidimensional performance system would be a triple line-based evaluation in which the employees are evaluated based on their financial performance, environmental performance, and social performance.[17]

Valutus: embedding corporate sustainability values in the decision-making process

Daniel Aronson created Valutus (which is Latin for values) to help managers embed the values of corporate sustainability into the decision-making process. Valutus identifies how firms and other organizations can add value through corporate sustainability and corporate responsibility. Valutus views leaders as the catalysts for corporate sustainability and have the ability to accelerate change when it is needed.[18]

Valutus approaches corporate sustainability from the perspective of an iceberg. The majority of the value of corporate sustainability is below the surface and, therefore, is not immediately identifiable by the observer. Daniel Aronson believes that there are inherent barriers by managers in perceiving the value of corporate sustainability, making it challenging to automatically include corporate sustainability in the decision-making process for the firm. The three barriers are: authority, periphery, and ROI.

Authority

Employees within the firm often do not have the authority to make changes based on their ideas and therefore have to persuade the decision makers to take the appropriate action. A common example is that decisions related to purchasing sustainable products from sustainable suppliers are usually centralized to top-level managers.

Periphery

Employees related to corporate sustainability projects are usually considered peripheral to the business and not as valuable as employees who directly generate revenue for the firm. This perceived "lack of importance" can diminish the valuable contribution of these employees and the corporate sustainability projects.

ROI

Decisions by managers integrate the financial impact of the decisions and the potential return on investment (ROI). As a result, corporate sustainability initiatives are evaluated based on the short-term return of the financial investment instead of the potential long-term benefits of the investment.

In order to unlock the submerged value of corporate sustainability initiatives, Mr. Aronson proposes five components which are: physics, lenses, actions, catalysts, and effort.

Physics

In the decision-making process, managers must understand all the interactions of any decisions related to corporate sustainability. For example, when the reduction of waste is considered, the focus should not be solely on the cost savings of the reduction of disposal costs, but should consider other tangible costs including transportation, storage, and liability costs.

Lenses

Managers need to understand the perspective of the firm's different stakeholders when making corporate sustainability decisions. The decisions made by the firm must coincide with the beliefs and needs of the stakeholders of the firm. As a result, decisions related to corporate sustainability must include how these decisions are viewed from different perspectives.

Actions

The actions and reactions of the employees are valuable tools in the development and implementation of a firm's corporate sustainability strategy. Therefore, the firm must support the actions of the employees in their development of new alternatives to the status quo focus of the corporate sustainability decision-making process.

Catalysts

An action by one employee can be a catalyst for the actions of many other employees. As a result, this catalyst creates a momentum in embracing new opportunities for corporate sustainability initiatives.

Effort

Positive results of corporate sustainability projects based on the collective effort of the employees of the firm should be celebrated. The projects should highlight the positive value added to the firm and to the firm's critical stakeholders. Furthermore, corporate sustainability commitment should be used as a tool to enhance the firm's competitive advantage by differentiating the firm from its competitors.[19]

Questions for thought

1. If corporate sustainability initiatives are "voluntary" actions by a firm, why would firms pay companies such as Goodera to help them develop corporate sustainability strategies?
2. Should you always make rational decisions? Why or why not?

3. Do you think you have "biases" when you make decisions? Explain.
4. Which biases do you think are the most common among managers?
5. Is there any limitations on the firm having a strong management control system?
6. Are there certain industries which do not need strong management control systems? If so, give some examples.

Notes

1 www.bloomberg.com/research/stocks/private/snapshot.asp?privcapId=285318252
2 www.forbesindia.com/article/brand-connect/conscious-capitalism-csr-sustainabil ity-and-beyond/51621/1
3 www.sify.com/finance/is-corporate-india-looking-at-csr-as-a-benevolent-activity-csr-tool-goodera-has-answers-news-business-sklkJLeciehff.html
4 T.K. Das and Bing-Sheng Teng. 1999. Cognitive Biases and Strategic Decision Processes: An Integrative Perspective. *Journal of Management Studies*. 36(6): 757–778.
5 Said Elbanna and John Child. 2007. The Influence of Decision, Environmental and Firm Characteristics on the Rationality of Strategic Decision-Making. *Journal of Management Studies*. 44(4): 565.
6 Said Elbanna and John Child. 2007. The Influence of Decision, Environmental and Firm Characteristics on the Rationality of Strategic Decision-Making. *Journal of Management Studies*. 44(4): 561–591.
7 T.K. Das and Bing-Sheng Teng. 1999. Cognitive Biases and Strategic Decision Processes: An Integrative Perspective. *Journal of Management Studies*. 36(6): 757–778.
8 Gilberto Montibeller and Detlof von Winterfeldt. 2015. Cognitive and Motivational Biases in Decision and Risk Analysis. *Risk Analysis*. 35(7): 1230–1251.
9 Daina Mazutis and Anna Eckardt. 2017. Sleepwalking into Catastrophe: Cognitive Biases and Corporate Climate Change Inertia. *California. Management Review*. 59(3): 90.
10 Daina Mazutis and Anna Eckardt. 2017. Sleepwalking into Catastrophe: Cognitive Biases and Corporate Climate Change Inertia. *California. Management Review*. 59(3): 74–108.
11 Louise Metcalf and Sue Benn. 2013. Leadership for Sustainability: An Evolution of Leadership Ability. *Journal of Business Ethics*. 112: 371.
12 Louise Metcalf and Sue Benn. 2013. Leadership for Sustainability: An Evolution of Leadership Ability. *Journal of Business Ethics*. 112: 369–384.
13 Kunal Basu and Guido Palazzo. 2008. Corporate Social Responsibility: A Process Model of Sensemaking. *Academy of Management Review*. 33(1): 125.
14 Kunal Basu and Guido Palazzo. 2008. Corporate Social Responsibility: A Process Model of Sensemaking. *Academy of Management Review*. 33(1): 122–136.
15 Francois Maon, Adam Lindgreen and Valerie Swaen. 2008. Thinking of the Organization as a System. The Role of Managerial Perceptions in Developing a Corporate Social Responsibility Strategic Agenda. *Systems Research and Behavioral Science*. 25: 413–426.
16 Diane-Laure Arjalies and Julia Mundy. 2013. The Use of Management Control Systems to Manage CSR Strategy: A Levers of Control Perspective. *Management Accounting Research*. 24: 284–300.

17 Jean-Pascal Gond, Suzana Grubnic, Christian Herzig and Jeremy Moon. 2012. Configuring Management Control Systems; Theorizing the integration of Strategy and Sustainability. *Management Accounting Research.* 23: 205–223.
18 https://valutus.com/
19 www.sustainablebrands.com/news_and_views/finance_investment/alissa_stevens/future_value_submerged_value_rop_other_facets_roi_s

4 Human resources and corporate sustainability

Introduction

This chapter examines the relationship between the firm and its employees. A firm can only survive in the long term if it has highly motivated employees who are committed to the goals of the firm and are loyal to the firm. For the employees, they must be in a job where they are satisfied with their current status and are fully engaged in their job functions. In this chapter concepts related to corporate sustainability that are discussed include: an overall framework relating human resources and corporate sustainability; socially responsible human resource management; job satisfaction; charismatic leadership; employee identity; employee recruitment; employee engagement; employee volunteerism programs; and employee trust. The chapter concludes with a discussion on SAP's commitment to hiring employees with autism and starts with a discussion on Tesco's non-conventional treatment of its employees.

Tesco's adventures in human resources

Tesco is Britain's largest supermarket chain with sales of almost £57 billion in 2018. It controls 27.3 percent of the UK grocery market and employs approximately 300,000 people in Britain. Yet, as with any major retailer, Tesco must revive underperforming stores in order to improve its financial condition. In January 2019, Tesco announced that it was going to close the fresh food counters in approximately 90 stores, which would result in firing up to 9,000 employees. At the end of May 2019, redundancy or severance payments were made to the employees that were fired. However, there was an administrative error which resulted in hundreds of fired employees receiving the wrong amount for their severance packages. For those employees that were overpaid, Tesco asked the former employees to return the money to Tesco. For those employees who were overpaid by more than £500, the employees could keep £100 and for those employees who were overpaid by less than £500 they could keep the full amount.[1] While asking for the money back due to Tesco's error may be perplexing, its determination of the amount to return was even more puzzling. For example, if the former employee was overpaid by £501, the employee would return £401 and keep £100. However, if the employee was overpaid by £499, the employee would keep the full amount.

This is not the first example of Tesco's unconventional treatment of its employees. In 2004, Tesco announced that it would eliminate sick pay in some of its stores in order to reduce "days off" cheaters. The Tesco spokesman at the time, Jonathan Church stated that:

> Our people tell us that unplanned absence is a real issue ... It impacts on our business as well as creating more work for people in store. These trials are about encouraging people to use planned absence (instead) whenever they can. If they need to take little Johnnie to the dentist, then we will bend over backwards to make that possible.

The structure of the sick pay developed by Tesco also raised some questions relative to the motivation of the employees. The sick pay schedule is structured so that workers would receive no pay at all for the first three days off for sickness, but on the fourth day they would be paid for not only the fourth day but also the three previous unpaid sick days. This could lead to the employees taking four or more days off in order to be paid for all the days. Jonathan Church admitted that "Obviously the trial is in its early stages and these are the kinds of issues we will need to look at." The selection of three sick days is most likely linked to the UK government regulations regarding sick leave. Employers must absorb the full cost of the first three days of sick leave, but after three days the sick pay becomes "statutory" and the employer can claim 80 percent of the amount from the UK government.[2] A comment by a former customer service assistant at Tesco posted on Glassdoor UK on May 21, 2019 stated that the non-paying of the first three sick days at Tesco is still in effect.[3]

One of Tesco's competitors, Asda, uses a carrot instead of a stick related to sick days. Asda offers prizes for low absenteeism, which could include an extra week's vacation or a weekend break or money vouchers. Asda also has programs for its employees including: family care leave, first day/half-day leave for parents taking their children to school and IVF leave.[4]

Overall framework relating human resources and corporate sustainability[5]

For the firm to effectively disperse its corporate sustainability commitment throughout the organization, the firm must understand the sequential process in order to establish and maintain the employee's complete commitment to the firm's corporate sustainability vision. There are four stages in this sequential process: planning and awareness; implementation and process development; monitoring and feedback; and revision and institutionalization. This sequential framework is shown in Figure 4.1.

Planning and Awareness	Implementation and Process Development	Monitoring and Feedback	Revision and Institutionalization
-Vision, mission and values	-Talent acquisition and development	-Employee surveys and interviews	-Goals and values
-Leadership	-Employee involvement and empowerment	-Review of policies and processes	-Structures
-Education	-Performance and rewards management	-Comparison of outcomes to standards/goals	-Supporting systems
-Communication	-Ethics management		-Learning

Figure 4.1 Overall relationship between human resources and corporate sustainability[6]

Planning and awareness

Vision, mission and values

The top-level managers of the firm must develop a comprehensive vision, mission, and values to develop an effective corporate sustainability strategy. A part of this process is ensuring that the corporate sustainability commitment is legitimized as an integral part of the firm's overall identity. In addition, the mangers must develop and maintain a values-driven culture which supports the corporate sustainability initiatives. In order to achieve a values-driven culture, the top-level managers must ensure that the vision, mission statement and description of the values coincide with the belief system supported by the firm's culture. If this message is not consistent to the employees, the top-level managers' credibility and their commitment to corporate sustainability will be questioned by the employees.

Leadership

The top-level managers must not only develop the firm's vision, mission, and values related to corporate sustainability, but they must also be able to convert their ideas into actions. The top-level managers must play a leadership role in guiding the employees into the most effective actions that will achieve the firm's goals related to corporate sustainability. The role of human resources within the firm is to ensure that the selection process for its top-level managers includes the skills set needed to not only embrace the value system related to corporate sustainability but also has the necessary abilities to formulate strategies and subsequently implement those strategies related to corporate sustainability.

Education and communication

A key step in any effective corporate sustainability strategy is to mobilize the collective employees' efforts toward corporate sustainability in order to increase the level of overall awareness. Increasing awareness of corporate sustainability for the employees can be accomplished through education and communication. The mediums for the communication could include firm statements and policies, employee bulletins, formal training sessions, town hall meetings, and departmental discussions.

Implementation and policy development

Talent acquisition and development

In order to effectively implement the corporate sustainability initiatives, the firm must rely on knowledgeable and devoted employees to the firm's corporate sustainability values. It is imperative that if a firm wants employees who are fully committed to corporate sustainability, the firm must be proactive in attracting employees who already have a willing commitment to help the firm achieve its corporate sustainability goals. These employees can be attracted to the firm through job postings and the description of the firm's corporate sustainability commitment on its website. In addition, potential employees may also research information from external sources to determine whether the firm's corporate sustainability goals align with their own goals. To incorporate the firm's values related to corporate sustainability into the decision-making process of the employees, the firm must create training and development programs related to corporate sustainability for its employees.

The firm should establish a corporate sustainability knowledge database which captures information related to the social and environmental issues impacting the firm. This database should also include comprehensive information on the interests and needs of its stakeholders as well as a detailed description of the corporate sustainability norms and standards related to the industries where the firm has operations.

The firm should also have a comprehensive education program to teach the necessary skills related to corporate sustainability initiatives. These training programs should include not only the current activities that are the responsibility of the employees but also how other operations connect the actions of all the different components of the firm's operations.

The education program should also include the opportunity for the employees to develop their cognitive aptitude so that they are highly competent in addressing complex corporate sustainability issues. This employee development program should be structured to ensure that the employees are able to see the "big picture" related to the firm's commitment to corporate sustainability.

Employee involvement and empowerment

The ability of the firm to allow employees to be involved and empowered gives the employees a strong sense of control over their job, which help facilitates the execution of the corporate's sustainability initiatives. Employees who can have direct input into the firm's operations are better able to directly improve the firm's productivity and profitability levels, which could resulting in the firm being able to allocate more funds for corporate sustainability initiatives.

There are many levels of employee involvement related to corporate sustainability. At the minimal involvement level, employees are informed about the firm's corporate sustainability decisions and initiatives. The next level would occur when top-level management asks lower-level employees to offer input and/or feedback about the firm's corporate sustainability initiatives through avenues such as open meetings, suggestion boxes, or committees. The next level is for the firm to allow employee empowerment, which give the employees the ability to make autonomous decisions related to corporate sustainability. At the highest level, employees provide the strategic direction of the firm's corporate sustainability commitment, which gives the employees an opportunity to have a voice in the firm's future corporate sustainability directions.

Performance and reward management

Employees are motivated based on expectancies or the probability that the employees can succeed in their tasks and the probability of receiving a reward of value for the completed task. As a result, the firm must incorporate in the employees' activities related to corporate sustainability an established reward system to ensure the employees are highly motivated to perform the tasks related to its corporate sustainability strategy.

Performance management is based on the firm focusing on the holistic approach of motivating its employees by not only rewarding past performance but also providing incentives for future employee performance. Therefore, top-level managers must design an incentive system in which the employees receive both extrinsic and intrinsic rewards for effectively completing tasks related to corporate sustainability initiatives. Extrinsic rewards are based on financial and career advancement achievements, while intrinsic rewards are based on the employees' perception of making a difference in the world based on their actions.

Ethics management

In order to be consistent with its value system, firms must not only follow the minimum legal standards, but they also must be proactive in their ethical standards if the firm is using corporate sustainability as a cornerstone dimension in its interactions with stakeholders. Within the firm, areas such as respect for human rights, embracing diversity, and providing equal employment opportunities need to be strictly monitored for both potential and current employees. Externally, the firm must ensure that its ethical value system is incorporated with its interactions with stakeholders through transparent communications.

Monitoring and feedback

Firms traditionally use a corporate sustainability audit in order to monitor and evaluate the actions of the firm as well as provide feedback to top-level managers if future adjustments need to be made to the corporate sustainability strategy. A corporate sustainability audit focuses on the firm's ethical, social, and environmental goals to determine the firm's overall corporate sustainability performance. A corporate sustainability audit would include obtaining data from the employees through surveys and interviews, a formal review of the policies and procedures related to corporate sustainability, and a calculation of any variances between the project's goals and the firm's actual performance.

Revision and institutionalization

When the actual performance of the firm does not equal the projected goals of the corporate sustainability initiatives, the firm must make revisions and subsequently institutionalize those revisions. The goals of the firm need to be evaluated to determine if the results were achievable and realistic. If it is determined that the variance is due to unrealistic expectations for the goals related to corporate sustainability, then the goals need to be revised. If the variance is due, in part, to lack of autonomy and a burdensome reporting hierarchy within the firm, then the structure of the firm needs to be revised. If the supporting systems within the firm are not able to provide the employees with the necessary resources, then the systems need to be revised. The key to this step in the process is for the top-level managers to learn from the firm's performance to ensure that negative variances will not occur in the future. Once these revisions have been made and top-level managers have captured knowledge through the learning process, these changes must become formalized and become an integral part of the future development of new corporate sustainability initiatives.[7]

Socially responsible human resource management

Socially responsible human resource management (SRHRM) incorporates the motivating of the firm's employees, resulting in positive work behaviors through the linking of social norms and organizational identity. A model depicting how SRHRM motivates positive employee work behaviors in shown in Figure 4.2.

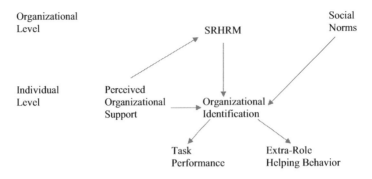

Figure 4.2 How SRHRM motivates positive employee work behaviors[8]

Organizational identification

The linchpin of the model is organizational identification, which is defined as the perceived sense of unity and belongingness that the employees have with their current employer. This sense of unity is part of social identity theory, which is based on the belief that employees tend to categorize themselves and their colleagues into social groups. Employees are part of social groups which share their same beliefs and interests, resulting in an enhancement of the level of self-esteem of the employees.

Social norms and organizational identity

A firm has institutional pressure to conform to social norms since its stakeholders expect the firm to conform to external social norms resulting in social legitimacy for the firm's operations. A firm's conformity to social norms can help the self-esteem of the employees, which leads to the employees having stronger levels of organizational identification.

Employees will evaluate their firm based on its commitment to corporate sustainability. As a result, successful commitments to corporate sustainability will be viewed favorably by the employees and will result in stronger employee identification with the firm. Adopting a performance evaluation and reward system based, in part, on the employee's commitment to corporate sustainability is a signal by the firm of its belief in the social norms guiding its corporate sustainability initiatives.

Perceived organizational support and organizational identification

Perceived organizational support (POS) is based on the employee's belief that the firm values his/her contributions and is concerned about his/her well-being. Actions that demonstrate the firm's commitment to its employees' well-being can include: adequate wages, fair working conditions, personal development opportunities, support for personal employee matters, and employee involvement in various activities within the firm.

As a result, POS influences the beliefs of the employees related to their legitimacy as organizational members. If the employees perceive themselves to be legitimate organizational members, they are more likely to bond themselves psychologically and emotionally to the firm. Therefore, there should be a positive relationship between POS and organizational identification.

SRHRM and organizational identification

By embracing the commitment of corporate sustainability, SRHRM practices are dedicated to ensuring conformance to social norms. This conformance increases the firm's external reputation in the view of its stakeholders. Therefore, a firm with a formal commitment to SRHRM enhances the level of organizational identification of the employees. The actions of the firm are consistent with the perception of the employees that the external reputation of the firm matches the values and beliefs of the employees. This assumption is based on the belief that a firm which is socially responsible toward its external stakeholders would also be socially responsible toward its employees.

Organizational identity and task performance/extra-role helping behavior

Organizational identity has a positive impact on employee work attitudes and behaviors. As a result, organizational identity reinforces the expectations of the employees and enhances their perceived status within the firm. This results in organizational identity for the employees' task performance. Task performance can be defined as the work activities described in an employee's formal job description.

Extra-role helping behavior is defined as the ability of an employee to aid the actions of other employees which are not included in the employee's job description. Task performance is regarded as one of the critical determinants of firm performance. Alternatively, extra-role helping behavior can yield many positive benefits for employees by enhancing firm effectiveness, interpersonal harmony, job performance, and job satisfaction.

Employees who have a strong organizational identification are more likely to devote extra effort in promoting the firm's collective interests and values by ensuring they are meeting their obligations to their job through their task performance. Employees are more likely to embrace extra-role activities if the firm has established strong cooperative norms. Cooperative norms are the shared beliefs that employees are expected to help each other in order to support each other and the overall objectives of the firm. Traditional cooperative norms include collaboration by sharing of information and assistance with task completion.

The employees who offer the extra help could be considered risk takers because this action is usually not recognized in the performance appraisal of the employee. As a result, the employee offering the help may not receive any formal benefits for the action, but the employee receiving the help could improve his/her performance appraisal by successfully completing the task. Therefore, the employee must have a strong commitment to the firm's organizational identity in order to take the "risk" of help others without receiving a guarantee that his/her effort will be recognized by his/her superior.[9]

Corporate sustainability and job satisfaction

The firm's corporate sustainability initiatives can play a critical role in the employee's interpretation of the intrinsic and extrinsic motivating factors needed to effectively implement the firm's social programs. The higher the intrinsic and extrinsic attributions that motivate employees, the higher the level of job satisfaction. An important factor to link the firm's commitment to corporate sustainability and the motivating factors of the employees is the role of charismatic leaders. The top-level managers must be leaders who capture the imagination of the employees and believe in the leader's vision pertaining to corporate sustainability. Based on the belief that employees will attribute the cause and result of their actions, employees will translate the commitment and successful results of their actions related to corporate sustainability initiatives into higher levels of job satisfaction. A model showing these relationships is presented in Figure 4.3.

Charismatic leadership and corporate sustainability–induced attributions

The charismatic qualities of the leader, including his/her values, have a direct influence on the employees' beliefs and values related to the firm. Charismatic

Figure 4.3 Corporate sustainability and job satisfaction[10]

behaviors such as inspiring a shared vison, establishing challenging goals, and caring for the well-being of the employees incorporate both intrinsic and extrinsic motivators for the employees. The charismatic leader represents the commitment to a values-driven strategic focus which is integrated into the day-to-day operations of the firm.

Intrinsic

Intrinsic motivations are considered to be selfless actions in which the ultimate objective is doing good and/or fulfilling the individual's obligations to society. Therefore, a charismatic leader motivates the employees to perform actions without consideration of his/her own self-interests. Charismatic leaders can create a collective identity of the employees within the firm which incorporates exemplary values that go beyond serving the self-interests of the employees. These values appeal to the greater good of the firm's stakeholders and society in general.

Extrinsic

Extrinsic motivators are motivators that satisfy the self-interests of the individuals and result in the individuals improving their own welfare. Charismatic leaders have a positive impact on extrinsic motivations of the employees by presenting an achievable future vision in which the employee's individual goals and the firm's overall goals can be achieved.

Job satisfaction

Both intrinsic and extrinsic motivators impact the level of job satisfaction of the employee. The employee's intrinsic motivators are influenced based on the perception of fairness by the employee. If the employee believes that the firm's corporate sustainability actions are fair, the employee will be positively motivated. The perception of fairness is based on both self-centered and other-centered criteria. Therefore, the interactions the firm has with both its employees and other stakeholders related to corporate sustainability impact the employee's work attitudes.

The employee's extrinsic motivators are based on his/her beliefs that the firm's corporate sustainability initiatives will project a positive image on the firm's stakeholders and will result in higher levels of financial performance. This financial improvement will result in higher levels of employee satisfaction since it will enhance the long-term sustainability of the firm. In addition, higher levels of financial performance not only have a favorable impact on the firm overall but also the potential financial rewards given to the employees.[11]

Employee identity and corporate sustainability

It is self-evident that the more skilled and qualified the employees are, the higher the chances that the firm will obtain and maintain financial success over the long term. The challenge for the firm is to attract and retain high-quality employees. Some of the characteristics of high-quality employees include intelligence, motivation, experience, vision, creativity, commitment, analytic abilities, and technology abilities. Daniel Greening and Daniel Turban argue that firms can use corporate sustainability commitment as an avenue to maintain these high-quality employees using social identity theory.[12]

Social identity theory

Social identity theory is based on the belief that the employee's self-value is influenced by being a member of an organization that has matching values and beliefs. Social identity theory proposes that the self-image of the employee is influenced by the image and reputation of the firm where he/ she works. As a result, potential and current employees who have strong views related to the firm's role in corporate sustainability initiatives will seek out firms for employment that also have those beliefs explicitly presented to the stakeholders. Employees want to work for these firms since the corporate sustainability "output" of the firm entails a sense of individual accomplishment for the employees.[13]

For current employees, social identity theory entrenches the positive intrinsic value of working for a firm which has a strong positive commitment to corporate sustainability. This connection between the firm and employee values is represented in Figure 4.4.

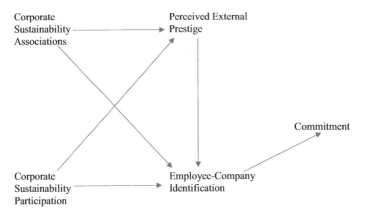

Figure 4.4 The components of social identity theory[14]

Corporate sustainability associations

Corporate sustainability associations are the perceptions the employees have of the firm's identity related to important societal issues. These are perceptions of the firm's external commitment to corporate sustainability. The employee will link these external actions of the firm with the firm's identity, which will be incorporated in the employee's perception of his/her identification with the firm.

Corporate sustainability participation

Corporate sustainability participation usually refers to employees volunteering to participate in corporate sustainability initiatives. Volunteering can be in the form of time and skills to provide service to local communities. However, corporate sustainability participation can also refer to employees being actively involved in the development and implementation of the firm's corporate sustainability programs. By encouraging the proactive participation of the employees in the creation of the corporate sustainability initiatives, the firm is able to strengthen the employees' identification with the firm and the social values of the firm.

Perceived external prestige

The employee's perception of corporate sustainability associations and participation directly impacts the level of perceived external prestige. The employee sees the actions through his or her cognitive lens in which the corporate sustainability initiatives generate overall goodwill to stakeholders. Since it is perceived as external prestige, the employee may evaluate the overall benefits and contributions at a higher value than other stakeholders. However, the important evaluation is the matching of the employee's social values with those actions of the firm.

Employee–company identification

Employee–company identification can be described as the ability of employees to identify with a firm where there is a sense of belonging and self-definition. As part of the identification process, employees not only seek firms to work for with similar beliefs but also seek firms that are distinctive in their ability to project those values to all stakeholders.[15]

Commitment

Commitment can be viewed as having three dimensions: affective commitment, continuance commitment, and normative commitment.

Affective commitment

Affective commitment can be described as the employee's willingness to accept the values of the firm, the willingness to exert effort to contribute to the success of the firm, and the desire to maintain membership in the firm. Therefore, affective commitment can be viewed as the level of affection the employee has for his or her job and can be defined as the employee's emotional attachment to, identification with, and involvement within the firm. If the employee and the firm both have a strong commitment to corporate sustainability, the employee will have a strong affective commitment since he/she believes in the values of the firm and wants the firm to succeed from both a financial and non-financial perspective.

Continuance commitment

Continuance commitment is the evaluation of the pros and cons for leaving the firm. As a result, continuance commitment can be defined as the employee's awareness of the costs associated with leaving the firm. If the employee has a strong continuance commitment, the perceived benefits of staying with the firm will outweigh the potential benefits of leaving the firm. Therefore, the employee will view commitment as the continuation of performing the responsibilities of the job within the existing firm. From a corporate sustainability perspective, employees will stay with a firm if they believe they can make a more effective contribution in helping the firm achieve its corporate sustainability goals than if they leave the firm.

Continuance commitment can also be strengthened by "side bets" that would be lost if the employee leaves the firm. Side bets could include firm pensions, comprehensive health insurance, financial allowances for housing, and education for the employee's children. These additional benefits of the job would be lost if the employee terminated his/her position and sought employment with another firm.

Normative commitment

Normative commitment refers to the sense of obligation for the employees to stay with the firm. This obligation is based on the perception that staying with the firm, even if the employee is not happy, is the morally correct thing to do to support the firm. Therefore, employees with a high level of normative commitment believe that they have a duty to stay with the firm.[16,17] Similar to continuance commitment, employees who are passionate about corporate sustainability believe that it is their duty to stay with the firm for the firm to be successful in achieving its corporate sustainability goals.

Employee recruitment and corporate sustainability

It is an underlying assumption that firms who can attract highly skilled, creative, and driven employees will have a competitive advantage in the marketplace. As the firm's most valuable resource, the decisions made by employees determine all the operations of the firm. As a result, it is imperative the firms use their corporate sustainability commitments as a recruiting tool to attract the best and the brightest employees. The corporate sustainability initiatives reveal the values of the firm and, therefore, are included in the "employee value proposition" in how potential employees determine which firm to work for. Corporate sustainability also gives the firm the ability to "humanize" in actions and present a more holistic perception of the firm since it demonstrates its commitment to stakeholders other than just shareholders. It is important since a paycheck may keep a person on the job physically, but it may not emotionally.

As a result, there are four factors that can improve the firm recruiting process by incorporating corporate sustainability in potential employee searches. The first factor is lack of awareness. Firms need to exploit their corporate sustainability commitments by including a description of corporate sustainability initiatives in overall summaries for potential employees to be aware of the type of programs currently being supporting. The firm should also let it be known that it is willing to explore new programs based on input received from employees.

The second factor is to ensure the potential employees are aware of the linkage between corporate sustainability and fulfillment of employees' needs. This could be based on a description of volunteer programs available or other activities the potential employee may want to be involved in if he/she decides to work for the firm. Another factor that would help fulfill the needs of the potential employee is the description of how the firm addresses the challenging balance between work and personal life. Having flexibility in hours, having the ability to commute, and having an on-site day care program are only a few examples under the umbrella of corporate sustainability of how potential employees can be enticed to work for the firm.

The third factor is to ensure potential employees know that their contributions are acknowledged and appreciated, not only for their efforts related to job performance but also for their performance in corporate sustainability initiatives. The potential employees must be made aware that their contributions do make a difference in society and that their efforts are valuable.

The fourth factor is ensuring the potential employees are aware that they will have some autonomy moving forward with their ideas related to corporate sustainability. The firm is purposely attracting not only excellent employees but also those who are passionate about corporate sustainability. Therefore, the firm must explicitly state that it not only encourages new ideas, but it will also champion and support these ideas through to fruition. If this supporting system is not in place, the employees will lose their bond of trust with the firm.[18]

Signaling theory

Signaling theory is based on the belief that potential employees do not have complete information about the firm before they are hired. Therefore, the potential employees look for "signals" from the firm based on information that is available to the public. These signals give a reference point for the potential employees to determine whether or not this is a desirable firm to work for where the individual's values coincide with the firm's values. Signaling allows the firm to present its commitment to all stakeholders, including potential employees, pertaining to corporate sustainability. These signals can identify the firm's internal commitment to corporate sustainability in the form of programs related to inclusion, gender equality, diversity, and other human resource related issues. These signals can also present information on the external commitment of the firm related to outreach programs, community support, and other avenues to aid its external stakeholders.[19]

Employee engagement and corporate sustainability

The results of a 2013 Gallup poll showed that only 13 percent of employees were engaged with their job globally. It is estimated that firms in the United States lose between $450 to $550 billion in productivity due to a lack of engagement by its employees. One solution to enhance the level of employee engagement within a firm is to incorporate a strong corporate commitment to corporate sustainability.

A firm with a strong commitment to corporate sustainability enables its employees to approach their jobs from a holistic perspective. Employees can strengthen their intrinsic rewards by wanting to perform well at work to support their emotional well-being in addition to the traditional financial and career-based rewards. The ability of the employees to show their whole self through

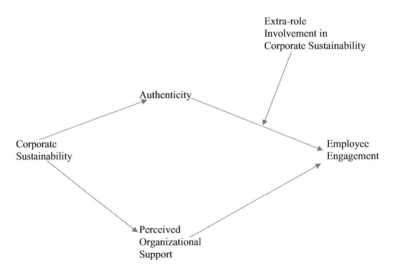

Figure 4.5 The relationship between corporate sustainability and employee engagement[20]

their work can enhance the level of employee engagement. The power of corporate sustainability related to employee engagement is that the employees find greater meaningfulness with their jobs if their sustainability values align. The key, however, is not in the firm's commitment through its mission or code of ethics statement, but rather in the implementation of firm actions supporting corporate sustainability. The firm's contribution to the greater good makes the employees feel better about themselves, which strengthens their identification with the value system of the firm. The overall relationship between corporate sustainability and employee engagement is presented in Figure 4.5.

The construct of employee engagement is based on three dimensions: authenticity, perceived organizational support, and extra-role involvement.

Authenticity

Authenticity refers to the content of the work which the employees are responsible for in successfully performing their jobs. If the type of content is aligned with their values, they are more engaged in performing the functions of their job. This engagement is referred to as the authenticity of the employee's job since the content is meaningful for the employee. Another component of authenticity is the workplace setting. The more positive the working climate is for an employee, the higher the level of psychological safety is perceived, which enhances the level of employee engagement.

The third component related to authenticity is the level of psychological availability. Do employees have the power and the authority to develop and implement decisions related to their job description? If they do have the autonomy to make these decisions, they perceive a higher level of authenticity in their jobs.

Perceived organizational support

Incorporated into the concept of psychological safety is perceived organizational support (POS). POS relies on the positive bond between the employees and the firm, and gives employees the ability to demonstrate more of their own self-worth without the fear of being subjected to negative consequences for their actions. Firms with strong corporate sustainability commitments can demonstrate the POS of their employees through their actions related to all its stakeholders. Employees interpret the signals set by the firms from its actions and this reassures the employees that their contributions to the firm are appreciated and valued by society. In addition, a strong corporate sustainability commitment is reflected in a well-run firm which embraces SRHRM practices. Furthermore, when employees see that the firm's stakeholders are being treated fairly, their expectations are that they will also be treated in the same manner.

Extra-role involvement

Extra-role involvement refers to activities by employees which are outside their job description. An example would be employees volunteering to help in the local community. Employee volunteering increases the self-value of the employees and strengthens their commitment to the firm. By being able to contribute their time and skills to community projects, the employees can enrich their contributions to society and are able to live out more of their real selves through their efforts to help others. The caveat with volunteering is that it must be perceived as "true" volunteering in which there will not be any negative consequences if the employees prefer not to volunteer. If the firm and/or peers put pressure on employees to perform volunteer activities, volunteering may foster employee disengagement.[21]

Employee volunteerism programs and corporate sustainability

The ability for the employee to be able to help the firm outside the work environment by providing benefits to the local community helps facilitate the employee's commitment to the firm. An employee volunteerism program is defined as a planned management event that attempts to motivate employees by enabling the workers to effectively volunteer under the sponsorship umbrella of the firm. A primary focus of these programs is to enhance the positive relationship with the firm's stakeholders in its local communities and provide a method to demonstrate the firm's commitment to corporate sustainability.

These programs make a public statement pertaining to the firm's corporate sustainability initiatives and can facilitate building a strong corporate culture within the firm. From the employee's perspective, employee volunteerism programs can yield five very positive outcomes: enhanced self-esteem, status security (reducing the threat of being fired), job enrichment (increasing the level of responsibility and satisfaction for the employee), increased practical skills, and the development of a more holistic perspective.

Employee volunteerism programs can be either inter-organizational or intra-organizational. Inter-organizational programs are ad hoc activities in which the employees identify the social programs they want to be involved in because it coincides with their own social values. Intra-organizational programs are designed by the firm in order to support philanthropic activities based on the firm's identification of the social programs it wants to endorse.

There are three traditional methods of structuring employee volunteerism programs: releasing time for volunteering, providing dollars-for-doers grants, and giving company-wide volunteer awards.

Releasing time for volunteering

One method used to sponsor employee volunteerism is to provide release time for the employees to volunteer with a non-profit organization of their choice. Under this program, the firm establishes a total number of yearly hours which eligible employees can volunteer. The firm would determine whether the employees would be paid for the hours during which they volunteer. Of course, a fully committed proactive firm would pay its employees for performing activities related to corporate sustainability initiatives.

Dollars-for-doers grants

Dollars for doers is a program in which the firm gives a financial contribution to an organization if an employee has served a specific number of volunteer hours for that organization. The benefit for employees is that they can emotionally support a social cause by not only volunteering their time but also by guiding financial resources for their social cause. This firmly entrenches the loyalty commitment the employees have with the firm. For the firm, these programs acknowledge its support for helping local communities. For the non-profit organization, it receives a double benefit from this program. The non-profit not only receives the volunteer hours from the employees, but it also receives a financial contribution from the firm.

Company-wide volunteer awards

A third method to structure employee volunteerism is to acknowledge the contribution of the employees through recognition and awards. Employees are recognized usually through either being given monetary or in-kind donations to support the charitable cause of their choice, or are given additional opportunities to volunteer in the future for social causes they believe in.[22]

Keurig Green Mountain is an example of a firm which uses a combination of these programs. Keurig Green Mountain has the Community Action for Employees Program (CAFÉ) which allows each full-time employee up to 52 paid volunteer hours annually to support community programs. In addition, Keurig Green Mountain sends nearly 100 employees on company-sponsored trips which go to coffee-growing and brewer manufacturing communities such as Peru, Brazil, and Costa Rica. Keurig Green Mountain also has a donations match program where it will match employees' donations to recognized charitable organizations up to a certain amount annually.[23]

Employee skills-based volunteerism

As the name implies, an employee skills-based program matches the skills, expertise, and talents of the employees with the specific needs of a non-profit organization. The specialized skills of the employees are used to strengthen the internal infrastructure of the non-profit organizations in order to build and sustain the organization's capacity to achieve both its short- and long-term objectives. For examples, certified public accountants can volunteer their accounting expertise to non-profits and top-level managers are able to draw on their vast experience related to strategic planning to help non-profits develop and implement goals.

Employees can do pro bono work where the employees contribute their expertise directly to a non-profit's internal operations. Pro bono work is usually a short-term commitment in which the volunteers use their expertise to address short-term issues or projects. An example of a pro bono project occurred when Capital One Brand Corps helped St. Joseph's Villa, a residential facility for special needs children in Richmond, Virginia. St Joseph's was struggling to reach its fundraising goals and needed help increasing both the number of donors and the average amount of the donations. Capital One used its expertise in direct mailing to help St. Joseph's develop a more engaging and efficient direct mail program to target more donors and larger donation amounts. After the first year of the program, St. Joseph's increased its existing donors by 41 percent and increased the overall response to the direct mail campaign by 51 percent.

A more comprehensive employee skills-based program focuses on continuously supporting the non-profit for the long term instead of through a single project. For the firms, the benefit of this consistent support is the ability to offer a way to expand its corporate philanthropy through its employees' commitment by increasing the social value of their skills for non-profits and the overall communities in need. Employees' skills can be used to aid the non-profits by developing the vision and strategy of the non-profit, developing and revising marketing programs, recommending new programs, and training the staff.

For example, a non-profit can develop a partnership with a Fortune 500 firm where the non-profit CFO can be matched with a person at a similar level within the firm. This relationship gives the non-profit an invaluable resource where the non-profit CFO seeks advice about issues which the corporate CFO may have had experience addressing in the past.

For the employees, skills-based volunteering gives them an opportunity to develop creative ideas and serves as a break from their jobs, which enhances their overall work experience. This type of volunteerism also can enhance the employees' organizational, leadership, communication, and decision-making skills which can facilitate career enhancement for the employees. This type of volunteering also opens new avenues for the employees to network with other people and to establish professional relationships with potential non-profit employers. A 2005 survey done by Deloitte on the impact of volunteering reported that over 80 percent of the respondents believed that volunteering enhances decision making, problem solving, and networking.[24]

Employee trust and corporate sustainability

In the pursuit to attract and retain high-quality employees committed to corporate sustainability, the firm must be able to develop and maintain a trusting relationship. The employees must be "guaranteed" that they will be treated and evaluated fairly in their jobs. A framework for the relationship between employee trust and corporate sustainability is shown in Figure 4.6.

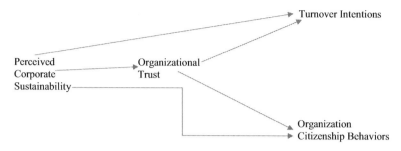

Figure 4.6 Employee trust and corporate sustainability[25]

Perceived corporate sustainability

The employees' perception related to the firm's commitment to corporate sustainability is paramount in the employees accepting and building a trusting relationship with the firm. These perceptions are based not only on corporate sustainability initiatives that have been developed and executed but also on the supporting culture of the firm that encourages the employees to incorporate the corporate's sustainability values in their actions. The employees' perceptions are based, in part, on people innately possessing moral duties of treating other people fairly and when unfair treatment of others is perceived, they will react accordingly.

Therefore, employees' perceptions are based not only on how they are treated by the firm but also how other stakeholders are treated by the firm. If the employees perceive that the firm is behaving in a socially irresponsible manner, the employees will be more likely to exhibit negative work attitudes and behavior. On the other hand, if the employees perceive that the firm is being socially responsible in its actions, the employees will have positive attitudes about the firm and subsequently will be motivated to be more productive in supporting the actions of the firm. This will result in the employees having a strongly entrenched, trusting relationship with the firm.

Employee trust

The actions taken by the firm send important signals to the employees about the firm's ethics and values, leading to the development of a trusting relationship. As a result, employee trust is an immediate outcome. If the firm has a strong positive corporate sustainability commitment, the employees will develop and maintain a high level of trust with the firm. Alternatively, if the firm acts in an irresponsible manner, the employees will lack a trusting relationship with the firm. If employees trust the firm, it will shape, in a positive manner, their attitudes and behaviors toward their employment and the firm overall.

Turnover intention

Turnover intention refers to the employee's intention to leave the firm based on being discontented or not being satisfied with his/her job and/or career opportunities to have a better opportunity with another firm. If the firm is acting in a responsible manner related to corporate sustainability, the threat of turnover intention decreases since the firm's commitment increases the level of content and satisfaction with his/her job position, resulting in the employee's perception that offers of employment from other firms are not as attractive.

Organizational citizenship behavior

Organizational citizenship behavior (OCB) refers to the discretionary actions which are perceived as "going the extra mile" to accomplish a task or address an issue. Employees employ OCB when they are committed to the firm and will exert extra effort in their actions to ensure the firm is successful. This behavior is perceived as "giving back" to the firm in exchange for the strong positive relationship the employees have with the firm. Therefore, when the employees perceive that the firm acts in a positive manner related to corporate sustainability, they will be more willing to demonstrate OCB as an acknowledgement of the positive actions by the firm.[26]

SAP: autism at work

According to the United Nations, 80 percent of people who have been diagnosed with autism are unemployed. In 2013, the German software company, SAP, started the Autism at Work program whose goal was to recruit and hire employees on the autism spectrum. By 2019, SAP had hired 160 employees in 13 countries under this program. One of the surprises SAP found from the program was the diversity of background experiences of the potential employees. SAP had received resumés from people who had degrees in history, literature, graphic design, and law.

The potential employees with autism are not given a traditional interview. They are given tasks such as team-building exercises in order for SAP to be able to observe their cognitive thinking in a non-conformist setting. Generally, employees with autism do not have fully developed social skills and do not enjoy interacting with other people. The Autism at Work program allows these employees to establish friendships with colleagues who are both autistic as well as those who are not. The SAP program assigns a mentor for the autistic employee to give advice and guidance throughout his/her career at SAP.

For the autistic employees, it gives them financial stability and more independence. In addition, they are grateful to SAP for giving them the opportunity to demonstrate their talents in a corporate setting where their contributions are acknowledged and rewarded. The employees also are able to see long-term career opportunities with SAP, which increases their engagement and commitment to SAP. The Autism at Work has a 90 percent retention rate.

SAP managers of employees with autism have said that they have become better managers as a result of being part of the Autism at Work program. The autistic employees can provide SAP with a very important analytical mindset, giving SAP the ability to think outside the common boundaries of traditional decision making. Common traits of autistic people are the ability to see patterns and an acute attention to detail. Both traits are paramount in software and other types of technology development. An additional benefit of the program is that the team spirit at SAP has improved significantly, which has had a positive impact on SAP's corporate culture.

In a program similar to SAP, HP Enterprise/DXC Technology's Dandelion Program for autistic employees in Australia focuses on a three-phase cycle. A fundamental starting point of the program is to identify the employee's strengths and not weaknesses. The first year, the employee with autism goes through a "job awareness" program in which the technical and social development of the employee are supported and monitored by their manager. The second phase focuses on the employee's "self-advocacy and self-determination," which focuses on the employee's understanding of how his/her actions impact the firm and how the employee is expected to contribute and perform in the same manner as every other employee at HP Enterprise. The third phase is the development of a long-term career growth strategy in which the employee is able to suit his/her future course within HP Enterprises with the help of mentors. Part of this long-term career development is giving the employee an opportunity to seek other roles within HP Enterprise in order to broaden the employee's perspective and allow other parts of HP Enterprise to benefit from the unique strengths of the employee. In 2017, HP Enterprise had 58 employees in the program who have jobs in cybersecurity, data analysis, and software testing, and all the employees have direct face-to-face contact with HP Enterprise's clients.[27,28,29]

Questions for thought

1. Do you think the employees at Tesco are upset about how the firm treats them? If so, why don't the employees leave Tesco?
2. Would you evaluate a firm's overall commitment to corporate sustainability before you apply for a job with that firm? Why or why not?
3. Would you want to participate in a volunteer program sponsored by your employer? Why or why not?
4. How loyal should you be to a firm? What are the pros and cons of being fiercely loyal to a firm?

5. Do you think you can trust any firm completely? If so, what factors would result in your complete trust? If not, what factors would result in your complete lack of trust?
6. What factors would have to take place in your job for you to be completely satisfied with your job?
7. Have you ever had a charismatic boss? If so, what attributes did the boss have that made him/her charismatic? If not, what attributes do you look for in an outstanding boss?

Notes

1 Alex Ralph. 2019. Tesco Asks Sacked Staff to Return Cash. *The Sunday Times.* June 20.
2 Sarah Ryle. 2004. Tesco Axes Sick Pay to Reduce 'Days Off' Cheats. *The Observer.* May 15.
3 www.glassdoor.ie/Benefits/Tesco-Sick-Pay-UK-BNFT72_E10250_N2.htm
4 Sarah Ryle. 2004. Tesco Axes Sick Pay to Reduce 'Days Off' Cheats. *The Observer.* May 15.
5 Helen Lam and Anshuman Khare. 2010. HR's Crucial Role for Successful CSR. *Journal of International Business Ethics.* 3(2): 3–15.
6 Helen Lam and Anshuman Khare. 2010. HR's Crucial Role for Successful CSR. *Journal of International Business Ethics.* 3(2): 12.
7 Helen Lam and Anshuman Khare. 2010. HR's Crucial Role for Successful CSR. *Journal of International Business Ethics.* 3(2): 3–15.
8 Jie Shen and John Benson. 2016. When CSR Is a Social Norm: How Socially Responsible Human Resource Management Affects Employee Work Behavior. *Journal of Management.* 42(6): 1725.
9 Jie Shen and John Benson. 2016. When CSR Is a Social Norm: How Socially Responsible Human Resource Management Affects Employee Work Behavior. *Journal of Management.* 42(6): 1723–1746.
10 Pavlos A. Vlachos, Nikolaos G. Panagopoulos and Adam A. Rapp. 2013. Felling Good by Doing Good: Employee CSR-Induced Attributions, Job Satisfaction, and the Role of Charismatic Leadership. *Journal of Business Ethics.* 118: 579.
11 Pavlos A. Vlachos, Nikolaos G. Panagopoulos and Adam A. Rapp. 2013. Felling Good by Doing Good: Employee CSR-Induced Attributions, Job Satisfaction, and the Role of Charismatic Leadership. *Journal of Business Ethics.* 118: 577–588.
12 Daniel W. Greening and Daniel B. Turban. 2000. Corporate Social Performance as a Competitive Advantage in Attracting a Quality Workforce. *Business and Society.* 39(3): 254–280.
13 Ibid.
14 Hae-Ryong Kim, Moonkyu Lee, Hyoung-Tark Lee and Na-Min Kim. 2010. Corporate Social Responsibility and Employee-Company Identification. *Journal of Business Ethics.* 95: 559.
15 Hae-Ryong Kim, Moonkyu Lee, Hyoung-Tark Lee and Na-Min Kim. 2010. Corporate Social Responsibility and Employee-Company Identification. *Journal of Business Ethics.* 95: 557–569.
16 John P. Meter and Natalie J. Allen. 1991. A Three-Component Conceptualization of Organizational Commitment. *Human Resource Management Review.* 1(1): 61–89.

17 Hae-Ryong Kim, Moonkyu Lee, Hyoung-Tark Lee and Na-Min Kim. 2010. Corporate Social Responsibility and Employee-Company Identification. *Journal of Business Ethics*. 95: 557–569.

18 Chitra B. Bhattacharya, Sankar Sen and Daniel Korschun. 2008. Using Corporate Social Responsibility to Win the War for Talent. *MIT Sloan Management Review*. 49(2): 37–44.

19 Daniel W. Greening and Daniel B. Turban. 2000. Corporate Social Performance as a Competitive Advantage in Attracting a Quality Workforce. *Business and Society*. 39(3): 254–280.

20 Ante Glavas. 2016. Corporate Social Responsibility and Employee Engagement; Enabling Employees to Employ More of Their Whole Selves at Work. *Frontiers in Psychology*. 7: 796. May 31.

21 Ante Glavas. 2016. Corporate Social Responsibility and Employee Engagement; Enabling Employees to Employ More of Their Whole Selves at Work. *Frontiers in Psychology*. 7: 796. May 31.

22 Shelly McCallum, Melissa Ann Schmid and Lawrence Price. 2013. CSR: A Case for Employee Skills-Based Volunteering. *Social Responsibility Journal*. 9(3): 479–495.

23 www.keuriggreenmountain.com/en/JobSeekers/WhyWorkHere/Sustainability. aspx

24 www.nationalservice.gov/sites/default/files/resource/Grantee%20TTA%20Calen dar%202015%20for%20Posting.pdf

25 S. Duane Hansen, Benjamin B. Dunford, Alan D. boss, R. Wayne Boss and Ingo Angermeier. 2011. Corporate Social Responsibility and the Benefits of Employee Trust: A Cross-disciplinary Perspective. *Journal of Business Ethics*. 102: 30.

26 S. Duane Hansen, Benjamin B. Dunford, Alan D. boss, R. Wayne Boss and Ingo Angermeier. 2011. Corporate Social Responsibility and the Benefits of Employee Trust: A Cross-disciplinary Perspective. *Journal of Business Ethics*. 102: 29–45.

27 https://news.sap.com/2017/04/autism-at-work-summit-2017-hiring-for-a-career- not-just-a-job/

28 www.sap.com/corporate/en/company/diversity/differently-abled.html

29 www.cbsnews.com/video/hiring-autistic-workers/

5 Organizational strategies and corporate sustainability

Introduction

Regardless of its commitment to corporate sustainability issues, every firm must be profitable and be financially sustainable. Its social mission and causes are of no value if the firm is in bankruptcy. This chapter addresses how a firm can use its overall strategic focus to obtain its social, environmental and financial goals. This triple bottom line approach is needed since both financial and non-financial goals can only be achieved through an independence of actions. Concepts that are discussed in this chapter include turning core competencies into corporate sustainability initiatives; the development of strategic sustainability value; corporate sustainability and Porter's five forces model; corporate diversification and corporate sustainability; corporate sustainability and competitive advantage; corporate sustainability and strategic implementation; and inclusive capitalism. The chapter begins with a discussion on how Outland Denim is helping anti-human trafficking and concludes with a discussion of Salesforce CEO Marc Benioff's views of inclusive capitalism.

Outland Denim: helping survivors globally

The origins of Outland Denim started when its founder, James Bartle, met with an anti-human trafficking group while attending a music festival. Based on that meeting, Bartle decided to travel to Asia to observe the vulnerability of young girls who were forced to work in the sex industry by human traffickers.

In response to that visit, Bartle set up the "Denim Project," which taught girls sewing and then used their skills to sew denim jeans. The making of jeans was based on his simple philosophy towards clothing. Bartle stated that "I've always lived in jeans. If you were going to produce anything, why wouldn't you produce the most staple part of a person's wardrobe? Jeans aren't a throw-away item, but something you keep for years."

Headquartered in Australia, Bartle created Outland Denim in order to give these young women a fresh start. The fundamental philosophy of Outland

Denim is the ability to empower disadvantaged and disenfranchised young women so that they are able to create a better life for themselves and their families. As a social enterprise, Outland Denim is committed to achieving performance goals beyond financial success. Outland Denim's dual mission is to address the social issues related to human trafficking as well as being a financially sustainable firm.

One of the biggest challenges for Outland Denim is the initial training of the women. Before they start at Outland Denim, the women do not have a clear understanding of the fashion industry or garment industry. In addition, making jeans is one of the most difficult garments to create. One of Outland Denim's goals is to train the women on every step in the jean manufacturing process. This type of job rotation increases the motivation of the employees and gives Outland Denim the flexibility to assign the women based on the needs of the workstation instead of the skills of the employee.

The 360-degree job rotation program takes over two and a half years to train the women so they can do every step in the jean manufacturing process. The employee's pay scale is based on factors such as punctuality, attitude at work, quality of work, and speed of work.

Both of Outland Denim's production facilities are located in Cambodia. One is located in Phnom Penh and the other in Kampong Cham. In these facilities, the work environment fosters not only the feeling of safety, but Outland Denim also addresses the employees' holistic needs through providing liveable wages, skills training, and personal development initiatives. Outland Denim hosts employee workshops in English in areas such as tailoring and financial budgeting. Outland Denim pays the women a living wage which does not include stringent output levels and mandatory overtime. In highlighting the value of the employees, before any pair of jeans leaves the factory, one of the seamstresses writes a message inside the pocket about herself. This creates an emotional bond between the seamstress and the customer.

Outland Denim has moved beyond its original mission by also expanding its employee base to include young female workers who are on the risk of falling into poverty, a contributing factor in human trafficking vulnerability. In addition, Outland Denim is committed to sourcing the most ethically and environmentally sound raw materials, which include organic cotton pocket lining and recycled packaging.

Outland Denim sources its denim from the company, Bossa Denim. Established in 1951, Bossa has always been actively involved in corporate sustainability issues. The production facility for the denim is located in Turkey and Bossa provides proof to Outland Denim that it is has favorable working conditions and gives its workers a fair living wage. Bossa uses organic cotton which is manufactured with 91 percent less fresh water than conventional cotton. Bossa also ensures the cotton farmers are using the best practices related to the use of water, fertilizers, chemicals, and other resources.

Bossa's environmental commitment includes designing a waste recovery system for its spinning mills, the utilization of natural dyes, the development of recycled cotton for blended denims, and reduction of its carbon dioxide emission levels.[1,2,3,4,5]

The Meghan Markle effect

During a tour of Australia in 2018, Meghan Markle, the Duchess of Sussex, was wearing Outland Denim jeans. After pictures were published of her wearing the jeans, the traffic on Outland Denim's website increased by 948 percent over a ten-day period. The increased level of sales allowed Outland Denim to hire between 15 and 30 new employees. In a speech at the University of the South Pacific, the Duchess of Sussex stated that "When girls are given the right tools to succeed, they can create incredible futures, not only for themselves but also for those around them."[6]

Social enterprise

Social enterprises can be either non-profit or for profit in nature. As was shown in the description of Outland Denim, social enterprises have both a financial and social mission. There are three major social enterprise models: opportunity employment, transformative products or services, and donating back.

Opportunity employment

The first model is opportunity employment. Outland Denim is an example of an opportunity employment model. In this model, the organization focuses on employing people who have barriers to being hired in a traditional employer setting. Other examples of organizations that use this model include Goodwill Industries, who provides job training and employment placement. The philosophy of Goodwill is "a hand up, not a handout" and implements this philosophy by employing those with limited financial resources to mend and repair used goods that could be resold to the general public.[7,8]

Transformative products or services

The second model is the development of transformative and innovative products or services by the organization.[9] Soles 4 Souls is an example of an organization that provides an innovative service by developing sustainable jobs collecting and distributing clothing and shoes globally. The mission of Soles 4 Souls is to disrupt the cycle of poverty by serving those in need, developing employment opportunities, and protecting the environment.[10]

Donating back

The third model is based on the organization donating a portion of its profits to social causes which are able to address basic unmet needs. Songs Against Slavery is an example of an organization which uses music to address unmet social needs through music. Songs Against Slavery inspires communities to fight against human trafficking by raising community awareness through benefit concerts and musician partnerships.[11,12]

What is the strategy of the firm?

A firm's strategy is the development and execution of the firm's future course of action to achieve long-term viability. The strategy of the firm incorporates the firm's vision and mission in the development of a strategic plan. This plan incorporates external factors such as the competitive environment and industry dynamics in order to be financially successful. At the corporate level, the firm decides what industries to compete in as well as determine how to enter new markets. Firms can enter a new market through mergers, acquisitions, joint ventures, or new business creation internally. Business level strategies refer to how the firm competes in the marketplace. Instead of asking the question "where does the firm compete?" the question to answer at a corporate level strategic focus, at the business level, the firm answers the question of "how will it compete in the marketplace?" The development of the firm's strategy is referred to as the strategic formulation process and the execution of the strategy is referred to as the strategic implementation process.

The strategic formulation process is based on the develop of a Strengths, Weaknesses, Opportunities and Threats (SWOT) analysis. The strengths identify areas in which the firm is performing at an above average level while weaknesses are areas in which the firm needs to make adjustments and improvements. Both strengths and weaknesses are internal in nature. Opportunities and threats are external factors that can impact the financial performance of the firm. Opportunities are future courses of actions the firm may capitalize on in the future. Examples of opportunities can include developing new products, expanding into a new industry, expanding into a new country, developing a new type of technology, and the identification of a new market opportunity. Threats are external factors that can have a negative impact on the firm. Traditional threats include: competition, government regulations, the economy, technology changes, changes in customer tastes, and changes in a country's demographics.

From a corporate sustainability perspective, the SWOT analysis is a key component for the firm to be able to incorporate the stakeholders' needs in the decision-making process. As the needs and expectations of the stakeholders shift, so do the potential opportunities to address the shifts, as well as the potential threats of now being aware of the shifts in the stakeholders' expectations.

Therefore, it is critical for the managers of the firm to understand that corporate sustainability should be considered a core competency for the firm. A core competency can be defined as a fundamental component which facilitates the firm's ability to compete in the marketplace. Core competencies could be customer service, technology trend setting, efficient manufacturing processes, an aggressive commitment to quality, and the image and reputation of the firm.

In order for the firm to be able to integrate corporate sustainability throughout the organization, the firm must be able to use resources and capabilities which are valuable, rare, difficult to imitate, and impossible to be challenged by substitutes. If the firm can do an effective job in the development of sustainability core competencies, the firm will be able to differentiate itself from its competitors and notify all existing and potential competitors that it has developed a sustainable competitive advantage.[13]

Turning core competencies into corporate sustainability initiatives

There are seven traditional core competencies which can be used by the firm to develop and implement the firm's corporate sustainability agenda. The first core competency is *strategic flexibility*. If a firm is able to adapt to a quickly changing competitive and industry environment, the firm is better able to match its resources on issues that will yield high performance levels. This quick adaptability is extremely valuable when a firm has to quickly adjust to shifting demands of its stakeholders related to corporate sustainability issues.

The second core competency is *strategic leadership*. By having strong leaders in management positions, it not only facilitates developing an effective operational strategy, but it also gives managers the ability to incorporate sustainability objectives into the firm's vision and mission used in the decision-making process.

The third core competency is *employee development* through the enhancement of employees' skills and capabilities. Employee development is useful in developing innovative products and solutions for corporate sustainability initiatives.

The fourth core competency is the development of *human capital*. The knowledge that the firm's employees obtain throughout their careers is invaluable in applying that expertise in the development and execution of the firm's corporate sustainability strategy.

The fifth core competency is the effective use of *new technology*. The use of new technology opens new opportunities for the firm to incorporate the needs and expectations of the stakeholders into the day-to-day operations of the firm, including addressing corporate sustainability issues.

The sixth core competency is engaging in *valuable strategies*. Firms that can reach out and develop joint ventures and other types of corporate partnerships can share knowledge with partners to increase the level of organizational learning. This learning can be applied to corporate sustainability issues.

The seventh core competency is the development of *new organizational structures and cultures*. If a firm has a strong positive corporate culture, the employees are united in their goal to help the firm achieve its short-term and long-term objectives. This culture also embraces a positive commitment to incorporate corporate sustainability in the decision–making process.[14]

The development of strategic sustainability value

The development of sustainability value is based on whether the actions required by the firm are internal or external and whether the time frame is current or future. The framework is shown in Figure 5.1.

The drivers in Figure 5.1 represent external factors that influence the strategic focus of the firm. These drivers could be based on the actions of competitors, changes in the competitive landscape of the industry, as well as representing the needs and expectations of the firm's stakeholders.

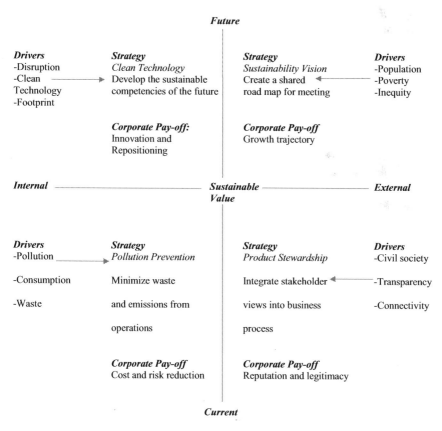

Figure 5.1 The development of strategic sustainable value[15]

Decision makers in the firm make decisions based on whether those decisions impact short-term results (current) and guide the firm into long-term strategic positioning (future). Short-term corporate sustainability strategies focus on areas such as cost reduction and efficiencies that have a positive impact on the firm's operations as well as serving the needs of its stakeholders. In using a long-term strategic focus, firms establish and announce to their stakeholders their long-term vision toward corporate sustainability issues. This commitment could include long-term investment in new technology which more effectively addresses the needs of its stakeholders. An example of this technology would be the development of alternative energy sources or the use of technology to develop products in countries where the customers have very low income levels.

For internal strategic focus, the firm would enhance its current internal capabilities which are directed related to the firm's core competencies. Investments for the firm internally would include the acquisition of new equipment or other resources in order to enhance its corporate sustainability strategic focus. These internal investments increase the firm's competitive advantage by increasing its ability to improve its relationship with its shareholders through increased financial performance as well as improving its relationship with its other stakeholders. The firm's external strategic focus refers to its ability to enhance formal relationships with its stakeholders through the enhancement of its reputation and legitimacy. The external focus includes comparing the corporate sustainability performance of the firm relative to other firms in the industry.[16]

Strategic corporate sustainability

Strategic corporate sustainability is the integration of corporate sustainability into the strategic focus of the firm. Strategic corporate sustainability is comprised of four components. The first component is incorporating the corporate sustainability initiative in the firm's strategic planning process. The second component is that any actions that have a corporate sustainability activity are directly related to the firm's core competencies. The third component is to ensure the stakeholders' needs are incorporated into the actions of the firm. The fourth component is the shifting of strategic focus and resources from a short-term to a long-term time horizon.

Therefore, strategic corporate sustainability involves a proactive integration of corporate sustainability issues in the decision–making process related to the day-to-day operations of the firm. The result of a strategic corporate sustainability philosophy is that there is a direct impact on the firm's operations on society and society has a direct impact on the firm. Alternatively, a responsive corporate sustainability strategy occurs when a firm is proactive in becoming involved in a corporate sustainability issue which is not directly related to the day-to-day operations of the firm.[17]

Corporate sustainability and Porter's five forces model

Michael Porter's five forces model identifies five different dimensions of competition in any given industry. The five forces are: threat of new entrants; bargaining power of suppliers; bargaining power of buyers; threat of substitute products or services; and rivalry among existing competitors.

Threat of new entrants

The threat of new entrants is based on the strength of the barriers of entry into the industry. In order for a new firm to enter the industry, the firm must be able to secure financial, human, and physical resources. In addition, factors such as brand recognition and brand loyalty also play a significant role in creating a barrier to entry. A barrier to entry is a component that hinders the ability of a new firm to enter the market place. If the existing firms in the industry have strong brand loyalty, it is extremely difficult for a new firm to take away market share from an existing firm. Therefore, this can be an extremely high barrier for new entrants to address before they establish a presence in the marketplace.

Firms that have a strong commitment to corporate sustainability can generate a desirable corporate reputation which is like brand loyalty. Customers that agree with the firm's philosophy related to corporate sustainability will be hesitant to buy their products from a competitor. Firms with a strong environmental commitment will make the necessary investments to be technological leaders in product design and manufacturing. If government regulations related to the natural environment become more stringent, firms that are proactive to the environment can quickly shift to address the requirements of the regulations. However, increasing government regulations can result in additional financial, human, and physical asset costs for firms that are considering entering the new industry. These additional costs will further raise the barriers of entry for any new firm.

Bargaining power of suppliers

Bargaining power of suppliers is based on who has the power in the relationship between the firm supplying raw materials and the buyer acquiring the raw materials. As a buyer firm gets larger, its power increases over its suppliers due to economies of scale. The more of a raw material a buyer purchases, the lower the cost per unit since the supplier may give a discount for larger volumes.

The scarcer the raw materials, the more valuable and important they become for the buyer to acquire. This scarcity relationship is demonstrated in the case presented in this textbook on cobalt mining in the Democratic Republic of Congo (DRC). Existing firms that have a strong relationship with suppliers of scare resources have created a significant competitive advantage over firms that do not have the same type of supplier relationship.

Another corporate sustainability issue related to increasing scarcity of raw materials is climate change. For example, in the food and beverage industry, firms are concerned about the availability of water and other food products as climate change forces farmers to adjust their farming strategies. As a result, there is an increased focus of farmers globally adopting sustainable and water-efficient agriculture methods in order to reduce the costs of farming. Those firms that have a positive relationship with suppliers related to corporate sustainability issues will be in a stronger competitive position to address the needs of all their stakeholders as compared with firms that lack this relationship.

Bargaining power of buyers

The reciprocal of the bargaining power of suppliers, the bargaining power of the buyers, also examines who has the power between the relationship of the buyers and suppliers from the buyer's perspective.

The more dependent suppliers are on selling their goods to the buyers, the more bargaining power the buyers have in the relationship. From a corporate sustainability perspective, buyers can demand the suppliers be certified by international organizational standards related to the natural environment, such as the International Organization of Standardization (ISO) 14000 system. To be certified for this standard, firms must have an environmental management system in place to minimize the environmental impact of their operations.

Global retailers, such as Walmart, demand that suppliers comply with their corporate criteria of acceptable products based on environmental sustainability including minimizing waste and the development of more efficient manufacturing processes.

Threat of substitute products or services

The threat of substitutes refers to alternative products or services which can satisfy most, if not all, of the customer's needs.[18] From a corporate sustainability perspective, shifts in stakeholder focus include society forcing firms to develop alternative products. There can be "perfect" substitutes such as the replacing of plastic straws with paper straws in many cities and countries globally. However, there are numerous examples where consumers have the option to support corporate sustainability causes by shifting their buying patterns. One area in which customers have shifted their focus is supporting products where child labor has been eliminated in the manufacturing process. For example, the Oliberte shoe line guarantees that no child labor was used in its manufacturing process. That is a viable alternative to Nike shoes, which have been accused of unethical working conditions in its outsourced factories for multiple decades. Another alternative to the global chocolate brands is

Equal Exchange Chocolates, which ensures that no child labor was used in the collection and manufacturing of its cocoa from the Ivory Coast, which has an estimated 250,000 child laborers.[19]

Rivalry among existing competitors

Rivalry among existing competitors refers to the intensity of a firm acquiring market share from other firms in the industry. This intensity is based on how strong the competitive advantages of the firms are in order to obtain gains in market share position. The competitive advantage of the firm is one explanation why a customer will purchase the product or service from the firm. As was stated earlier in the chapter, firms that have a strong commitment to corporate sustainability are able to use this commitment to enhance the firm's ability to differentiate its product relative to its competitors.[20]

Corporate level strategies

Corporate diversification and corporate sustainability

Related diversification strategies

Diversification occurs when a firm expands from a single market focus to multiple markets. There are many benefits for firms to move to a diversified corporate level strategy. Among those benefits are the ability to grow beyond its existing markets, to be able to create or enhance the firm's competitive advantage, to maneuver around the firm's existing competitors. Diversification can generally be separated into two major categories: related and unrelated. Related diversification refers to a diversification strategy in which there is a connection among the different business units. This connection could be based on a similar manufacturing process or catering to similar customers with its products. For example, Exxon/Mobil has a related diversification strategy due to the manufacturer process. Exxon/Mobil takes petroleum and converts it into petroleum-based produces including gasoline, oils, lubricants, and chemicals. The Walt Disney Company is an example of a firm which has a related diversification strategy based on developing products and services to families. Its television shows, movies, theme parks, licensed toys, and other merchandise all target family units.

Larger firms who have the benefits of economies of scale are having to generate lower overall average costs of providing corporate sustainability attributes when compared with smaller firms. As a firm becomes more diversified, there are not only benefits of economies of scale but also economies of scope. A diversified firm can spread the cost of corporate sustainability investments over many products and services. The resulting positive reputation and goodwill would also be spread across the firm's multiple divisions both domestically and globally.[21]

As a firm increases its level of diversification, the range of stakeholder demands and social issues of its different business units will increase, requiring a comprehensive response to the demands and issues. A firm's diversification strategy increases potential managerial risk, which can be reduced through a positive supportive relationship with stakeholders.

A firm that engages in addressing responses to stakeholders in a proper and timely fashion will significantly reduce the firm's level of risk. As a result, if a firm makes investments in corporate sustainability initiatives such as environmentally friendly manufacturing, labor relations, and transparent corporate governance programs, it can reduce the level of firm risk by minimizing the costly problems with regulations, activists, and consumers. Furthermore, charitable donations and other acts of philanthropy generate positive goodwill, which increases the firm's reputation from the perspective of its stakeholders. Therefore, firms are motivated to invest in corporate sustainability initiatives to protect their brand name and reputations across various business unites.

Stakeholders in different industries and different geographic markets view corporate sustainability issues from different levels of importance. Therefore, a significant level of diversification can potentially increase the pressure from a more extensive group of stakeholder needs and demands. As a result, diversified firms will face a larger number of critical stakeholders who have significant levels of power, legitimacy, and urgency than those firms who are not diversified.

Unrelated diversification

An unrelated diversification refers to the composition of business units in the firm's portfolio. The business units of an unrelated diversification firm do not have any connection with each other. As a result, there is no connection or relatedness among the different business units.

As a result, the number and diversity of the stakeholders may be higher for those firms which have an unrelated diversification strategy. The firm will potentially have less overlapping of the same stakeholders and its needs than a firm which has a related diversified corporate level strategy. Therefore, there is a significant additional burden for unrelated diversified firms since they may be forced to address more stakeholders and a higher level of diversity of stakeholder needs than those of a related diversified firm.

Social issues and the needs and expectations of the stakeholders, which can vary significantly from one industry to another, include: environmental protection; humanitarian contributions; governance transparency; labor policy; employee relations; workforce diversity; and product related responsibility. General Electric (GE) is an example of an unrelated diversified firm with divisions in industries such as energy infrastructure, aviation, and financial services. The stakeholder demands for GE's Capital division (financial services) related to corporate sustainability are very different than GE Aviation and GE Energy Infrastructure. Alternatively, a company like Coca-Cola, which has a related diversified strategy based on beverages, has the same stakeholders and similar needs and expectations related to Coke's environmental commitment to issues such as the environmental impact of plastic packaging and use of water for Coke's carbonated beverage, sports drinks, and bottled water markets.[22]

In addition, factors such as government regulations and expectations can vary significantly from one industry to another for unrelated diversified firms. This variance in addressing the needs of the government can force unrelated diversified firms to implement more corporate sustainability initiatives in order to meet the government needs in multiple industries.

Furthermore, since unrelated diversified firms do not have the synergistic advantages of shared costs, knowledge, and branding that occurs in related diversified firms, unrelated diversified firms have the opportunity to create market intangible assets such as reputation, brand, and customer loyalty through its corporate sustainability initiatives. This will allow an unrelated diversified firm to enhance its competitive advantage in different industries through a unified corporate sustainability commitment.[23]

International diversification

As is the case with unrelated diversified firms, once a firm moves beyond its country of origin, the number of stakeholders' demands increases with a higher level of diversity in the stakeholders. Stakeholders in different countries and different regions give different levels of priorities related to corporate sustainability issues. These differences in priorities are due, in part, to differences in cultural and religious backgrounds. For example, in some countries gender equality is a paramount social issue, while in other countries the issue is not considered a priority.[24]

A report by the non-profit, Equal Measure 2030, found great disparity in gender equality globally. Although the findings from 129 countries showed that no country was at 100 percent gender equality based on their evaluation, four Scandinavian countries were at the top of the listing: Denmark 89.3, Finland 88.8, Sweden 88.0, and Norway 87.7. The four countries with the lowest scores related to gender equality were: Yemen 44.7, Congo 44.0, DRC 38.2, and Chad 33.4.[25]

Therefore, if the firm had operations in both Denmark and Chad, there would be a fundamental difference in how stakeholders in those two countries would view the importance of gender equality. For Asian countries, there is a top priority of ensuring lifetime employment for its employees, while other countries in North America and Europe do not view lifetime employment as a viable option for employees of their firms.

Furthermore, issues related to environmental protection and climate change have significant variances in importance in how these issues should be addressed globally. Countries with comprehensive environmental regulations will demand monitoring and compliance, as well as being proactive addressing environmental issues. Countries with weaker environmental regulations will not demand the same level involvement of the firm addressing environmental issues. Geographically diversified firms will have to address the comprehensive needs of a larger number of salient stakeholders who have power, legitimacy, and urgency than domestic-based firms.[26]

Business level strategies

Corporate sustainability and competitive advantage

The relationship between corporate sustainability and competitive advantage is depicted in Figure 5.2.

Due to the firm's commitment to corporate sustainability, the perceived image and reputation of the firm is strengthened from the perspective of its stakeholders. Therefore, the firm is better able to attract and retain its customers due to the shared belief that corporate sustainability initiatives are important for all stakeholders, including society. The firm's image and reputation also increase the effective recruitment, motivation, and retention of employees. Therefore, a firm's commitment to corporate sustainability will enhance the firm's competitive advantage.

By having loyal customers and employees, the firm can not only generate positive financial gains from their commitment but also establish and maintain employee and customer loyalty, blocking existing and potential competitors from

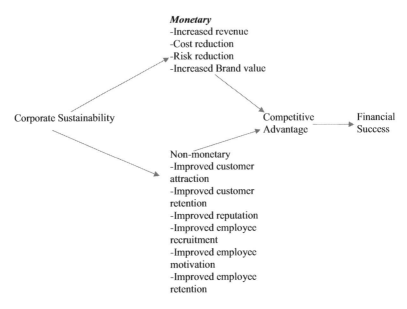

Figure 5.2 The relationship between corporate sustainability and competitive advantage[27]

taking away the firm's customers or employees. As a result, the firm is able to present a unique narrative to its stakeholders which results in its stakeholders agreeing and supporting the firm through purchasing its products from the customers and developing new innovative processes and products from its employees.[28]

Corporate sustainability used for differentiation

A firm's commitment to differentiation is based on presenting a unique product or service to the marketplace. One dimension that firms can use to separate products from competitors' products is based on its commitment to corporate sustainability. The firm's corporate sustainability initiatives can be presented to the customer as part of the holistic experience of purchasing the product or using the service. In addition, when firms are able to develop a new production process and/or a process innovation, the result of this technological advancement could produce a product which is not only unique but could also have a positive environmental impact by reducing the amount of material, energy, raw materials, and increases in recycled materials as part of the production process.

Another component of developing a higher level of differentiation in the firm's products is having a stellar corporate reputation. Firms that are diligent in protecting their reputations through actions, including their commitment to corporate sustainability. will be rewarded by consumers who perceive the firm as reliable, honest, and trustworthy.[29]

Product differentiation

Product differentiation is critical for the success of the firm since it creates barriers to entry for potential competitors, it protects against imitation by current competitors, and it enhances the level of customer loyalty to the firm. Product differentiation can include advances in technology, developing more innovative features, producing high quality standards, and improving customer service and the reputation of the firm. The reputation of the firm can be enhanced through social and environmentally responsive products under the realm of corporate sustainability.

Product quality differentiation

Product quality differentiation is based on several characteristics of the product including performance, durability, reliability, and consistency based on specification. By having a premium quality product, the firm is able to develop a premium image of the products which enhances the firm's competitive advantage.

Product innovation differentiation

Through product and process engineering, the firm can develop product innovation that separates the features of its product from those of its competition. Therefore, the ability of the firm to use research and development investments to develop truly unique features for its products gives the firm another dimension of differentiation.

Corporate sustainability and product differentiation

Firms can use corporate sustainability commitments to capture increased value of the products and the firm through stakeholder management by incorporating it into the firm's strategic focus. The firm's corporate sustainability strategy can be used to create competitive advantages by favorably positioning the firm's products in the minds of the customers by building and maintaining a reputation which focuses on environmental and/or socially responsible activities.

This perception by the customers can be developed through total quality management programs, being proactive in managing the firm's stakeholders, and marketing the firm's corporate and sustainability commitment through branding and communications. By having a strong corporate sustainability commitment, the firm can attract and retain highly skilled employees who are able to develop higher quality and more innovative products and be better able to find solutions to problems. Through a strong total quality management program, the firms can improve the processes which impact corporate sustainability including: elimination of waste, minimizing pollution, and eliminating the exposure employees would have to unhealthy working conditions.

The firm is also able to improve its reputation, which can create more favorable relationships with its stakeholders. A firm's reputation is unique so it is an extremely valuable intangible resource which can be difficult to imitate by existing competitors. The value added by the firm's reputation includes strengthening the firm's relationship with its customers by building customer loyalty and brand identification. Therefore, a strong corporate sustainability commitment will encourage firms to better understand their customers' demands and be more proactive in responding to the customers' needs, rationales, and beliefs.

For countries with emerging economies, firms who make products in those countries and export the products may have difficulties due to the perception that the products lack acceptable quality. In addition, there may be a perception of an inferior image and reputation for products developed in that country. Firms can use investments in corporate sustainability initiatives as an opportunity to enhance the level of differentiation of its products when exporting to countries with developed markets. Figure 5.3 shows the

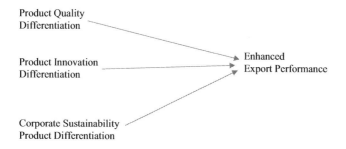

Figure 5.3 The relationship between product differentiation, corporate sustainability, and export performance[31]

relationship between product differentiation and export performance for firms in emerging economies.[30]

Corporate sustainability and strategic implementation

When focusing on implementing its strategy, a firm focuses on four different perspectives: financial, customer, internal process, and learning and growth.

Financial perspective

The financial perspective focuses on the financial costs to address the implementation process, as well as the projected financial performance of the successful implementation of the strategy. Therefore, financial perspective is the allocation of the resources needed in order to serve the needs of the stakeholders in implementing the firm's strategy. Components of the financial perspective include revenue growth, productivity growth, and asset utilization.

Customer perspective

The customer perspective refers to the customer and market segments that are targeted with the strategic focus of the firm. It is the customer perspective that firms use in the establishment of the strategic objectives, strategic measurements, and the development of customer value to effectively compete in the marketplace. The customer perspective drives a firm to develop and maintain its competitive advantage to ensure its long-term survival. Components of the customer perspective include market share, customer acquisition, customer retention, customer satisfaction, and customer profitability.

Internal process perspective

The internal processes are those activities within the firm such as operational processes, customer management processes, innovation processes, regulatory processes, and after sale service processes.

Learning and growth perspective

The learning and growth perspective is based on the development of the proper infrastructure to achieve the effective execution of the goals of the previous three perspectives. The critical components of this perspective include qualification and motivation of the employees and the establishment of goal orientation so that the employees have a vested interest in the firm's achievement of its goals. Components of the learning and growth perspective include employee retention, employee productivity, and employee satisfaction.

For firms that want to embrace corporate sustainability, the focus must be on the three critical dimensions of sustainability: economic, environmental, and social issues. Managers should be able to identify and capitalize on opportunities for simultaneous improvement in all three dimensions in the development of a strong commitment to corporate sustainability. Firms whose vision includes integrating corporate sustainability in the implementation of its strategic focus will develop an additional corporate sustainability perspective.

Corporate sustainability perspective

A firm with a commitment to corporate sustainability must be able to incorporate its commitment in its implementation process. By integrating the firm's corporate sustainability strategy, the firm will ensure that the actions taken by the firm coincide with the firm's corporate sustainability commitment. Figure 5.4 highlights the process of incorporating corporate sustainability in the strategic implementation process.

The components of the corporate sustainability perspective are customized to the stakeholders' needs and demands for that firm's strategic business unit (SBU). A firm's SBU is equivalent to a division of the firm. Each SBU of the firm must tailor its corporate sustainability to address the needs of the SBU's critical stakeholders. Furthermore, the SBU's strategic focus must be in harmony with the firm's corporate sustainability initiatives that are implemented by the SBU.

After the SBU has identified potential environmental and social exposure, it must develop a corporate sustainability strategic focus in order to assure that the SBU has addressed the relevant issues. Environmental issues can include air, water and soil emissions, waste, materials used, energy intensity, noise and vibrations, waste heat, radiation, and direct interventions on nature. Social exposure issues relate to specific issues that impact

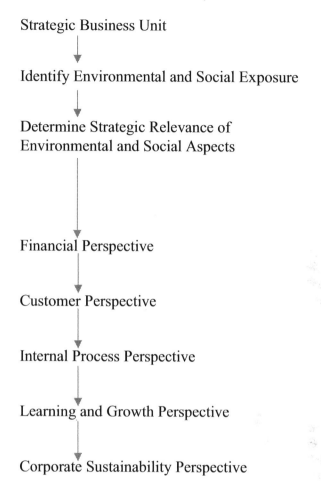

Figure 5.4 Incorporating corporate sustainability in the strategic implementation process[32]

stakeholders internally, along the firm's value chain, in the local community and society.[33]

After the strategic implementation process

After the firm has developed and executed its strategic implementation strategy, the competitive advantage related to corporate sustainability will be integrated into the decisions and actions of the firm. The results of this successful integration should result in eight different dimensions.

Shift from efficiency to strategy

The strategic focus of the firm should be based on building capabilities around achieving strategic goals which move beyond legal compliance and the traditional efficiency approach toward sustainability. Instead of just focusing on compliance and cost minimization through efficiency enhancements, the firm needs to focus on strategic investments in research and development which move beyond the minimal standards and expectations and increase the level of flexibility in the decision-making process.

Introducing new tools and techniques

The firm can introduce stakeholder evaluation techniques such as using the triple bottom line performance measurement. The 3P's of the triple bottom line are people, planet, and profit. The firm would establish measurable goals related to corporate sustainability performance, the firm's performance related to the natural environment, and financial performance. This serves not only to increase the formal accountability of the firm, but it also increases the level of transparency in the communication of information by the firm to its stakeholders.

Linking operational processes to sustainable strategy

After the successful implementation of the firm's strategy, which integrated corporate sustainability initiatives, the firm can convert successful experimental operational projects into standard operating procedures for the firm. New innovations that had been piloted on a small-scale execution can now be embraced firm wide as the company grows and expands its presence. For example, a firm may try to use alternative energy sources in one facility and after a successful outcome, the firm can implement the same strategy to other facilities.

Creating new product and service process improvement opportunities

A strategic approach to corporate sustainability can result in the firm looking for new opportunities to explore other potential markets, to reinvent existing products, and to add value to both products and services.

Creating enabling structure and design

The development of a corporate sustainability perspective in the firm's quest for a sustainable competitive advantage can result in the firm adjusting its organizational structure and design. The adjustment of the firm's structure can result in enhancing the firm's ability to quickly respond to environmental and social issues. These adjustments in the structure can also result in the firm developing stronger positive relationships with its stakeholders.

Building employee knowledge and commitment

The firm's competitive advantage is based, in part, on the knowledge and commitment of its employees. By addressing corporate sustainability issues in the firm's development of its competitive advantage, the firm is able to entrench its vision to its employees. As a result, the firm is able to benefit from the employees' knowledge and commitment in the development of innovative solutions to issues that are both related and unrelated to corporate sustainability.

Executive leadership and stewardship

For the firm to develop an effective strategy which incorporates corporate sustainability, the firm must encourage management to take a true leadership position. The top-level managers must support the firm's commitment in the development of sustainable products, services, and processes for both existing and future markets.

Developing differentiated stakeholder strategies

The firm is able to design and implement different strategies which reflect the needs and interests of its different stakeholders. This flexibility is based not only on the knowledge and the commitment of the employees and top-level managers but also on adjusting the firm's structure to develop a more fluid information flow for its stakeholders. This flow of information allows the firm to quickly address any adjustment needs based on the shifts in the expectations of its stakeholders.[34]

Inclusive capitalism

Inclusive capitalism can be defined as capitalism which acknowledges economic inclusion, human development, social inclusion, environmental sustainability, and political inclusion.

Inclusive capitalism attempts to answer the question of what role business should play in society. Inclusive capitalism focuses on the mission of firms to act in a more inclusive way to impact society, which includes fairness, sustainability, conscious, pro-social, and being responsible. The Ford Foundation defines inclusive capitalism as one in which there are a vast number of opportunities for individuals so that the standards of living improve for all and prosperity is widely shared.

There are different viewpoints about the true purposes of firms: delivering excellent goods and services, providing livelihoods and meaning to employees, producing financial returns to investors, doing no harm by imposing no negative externalities, and doing good by producing positive externalities. While the production of products, providing wages to employees, and financial returns to investors are traditional purposes of the firm, inclusive capitalism is based on the fourth and fifth viewpoints of doing no harm and doing good.

There are three types of actors who can create a more inclusive capitalism: the core, the suppliers, and the context setters.

The core

The core or the heart of inclusive capitalism is based on the relationship between business leaders and customers, employees, and other relevant individuals. It is these long-term relationships that are the keystone in the establishment of the firm's philosophy regarding inclusive capitalism.

The suppliers

The suppliers are one ring beyond the core and include the supply chain; professional services such as law, accounting, and consulting firms; and the development of knowledge such as science, research and development, and capital management firms.

The context setters

At the outer ring are the context setters. The context setters are the traditional external stakeholders whose membership includes labor unions, society, media, philanthropy, government regulators, local communities, and business associations.

There are numerous avenues available to a firm to promote inclusive capitalism, which include networking with other business leaders, the development of research, community organizing, being an advocate, establishing new standards for the firm, business education, public engagement, and advisory services.[35]

Marc Benioff and inclusive capitalism

Headquartered in San Francisco, Salesforce is a customer relationship management (CRM) software company started in 1999. Salesforce believes that culture is its greatest competitive advantage by engaging its employees resulting in innovative processes which effectively service the needs of its customers. Salesforce's culture is centered around four pillars, which are trust, customer success, innovation, and equality. Its commitment to equality allows Salesforce to attract and retain the best employees globally. Its focus on innovation has resulted in the most comprehensive CRM system in the industry. Salesforce's commitment to trust and customer success has resulted in it reaching over $13 billion in annual sales, a rate quicker than any other enterprise software company in history.[36]

Salesforce is a founder, member, and champion of the 1-1-1 model of corporate sustainability commitment. Salesforce, along with other firms, has pledged to dedicate 1 percent of employee's time, 1 percent of product, 1 percent of profit and/or 1 percent of equity to improve the world. In 2019, 8,500 firms had made the 1-1-1 pledge in 100 countries with an estimated $1 billion given in donated volunteer hours, product licenses, pro bono resources, and philanthropic funding.

The co-CEO of Salesforce, Marc Benioff, has a vision in which everyone is able to receive the benefits of the digital age. Benioff's vision is based on the belief that this inclusion can occur through a stronger education system, more inclusive businesses, and a more sustainable environment. Benioff warned that:

> Every company and every CEO had better be ready to answer ... to their values. Business is the greatest platform for change ... We believe we have to bring everyone in, everyone has to come into the fourth industrial revolution. It's inclusive capitalism. Nobody will be left behind.

Benioff is personally committed to inclusive capitalism by donating $15 million to support public schools near Oakland, California and by supporting Saleforce's push for LGBTIQ equality in the state of Indiana. Salesforce also has the largest on-site water recycling system in a commercial high-rise building built in the United States.

Benioff cites the global reach of artificial intelligence as an example of how the global community should be included in the discussions which impact their lives.[37] Benioff continues by stating that "we all have a higher responsibility especially as AI gets released to the whole world."

Technology needs to be viewed as a method used to empower people in decisions that impact their daily lives. As technology changes, so do the skills sets needed to be interconnected with the technology. Technology should be used to inspire people all over the world to improve their lives. Therefore, firms must listen to their stakeholders including its customers, employees, and executives in order to develop an explicit determination of its value system. It is also imperative that the value system be aligned with the greater good of society. Benioff observes that "Technology is not good or bad, it is what you do with it."[38]

Questions for thought

1. After reading about Outland Denim's commitment to social causes, would you be more likely to buy a pair of jeans from them?
2. Do you think social enterprise is a fad or a long-term trend? Explain your answer.
3. Would you be more likely to buy a product or use its services if the firm has a strong corporate sustainability commitment?
4. Would you be willing to pay a premium price for a firm's product or service where the firm has a strong corporate sustainability commitment?

5. Identify and explain three corporate sustainability challenges for a firm that is diversified.
6. Do you think inclusive capitalism is a fad or a long-term trend? Explain your answer.

Notes

1   https://outlanddenim.com/pages/our-story#number4
2   https://outlanddenim.com/pages/our-process#number2
3   https://outlanddenim.com/pages/our-business-model
4   https://outlanddenim.com/pages/our-supply-chain#number4
5   www.fashionrevolution.org/fashion-revolution-caught-up-with-james-bartle-foun der-and-ceo-of-outland-denim/
6   Chrissy Rutherford. 2018. Meghan Markle Helped Create 30 New Jobs for At-Risk Women By Wearing These Jeans. *Harpers Bazaar.com*. October 29.
7   www.goodwill.org/about-us/
8   https://socialenterprise.us/about/social-enterprise/
9   https://socialenterprise.us/about/social-enterprise/
10 https://soles4souls.org/about-us/
11 www.facebook.com/pg/SAS27million/about/?ref=page_internal
12 https://socialenterprise.us/about/social-enterprise/
13 William B. Werther, Jr. and David Chandler. 2011. *Strategic Corporate Social Responsibility: Stakeholders in a Global Environment*. Sage Publications: Los Angeles, CA.
14 Dexter Dunphy, Andrew Griffiths and Suzanne Benn. 2007. *Organizational Change for Corporate Sustainability: A Guide for Leaders and Change Agents of the Future*. Second Edition. Routledge: New York.
15 Dexter Dunphy, Andrew Griffiths and Suzanne Benn. 2007. *Organizational Change for Corporate Sustainability: A Guide for Leaders and Change Agents of the Future*. Second Edition. Routledge: New York. 165.
16 Dexter Dunphy, Andrew Griffiths and Suzanne Benn. 2007. *Organizational Change for Corporate Sustainability: A Guide for Leaders and Change Agents of the Future*. Second Edition. Routledge: New York.
17 Abagail McWilliams and Donald Siegel. 2001. Corporate Social Responsibility: A Theory of the Firm Performance. *Academy of Management Review*. 26(1): 117–127.
18 www.sasb.org/blog/five-forces/
19 www.endslaverynow.org/blog/articles/products-made-by-child-labor-with-alterna tive-options
20 www.sasb.org/blog/five-forces/
21 Abagail McWilliams and Donald Siegel. 2001. Corporate Social Responsibility: A Theory of the Firm Performance. *Academy of Management Review*. 26(1): 117–127.
22 Jingoo Kang. 2013. The Relationship between Corporate Diversification and Corporate Social Performance. *Strategic Management Journal*. 34: 94–109.
23 Dina Patrisia and Sshabbir Dastgir. 2017. Diversification and Corporate Social Performance in Manufacturing Companies. *Eurasian Business Review*. 7: 121–139.
24 Jingoo Kang. 2013. The Relationship between Corporate Diversification and Corporate Social Performance. *Strategic Management Journal*. 34: 94–109.
25 Equal Measures 2030. *Harnessing the Power of Data For Gender Equality*.
26 Jingoo Kang. 2013. The Relationship between Corporate Diversification and Corporate Social Performance. *Strategic Management Journal*. 34: 94–109.

27 Manuela Weber. 2008. The Business Case for Corporate Social Responsibility: A Company-level Measurement Approach for CSR. *European Management Journal.* 26: 250.

28 Manuela Weber. 2008. The Business Case for Corporate Social Responsibility: A Company-level Measurement Approach for CSR. *European Management Journal.* 26: 247–261.

29 Abagail McWilliams and Donald Siegel. 2001. Corporate Social Responsibility: A Theory of the Firm Performance. *Academy of Management Review.* 26(1): 117–127.

30 Dirk Michael Boehe and Luciano Barin Cruz. 2010. Corporate Social Responsibility, Product Differentiation Strategy and Export Performance. *Journal of Business Ethics.* 91: 325–346.

31 Dirk Michael Boehe and Luciano Barin Cruz. 2010. Corporate Social Responsibility, Product Differentiation Strategy and Export Performance. *Journal of Business Ethics.* 91: 328.

32 Frank Figge, Tobias Hahn, Stefan Schaltegger and Marcus Wagner. 2002. The Sustainability Balanced Scorecard – Linking Sustainability Management to Business Strategy. *Business Strategy and the Environment.* 11(5): 277.

33 Frank Figge, Tobias Hahn, Stefan Schaltegger and Marcus Wagner. 2002. The Sustainability Balanced Scorecard – Linking Sustainability Management to Business Strategy. *Business Strategy and the Environment.* 11(5): 269–284.

34 Dexter Dunphy, Andrew Griffiths and Suzanne Benn. 2007. *Organizational Change for Corporate Sustainability: A Guide for Leaders and Change Agents of the Future.* Second Edition. Routledge: New York.

35 Peter Tufano, Peter Moores Dean and Tony Siesfeld. 2018. *The State and Direction of Inclusive Capitalism.* Said Business School. University of Oxford: Oxford, UK.

36 Salesforce. *FY19 Stakeholder Impact Report: Blazing a Trail toward a Better, More Equal World.*

37 Yolanda Redrup. 2018. Businesses Must Drive 'Inclusive Capitalism': Salesforce's March Benioff. *Financial Review.* September 26.

38 www.marketing-interactive.com/salesforce-ceo-marc-benioff-on-the-fourth-industrial-revolution-and-inclusive-capitalism/

6 Ethics and organizational culture

Introduction

Ethics and corporate sustainability are synonyms in their focus of how the actions of one person can impact many people. The decision-making process of a manager should be based on ensuring the decisions and actions by the firm are beneficial to its stakeholders. It is the accountability and responsibility of the behavior of humans that shape society as the foundations of ethical behavior. Both ethics and corporate sustainability should be integrated as part of the manager's decision-making process instead of being afterthoughts. In this chapter, some concepts that are presented include the relationship of corporate sustainability with the philosophical foundations of ethics; corporate citizenship; corporate reputation; corporate philanthropy; human rights; whistleblowing; and corporate culture. The chapter concludes with a discussion of the unethical behavior of Juul Labs. The chapter begins with a discussion how the co-founders of the company Patagonia are helping to save Patagonia.

How Patagonia is saving Patagonia

The former CEO of Patagonia, Kristine McDivitt Tompkins, and her late husband, Douglas Tompkins, who founded the North Face and Esprit clothing companies, were on a mission to convert ranching and farming land in the Patagonia Region of Peru into national parks. Starting in 1991, the couple put $345 million into buying large tracts of land in the region. Both Douglas and Kristine had a strong connection with the Patagonia clothing company. In 1968, Doug spent six months traveling through Patagonia with the company's eventual founder, Yvon Chouinard. In 1973, Kristine helped Yvon Chouinard create Patagonia Inc. In 1990, Doug created the Foundation for Deep Ecology, which supports environmental activism.

Douglas and Kristine married in 1993 after she had retired as CEO from the Patagonia clothing company. They moved to Patagonia and lived together until Doug's tragic death while kayaking with Yvon Chouinard in southern Chile in December 2015.

Douglas Tompkins had visited Patagonia for the first time in 1961 and returned 30 years later to acquire 42,000 acres of mostly primeval rainforest in the Los Lasog region of Chile to protect it from future exploitation. The following year, in 1992, Doug created the Conservation Land Trust to manage the land purchases.

Douglas and Kristine continued buying land including 208,000 acres near the Corcovado volcano with philanthropist Peter Buckley as a partner. They also acquired over 700,000 acres in a temperate rain forest region of Chile which includes the millenary alerce tree, which is a relative of the California Redwood.

When the Tompkins Conservation group bought a 764,000 acre sheep farm in Valle Chacbuco, local ranchers and farmers objected stating that their traditional livelihoods were being disrupted. However, Tompkins Conservation took down more than 400 miles of fencing, removed 25,000 sheep and built high-end lodges, campgrounds, hiking trails and roads, and reintroduced wildlife to their natural habitats. This transformation of the land generated new job opportunities for the local people.

The Tompkins created the Tompkins Conservation to be used as an umbrella group of conservation initiatives that they had initially invested in Patagonia. In 2018, the foundation proposed to donate over one million acres of their preserved and restored land to the government of Chile on the condition that the government would add additional land and would create a Patagonian national park network. The Chilean government agreed and contributed an additional nine million acres and created five new national parks and expanded the area of three additional national parks. Ms. Tompkins commented that the partnership should be used as "a real model to do large-scale conservation and create national parks in a public-private way."

The ten-million acre national park system is more than three times the size of the Yosemite and Yellowstone national parks in the United States combined and it expands Chile's national parklands by almost 40 percent. A number of endangered animals live in the new national parks, including pumas, condors, flamingos, and endangered deer species.[1,2]

The role of game-changing tourism

The donation of the land and the establishment of the national parks is only the first step in the development of an area which will bring the greatest good for the greatest number of people. The challenge is for the 60 local communities across the region to develop tourism ventures that will give the needed funding in order to sustain the financial support of the national parks. The parks which span the distance of 1,700 miles can link the local communities together, and be able to generate future opportunities for the local people. Kristine Tompkins stated, "We want local people to have a sense of ownership and pride. They will become the first line of defense in conservation." Some of the major national parks in the Patagonia region of Chile, including Punta Arenas, Puerto Montt, Balmaceda, and Torres del Paine, already have a comprehensive tourist infrastructure; however, there are other areas which do not have these resources.

The Tompkins Conservation has sent teams to travel to the different areas around the national parks to explain that the vision of the national park is to restore the landscape to its natural state and be able to reintroduce endangered species. Due to these actions, the foundation is attempting to encourage local people to establish tourist services that will generate income as well as protect the long-term preservation of the natural indigenous habitat. The foundation wants the communities to develop low-impact accommodation, guide and transport services, and cultural tours.

The Tompkins Conservation has also set up the Friends of the Parks (Amigos de los Parques) program, which encourages Chileans to be proud of their national park system. The program also provides a private-public fund which uses money in order to ensure that the parks are properly maintained. The program also created the Route of Parks program, which is used to promote the Patagonia national parks locally, nationally, and internationally.[3]

Ethics and corporate sustainability

As human beings, we are ultimately responsible and accountable for our actions to society. As employees, we are responsible not only for our individual actions but also for the actions implemented by our firm in its day-to-day operations. This accountability and responsibility is the foundation of the definition of ethics and business ethics.

Ethics can be defined as the values used by an individual in order to interpret whether a particular action or behavior is considered to be acceptable and appropriate. Business ethics can be defined as the collective values of a business organization that can be used to evaluate whether the aggregate behaviors of the organization's collective members are considered to be acceptable and appropriate.

From a corporate sustainability perspective, the ethical commitment of the employees of the firm is converted into the ethical actions of the firm. By addressing the needs of its stakeholders, the firm is able to not only "do the right thing" but also establish and maintain critical reciprocal relationships with its stakeholders. In guiding the ethical conduct of its employees, firms must be able to incorporate seven basic principles in its overall ethical philosophy. The seven guiding principles are:

1. *Fidelity*: The ability of the employees to fulfill explicit and implicit promises.
2. *Reparation*: The ability of the employees to be able to repair the consequences of previous wrongful acts.
3. *Gratitude*: The ability of the employees to show thanks and gratitude for the kindness of the actions of others.

4. *Justice*: The ability of the employees to see that all resources are distributed objectively and fairly.
5. *Beneficence*: The ability of the employees should facilitate the actions that improve the lives of others.
6. *Self-improvement*: The ability of the employees to intrinsically improve themselves through virtue and intelligence.
7. *Noninjury*: The ability of the employees to not cause harm to others.

The seventh principle of noninjury is directly related to corporate sustainability. By understanding and accommodating the needs of its stakeholders, the firm has the ability to ensure that no harm should come to its stakeholders.[4]

The interconnection between ethics and corporate sustainability

There are three major ethical theories which can be directly linked with corporate sustainability. The three ethical theories are utilitarianism, the ethics of rights, and contractualism.

Utilitarianism

The theory of utilitarianism is based on the philosophy of the greatest good for the greatest number of people. Its ethical focus relies on the belief that it is beneficial to do as much good as possible when an individual makes a decision. This maximization of the total sum of well-being of society relates directly into identifying and serving the needs of as many people as possible, which includes the stakeholders of the firm. The impact of the decisions based on utilitarianism philosophy can vary based on the time horizon. For example, firms that have reduced their greenhouse gas emissions may have limited impact on society in the short term but could have significant utilitarianism benefits globally in the long term.

The ethics of rights

The rights of stakeholders, including the firm's suppliers, customers, and employees, are incorporated into the firm's corporate sustainability strategy. Therefore, the corporate sustainability philosophy of the firm will emphasize the rights and moral dignity of all its stakeholders that are impacted by the actions of the firm. A cornerstone component of the stakeholders' ethical rights is respect. The firm must acknowledge and develop a mutually respectful relationship with its stakeholders as part of its commitment to protect the rights of its stakeholders. This commitment to rights is critical in a global context where the respect for individuals can vary significantly due to different beliefs and cultures. Firms can use their corporate governance structures as monitoring and validation processes to ensure that the firms are not violating the rights of its stakeholders.

Contractualism

The underlying premise of contractualism is that there are normative truths in which there is an understanding that individuals agree to the social contracts of society. A normative truth is validated when all relevant and reasonable individuals agree or should agree with the actions related to the normative truth. The firm's corporate sustainability philosophy will embrace contractualism by incorporating the key concepts of reciprocity and mutual acceptability in its decision-making process. A firm with a strong corporate sustainability commitment needs to ensure that it takes into account the general and mutual acceptability of all its important business decisions.[5]

Corporate citizenship and corporate sustainability

Corporate citizenship can be defined as the perceived obligation a firm has to be a good member of society. This belief is based on the interaction of the firm and its stakeholders, and acknowledges that the firm's role can evolve over time. Therefore, corporate citizenship incorporates the values and vision of the firm's corporate sustainability strategy.

There are seven fundamental dimensions of corporate citizenship: citizenship concept; strategic intent; leadership; structure; issue management; stakeholder relationships; and transparency.

Citizenship concept

The citizenship concept can be defined as the total actions taken by a firm related to obligation and corporate sustainability. These activities include actions related to ethics, philanthropy, stakeholder management, social responsibilities, and environmental responsibilities. The citizenship concept for the firm can be at one extreme focusing on financial goals to the other extreme focusing on being instrumental in making fundamental changes for society.

Strategic intent

Strategic intent refers to the firm's goals and objectives based on its corporate citizenship philosophy. A firm's strategic intent focuses on minimizing specific reputational risks and maximizing specific reputational benefits in both the competitive marketplace and society. Strategic intent can be as simple as being in legal compliance to the more comprehensive development of new markets that impact social change.

Leadership

From a corporate citizenship perspective, leadership is the degree to which top-level managers lead and support the firm's commitment to corporate citizenship initiatives. It is expected that an effective leader would be well informed about the firm's corporate citizenship activities and his/her actions would be consistent with the corporate citizenship vision. In other words, do they not only "talk the talk" but also "walk the walk." The firm's level of leadership can go from offering lip service to citizenship issues to being visionaries and trend setters leading to future social change.

Structure

The structure refers to how the firm is able to incorporate corporate citizenship actions within the decision-making process. Firms that have a strong commitment to corporate citizenship develop cross-functional committees in order to integrate the courses of action instead of managing citizenship from isolated functional "islands." The structure of the firms related to incorporating corporate citizenship actions within the firms can be a continuum from being marginalized to being fully integrated and part of the mainstream decision-making process at the other end of the spectrum.

Issues management

Issues management refers to the process used by the firm to address citizenship issues when they develop. The level of responsiveness to addressing the issues can be from being defensive at one end of the continuum all the way to heling define future issues at the other end.

Stakeholder relationships

Stakeholder relationships refer to how engaging the firm is related to its interaction with its stakeholders. This engagement refers not only to the information flow between the firm and its stakeholders but also how the firm addresses the needs and expectations of its stakeholders. This relationship can run the spectrum of being a unilateral or one-way relationship to developing multi-organizational alliances at the other end of the spectrum.

Transparency

Transparency refers to the level of openness of the firm related to disclosing its financial, social, and environmental performance. Firm level of transparency can range from only disclosing information to ensure that the firm is not attacked by its stakeholders at one end of the spectrum, to providing full disclosure of all its performance measurements at the other end of the spectrum.

The evolution of corporate citizenship

The evolution of corporate citizenship can be presented in stages from minimal or elementary to the encompassing transforming stage. The five different stages are presented in Table 6.1.

Stage 1: elementary

At the minimal or elementary stage, the firm's commitment to corporate citizenship is underdeveloped and reactive. Top managers are either uninterested or indifferent toward citizenship issues and there is minimal or only one-way interaction with the firm's stakeholders. The focus of firms in Stage 1 is not ethical based, but it is based on legal compliance. Lawful activities are equated with ethical activities. The monitoring of compliance is usually done within the legal and human resources department. The activities of the firm are evaluated to prevent harm to the firm's reputation. The primary and dominant stakeholder is the shareholder and the primary vision of the firm's commitment to citizenship is to maximize the financial returns to the shareholders.

Stage 2: engaged

There is a fundamental shift that occurs when a firm moves from Stage 1 to Stage 2. In Stage 2, the firm becomes engaged with developing and implementing its

Table 6.1 Stages of corporate citizenship[6]

	Stage 1 Elementary	Stage 2 Engaged	Stage 3 Innovative	Stage 4 Integrated	Stage 5 Transforming
Citizenship concept	Jobs, profits, and taxes	Philanthropy environmental	Stakeholder management	Sustainability triple bottom	Change the game
Strategic intent	Legal compliance	License to operate	Business case	Value proposition	Market creation or social change
Leadership	Lip service, out of touch	Supporter, in the loop	Steward, on top of it	Champion, in front of it	Visionary, ahead of the pack
Structure	Marginal: staff driven	Functional ownership	Cross-functional coordination	Organizational alignment	Mainstream: business driven
Issues management	Defensive	Reactive, policies	Responsive, programs	Pro-active, systems	Defining
Stakeholder relationships	Unilateral	Interactive	Mutual influence	Partnership	Multi-organization alliances
Transparency	Flank protection	Public relations	Public reporting	Assurance	Full disclosure

strategy related to corporate citizenship. The philosophy of the firm moves from focusing primarily on its shareholders to a more broadened scope of stakeholders. The citizenship concept includes areas such as philanthropy and environmental protection.

Firms at this stage develop policies to ensure that its actions would not have a negative impact on its reputation. The policies that are created will exceed the legal compliance requirements that are acceptable in Stage 1 in areas such as employment, health and safety, and environmental practices. Department units are now accountable for ensuring actions coincide with the overall corporate citizenship focus of the firm. The leaders of the firm are now part of the information flow and support the citizenship commitment of the firm.

When firms in Stage 2 are no longer defensive when an issue related to citizenship needs to be addressed, the firms are still reactive in their actions. As a result, firms in Stage 2 may establish performance standards related to areas such as the protection of human rights, gaining quality certifications, and ensuring more transparency related to financial and other types of disclosures.

The firm's communication with its stakeholders becomes a dialogue and the firm encourages input from both internal stakeholders such as its employees, as well as traditional external stakeholders.

Stage 3: innovative

In Stage 3, firms identify responsibilities to both shareholders and stakeholders and expect to be held accountable for performance. As a result, Stage 3 firms embrace stakeholder management and are responsive to stakeholder needs and in finding solutions to corporate citizenship issues. This responsibility and accountability to stakeholders are reflected in the shared mutual influence the firm and stakeholders have on each other. This mutual influence is based on increased consultation with its stakeholders, as well as addressing the needs from a diversity of stakeholders by opening a clearly established two-way communication.

The leaders of the firm are stewards in protecting the citizenship commitment. The structure of the firm is organized to receive cross-functional benefits of the coordination of different corporate citizenship initiatives. The social agenda of Stage 3 firms is one that focuses on employee recruiting, retention, and the firm's reputation. The environmental agenda would be dominated with issues such as reduction of risk and the life-cycle costs of the firm's products. As a result, firms would begin to monitor social and environmental performance and would publicly release performance results in these areas.

Stage 4: integrated

In Stage 4, the firm has moved to become fully integrated in its actions related to corporate citizenship in every area throughout the firm. The firm declares to its stakeholders that it will be evaluated not only on financial performance but also on corporate sustainability performance and environmental performance. This holistic declaration of the triple bottom line sends a message to the stakeholders that the firm will validate and disclose its performance on these three criteria. The leaders of the firm become champions for new ideas to further enhance the firm's commitment to corporate citizenship. Firms in Stage 4 are proactive in anticipating shifts in stakeholders' needs before they occur. This anticipation allows the firms to effectively address the stakeholders' needs on a "real-time" basis since the firm views stakeholders as partners. Stage 4 firms view social, environmental, and economic sustainability as being necessary conditions for the long-term survival of the firm.

Stage 5: transformative

At Stage 5, the firm is no longer a player of the game, but becomes the firm that changes the rules of the game. The strategic intent of the firm is to fully expect social change to occur based on the actions of the firm. The leaders of Stage 5 firms are visionaries who understand how not only the competitive environment will change in the future but also how the responsibilities of the firm will change based on the shift of stakeholders needs and expectations. The corporate sustainability strategy of the firm embraces not only the execution of the firm's citizenship actions but also the innovative development of new ideas that could be adopted in the future. Firms in Stage 5 have full disclosure of operations because not only do they have nothing to "hide," but they want to demonstrate to stakeholders how this transforming commitment to corporate citizenship is beneficial to both the firm and its stakeholders.[7]

Corporate reputation and corporate sustainability

Corporate reputation can be defined as the overall evaluation by an individual or entity that reflects the extent to which the perception of the firm is either substantially good or bad.

The firm's reputation is not just an acceptable dimension of a firm's operations, but it can increase the overall value of the firm. Everyday decisions made by the firm's stakeholders are based on the firm's reputation. A simple example is when you ask a friend or neighbor for a recommendation of a service such as a plumber or electrician. The recommendation of that friend can have a significant impact on whether you use that service. Therefore, the reputation of the plumber is critical in not only keeping the current customers happy but also a major impetus in the acquisition of new customers. This action is similar to identifying the reputation of the firm in determining what type of interaction each stakeholder will have with the firm. Therefore, the firm's reputation sends a message to stakeholders of the stakeholders' expectations of the interactions with the firm.[8]

Corporate reputation is a critical intangible asset created by a firm in which the past actions of the firm create a sustainable image of what stakeholders believe are the values and motivations for the firm, including the firm's commitment to being trustworthy, consistent, and fair. The perceived reputation of a firm by its stakeholders can be considered as the most valuable intangible resource because of the uniqueness and importance of the firm's reputation.

The firm's reputation reduces the level of uncertainty when stakeholders interact with the firm since the stakeholders can draw on the firm's past actions in the determination of types of interactions that will take place between the firm and its critical stakeholders. Therefore, a firm's corporate reputation gives the firm the opportunity to separate itself from its competitors and create a sustainable competitive advantage.

Stakeholders evaluate the firm's reputation based on its actions related to factors such as the quality of services and products, the level of corporate transparency, and the firm's commitment to corporate sustainability issues. Therefore, if a firm has a strong positive reputation, it will receive numerous short-term and long-term benefits.

The firm will be able to capture cost savings since suppliers and employees want to be associated with the firm. This will result in the suppliers potentially offering lower prices for their products and employees being willing to stay with the firm even if the firm's competitors are offering higher wage rates. In addition, the firm's reputation enhances the level of loyalty the employees have for the firm, which results in lower turnover of the employees. The reduction of turnover leads to cost savings including employee recruitment and training costs.

Firms with a positive reputation will also have access to capital at a lower interest rate since the lender perceives that the firm is a lower risk than other firms who do not have the same level of reputation. Firms with strong positive reputations also can charge a premium for products and services since customers want to buy their products.

A firm's reputation is supported by its commitment to corporate sustainability issues. As a result, a firm that wants to strengthen and protect its

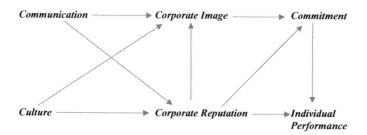

Figure 6.1 The interconnected relationships of corporate reputation[9]

strong positive reputation will embrace the development and implementation of its comprehensive corporate sustainability strategy. The actions of the firm related to corporate sustainability provide legitimacy by the firm to its stakeholders that it is committed to listening to the needs and expectations of the stakeholders. Figure 6.1 highlights the interconnected relationship between corporate reputation, communication, corporate culture, corporate image, organizational commitment, and individual performance.

Communication

Corporate communications can be defined as the process through which stakeholders develop the firm's perception using information related to its identity, image, and reputation. Therefore, communication is a critical tool used by the firm to present its reputation in a favorable light. The firm can use its communication channels to develop long-term relationships with its stakeholders based on its transparency of providing information which supports the stakeholders' perception of its reputation.

Corporate culture

Corporate culture can be defined as the shared values and beliefs of the employees within the organization. As is the case with corporate reputation, the firm's culture is a valuable, intangible asset that is unique and can enhance the firm's competitive advantage. The dimensions of corporate culture include the firm's beliefs and organizational values, the explicit and formal knowledge of the firm's operations, and the firm's future vision. The firm's culture can have a significant impact on the firm's reputation due to its influence on employee morale, innovation, and quality of the firm's products and services, providing its customers with its excellent service, and increasing the financial performance of the firm. A firm's culture which supports the commitment to corporate sustainability issues such as social responsibility, environmental sustainability, and ethical commitment will enhance the firm's image and reputation.

Corporate image

Corporate image can be defined as the way the firm organizes and operates its activities and conducts its business. Corporate image can be viewed as the net result of the knowledge, beliefs, ideas, feelings, and impressions of a firm. The firm's corporate sustainability commitment is based on the two-way interaction with its corporate image. The firm's corporate sustainability initiatives can influence the firm's image and the firm's image can impact the firm's corporate sustainability vision.

Organizational commitment

The employee's commitment to his/her job is based on his/her perception of the firm's work environment and overall values. If employees are highly committed, they will exert higher levels of effort and energy in their work. The firm's commitment to corporate sustainability initiatives can enhance the employees' commitment by being more motivated to achieve the firm's financial and non-financial goals. In addition, an employees' strong commitment can result in an increased self-esteem level which results in a higher level of satisfaction at the workplace. A strong commitment also increases the level of trust the employee has with the firm, which increases the employee's level of loyalty.

Individual performance

Individual performance can be defined as the set of behaviors or actions of an employee which are measured against the goals and objectives of the firm. Corporate reputation can enhance the employee's individual performance by motivating the employee to protect and enhance the firm's reputation through his/her actions. Furthermore, since it is expected that employees agree with the firm's corporate sustainability strategy, the employees will have a strong sense of commitment since their actions have a direct impact on the success of the corporate sustainability initiatives.[10]

Corporate philanthropy and corporate sustainability

Firms fund philanthropic programs as part of their corporate sustainability strategic focus. These programs give the firms an opportunity to "give back" to society by providing resources to enhance individuals within local communities. There are also benefits for firms to invest in philanthropic projects. Philanthropic programs in education and training not only increase the skills of the individuals but also facilitate the learning process for society and as potential employees from the firms that finance the education-based programs.

Philanthropic initiatives also can improve the quality of life of the local community, which increases the desirability of individuals moving into the area, thereby increasing the recruiting base for the firm in the community. In addition, philanthropic programs can increase the quality of local research and development institutions, improve the quality of the physical infrastructures, and enhance the development of the sustainable use of natural resources.

Philanthropy can also encourage the development of supplier and technology clusters, which is beneficial to existing firms located in the cluster area. Due to the close proximity of supporting firms in the cluster, existing firms' productivity can be greatly enhanced due to the efficiencies created by the closeness of the supporting firms.[11]

Strategic configurations of corporate philanthropy

One approach firms take regarding corporate philanthropy is to view their commitments based on market and competence orientation. Market orientation occurs when firms view corporate philanthropy as a tool to be used to address the demands of external stakeholders. The use of corporate philanthropy supports and enhances the image and reputation of the firm, which strengthens its competitive advantage through a strong positive relationship with its stakeholders.

The firm's competency orientation is based on the approach of using corporate philanthropy to address internal goals. Competency-oriented firms use their abilities and core competencies to develop and execute corporate philanthropic programs. The four strategic configurations that are classified based on competency and market orientation are: peripheral philanthropy, dispersed philanthropy, constricted philanthropy, and strategic philanthropy. These configurations are shown in Table 6.2.

Peripheral philanthropy

A firm with a high market orientation and low competency orientation is considered to have a peripheral philanthropy. Peripheral philanthropy firms use stakeholder demands and expectations in the development of corporate philanthropy strategies. These firms do not draw on capabilities and expertise in creating corporate philanthropy initiatives, but instead focus on philanthropy from a marketing perspective to enhance image and reputation. Since actions are not linked to core competencies, it could raise suspicions from stakeholders that the actions of firms are not genuine or sincere, but the actions are instead being used to present a better "appearance" of the firm.

Dispersed philanthropy

A firm with a low market and low competence orientation is considered to have a dispersed philanthropy configuration. A dispersed configuration lacks a concentrated strategic focus on its philanthropic actions. As a result, the philanthropic actions are usually uncoordinated and there is no formalized evaluation process for either the actions or the results of the actions. This lack of coordination results in the firm doing small unconnected programs which

Table 6.2 Strategic configuration of corporate philanthropy[12]

	Low competence orientation	*High competence orientation*
High market orientation	Peripheral philanthropy	Strategic philanthropy
Low market orientation	Dispersed philanthropy	Constricted philanthropy

are not supported by the firm's capabilities or its core competencies. In addition, the lack of a formal process and a coordination mechanism for its philanthropic activities can raise concerns by its stakeholders related to the credibility and motives of its philanthropic actions.

Constricted philanthropy

A firm with a low market and high competence orientation is considered to have a constricted philanthropy configuration. A firm using a constricted philanthropy strategy will use its synergistic benefits of having its philanthropy strategy being based on its capabilities and core competencies. Through the connectedness of its operations and its philanthropic initiatives, constricted philanthropic firms can strengthen the loyalty and commitment of employees. In addition, constricted firms can also strengthen and develop additional capabilities and core competencies whose benefits would be shared throughout the firm. The limitation of this strategy is that these actions may not directly address the specific needs of its stakeholders. As a result, there may be a perception from the firm's stakeholders that the firm is ignoring their needs and expectations.

Strategic philanthropy

A firm with a high market and a high competence orientation is considered to have a strategic philanthropy configuration. A strategic configuration is considered to be the most effective approach because it addresses both internal and external issues related to philanthropy. Through its high market orientation, the firm addresses the needs and expectations of its stakeholders, and through its high competency orientation, the firm draws on its capabilities and core competencies in the development and execution of its philanthropic vision. The use of its capabilities and core competencies enhances its competitive advantage, which results in giving the firm the ability to create new market opportunities. In addition, a strategic philanthropic configuration is very desirable for employees who agree with the philanthropic vision of the firm. This results in the firm being more effective in its recruiting, as well as developing and keeping its highly motivated workforce. This highly motivated workforce encourages innovative ideas which result in better serving the needs of its stakeholders, including increasing customer demand for its products resulting in a stronger financial performance of the firm.[13]

Human rights and corporate sustainability

Human rights can be perceived as moral rights of individuals in the consideration of providing the basic right to be able to live one's life with dignity. These are rights which every human has and are independent of the person's membership into a specific nation, class, sex, ethnic, religious, or sexual group. Therefore, it is a human right to live in freedom and autonomy. A violation of human rights is a form of humiliation because the action disregards the person's value as a human being.[14]

It is from the duty of protecting people that a firm incorporates its corporate sustainability perspective. Through guidance such as the Universal Declaration of Human Rights, firms are able to demand that the human rights of its stakeholders be not violated. By incorporating human rights into its corporate sustainability strategy, firms can establish criteria with which they expect stakeholders such as suppliers to comply in order to continue the relationship with the firm. A firm's commitment to human rights can evolve over time. The case study in this textbook on Global Outsourcing of Nike highlights how Nike's commitment to human rights has become more comprehensive due to external pressure from its stakeholders.

Universal Declaration of Human Rights

Developed by Eleanor Roosevelt when she was chair of the United Nations Human Rights Commission, The Universal Declaration of Human Rights has become the cornerstone for global human rights.[15]

Presented in Paris on December 10, 1948 The Universal Declaration of Human Rights established a common standard against which the rights of individuals can be measured around the world. The declaration has been translated into over 500 languages and is the framework used globally to identify both positive and negative actions related to human rights. There are 30 Articles in the declaration. An abridged summary of the Articles is presented in Table 6.3.

The Universal Declaration of Human Rights has become the foundations for any firm to develop its human rights policy. Through the presentation of the 30 Articles, this declaration highlights the goal for human rights of everyone in the world to be supported and defended based on the true value of human rights for every individual.

Whistleblowing and corporate sustainability

Whistleblowing can be defined as a disclosure of information on a public record by a person who has privileged access to the organization's data or information about illegality or wrongdoing which could implicate the organization to an external entity.

The origin of the term whistleblowing comes from law enforcement officers in the nineteenth century who blew whistles to stop illegal behavior. Whistleblowing is also linked to referees blowing a whistle to stop play in a sporting match. There are six steps in the whistleblowing process for an individual. They are: the act of disclosing damaging news; the identification

Table 6.3 An abridged summary of The Universal Declaration of Human Rights[16]

Article 1

All human beings are born free and equal in dignity and rights.

Article 2

Everyone is entitled to all the rights and freedoms without distinction of any kind, such as race, colour, sex, language, religion, political or other opinion, national or social origin, property, birth or other status.

Article 3

Everyone has the right to life, liberty and security of person.

Article 4

No one shall be held in slavery or servitude; slavery and the slave trade shall be prohibited in all their forms.

Article 5

No one shall be subjected to torture or to cruel, inhuman or degrading treatment or punishment.

Article 6

Everyone has the right to recognitions everywhere as a person before the law.

Article 9

No one shall be subjected to arbitrary arrest, detention or exile.

Article 10

Everyone is entitled in full equality to a fair and public hearing by an independent and impartial tribunal.

Article 11

Everyone charged with a penal offence has the right to be presumed innocent until proved guilty according to law.

Article 13

Everyone has the right to freedom of movement within the borders of their country and the freedom to leave any country.

Article 14

Everyone has the right to seek and to enjoy in other countries asylum from persecution.

Article 15

Everyone has the right to a nationality.

Article 16

Men and women of full age, without any limitation due to race, nationality or religion have the right to marry and to have a family.

Marriage shall be entered into only with the free and full consent of the intending spouses.

Article 17

Everyone has the right to own property alone as well as in association with others.

Article 18

Everyone has the right to freedom of thought, conscience and religion.

Article 19

Everyone has the right to freedom of opinion and expression.

Article 20

Everyone has the right to freedom of peaceful assembly and association.

Article 21

Everyone has the right to take part in the government of their country, directly or through freely chosen representatives.

(Continued)

Table 6.3 (Cont.)

Article 23

Everyone has the right to work, to free choice of employment, to just and favourable conditions of work and to protection against unemployment.

Everyone, without any discrimination has the right to equal pay for equal work.

Article 24

Everyone has the right to rest and leisure, including reasonable limitation of working hours and periodic holidays with pay.

Article 25

Everyone has the right to a standard of living adequate for the health and well-being of him or herself and his or her family including food, clothing, housing and medical care and necessary social services.

Motherhood and childhood are entitled to special care and assistance.

Article 26

Everyone has the right to education, Education shall be free, at least in the elementary and fundamental stages. Elementary education shall be compulsory.

Article 27

Everyone has the right freely to participate in the cultural life of the community, to enjoy the arts and to share in scientific advancement and its benefits.

Article 29

Everyone has duties to the community in which alone the free and full development of his/her personality is possible.

Article 30

Nothing in this Declaration may be interpreted as implying for any State, group or person any right to engage in any activity or to perform and any act aimed at the destruction of any of the rights and freedoms set forth herein.

of the agent for the whistleblower; the subject of the disclosure involving wrongdoing; the organization that is held responsible for the act of wrongdoing; the disclosure recipient; and the outcome of the whistleblowing process.

A core tenet of a whistleblower action is to deliberately release information in order to achieve the disclosure of the information to a third party. The releasing of information is usually done through unconventional and anonymous methods since the traditional methods of monitoring, auditing, and formal communication have failed to bring the information to the attention of those individuals with the authority to investigate and resolve the issue.

The actions of the whistleblower are based on two dimensions, which is the nature of the perceived activity and the expression of concern by the whistleblower. The specific actions taken by the whistleblower are shown in Table 6.4.[17]

Table 6.4 Actions taken by a whistleblower[18]

	Nature of the perceived activity that is creating concern by the employee			
	Illegal, immoral or illegitimate		Not illegal, immoral or illegitimate	
	Decision by the employee to stay or leave the firm			
Expression of employee concern	Stay	Leave	Stay	Leave
External dissent to someone who can take action	External whistleblowing	Exit with public protest	Secret sharing	Exit with secret sharing
Internal dissent to someone who can take action	Internal whistleblowing	Protest during exit interview	Employee participation, grievance	Explain reason for resignation in exit
Dissent in some other form	Discussion, confrontation with wrongdoer	Exit with notice to wrongdoer	Sabotage, strikes	Sabotage, strikes with exit
No expressed dissent	Inactive observation	Inactive departure	Silent disgruntlement	Silent departure

Corporate culture and corporate sustainability

Corporate culture can be defined as the shared values and beliefs of employees within an organization. A strong positive corporate culture can reinforce the values and beliefs of the employees related to the firm's commitment to corporate sustainability. The firm's culture is based on the norms and behavior patterns of the employees and can be structured based on three components: artifacts, shared values, and basic assumptions.

Artifacts

Artifacts are representations of the firm based on what is seen and heard within the firm. Artifacts can also be the language used in the workplace as well as how people dress and the types of stories related to the workplace that are told to the employees.

Shared values

Shared values refer to the learning process by employees pertaining to what is acceptable and unacceptable behavior. The origin of the shared values initially come from the founder of the firm, but those values can change over time based on shifts in societal values, as well as the values of firm leadership subsequent to the founder.

Based assumptions

Basic assumptions refer to the agreed starting point for decision making in the firm. It is through the basic assumptions that corporate sustainability will be incorporated into the decision-making process. A firm with a strong corporate sustainability commitment will have integrated the needs of its stakeholders in the decisions made by the firm. Therefore, basic assumptions are the foundation of the decision-making process.

How to change the culture to embrace corporate sustainability

For firms that do not have a strong commitment to corporate sustainability, there is a process which can adjust the culture to embrace corporate sustainability. The three-step process allows the top-level managers to make adjustments to the firm's culture.

Stage 1: unfreezing

The first step is to unfreeze the employees' existing beliefs. The unfreezing occurs when top-level managers present a future vision of the firm where the existing beliefs no longer support that vision. For example, if the top-level managers do not believe that the employees are fully committed to the corporate sustainability initiatives, the managers will convince the employees that their beliefs need to be adjusted. The unfreezing is a critical and difficult step because individuals are usually comfortable in their current beliefs and will be resistant to accept changing those beliefs.

Stage 2: moving

In Stage 2, top-level managers shift the beliefs of the employees to support the new future vision of the firm. It is in this stage that employees must accept that their beliefs need to be adjusted in order to ensure that they understand what acceptable and unacceptable behavior is. Stage 2 will potentially result in employees that do not agree with the new belief structure leaving the firm. In addition, management must be wary of employees who do not accept the new beliefs, but who want to continue working for the firm. These employees must ultimately leave the firm either voluntarily or involuntarily because the culture must be able to thrive with employees who believe in the new vision.

Stage 3: freezing

In Stage 3, the top-level managers have "locked" in the new belief structure of the employees. It is at this final stage that the recalibration of the firm's culture is complete. In this stage, top-level managers clearly identify the expectations of the employees and implement a reward and punishment mechanism to ensure that the employees are fully committed to the new culture.[19]

From a corporate sustainability perspective, this three-stage process is an effective tool that can be used by managers if they perceive that the employees of the firm are not fully committed to the firm's corporate sustainability vision. For example, the firm may incorporate more information on its commitment to the corporate sustainability vision in its training program with the explanation as to why it is important to be fully committed. Based on the presentation of information, the managers can move the firm's culture to the new belief structure and then refreeze or entrench the new beliefs within the firm's culture.

The unethical behavior of Juul Labs

> We don't want this to be a glamorous lifestyle product . . . This is a serious product with a serious purpose.[20]
>
> Juul co-founder Adam Bowen in August 2018

In a survey released in November 2018, results showed a huge increase of young consumers using e-cigarettes. From the spring of 2017 to the spring of 2018, the number of high-school students in the United States who used e-cigarettes increased by 78 percent. A total of 3.05 million high-school students used e-cigarettes, which translated to one in every five high-school students in the United States. The study also showed that e-cigarettes used by middle-school students had increased by 48 percent during the same time period to 570,000 students or 4.9 percent of the overall student population in middle schools in the United States. Furthermore, vaping facilitated the increased use of tobacco products by 38 percent in high-school students and by 29 percent among middle-school students from 2017 to 2018.[21]

Juul is a type of e-cigarette which delivers a power dose of nicotine in a patented salt solution which closely mimics the feeling of inhaling cigarettes. The Juul device can easily fit into a pocket and is plugged into a USB drive of a laptop to be recharged. Juul liquids come in flavors such as Crème Brule, Fruit Medley, and Mango, which eliminates the potential harsh taste of smoking tobacco. The minimal vapor and smell produced by the Juul device also makes it harder to detect as compared with other e-cigarettes. The concentration of nicotine in Juul's liquid is 5 percent nicotine concentration, which is significantly higher than other commercially available e-cigarettes. One liquid pod delivers the equivalent nicotine to a pack of cigarettes. The Juul starter kit, which includes the device, a charger, and four flavor pods, retails for $50. The liquid pods are sold separately at an average price of $4.25, which is less than a retail pack of cigarettes.[22]

The marketing of Juul

Juul used celebrities and social media influencers to target young users. Mitch Zeller, director of the Food and Drug Administration's (FDA) Center for Tobacco Products, stated that "Juul engaged in a wide variety of promotional activities and outreach efforts to persuade potential customers, including youth, to use Juul products."

From February 2017 to January 2018, one-quarter of users who shared tweets from the official Juul vapor Twitter account were under the age of 18 years. After the FDA started to investigate Juul in May 2018, Juul created a VIP portal for celebrities on its website which offered codes so that the celebrities could order vaporizers and refill pack for $1 each. Juul stated that it required the celebrities to agree to not promote Juul to children or teens who were under the legal smoking age. Juul also stated that it only targeted celebrities who were already using the product.[23]

The FDA accused Juul of illegally marketing its products as a safer alternative to smoking tobacco. The acting FDA commissioner, Dr. Ned Sharpless, stated that:

> Regardless of where products like e-cigarettes fall on the continuum of tobacco product risk, the law is clear that, before marketing tobacco products for reduced risk, companies must demonstrate with scientific evidence that their specific product does in fact pose less risk or is less harmful. Juul has ignored the law and, very concerningly, has made some of these statements in school to our nation's youth.[24]

Juul claims that it never targeted underage users, but after an investigation started by the FDA and the Federal Trade Commission, Juul closed its US Facebook and Instagram accounts and stopped selling sweet and fruity flavors in US retail stores. Flavored liquids such as mint and menthol represent over 80 percent of Juul's sales in the United States.[25]

The financial cost for Juul

The tobacco company, Altria, bought a 35 percent equity in Juul for $12.8 billion in December 2018. Altria had perceived the Juul investment as an additional opportunity for future growth of nicotine-based products since Juul's market share of e-cigarettes in the United States was over 70 percent.

Altria was negotiating with another tobacco giant, Philip Morris International, to merge together in an estimated $200 billion deal. Altria, which makes Marlboro cigarettes with other brands, was initially part of Philip Morris but had become a separate independent firm in 2008.

Altria and Philip Morris had created a joint venture to develop its own cigarette alternative, which is based on a heat and no burn tobacco device called IQOS. IQOS has been approved by the FDA while Juul's device has not been approved by the FDA. Due to the growing legal concerns related to Juul, Altria and Philip Morris announced that they would cancel the talks of merging the two companies.

On September 25, 2019, the CEO of Juul, Kevin Barnes, stepped down from his position due to the pressure of Juul being a party to multiple federal investigations. Kevin Barnes was replaced with an executive from Altria, K. C. Crosthwatie.

Stefanie Miller, a co-founder of Sandhill Strategy which does consulting with investment firms on issues related to regulatory policies, stated that "Juul is the face of the current public health crisis ... To see the top head roll is a sign to public health, investors, to everyone that they know they need to make some changes."

With the announcement of the new CEO, Juul also announced that it would not challenge the US government's proposal to ban most flavored e-cigarettes, which would cripple Juul's US sales. Juul also agreed to stop its marketing campaigns titled "Make the Switch," which portrayed that e-cigarettes were safer than traditional cigarettes.

Initially, health officials in the United States viewed e-cigarettes as a safer alternative to smoking and allowed Juul to sell its products before they were reviewed by the FDA. The FDA has required Juul to apply for FDA approval by May 2020 or they would no longer be able to sell their products in the United States.[26,27]

The health cost of vaping

By September 2019, health officials in the United States were investigating 530 confirmed and probable cases of pulmonary illness due to vaping and the use of e-cigarette products. Seven people had died due to pulmonary illness caused by vaping. It is believed that the chemical exposure related to vaping and the use of e-cigarettes caused inflammation or damage to the lungs. It was also concluded that many of the illnesses are related to the people vaping using cannabis-related products including THC (tetrahydrocannabinol), which is the active ingredient in marijuana. Many of the THC products contain large levels of vitamin E acetate, which is used to thicken the vaping liquid but damages the lungs.[28]

Questions for thought

1. Why do you think Kristine and Douglas Tompkins had such a strong commitment to environmental sustainability?
2. How often do you take a utilitarianism approach when you make decisions?
3. Give an example of three social contracts individuals make with society.
4. What stage of corporate citizenship do you think most Fortune 500 companies are currently in due to their actions?

5. How important is the firm's corporate reputation when you decide which firm you want to work for?
6. Give an example of corporate philanthropy that has occurred in your local community and describe its purpose.
7. What are the types of challenges related to human rights when outsourcing manufacturing processes?
8. How easy or difficult is it for a firm to change its corporate culture?

Notes

1 Pascale Bonnefoy. 2018. With 10 Million Acres in Patagonia, a National Park System is Born. *The New York Times*. February 19.
2 Greg Dickinson. 2018. How the Former CEO of Patagonia Clothing is Saving One of the World's Most Beautiful Regions. *The Telegraph*. January 31.
3 Isabel Choat. 2019. Why Chile's Route of Parks Will Be a 'Game Changer for Tourism'. *The Guardian*. September 26.
4 Peter A. Stanwick and Sarah D. Stanwick. 2016. *Understanding Business Ethics*. Third Edition. Sage Publications: Thousand Oaks, CA.
5 Claus Strue Frederiksen and Morten Ebbe Juul Nielsen. 2013. *The Ethical Foundations for CSR*. From John O. Okpara and Samuel O. Idownu. Editors. *Corporate Social Responsibility: Challenges, Opportunities and Strategies for 21st Century Leaders*. Springer: New York. 17–33.
6 Philip Mirvis and Bradley Googins. 2006. Stages of Corporate Citizenship. *California Management Review*. 48(2): 108.
7 Philip Mirvis and Bradley Googins. 2006. Stages of Corporate Citizenship. *California Management Review*. 48(2): 104–126.
8 Peter A. Stanwick and Sarah D. Stanwick. 2016. *Understanding Business Ethics*. Third Edition. Sage Publications: Thousand Oaks, CA.
9 Maria da Graca Marques Casimiro Almeida, Arnaldo Fernandes Matos Coelho. 2019. The Antecedents of Corporate Reputation and Image and Their Impacts on Employee Commitment and Performance: The Moderating Role of CSR. *Corporate Reputation Review*. 22(1): 14
10 Maria da Graca Marques Casimiro Almeida, Arnaldo Fernandes Matos Coelho. 2019. The Antecedents of Corporate Reputation and Image and Their Impacts on Employee Commitment and Performance: The Moderating Role of CSR. *Corporate Reputation Review*. 22(1): 10–25.
11 Michael E. Porter and Mark R. Kramer. 2002. The Competitive Advantage of Corporate Philanthropy. *Harvard Business Review*. December: 56–69.
12 Heike Bruch and Frank Walter. 2005. The Keys of Rethinking Corporate Philanthropy. *MIT Sloan Management Review*. 47(1) Fall: 51.
13 Peter A. Stanwick and Sarah D. Stanwick. 2016. *Understanding Business Ethics*. Third Edition. Sage Publications: Thousand Oaks, CA.
14 Florian Wettstein. 2012. CSR and the Debate on Business and Human Rights: Bridging the Great Divide. *Business Ethics Quarterly*. 22(4): 739–770.
15 www.humanrights.com/voices-for-human-rights/eleanor-roosevelt.html
16 www.un.org/en/universal-declaration-human-rights/
17 Peter B. Jubb. 1999. Whistleblowing: A Restrictive Definition and Interpretation. *Journal of Business Ethics*. 21: 77–94.
18 Peter B. Jubb. 1999. Whistleblowing: A Restrictive Definition and Interpretation. *Journal of Business Ethics*. 21: 80.

19 Peter A. Stanwick and Sarah D. Stanwick. 2016. *Understanding Business Ethics.* Third Edition. Sage Publications: Thousand Oaks, CA.

20 Jennifer Maloney and Betsy McKay. 2019. Teen Vaping Didn't Cool Juul's Celebrity Push. *The Wall Street Journal.* September 28.

21 Betsy McKay. 2018. Youth Use of E-Cigarettes Jumped 78%, Government Study Shows. *The Wall Street Journal.* November 15.

22 Anne Marie Chaker. 2018. Schools and Parents Fight a Juul E-Cigarette Epidemic. *The Wall Street Journal.* April 4.

23 Betsy McKay. 2018. Youth Use of E-Cigarettes Jumped 78%, Government Study Show. *The Wall Street Journal.* November 15.

24 Sheila Kaplan and Matt Richtel. 2019. Juul Illegally Marketed E-Cigarettes, F.D.A. Says. *The New York Times.* September 11.

25 Jennifer Maloney and Betsy McKay. 2019. Teen Vaping Didn't Cool Juul's Celebrity Push. *The Wall Street Journal.* September 28.

26 Sheila Kaplan and Matt Richtel. 2019. Juul Illegally Marketed E-Cigarettes, F.D.A. Says. *The New York Times.* September 11.

27 Sergei Klebnikov. 2019. Philip Morris International and Altria Call Off $200 Billion Merger. *Forbes.* September 25.

28 Brianna Abbott. 2019. What We Know about Vaping-Related Illness. *The Wall Street Journal.* September 20.

7 Corporate sustainability reporting, performance, and corporate compliance

Introduction

For a firm's stakeholders to build and maintain corporate trust, the firm must "prove" that it is consistent with its decisions and actions related to corporate sustainability. Firms must demonstrate to stakeholders that their commitment to sustainability issues is sincere by providing goals and objectives related to corporate sustainability, as well as whether the firms have achieved these goals. By presenting a triple bottom line approach of measuring its financial, social, and environmental performance, the firm can give the necessary information to its stakeholders for a comprehensive evaluation of its operations. Firms also need to demonstrate that their actions comply with rules and regulations established by internal and external monitoring mechanisms. In this chapter, some of the concepts that are presented include: triple bottom line; benefit corporations; the UN Sustainability Development Goals; reputation risk management; corporate governance; the board of directors; social and environmental accounting; and corporate sustainability reporting. The chapter begins with how Levi Strauss is using the triple bottom line to measure its performance and concludes with a discussion of how Novozymes is using the UN Sustainable Development Goals in order to reach both its financial and non-financial goals.

Levi Strauss and the triple bottom line

Named after the gold rush entrepreneur, Levi Strauss has focused on the triple bottom line for over a century. Levi Strauss commercialized the develop of extremely sturdy riveted denim jeans and overalls and revolutionized the clothing industry. After reaping the financial benefits of his firm, Strauss gave much of his money away to fund local orphanages and university scholarships. The continuing legacy of Strauss' commitment to employees and other stakeholders was demonstrated when the firm continued to pay its employees after the Levi Strauss factory was destroyed in the 1906 San Francisco earthquake. This belief to serve its stakeholders continues today under the firm's philosophy of "profits through principles."

As a pioneer in the develop of a reciprocal relationship with its stakeholders, Levi Strauss introduced its Terms of Engagement, which was its code of conduct for its suppliers in 1991. The Terms of Engagement includes requirements related to improving employees' health, financial literacy, and future opportunities. Levi Strauss's expectations of its suppliers include the use of sustainable cotton farming and the development of water reduction in the manufacturing process.

An example of how Levi Strauss has used technology to reduce the environmental impact in the manufacturing process occurs in how the firm creates a distressed look for its denim products. In the past, employees had to scrub denim jeans with sandpaper for 20 minutes and then put the jeans in a chemical solution to transform the denim into a well-worn look. Levi Strauss now uses a laser that is programmed to etch faded creases into the jeans based on a pattern that has been developed in the laser machine's software.[1]

Levi Strauss's holistic view of the triple bottom line can be seen in the development of the Wellthread brand. The mission of this brand is to develop jeans which consumers will be wearing in 2050. Levi Strauss understands that the average US consumer discards 80 pounds of clothing annually of which the vast majority ends up in landfills. This action is not a sustainable disposal of used clothing. The estimated 14 billion tons of clothing that are discarded annually across the United States result in a potentially renewable resource being wasted that could be captured to be used in the next generation of clothing.

Levi Strauss uses recycled textiles, plastics, and aluminum in its Wellthread brand of clothing. The company has developed a design center to incorporate these recycled products into its clothing design. The designers are motivated to design clothes which can be manufactured in a more efficient process which incorporates not only recycled materials but also develops designs which make the recycling process easier when the clothing is disposed of by consumers.

The clothing of the capsule collection within the Wellthread brand is made from a single material. For example, the T-shirts are 100 percent cotton while the fleece lining of a jacket is 100 percent plastic-based polyester and can be removed from the 100 percent cotton-based hemp denim made outer shell. This creates efficiency in the future sorting of these materials since each type of material can be separated more easily and sent to its corresponding recycling center.[2]

Chip Berg, CEO of Levi Strauss, stated that "I hope I don't live to regret these words, but I think we have an opportunity to show that you can run a company with profits through principles … and be thinking about not just shareholder returns, but stakeholder returns more broadly." Berg continues by saying that firms have a moral obligation to address societal issues and that "If you sit on the sidelines on some of these things, you're not really doing what companies have the potential to do."[3]

Triple bottom line

The triple bottom line approach is based on the ability to measure the performance of a firm from multiple perspectives related to corporate sustainability. The firm measures not only its financial performance but also its social and environmental performance. By including these three measurements, the firm is able to present an all-inclusive report which provides relevant information to the needs of its diverse stakeholders globally. The triple bottom line is also known as 3BL (3 Bottom Line) or by the phase "People, Planet, Profit."

By focusing on three performance measurements, the triple bottom line centers on the vested interests of all the firm's stakeholders instead of just on the shareholders. In addition, by implementing a triple bottom line approach to performance, the firm is encouraged to establish social and environmental objectives as well as benchmarking financial goals. Once these goals have been established, it is easier for firms to justify the interconnection between succeeding in its social and environmental performance and also succeeding in its financial goals. The establishment of these triple objectives also increases the level of transparency of the actions of the firm by enhancing the ability of the stakeholders to effectively evaluate the holistic performance of the firm.

For environmental-based objectives, the firm usually focuses on the amount of resources that are used in its operations such as energy, land, and water. The environmental performance of the firm also focuses on the generation of by-products during the manufacturing process such as waste, air emissions, and chemical materials. The firm's social performance traditionally has focused on how the firm and its suppliers have positively and negatively impacted the local communities where the firm has operations. Just as society evolves over time, so does the firm's measurement of its triple bottom line commitment by adjusting the benchmarks and goals in serving the needs of its stakeholders.

The benefit corporation

The benefit corporation (B Corp) embraces the triple bottom line approach in a formalized process through a certification process. B Corps are certified by the non-profit organization B Lab. B Corps must have three criteria which are not required by publicly traded corporations: (1) the firm must meet comprehensive and transparent social and environmental standards; (2) the firm must meet higher legal accountability standards than traditional firms; and (3) the firm must build business constituencies for public policies and support sustainable business.

In order for the firm to be certified as a B Corp, the firm must complete a stakeholder impact assessment and incorporate its social and environmental objectives into its mission and legal framework. The firm must also sign a "Declaration of Interdependence" which acknowledges its interdependent commitment with its stakeholders. A B Corp firm must also publish an annual benefit report, which is an evaluation of how well the firm was able to achieve its financial, social, and environmental goals. The benefits of a firm being B Corp certified include the ability to: increase its level of profitability, attract more investors, generate positive press, preserve the mission of the firm, and enhance political commitment to the values and ideals which are represented by the B Corp certification.[4]

United Nations Sustainability Development Goals

In September 2015, the United Nations General Assembly adopted the 2030 Agenda for Sustainable Development which included 17 Development Goals based on the philosophy of "leaving no one behind" in the world. The 17 goals are: no poverty; zero hunger; good health and well-being; quality education; gender equality; clean water and sanitation; affordable and clean energy; decent work and economic growth; industry, innovation, and infrastructure; reduced inequality; sustainable cities and communities; responsible consumption and production; climate action; life below water; life on land; peace and justice and strong institutions; and partnerships to achieve the goals.

Goal 1: no poverty

The target of this goal is to eradicate extreme poverty by 2030, for all people globally as measured based on people living on less than $1.25 a day. Goal 1 also includes ensuring that all men and women, in particular the poor and vulnerable, have equal rights to economic resources. Goal 1 also focuses on reducing the exposure of the poor to climate-related extreme events and other economic, social, and environmental shocks and disasters. In addition, Goal 1 incorporates the creation of sound policy frameworks at the national, regional, and international levels which are pro-poor and gender-sensitive development strategies.

Goal 2: zero hunger

Goal 2 refers to ending hunger, achieving food security, improving nutrition, and promoting sustainable agriculture by 2030. Goal 2 includes ending all forms of malnutrition and reducing stunted growth of children under five years of age, as well as addressing the nutritional needs of adolescent girls, pregnant and lactating women, and older people. Goal 2 also incorporates the ability to ensure sustainable food production systems as well as maintaining the genetic diversity of seed cultivated plants, farmed and domesticated animals, and their related wild species.

Goal 3: good health and well-being

The objective of Goal 3 is to reduce the global maternal mortality ratio to less than 70 per 100,000 live births. Goal 3 strives to end preventable deaths of newborns and children under five years of age. Ending the epidemics of AIDS, tuberculosis, malaria, neglected tropical diseases, and water-borne diseases are also part of Goal 3. Goal 3 also focuses on ensuring, by 2030, universal access to sexual and reproductive health-care services, as well as providing universal health coverage.

Goal 4: quality education

Goal 4 is based on the desire for all girls and boys to complete free, equitable, and quality primary and secondary education by 2030. The goal also focuses on providing equal access for all women and men to affordable and quality technical, vocational, and university education by 2030. Goal 4 emphasizes the need for all youth and a substantial proportion of adults to achieve literacy and numeracy.

Goal 5: gender equality

Goal 5 focuses on the ability to end all forms of discrimination against all women and girls globally by 2030. In addition, Goal 5 states that all forms of violence against women and girls should be eliminated, including human trafficking and sexual exploitation. Goal 5 also presents the objective of the elimination of all harmful practices against girls including forced marriage and female genital mutilation.

Goal 6: clean water and sanitation

The 2030 goal for Goal 6 is to achieve universal and equitable access to safe and affordable drinking water for everyone in the world. Goal 6 also focuses on the ability to achieve access to adequate and equitable sanitation and hygiene. Another focal point of Goal 6 is to protect and restore water-related ecosystems and implement integrated water resources management globally.

Goal 7: affordable and clean energy

Goal 7 focuses on the ability to ensure universal access to affordable, reliable, and modern energy services by 2030. This goal includes increasing the level of renewable energy globally as well as focusing on doubling the global rate of improvement in energy efficiency.

Goal 8: decent work and economic growth

Goal 8 focuses on sustaining a 7 percent per capita economic growth based on gross domestic product growth in the least developed countries. In addition, Goal 8 seeks to increase the levels of economic productivity through diversification, technological upgrading, and innovation.

Goal 9: industry, innovation, and infrastructure

Goal 9 focuses on the ability to develop quality, reliable, sustainable, and resilient infrastructure both regionally and across borders to support economic development and human well-being by 2030. Goal 9 also focuses on the promotion of inclusive and sustainable industrialization, as well as increasing the access of individuals to small-scale firms and other enterprises.

Goal 10: reduced inequality

Goal 10 focuses on the ability to progressively achieve and sustain income growth for the bottom 40 percent of the population at a higher rate than the national average. It also focuses on empowering and promoting social, economic, and political inclusion for all regardless of age, sex, disability, race, ethnicity, origin, religion, or economic status. Another area Goal 10 focuses on is to ensure equal opportunity and reduce the inequalities of outcomes, including the elimination of discriminatory laws, policies, and practices.

Goal 11: sustainable cities and communities

Goal 11 includes the ability to ensure access for everyone to adequate, safe, and affordable housing and basic services. By 2030, Goal 11 also proposes that everyone should have access to safe, affordable, accessible, and sustainable transportation systems. This goal also focuses on enhancing inclusive and sustainable urbanization and providing additional protection and safeguards for the world's cultural and natural heritage sites.

Goal 12: responsible consumption and production

Goal 12 states the desire to achieve sustainable management and efficient use of natural resources by 2030. In addition, Goal 12 focuses on reducing by half the amount of global food waste per capita.

Goal 13: climate action

Goal 13 focuses on strengthening the resilience and adaptive capacity to climate-related hazards and natural disasters globally by 2030 and integrating climate change measures into national policies, strategies, and planning. Goal 13 also proposes improving education, awareness-raising, human, and institutional capacity to address issues related to climate change mitigation, adaptation, and impact reduction.

Goal 14: life below water

Goal 14 focuses on preventing and significantly reducing marine pollution of all kinds by 2025 including marine debris and nutrient pollution. Goal 14 has a number of objectives which should be accomplished by 2020. These objectives include managing and protecting marine and coastal ecosystems, regulating harvesting and ending illegal and overfishing globally, conserving at least 10 percent of coastal and marine areas, being consistent with national and international laws, and prohibiting fishing subsidies which contribute to overcapacity and overfishing.

Goal 15: protect, restore, and promote sustainable use of terrestrial ecosystems

The objectives for Goal 15 by 2020 are to ensure the conservation, restoration, and sustainable use of terrestrial and inland freshwater ecosystems and to promote the implementation of sustainable management of all types of forests. This management includes stopping deforestation, restoring degraded forests, and substantially increasing reforestation globally. By 2030, the objective of Goal 15 is to ensure the conservation of mountain ecosystems including their biodiversity.

Goal 16: peace and justice and strong institutions

The targets for Goal 16 include a significant reduction of all forms of violence and related deaths globally; the ending of abuse, exploitation, and trafficking of children; promoting the rule of law at national and international levels; reducing corruption and bribery; accountability and transparency of government decision making; and providing good governance globally.

Goal 17: partnerships for the goals

The financial targets of Goal 17 include strengthening domestic resource mobilization, mobilizing additional financial resources for developing countries, assisting developing countries in attaining long-term debt sustainability, and encouraging investment development globally.

The technology targets of Goal 17 include encouraging cooperation between countries and regions related to science, technology, and innovation, and promoting the development, transfer, and dissemination of environmental sound technologies.

Goal 17 also encourages the development of multi-stakeholder partnerships in which partners can mobilize and share knowledge, expertise, technology, and financial resources to help in the achievement of the sustainable development goals in all countries.[5]

Reputation risk management and corporate social sustainability

Reputation

A firm's reputation can be defined as the perception of the trustworthiness and reliability of the firm's overall performance by the firm's stakeholders over time. The perceived reputation of the firm by its stakeholders is based on financial performance, quality and leadership abilities of management, social and environmental performance, employee treatment and quality, and the quality of the goods and services provided.[6] A firm's reputation can also be impacted by its perceived emotional appeal the stakeholders associate with their interactions with the firm. In order to integrate the emotional commitment by the stakeholders, the firm must ensure that it provides transparency, accountability, consistency, authenticity, and reliability of its communications and actions. If this positive relationship is not forged between the stakeholders and the firm, the consequences of this failed relationship can generate negative reputation and social risks.

Reputation risk

Reputation risk can be defined as the range of possible gains and losses in the reputational capital of the firm. Reputational capital is the goodwill that has been generated between the firm and its stakeholders. Therefore, the level of risk of the firm's reputation is directly related to the support the stakeholders have for the firm's operations. As a result, it is critical that any source of potential reputation risk is well monitored and managed by the firm since the firm's stakeholders have the power to increase or decrease the level of reputation capital.

Social risks

Traditional risks include economic, political, and technical risk which the firm must manage to increase its reputational capital. Social risk includes human rights, labor standards, and environmental standards. As the firm expands globally, these social risks increase due to the increased complexity of doing business in other countries. Factors such as global value chains and shifting global demographics increase the challenges a firm has in its ability to minimize its social risks to protect its reputational capital. Globally, different stakeholders can transmit different levels of social risk from different entry points in different countries and different divisions of the firm. The impacts of social risk on the firm are shown in Figure 7.1.

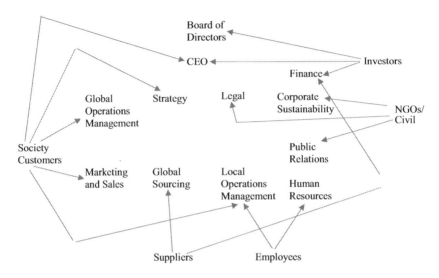

Figure 7.1 Global social risk points[7]

Customers

Customers have a significant impact on the level of social risk that occurs within a firm. The impact includes the relationship the customers have with the firm's global and local operations, the firm's marketing and sales relationship with its customers, the firm's strategy, and the firm's vision. Through the transparency of information, the customers can evaluate the firm's commitment to corporate sustainability issues related to the firm's operations around the world. Furthermore, the customers evaluate the firm's marketing strategy in order to determine if they are being treated in a respectable manner where the firm is accountable for its actions. The ever-changing demands of the customers require the firm to make adjustments to its vision from the CEO as well as the firm's overall strategy.

Suppliers

The suppliers have a direct impact on the firm's global sourcing operations. As a result, the firm must be aware of its suppliers' commitment to corporate sustainability in order to ensure that the firm's reputation is not negatively impacted by the actions of the suppliers. This "guilt by association" risk occurs when suppliers increase social risk by violating the human rights of its employees through the negative treatment of employees in the supplier's facilities. While the supplier is the responsible party for the violation, the stakeholders of the firm may perceive the brand name on the product as the party that should be held accountable for any corporate sustainability violation.

Employees

The employees have a direct impact on the firm's human resources strategy as well as the management of the firm's local operations. The employees are obviously an extremely critical stakeholder and the firm's reputation can be significantly damaged if the employees publicize negative attributes of the firm. A disgruntled employee or ex-employee description of a toxic work environment can have negative repercussions throughout the firm. From a corporate sustainability perspective, the firm's employees are on the "front lines" relative to both the firm's commitment and execution of its corporate sustainability vision. As a result, if employees view the firm as being hypocritical related to its actions versus its commitment, there is a real danger that other stakeholders will adjust their perceptions based on this "insider" information.

NGOs/civil society

As an external stakeholder who has a vested interest in monitoring the firm's reputation and corporate sustainability, NGOs and the civil society (concerned citizens) interact and communicate with the firm's corporate sustainability and public relations representatives. NGOs and concerned citizens expect transparency in both the actions and information about the firm. Therefore, if NGOs and concerned citizens perceive that the firm is not making a good faith effort to address the needs of the stakeholders, these stakeholders can publicly complain in order to make other stakeholders aware of their lack of satisfaction. Some firms can underestimate the power of NGOs and the civil society since they are not directly "involved" in the business transactions of the firm. However, this is a dangerous belief to have since NGOs such as Amnesty International and Greenpeace have the global power to persuade other stakeholders of the validity of the firm's commitment to corporate sustainability, which can impact the firm's reputation.

Investors

The investors are evaluating the firm's commitment to corporate sustainability using a financial lens. Therefore, investors focus on how the decisions and actions of the firm impact its financial performance. However, enlightened investors view the firm holistically and understand that serving the needs of all its stakeholders results in the firm achieving a superior financial performance. Investors use their money as an indicator of the firm's reputation. If the investors believe in the vision of the firm and believe it will increase its financial performance, the firm is rewarded with additional capital investments. Alternatively, if the investors believe that it is moving down the wrong course, they will withdraw their investment in the firm. Therefore, metrics such as "total market capitalization" help determine the firm's financial reputation since the investors have factored in the future growth of the firm into the firm's stock price. From a corporate sustainability perspective, investors can view investments into corporate sustainability initiatives as either a required investment to serve the needs of the stakeholder, or these investments are viewed as a waste of money since it is not directly linked with a financial outcome. As was mentioned previously, how corporate sustainability investments are perceived are based on how important the investors view serving the needs of other stakeholders.[8]

Corporate governance and corporate sustainability

Corporate governance can be defined as the system that is implemented by a firm to control and direct its operations and the operations of its employees. It is through the corporate governance system that the firm's stakeholders can evaluate whether their needs and expectations are being addressed in a satisfactory manner.[9] The primary component of a firm's corporate governance system is the board of directors.

Board of directors

The board of directors is responsible for representing the interests of the stockholders. This responsibility, which is called agency theory, is based on the belief that the managers of the firm are "agents" of the stockholders since the managers are making decisions pertaining to the operations of the firm on behalf of the stockholders. As a result, the board of directors acts as a corporate governance mechanism to ensure that the managers or agents do their job in maximizing the financial return for the stockholders.

Board members can be classified as either inside or outside board members. An inside board member has direct financial ties to the firm. Any employee of the firm is an inside board member. If the board member does not have direct financial ties with the firm, the board member is classified as an outside member. Since the board is responsible for protecting the investments made by the stockholders, the criteria for selecting board members includes evaluating honesty, integrity, loyalty, responsibility, fairness, and good corporate citizenship.

The role of the board of directors assumes that the actions of the board represent the objectives and needs of not only the stockholders but all stakeholders. This holistic approach to accountability and responsibility ensures that the firm has a strong positive long-term relationship with its stakeholders. There are five different types of board of directors. The five types are shown in Figure 7.2.

Figure 7.2 Types of boards of directors[10]

Passive board

A passive board is often referred to as a "rubber stamp" board since it approves the recommendations made by the firm's management without any opposition. The board signs off or stamps its seal of approval without challenging any of the proposals made by management.

Certifying board

The certifying board of directors verify and subsequently certify the actions of the firm. A certifying board acknowledges through its verification process that the firm is abiding by all the rules and regulations that are within its jurisdiction. If the verification process uncovers violations, the board expects the managers of the firm to correct those violations.

A certifying board can communicate to the firm's stakeholders that they are in legal compliance. The role of outside board members is critical in a certifying board since it has an external perspective on the actions of the firm and may identify potential problems earlier than the firm's management.

Engaged board

The engaged board moves from being a passive monitor of the actions of management to becoming engaged in the strategic focus of the firm. An engaged board provides advice and support to management in the decision-making process. An engaged board judges the performance of the CEO and helps guide the actions of the top-level executive. An engaged board will also seek information externally in order to give more breadth and diversity in making recommendations to the top management of the firm.

Intervening board

An intervening board moves forward in its level of involvement in the decision-making processes of the top-level managers in the firm. An intervening board is actively involved in all the major decisions of the firm. As a result, the board meets frequently and focuses intensely on all issues under its review.

Operating board

The operating board is the most involved type of board of directors. The operating board makes key decisions for the firm. The responsibility of the top-level management is to execute the recommendations made by the board. The management of the firm draws on the expertise and skills of the board members to develop the strategic focus of the firm.[11]

Corporate governance mechanisms

There are three types of mechanisms, institutional level, firm level, and group level, that can be used by a firm to monitor its operations and its strategic focus.

Institutional level corporate governance mechanisms

Firms are pressured by the external environmental factors to adopt certain monitoring and communicating mechanisms, which include corporate sustainability reports. Therefore, firms are required to continuously adapt their structure and policies to shifting instructional norms within its cultural context to protect its long-term survival. This institutional alignment is based on not only changing government regulations but also matching the practices that are changing by competitors. The corporate sustainability reports reflect these institutional shifts by presenting a fulfillment of the firm's current commitments to its stakeholders and society. The institutional level industry-based environments of the firms are either rule-based or relation-based.

For a rule-based environment, regulations are transparent and efficient and, therefore, the information provided by the firms is credible. A relation-based environment does not demand the same level of transparency since the industry develops self-regulations instead of having the government implement required compliance to established regulations. This lack of mandatory compliance triggers a high level of mistrust related to the information provided by the firm since it is perceived to be voluntary by the firm's stakeholders.

Firm level corporate governance mechanisms

The firm level corporate governance mechanism is primarily based on the actions carried out by the firm's board of directors. The role of the board is to be a liaison between the shareholders and the firm's management in both an advisory and monitoring capacity. If the board is proactive toward serving the needs of the stakeholders, the firm will be more likely to produce a comprehensive transparent corporate sustainability report. In addition, if the board is proactive in its advisory role within the firm and the firm encourages and implements the recommendations of the board, the board's actions can be extremely effective in identifying and resolving any issues related to corporate sustainability.

Group level corporate governance mechanism

The group level corporate governance mechanism refers to the size and composition of the board of directors. While there is a uniform optimal size of the board of directors, the number of board members needs to be consistent with the size of the firm and the type of participation the firm expects from the board. However, it is expected that a smaller board size may be more effective in presenting their ideas to management in areas such as strategy and addressing the needs of its stakeholders due to fewer problems related to communication and coordination. A smaller board size also may result in the firm's developing a more effective means to connect with its external stakeholders, including providing a detailed comprehensive corporate sustainability report.

Furthermore, the diversity of the board and the number of outside board members who do not have a direct financial relationship with the firm can also impact the firm's interaction and communications with stakeholders. It is expected that diversity in the background of the board members will yield a high level of diversity in the decision-making process. This diversity would, therefore, be transferred into a diverse analysis of the needs of the stakeholders and a diverse presentation of ideas on how to effectively communicate to the stakeholders. Firms that have a high level of diversity and outside board members are more likely to have a comprehensive corporate sustainability report and are expected to have a more optimal two-way interaction with the firm's stakeholders.[12]

Seven guidelines for effective corporate governance

In order to be effective in the development and execution of corporate governance systems, there are seven guidelines which can help guide this process. The seven guidelines are: embracing stakeholders; monitoring international subsidiaries; knowledge of the board members; looking at the big picture; compensation; succession planning; and corporate compliance.

Embracing stakeholders

The first guideline is that corporate governance guidelines should not solely focus on monitoring quarterly results for the firm's shareholders. The corporate governance guidelines should be holistic in nature and embrace not only shareholders but also other stakeholders such as customers, employees, and society.

Monitoring international subsidiaries

Corporate governance guidelines and monitoring should occur not just in the firm's country of origin but also in all its foreign-based subsidiaries. Firms should expect the same type of monitoring and due diligence in all its global operations. Therefore, it is unacceptable for firms to have a "rubber stamp" corporate governance in place that is controlled by corporate headquarters. The foreign-based board of directors should have competent, committed, and independent local board members. In addition, the subsidiary boards should be chaired by a member of the local board of directors instead of a member of the firm's management team.

Knowledge of board members

The board of directors should have the same breadth of knowledge pertaining to the firm's markets, products, and operations as does the top management team. This knowledge is critical in order for the board of directors to direct and control the operations of the firm. It is also beneficial to have diversity in the background of the board members to ensure that different perspectives are presented related to how the firm addresses the needs of its stakeholders.

Looking at the big picture

The board needs to develop comprehensive measures to identify how the firm can maintain and enhance its ability to differentiate itself from its competitors based on stakeholder demands from customers, stockholders, employees, and society.

Compensation

The board must ensure that the compensation related to the board, management, and the employees is equitable and is based on internal, external, and company performance.

Succession planning

Effective succession planning is a key responsibility of the board of directors. The board should establish a sustainable, competent succession planning system which would result in the smooth transition for key players in the firm.

Corporate compliance

One of the primary functions of the board of directors is to ensure the firm is in compliance with all rules and regulations. Therefore, the board must be responsible for an effective review of its internal and external auditing process; the verification of the firm's financial reporting; an evaluation of its risk management; an evaluation of its information technology governance and communication; and its legal and ethical compliance.[13]

Corporate governance and stakeholders

Each of the firm's stakeholders establishes their own list of demands regarding what should be incorporated into the corporate governance system of the firm. The employees, suppliers, and the local community want and expect to have an honest and transparent relationship with the firm. As a result, the relationship between the firm and its stakeholders is based on established

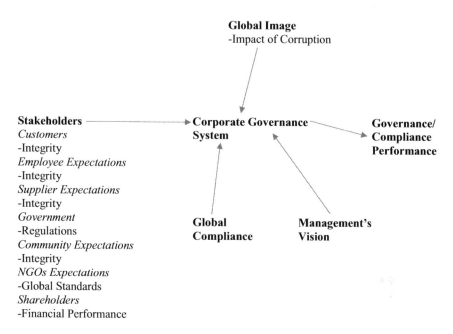

Figure 7.3 The relationship between stakeholders and corporate governance[14]

mutual integrity. Since the shareholders expect the firm to strive for optimal financial performance, the shareholders will support any actions within the corporate governance system which will increase the financial performance of the firm. The local and national governments in the countries where the firm has operations expect the firm to follow all laws and regulations related to its global operations. NGOs demand that the firm respect the global human and worker rights for all individuals who have a direct or indirect relationship with the firm around the world.

In addition to input by the stakeholders, the firm seeks guidance in the establishment and revision of its corporate governance system based on global compliance standards and the ability to protect its global reputation. The net result of these interactions should be a firm with a strong global corporate governance system which serves the needs and expectations of its stakeholders. Figure 7.3 shows the relationship between stakeholders and the firm's corporate governance system.

Social and environmental accounting

Social and environmental accounting (SEA) can be described as the preparation and publication of an evaluation made by the firm related to its social, environmental, employee, community, customer, and other stakeholder interactions. This evaluation process would include both the positive and negative consequences of those activities of the firm. While this evaluation can include financial reporting, the report would usually be dominated by a combination of quantified non-financial information and descriptive, non-quantified information. The primary focus of the report is describing how the firm has addressed its accountability to its stakeholders.[15] There are three broad perspectives on how stakeholders view SEA, which are: business case, stakeholder-accountability, and critical theory.

Business case

The business case perspective is one in which shareholders view corporate sustainability and SEA based on financial returns of the firm's actions. Supporters of this viewpoint tend to ignore, deny, or gloss over conflicts of interest in business-society relationships.

Corporate sustainability and SEA are viewed as extensions of the managers' existing toolkit to increase the wealth of the shareholders. There are numerous financial benefits for firms embracing corporate sustainability and SEA, which include the ability to create financial value; the ability to attract long-term capital and acquire favorable financing conditions; the ability to attract and motivate employees; the improvement of the firm's management system; an increase in risk awareness; the encouragement of innovation; the ability to develop continuous improvement; the ability to enhance the firm's reputation; the ability to provide transparency with its stakeholders; and the ability to maintain the firm's license to operate.

Business case firms will report on actions related to SEA issues which support their strategic focus. Focusing on corporate sustainability issues allows the firm to be able to mitigate risk, protect corporate brands, and enhance and maintain competitive advantage. Firms can use SEA in order to demonstrate to its stakeholders that its actions have a positive impact on society which will reduce the threat of protests from NGOs and activists. As a result, the business case supports the view of firms managing their social and environmental activities as part of their core business activity. The ability to manage and respond to stakeholder expectations through corporate sustainability and SEA is perceived by firms as "enlightened self-interests" through integration.

Therefore, SEA is used by the firm to manage threats to its organizational legitimacy such as potential challenges to its core values like conflicts of interest between the firm's actions and the demands of its key stakeholders. Concerns related to a firm's legitimacy are usually based on perceived instead of real conflicts of interest and its stakeholders. As a result, firms will use SEA as a demonstration that they are capable of self-regulating themselves on social and environmental issues and they do not need the government to establish rules and regulations to guide their behavior.

Stakeholder-accountability approach

The stakeholder-accountability approach is based on the belief that even though stakeholders share common interests, there can also be potential conflicts of interest among the stakeholders. The underlying philosophy of this approach is one of fair corporate accountability based on stewardship to both the financial success of the firm and the ability to achieve its social objectives. The firm has to have plural accountability of its actions in order to be responsible to the multiple constituencies related to the interests of the stakeholders. It is based on this belief of serving the needs of the stakeholders such as employees, consumers, and local communities that stakeholders have the right to know the actions of the firm and then have the right to respond to those actions through rewards or sanctions depending on whether or not the firm's actions support the needs and expectations of the stakeholders.

The stakeholder-accountability approach is perceived to be mutually beneficial for the firm and its stakeholders. For example, if the firm treats its employees fairly and equitably, it will be rewarded with increased levels of productivity. Alternatively, firms that embrace corporate sustainability initiatives develop a social "license" to operate and, subsequently, this gives them the ability to develop strong long-term relationships with the local community.

The stakeholder-accountability framework acknowledges that the firm has significant economic, social, and political power which impacts its stakeholders and can use its financial, human, and community resources to address the internal financial demands of the firm as well as the needs of its stakeholders. Therefore, the firm's stakeholders seek and demand transparency of information since this is an important monitoring tool in the behavior and actions of the firm.

Critical theory approach

The critical theory approach is based on the belief that a capitalist society does not require real accountability of the firm and that the imbalance of power and resources allows the firms freedom to do what they want without being limited by the constraints of the demands of stakeholders. The underlying assumption of the critical theory approach is the government globally allowing firms to police themselves through voluntary codes of conduct with the results of the firms focusing on achieving goals related to best practices instead of ensuring compliance with non-existent government rules and regulations. The comparison of the three approaches is shown in Table 7.1.[16]

Table 7.1 A comparison of the three different approaches related to corporate sustainability and social and environmental accounting[17]

	Business case	Stakeholder accountability	Critical theory
Purpose	– CS/SEA is viewed as an extension of a manager's existing toolkit for enhancing shareholder value – CS/SEA should result in improved reputation, social marketing, and employee relations	– CS/SEA should increase the accountability and transparency of firms – Accountability and transparency are central components of a democratic society	– CS/SEA should expose the contradictions and exploitative aspects of the capitalist system – Environmental degradation and social inequities should be highlighted.
Key assumptions	– Shareholder is the most important stakeholder – Focus on stakeholder management instead of stakeholder accountability	– Various stakeholders have "information rights" which must be acknowledged in the decision-making process of the managers – Shareholder may not be the most important stakeholder	– Skeptical about the potential for "real accountability" in a capitalist society
Regulation	– Favors self-regulation – Government regulations are too costly and inflexible	– Regulation is necessary to ensure balanced reporting for accountability, monitoring, and decision-making purposes	– Legislation is important in securing information rights
Role of stakeholders	– CS/SEA will involve consulting with stakeholders	– Stakeholders must meaningfully participate in firms' decisions and reporting	– Meaningful engagement is unlikely within current governance structures
Future of CS/SEA	– CS/SEA requires more focus on performance measures and benchmarking techniques	– Operationalization of CS/SEA is inevitably political – Government intervention is required to develop meaningful accountability measures	– Current economic system requires radical change – Stakeholders may do better to rely on externally prepared "anti-reports" from NGOs

CS = Corporate sustainability
SEA = Social and environmental accounting

Corporate sustainability reporting

Corporate sustainability reporting is based on the presentation of information to the firm's stakeholders that identifies its commitment to corporate sustainability through both actions and future goals. This type of reporting can take many forms but is usually either included within the firm's annual report or presented as a stand-alone report. Both voluntary and mandatory information is presented within the report with the identification of specific corporate sustainability initiatives either ongoing, having just been completed, or being executed in the future.[18]

The determination of the level of corporate sustainability reporting that is presented by a firm is based on firm size, profitability, and industry. The larger the firm, the higher the expectations of the firm's stakeholders to present a comprehensive corporate sustainability report. The higher level of profitability will also increase the incentive to present a comprehensive corporate sustainability report since the firm has demonstrated that its commitment to its sustainability initiative did not hinder its level of profitability. Peer pressure from other firms in the same industry can "force" a firm to present a comprehensive report if its competitors are also presenting their full commitment to corporate sustainability through reporting.[19]

The benefits of corporate sustainability reporting

From an institutional theory perspective, the external environment of the firm influences what is disclosed and how it is disclosed. Firms may be coerced into disclosing information based on rules and regulations. Firms may make disclosures to mimic the reporting practices of its competitors. Firms are also expected to make disclosures based on the normative nature of fulfilling the professional expectations of being in compliance with reporting standards and guidelines of industry-based organizations.

From a legitimacy theory perspective, firms are expected to make corporate sustainability disclosures based on an implicit social contract between the firm and society. As a result, society grants legitimacy to the firm and its operations in exchange for the firm complying with societal norms and expectations. The firm is also bound by implicit contracts with stakeholders. The diversity of stakeholders results in the stakeholders not only having different perspectives on corporate business conduct but also varying in their ability to impact the firm's activities and legitimacy. Challenges to the firm's legitimacy by its stakeholders can include actions such as consumers boycotting products, employees withholding their loyalty, and governments imposing rules and sanctions on the behavior of the firm.

One of the issues related to the use of the corporate sustainability report as a form of legitimacy occurs when corporate and societal values diverge. For example, legitimacy of the firm can be challenged when the firm is accused of pursuing strategies that change the perceptions of responsibility to its stakeholders without changing the behavior of the firm. A threat to the firm's legitimacy can also occur when it is perceived as deflecting attention away from the issues of concern to the stakeholders to other issues.

The advantages and disadvantages of voluntary and mandatory corporate sustainability reporting

The evolution of the corporate sustainability report is based on the continuous development of guidelines, standards, and regulations. This continuous guidance allows firms to develop reports that address the needs of stakeholders globally. While these guidelines are non-binding, it gives firms the opportunity to consider input from diverse sources which can broaden the firm's perspective on how it approaches communicating its corporate sustainability commitment to stakeholders. These diverse sources include not only different levels of governments but also NGOs such as industry associations and multi-stakeholder initiatives. Firm may also include certifications of standardized processes as part of its reporting to ensure its stakeholders have accurate information not only on how the firm is monitored related to corporate sustainability initiative but also in measuring of the results of its actions.

The information reported in corporate sustainability reports can be classified as either voluntary or mandatory. A comparison of the advantages and disadvantages of voluntary and mandatory corporate sustainability reports is shown in Table 7.2.

Voluntary corporate sustainability reporting

Voluntary corporate sustainability reports are the foundation from which firms can externally communicate social, environmental, and economic performance to global stakeholders. The guidelines and standards used in the voluntary reports can reflect diverse international reporting frameworks and attempt to highlight the synergies that are created among corporate sustainability initiatives of the firm. The voluntary reports are a vehicle used by the firm to tell its narrative of how it integrates its corporate sustainability vision with its actions. In addition, this type of reporting will also focus on the integration and harmonization of the corporate sustainability actions with financial operations. While voluntary reporting allows more flexibility and creativity in the presentation of information to stakeholders, it may not have the same evaluation rigor of reports that have been mandated by a stakeholder which is traditionally a government-based agency.

Table 7.2 Advantages and disadvantages of voluntary and mandatory corporate sustainability reporting[20]

| | Corporate sustainability reporting | |
	Voluntary	*Voluntary*
Advantages	– Supports voluntary commitment to corporate – More flexibility in reporting – More adaptable to external environmental changes	– Holistic reporting of positive and negative content – More balanced reporting – High quality of reporting – More credible disclosure – More consistent disclosure – Better year-on-year comparison of sustainability performance against set objectives – Better comparability of reports among companies
Disadvantage	– Incomplete reporting – Reluctance in reporting behavior – Focus on positive content – Less transparency – Less credible disclosure – Fewer comparable reports	– No evidence to state that mandatory reporting significantly impacts corporate accountability and the quality of corporate sustainability reports – High cost of command and control regulation – Stifles innovation and creativity in reporting – Inflexible to changes in the external business environment – Contrary to the belief that corporate sustainability reporting is voluntary

Mandatory corporate sustainability reporting

The alternative to voluntary corporate sustainability reporting is when a firm is required to publish its activities that are related to corporate sustainability. This mandatory type of reporting is usually required by a government agency as a necessary requirement to continue to operate in the marketplace. The reporting is based on a regulatory framework designed by the government to monitor and validate the actions of the firm.

A major proposed benefit of mandatory reporting is that it would prevent firms from misleading its stakeholders through false or incomplete information by using the report as a method to manage its public image. An additional benefit is that the firm is required to report both negative and positive actions related to corporate sustainability issues, resulting in a more balanced report. Furthermore, a mandatory report will have the same criteria from year to year which makes it easier for stakeholders to compare the firm's actions over an extended period of time.

A limitation of mandatory reporting is the perception by the firm that it would only report the bare minimum information and would view the reporting as a "cost" of doing business instead of an "opportunity" to develop more meaningful relationships with stakeholders. Therefore, mandatory reports may only present the bare minimum information about the firm's behavior related to corporate sustainability issues, which has a potentially negative impact on the firm's image and reputation. In addition, mandatory reporting is contradictory to the underlying belief by its stakeholders that the firm wants to report corporate sustainability actions on a voluntary basis.[21]

Corporate sustainability reporting and corporate reputation

Corporate sustainability reports are also a communication channel when there is a potential threat to the firm's corporate reputation. The disclosure of the action in question and the current and future response to the consequences of the action are paramount from the firm's stakeholder perspective since the stakeholders expect the firm to have a specific course of action to resolve the issue. It is imperative that the stakeholders "believe" that the firm is acting in good faith to resolve the issue. Therefore, firms have different approaches to take when addressing a threat to their reputations based on a previous action or inaction. The different approaches are shown in Table 7.3.

Novozymes: using UN Sustainable Development Goals in order to become an industry leader

Novozymes is a Danish biotechnology firm which has integrated the United Nations Sustainable Development Goals (SDGs) into decision making across its organization. The Sustainable Development Goals influence firm decisions

Table 7.3 Different responses to attacks on a firm's corporate reputation[22]

Strategy	Explanation
Denial	The firm does not believe it is responsible for the negative act and therefore denies any responsibility. Silence is considered a variation of denial.
Evading responsibility due to:	
Provocation	The firm goes on the offensive by challenging the actions of the party that is accusing it of wrongdoing.
Defeasibility	The responsibility of the negative act cannot be proven due to lack of information, volition, or it would be unfair to hold the firm responsible for the act.
Accident/good intentions	The responsibility of the firm is reduced due to the lack of control over the offensive act. While the net result of the act was negative, the motives of the firm were good and the results of the firm's actions could not have been anticipated.
Reducing offensiveness of the event by means of:	
Bolstering	The party accusing the firm of the offensive act provides information about other aspects of the firm's behavior that are positive which therefore contrast with the negative act.
Minimization	The impact of the negative act may be downplayed even though responsibility is acknowledged.
Differentiation	The specific negative act can be distinguished from negative acts by the firm's competitors. Therefore, even though a negative act was committed, other firms has done much worse acts.
Transcendence	The context of the offensive act is identified so that the act's offensiveness is transcended. For example, laying off workers is explained in terms of ensuring the long-term financial viability of the firm.
Attack accuser	The level of offensiveness of the negative act can be reduced if the firm can create an impression in which the accuser is somehow responsible for or deserves to have the consequences happen to them. For example, in the Bhopal chemical accident, many people died within a close proximity of the chemical plant. An attack accuser strategy would state that it was the government of India's fault for not clearing the shanty towns and its habitants which were located near the facility.
Compensation	While the offensiveness of the act is not challenged by the firm, the firm can reduce the impact of its stakeholders by offering compensation to those parties that have been negatively affected.
Corrective action	Corrective action is based on the promise to either make good on the impact of the offensive act or the firm acts to ensure that the offensive act will not happen again. This strategy may or may not include having the firm admit responsibility for the act.
Modification	The firm accepts responsibility for the offensive act and asks for forgiveness.

from innovation and product development and strategy, and the development of company-wide goals. This integration of the goals is beneficial in many ways for the firm, including Novozymes' recruitment process.

When Anne Sophie Bisbjerg Lee, vice-president of people and organization for Novozymes, interviews job candidates, two questions frequently asked by the candidates are: how is the company creating a positive impact on the local community and society; and how can employees make a positive individual impact on society? Ms. Bisbjerg Lee stated, "The sustainability agenda is definitely climbing up the ranks of the topics they want to discuss ... They're looking for meaningful work."[23]

Novozymes' purpose is to find biological answers to develop better lives in a more populated world. This purpose can be achieved by working with its customers, consumers, governments, and academia to find sustainable answers that the world needs. The goals of Novozymes in serving the world's needs are to save 60 million tons of carbon dioxide by developing low-carbon fuels by 2022; provide water so that over 4 billion people have access to water by providing laundry solutions that replace chemicals by 2022; and generate 500,000 tons of food by improving efficiency from farm to table by 2022.[24] Novozymes' global goals for sustainability are based on the UN Sustainable Development Goals. Novozymes has direct objectives related to 13 of the 17 goals.

Goal 2: zero hunger – Novozymes' response

By 2030, ensure that sustainable food production systems and resilient agricultural practices that increase productivity and production are implemented through a partnership with DSM Nutritional Products. DSM is the world's largest poultry and swine producer and Novozymes is developing animal feed enzyme solutions in order to produce more meat through sustainable and economical methods.

Goal 4: quality education – Novozymes' response

By 2030, ensure that all learners acquire the knowledge and skills that are needed to promote sustainable development. Novozymes has established the EDUCATION project in Brazil, which is based on the development of three app-based books which help teachers and scientists. The app books discuss the SDGs and how biology can be used to contribute to solving sustainability issues.

Goal 5: gender equality – Novozymes' response

The target for Novozymes is to ensure women's full and effective participation and equal opportunities for leadership roles in all forms of decision-making political, economic, and public forums. Novozymes has a target of having 30 percent of all senior management positions held by women in

2020. In Denmark, Novozymes is a member of the Gender Diversity Roundtable where top business leaders in Danish Business meet to facilitate the process of giving more women opportunities in leadership roles.

Goal 6: clean water and sanitation – Novozymes' response

The target for Novozymes is to improve water quality by reducing pollution, eliminating dumping, and minimizing the release of hazardous chemicals and materials. It also plans to reduce the proportion of untreated waste by half by 2030. Novozymes has an enzymatic solution which can be used in the textile industry to combine processes and save significant amounts of water. In the pulp and paper industry, a Novozymes' solution helps customers to reduce toxins in the effluent water which is generated during the production process. In China, Novozymes has microbial wastewater treatment solutions which ensure compliance of factories related to discharge of wastewater as well as improving the availability of water in the local communities.

Goal 7: affordable and clean energy – Novozymes' response

Novozymes' target is to increase the share of renewable energy in the global energy mix by a substantial level. The target is based on Novozymes' ability to enhance international cooperation to facilitate access to clean energy research and technology. This technology includes renewable energy, energy efficiency, and advanced and cleaner fossil-fuel technology. Novozymes has collaborated with Beta Renewables in Italy to establish the first biorefinery in the world designed to produce cellulosic bioethanol from agricultural residues and energy crops. In addition, the plant is entirely self-sufficient in its consumption of energy.

Goal 8: decent work and economic growth – Novozymes' response

The target for Novozymes is to progressively improve through 2030 the efficiencies of global resources through adjustments in consumption and production and attempts to decouple economic growth from environmental degradation. Since 2009, Novozymes has decoupled absolute water and energy consumption from business growth. In numerous production facilities, Novozymes has installed biogas reactors to utilize wastewater, which creates carbon and energy savings.

Goal 9: industry, innovation, and infrastructure – Novozymes' response

The target for Novozymes is to enhance scientific research and upgrade the technological capabilities of industrial sectors focusing on developing countries. By 2030, Novozymes wants to encourage innovation and substantially increase the number of research and development workers. At Novozymes, more than 20 percent of its global workforce is employed in research and development. The company spends approximately 13 percent of its revenue on research and development. With its partner, the Henning Holck Larsen Foundation, Novozymes has an agreement to advance the relationship between Denmark and India by developing scientists through the broadening of their scientific and international work experience.

Goal 11: sustainable cities and communities – Novozymes' response

The target for Novozymes is to make cities and human settlements inclusive, safe, resilient, and sustainable. By 2030, Novozymes wants to reduce the adverse per capital environmental impact of cities by focusing on air quality and waste management. In the UK, Novozymes is partnering with DONG Energy to deliver enzymes which recycle and convert waste from almost 110,000 UK homes into recycled materials that are converted into biogas. The biogas is an alternative green power which is used to generate approximately 5 mega (million) watts of electricity, enough power to support 9,500 typical UK households.

Goal 12: responsible consumption and production – Novozymes' response

The target for Novozymes is to achieve sustainable management and efficient use of natural resources by 2030. The enzymes that Novozymes uses in detergents so that laundry can be washed at lower temperatures results in saving energy without impacting the cleaning performance of the products.

The second target is for Novozymes to encourage companies, especially large and multi-national corporations (MNCs), to adopt sustainable practices and be able to integrate sustainability information into the MNCs' reporting. Novozymes develops reports that can connect the firm's business model, strategy, targets, and performance through integrated financial and sustainability data.

Goal 13: climate action – Novozymes' response

The target for Novozymes is to integrate climate change measures into governmental policies, strategies, and planning. In 2016, the customers of Novozymes reduced an estimated 69 million tons of CO_2 emissions by using its products, equal to taking approximately 30 million cars off the road. In addition, Novozymes was able to decouple absolute CO_2 emissions from business growth by not increasing energy use as sales grew. It also invested in renewable energy sources.

Goal 15: life on land – Novozymes' response

The target of Novozymes is to promote the implementation of sustainable management for all types of forests, halt deforestation, restore degraded forests, and substantially increase afforestation and reforestation around the world. Novozymes implements this target through the development of its supplier program on responsible sourcing, which ensures that its directly sourced agricultural raw materials do not originate in areas of deforestation. In addition, Novozymes supports the United Nations Convention on Biological Diversity, which focuses on fair and equitable sharing of the benefits arising from the utilization of genetic resources.

Goal 16: peace and justice and strong institutions – Novozymes' response

The target for Novozymes is to substantially reduce corruption and bribery in all its forms. Novozymes is committed to fair business practices and upholding the values of transparency and accountability to ensure business integrity from both a legal and business ethics perspective.

Goal 17: partnerships for the goals – Novozymes' response

The target for Novozymes is to encourage and promote effective public, public–private, and civil society partnerships. These partnerships include its Partnering for Impact program which focuses on creating transformational change and having a significant positive impact on society by partnering with customers, governments, suppliers, and academia. Novozymes has partnered with the United Nations Sustainable Energy for All initiative and has started the Sustainable Bioenergy Accelerator program with the UN Food and Agriculture Organization as a partner. The programs focus on accelerating the use of sustainable bioenergy for power and fuel as well as presenting sound environmental management programs focusing on energy and food security needs.[25]

Questions for thought

1. Do you think many customers realize Levi Strauss's commitment to the triple bottom line when they buy jeans? Why or why not?
2. Why do you think that more companies do not embrace a triple bottom line performance measurement system?
3. How realistic are the United Nations Sustainability Development Goals? Is their sole purpose to achieve these goals by 2030?
4. How important is a firm's reputation? Give an example of a firm that quickly lost its positive reputation.
5. Of the five types of boards of directors, which do you think is the most common in the United States? Do you think there would be a different answer if focusing on European firms?
6. Look at the corporate sustainability reports of three firms in the same industry. Which components are similar and which components different?

Notes

1 Andrew Edgecliffe-Johnson. 2019. Levis Strauss Bets Moral Mission Can Survive Public Markets. *Financial Times*. October 9.
2 Elizabeth Segran. 2019. Levi's Wants to Invent the Jeans You'll Be Wearing in 2050. *Fast Company*. November 11.
3 Andrew Edgecliffe-Johnson. 2019. Levis Strauss Bets Moral Mission Can Survive Public Markets. *Financial Times*. October 9.
4 Peter Stanwick and Sarah Stanwick. 2016. *Understanding Business Ethics*. Third Edition. Sage Publications: Thousand Oaks, CA.
5 www.un.org/development/desa/disabilities/envision2030.html
6 Jan Bebbington, Carlos Larrinaga and Jose M. Moneva. 2008. Corporate Social Reporting and Reputation Risk Management. *Accounting, Auditing & Accountability Journal*. 21(3): 337–361.
7 Christine K. Jacob. 2012. The Impact of Financial Crisis on Corporate Social Responsibility and Its Implications for Reputation Risk Management. *Journal of Sustainability Science and Management*. 2(2): 264.
8 Christine K. Jacob. 2012. The Impact of Financial Crisis on Corporate Social Responsibility and Its Implications for Reputation Risk Management. *Journal of Sustainability Science and Management*. 2(2): 259–275.
9 Peter Stanwick and Sarah Stanwick. 2016. *Understanding Business Ethics*. Third Edition. Sage Publications: Thousand Oaks, CA.
10 Peter Stanwick and Sarah Stanwick. 2016. *Understanding Business Ethics*. Third Edition. Sage Publications: Thousand Oaks, CA. 100.
11 Peter Stanwick and Sarah Stanwick. 2016. *Understanding Business Ethics*. Third Edition. Sage Publications: Thousand Oaks, CA.
12 Maria del Mar Miras-Rodriguez and Roberto Di Pietra. 2018. Corporate Governance Mechanisms as Drivers that Enhance the Credibility and Usefulness of CSR Disclosure. *Journal of Management and Governance*. 22: 565–588.
13 Martin Hilb. 2010. Redesigning Corporate Governance: Lessons Learnt From the Global Financial Crisis. *Journal of Management and Governance*. 15: 533–538.
14 Peter Stanwick and Sarah Stanwick. 2016. *Understanding Business Ethics*. Third Edition. Sage Publications: Thousand Oaks, CA. 104.
15 Rob Gray. 2000. Current Developments and Trends in Social and Environmental Auditing, Reporting and Attestation: A Review and Comment. *International Journal of Auditing*. 4: 247–268.
16 Judy Brown and Michael Fraser. 2006. Approaches and Perspectives in Social and Environmental Accounting: An Overview of the Conceptual Landscape. *Business Strategy and the Environment*. 15: 103–117.
17 Judy Brown and Michael Fraser. 2006. Approaches and Perspectives in Social and Environmental Accounting: An Overview of the Conceptual Landscape. *Business Strategy and the Environment*. 15: 114.
18 Jan Bebbington, Carlos Larrinaga and Jose M. Moneva. 2008. Corporate Social Reporting and Reputation Risk Management. *Accounting, Auditing & Accountability Journal*. 21(3): 337–361.
19 Maria del Mar Miras-Rodriguez and Roberto Di Pietra. 2018. Corporate Governance Mechanisms as Drivers that Enhance the Credibility and Usefulness of CSR Disclosure. *Journal of Management and Governance*. 22: 565–588.
20 Christian Herzig and Anna-Lena Kuhn. 2017. Corporate Responsibility Reporting. In eds. Andreas Rasche, Mette Morsing and Jeremy Moon. *Corporate Social Responsibility: Strategy, Communication and Governance*. Cambridge University Press: New York. 205.

21 Christian Herzig and Anna-Lena Kuhn. 2017. Corporate Responsibility Reporting. In eds. Andreas Rasche, Mette Morsing and Jeremy Moon. *Corporate Social Responsibility: Strategy, Communication and Governance.* Cambridge University Press: New York. 187–219.
22 Jan Bebbington, Carlos Larrinaga and Jose M. Moneva. 2008. Corporate Social Reporting and Reputation Risk Management. *Accounting, Auditing & Accountability Journal.* 21(3): 343.
23 Sarah Murray. 2019. Jobseekers Want Employers to Commit to Meaningful Social Impact. *Financial Times.* October 20.
24 www.novozymes.com/en/about-us
25 Novozymes-and-the-SDGs-June-2017.pdf

8 Suppliers, governments, and NGOs

Introduction

While it is common to think that the three most important stakeholders would be shareholders, employees, and customers, that is not always the case. Three additional critical stakeholders for a firm are its suppliers, governments, and NGOs. Depending on the issues and circumstances, any stakeholder could become top priority for a firm. Therefore, it is critical for firms to ensure that there is a strong positive relationship with all stakeholders. Corporate sustainability issues related to global supply chain, government regulations, or protests from NGOs can create permanent financial and reputational damage to firms. In this chapter some of the concepts that are discussed include: global supply chains; purchasing social sustainability; sustainable transportation; and the role of governments and NGOs. The chapter begins with a discussion of IKEA's sustainable supply chain and concludes with a discussion of the philanthropic work of the Bill and Melinda Gates Foundation.

IKEA's sustainable supply chain

IKEA's global supply chain strategy is based on the philosophy of purchasing instead of trading. From IKEA's perspective, trading is a transactional short-term relationship with its suppliers and purchasing is the establishment of long-term relationship with its suppliers. Under IKEA's previous trading model, it would demand a certain level of quality, service, price, environmental responsibility, and social responsibility from its suppliers. Under the purchasing relationship, IKEA partners with the suppliers to develop acceptable solutions to these issues. As a result, IKEA is working with its suppliers to achieve optimal production conditions which positively impact both partners. This continuous development process further entrenches the co-dependence and support IKEA and the suppliers have for each other.

Since this co-dependence is paramount in the relationship between IKEA and its suppliers, IKEA has an extremely rigorous selection process for its suppliers. The suppliers are evaluated on a number of different criteria including: management style and attitude; financial performance; the ability to source raw materials; the type of production equipment; the ability to support IKEA in its product development; the supplier's quality performance, social performance, and environmental performance; and employee working conditions.[1]

IKEA's code of conduct

IKEA's code of conduct was established in 2000 and is formally titled *The IKEA Way on Purchasing Home Furnishing Products (IWAY)*. It is commonly known as IWAY. IWAY describes the minimum requirements for social and working conditions along with the environmental demands of suppliers. The code was developed in order to ensure that IKEA's position is clear to its suppliers and other stakeholders. The IKEA concept is based on the vision of creating a better life every day for people around the world. This vision is accomplished through offering functional home furnishing products of high quality that are manufactured under acceptable working conditions by suppliers that care about the natural environment. IKEA also identifies its responsibilities to its suppliers including: being reliable, adapting its products to production demands, contributing to efficient production, caring about the environment, supporting material and energy saving techniques, taking a comprehensive view of the protection of working conditions, respecting different cultures, and having clear and mutually agreed upon commercial terms.

IKEA's expectations of its suppliers

Legal requirements

Every supplier must comply with all national laws and regulations and all international conventions pertaining to social and working conditions, child labor, and the protection of the environment.

Social and working conditions

Suppliers must agree to provide a healthy and safe working environment; pay at least the minimum legal wage and compensate for overtime; and ensure acceptable working conditions including reasonable privacy, quietness, and personal hygiene. Suppliers must not use child labor, use forced or bonded labor, discriminate, use overtime illegally, prevent the formation of labor unions, or accept any type of harassment or any other mental or physical abuse of its workers.

Environment and forestry

IKEA's suppliers must agree to work to reduce waste and emissions to the air, ground, and water; have safety procedures for handling chemicals, including the proper procedures designed for the handling, storage, and disposal of hazardous waste in an environmentally safe manner; be active in the recycling and reusing of materials and products; and use wood from well-managed and sustainable areas. Suppliers are not allowed to use wood originating from national parks, nature preserves, or intact natural forests.[2]

IKEA's staircase framework

The IWAY philosophy of IKEA has led to the development of a staircase framework which enables IKEA's suppliers to improve their overall performance. There are four levels to the framework, which are presented in Table 8.1.

Level 1

In Level 1, IKEA establishes the supplier requirements related to social and working conditions as well as wood merchandise before the supplier can start a business relationship with IKEA. The requirements refer to not using child or forced labor and to having no wood used from intact natural forests or high conservation value forests. In addition, suppliers who are delivering products to IKEA that contain solid wood, veneer, plywood, and layer-glued wood must complete a Forest Tracing System document to verify the origin of the wood.

Level 2

Once the supplier has fulfilled the minimum requirements established by IKEA, the supplier can start doing business with IKEA. At Level 2, the supplier must fulfil the IWAY requirements related to outside environment, social and working conditions, and sustainable management of its wood products. Since Level 2 is the critical step in the staircase, IKEA concentrates on ensuring that all of its suppliers fulfill the minimal obligations of the IWAY program.

Level 3

At Level 3, the supplier must receive certification of its operations based on the requirements by IKEA. The certification requires that the suppler be able to maintain the IWAY standards at its factories and be able to establish goals and plans on how to make continuous improvements related to the outside environment, social and working conditions, and wooden merchandise.

Table 8.1 IKEA's staircase model[3]

Level 1	Level 2	Level 3	Level 4
Start-up requirements and action plan to achieve level 2	Fulfillment of minimum requirements, IWAY standard	Fulfillment of IKEA level 3 standards	Fulfillment of official standards, third-party certificate
Outside environment			
Action plan to achieve level 2	IWAY outside environmental requirement	Supplier environmental assurance	ISO 14001
Social and working conditions			
No forced/bonded child labor	IWAY social and working condition requirement	Social and working conditions	Future official standards recognized by IKEA
Wooden merchandise			
No wood from intact natural or high conservation forest unless certified	IWAY forestry requirement	Wood procurement and forestry	Well-managed forests certified by an official standard recognized by IKEA

Level 4

For a supplier to achieve Level 4 status, it must have its processes certified according to an official standard recognized by IKEA. Once a firm has reached Level 4, IKEA will likely aid the supplier in the certification process.[4]

Corporate sustainability and global supply chains

In the past, supply chain issues for firms included areas such as the ability to integrate processes across supply chain partners, the cost-efficiency of supply chains, and the ability to offer superior customer service. However, stakeholders of firms are putting increased scrutiny on firms in their social sustainability commitment related to supply chains. Stakeholder concerns include the social impact of outsourcing to developing countries and the social and environmental impact of production and consumption through firm activities such as reverse logistics, environmental management, and supply chains.

Reverse logistics

Reverse logistics refers to the firm's logistics strategy related to product returns, source reduction, recycling, material substitution, reuse of materials, waste disposal and refurbishing, repair, and remanufacturing. Stakeholders are interested in how firms take accountability and responsibility to address these issues using a corporate sustainability focus. This closed loop supply chain will continue to be a major component in the firm's ability to demonstrate its corporate sustainability commitment. The complexity of reverse logistics is based on the integration of these issues throughout the entire supply chain of the firm from the end user customers back to the original suppliers of raw materials.

Environmental supply chains

A firm's strategy is related to identifying the total environmental impact of the supply chain from both a resources and ecological footprint perspective. The "greening" of the supply chain can result in the firm saving resources, eliminating or reducing waste, and improving the firm's level of productivity and its competitive advantage. Some examples of the greening initiative includes the firm designing products for easier disassembly and remanufacturing. Other focal points include using sustainable raw materials, the use of renewable energy sources, the use of environmentally friendly transport modes, and the ability to utilize the maximum capacity of production facilities and transportation modes.[5]

Factors influencing corporate sustainability and supply chains

There are several factors within the firm's culture that impact the importance of corporate sustainability and its global supply chains. Four of those major components are: knowledge enhancing mechanisms; knowledge controlling mechanisms; firm-specific assets; and corporate history.

Knowledge enhancing mechanisms

Knowledge enhancing mechanisms are used to maintain and enhance the knowledge of the managers in incorporating sustainability in the decision-making process. Internal knowledge enhancement is achieved through employee training which focuses on corporate sustainability issues such as the firm's code of conduct. This training is useful in the development of common beliefs of managers in how corporate sustainability issues are identified and are subsequently resolved.

External knowledge enhancing mechanisms refer to the development of a common frame of reference between the firm and its suppliers. This common frame of reference can be achieved through frequent dialogue and visits to the firm's suppliers, as well as formal and informal supplier training.

Knowledge controlling mechanisms

Knowledge controlling mechanisms refer to the firm integrating its code of conduct into the employee performance measurement system. By including the code as part of the annual evaluation of employees, employees are motivated for their behavior to be within the code and ensure their interactions with the firm's stakeholders are acceptable. Another knowledge controlling mechanism is the appointment by the firm of change agents who are expected to monitor the employees' commitment to working within the guidelines of the code of conduct. Each purchasing team at IKEA has goals related to prices, volume, inventory turnover, delivery performance, quality performance, and IWAY fulfillment.

Firm-specific assets

Firm-specific assets refer to the size of the firm, the design of the firm's global supply chain, financial resources, and the firm's reputation. The more resources the firm has, the higher the supplier's level of motivation to become a partner with the firm. Therefore, the supplier will ensure that it meets the minimum requirements established by the firm related to the code of conduct and corporate sustainability initiatives. Furthermore, fulfilling the rigorous firm standards can be beneficial for the supplier to develop relationships with other firms.

Corporate history

By embracing corporate sustainability initiatives in the past and having a tradition of working with environmental and social issues, the firm is likely to have a comprehensive code of conduct with a performance evaluation system integrated into the operations of the firm. This historical view can come from the original founder or seminal top-level managers in the past who have guided the firm throughout its history in embracing ethical and corporate sustainability initiatives. This historical reference point is invaluable in demonstrating to suppliers how important it is for the supplier to agree to the firm's vision. This historical perspective also facilitates a deep-rooted acceptance and commitment from the firm's long-standing suppliers and serves as a role model for future suppliers.[6]

Purchasing social sustainability

The purchasing function is a unique boundary-spanning relationship between the firm's stakeholders such as buyers, suppliers, contractors, and the community. The socially responsible purchasing activities can result in the development of a positive impact on the firm's supply chain partners and the firm's reputation. Purchasing social sustainability (PSS) can include activities of the firm such as environmental purchasing, sourcing from minority-owned suppliers, and the monitoring of human rights conditions of the outsourced factories.

The financial benefits of PSS can lead to cost reduction by improving the organizational learning and the suppliers' performance. By working with its suppliers, the firm is able to facilitate changes to the suppliers' processes, product design, and packaging which can have a positive financial impact on the suppliers' financial performance. This reciprocal relationship enhances the ability of the firm and its suppliers to entrench a long-term relationship instead of a short-

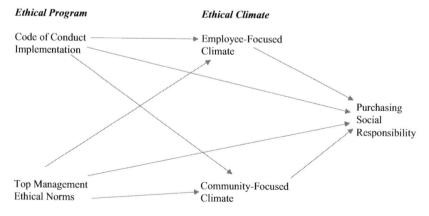

Figure 8.1 The relationship of purchasing social sustainability[7]

term transactional relationship, benefitting both sides financially. As a result, not only does this relationship improve the reputation of the firm, but it also improves the brand image and goodwill among the firm's stakeholders. The development of a strong positive image, reputation, and goodwill allows the firm to develop a stronger competitive advantage in the marketplace. Stakeholders prefer to interact with firms that have a strong positive image and reputation.

For the firm to effectively execute PSS, the firm must establish the current ethical programs which are supported by a proactive ethical climate. The relationship of these concepts is shown in Figure 8.1.

Ethical programs

Code of conduct implementation

The establishment of a code of conduct is imperative for the firm to demonstrate to its suppliers and its other stakeholders what the expectations and requirements are for both sides of the stakeholder relationship. The enforcement of the code of conduct is necessary to embrace the positive social sustainability corporate culture which guides the decision-making process for both the firm and its stakeholders. Therefore, a comprehensive code of conduct can establish the internal "rules of the game" for the firm by fortifying the firm's ethical and social sustainability commitment. As a result, code of conduct implementation has a direct impact on PSS, as well as an indirect result through the employee- and community-focused climate of the firm.

Top management ethical norms

It is critical for any proactive ethical and social sustainability commitment to be embraced by top-level management. To have firms that are focused on social sustainability, the firms must have socially responsible managers who influence the ethical behavior. Leading by example, the top-level managers are looked upon to be ethical leaders, which encourages the other employees to move beyond just strictly following the established codes of conduct. As a result, the top-level managers are needed to not only develop a supportive ethical climate but also ensure that its constituents behave and make decisions in an ethical manner including their focus on corporate sustainability issues. Therefore, the top management ethical norms have a direct impact on PSS and an indirect impact through the employee- and community-focused climate.

Ethical climate

Employee-focused climate

An employee-focused climate refers to the individual ethical values of the employee which can be impacted by the ethical commitment and responsibilities implemented by the firm through its code of conduct. The code of conduct is a tool the firm uses to respect employees and strengthen the positive ethical culture of the firm. The firm's climate is strengthened through providing guidance to the employees in the determination of what is acceptable and unacceptable ethical behavior. As a result, in an employee-focused climate, the employees perceive that decisions should be made under the umbrella of ensuring the well-being of the employees of the firm. Therefore, it is expected that the employee-focused climate will have a direct impact on the PSS focus of the firm.

Community-focused climate

A community-focused climate refers to external stakeholders where a dominant focus in this model is on suppliers. The firm's code of conduct also impacts the relationship the firm has with its external stakeholders as a response to demonstrating its social legitimacy in operating and providing goods to other entities. This demonstration of the firm's ethical and social sustainability commitment strengthens the firm's positive reputation. As a result, in a community-focused climate, the employees perceive that decisions should be based under the umbrella of ensuring the well-being of the firm's community of stakeholders. Therefore, it is expected that the community-focused climate will have a direct impact on the PSS of the firm.[8]

Sustainable transportation

There are three major factors where transportation has a potential impact on sustainability: economic, social, and environmental. The economic impacts of transportation are traffic congestion, mobility barriers, accident damages, facility costs, consumer costs, and the depletion of non-renewable resources. The social impact of transportation includes inequity of impacts, mobility disadvantages, health impacts, impacts on community interaction and livability, and aesthetics. The environmental impacts of transportation are air and water pollution, habitat loss, and depletion of non-renewable resources.

There are simple and comprehensive sustainable transportation actions available for various stakeholders including individuals and local communities. Simple sustainable transportation actions include transportation fossil fuel consumption reduction, vehicle pollution emissions reduction, increasing per capital vehicle mileage, higher transit ridership, and lower transport land consumption. Simple sustainable transportation actions can be effective, but they fail to provide an effective plan to guide future transportation activities. Simple actions can overlook critical factors such as community livability and equity. They may focus on addressing only one or two specific objectives while not considering solutions which provide modest benefits to multiple stakeholders.

Alternatively, comprehensive sustainable transportation actions can have a range of potential impacts. Table 8.2 through 8.4 show a listing of comprehensive sustainable transportation activities related to economic, social, and environmental objectives.

This triple bottom line approach to sustainable transportation highlights the interdependence of the objectives of stakeholders related to corporate sustainability. While many people view sustainable transportation through a narrow lens of sustainability, the objectives listed in Table 8.2 through 8.4 highlight the inherent complexities in identifying transportation issues and the development of a solution to these issues.

Table 8.2 Economic comprehensive sustainable transportation activities[9]

Objective	Activity	Direction
Accessibility – commuting	–Average commute travel time	Less is better
Accessibility – land use mix	–Number of job opportunities and services within a 30-minute travel distance	More is better
Accessibility – smart growth	–Planning practices that lead to more accessible, clustered, mixed, and multi-modal development	More is better
Transport diversity	–Travel portions based on walking, cycling, rideshare, public transit, and telework	More is better
Affordability	–Portion of household expenditures devoted to transport by 20% lowest-income households	Less is better
Facility costs	–Per capita expenditures on roads, traffic services, and parking facilities	Less is better
Planning	–Degree to which transportation institutions reflect least-cost planning and investment practices	More is better

Table 8.3 Social comprehensive sustainable transportation activities[10]

Objective	Activity	Direction
Health and fitness	–Percentage of population that regularly walks and cycles	More is better
Community livability	–Degree to which transport activities improve community living conditions	More is better
Equity – fairness	–Degree to which transport costs reflect full costs unless a subsidy is specifically justified	More is better
Equity – non-drivers	–Quality of accessibility and Services for non-drivers	More is better
Equity – disabilities	–Quality of transport facilities and services for people with disabilities	More is better
Non-motorized transport Planning	–Degree to which impacts on non-motorized transport are considered in transportation modelling and planning	More is better
Citizen involvement	–Public involvement in transport planning process	More is better

Table 8.4 Environmental comprehensive sustainable transportation activities[11]

Objective	Activity	Direction
Climate change emissions	-Per capita fossil fuel consumption, and emissions of CO_2 and other climate change emissions	Less is better
Other air pollution	-Per capital emissions of conventional air pollutants such as carbon monoxide and nitrogen oxide	Less is better
Noise pollution	-Portion of population exposed to high levels of traffic noise	Less is better
Water pollution	-Per capital vehicle fluid losses	Less is better
Land use impacts	-Per capital land devoted to transportation facilities	Less is better
Habitat protection	-Preservation of wildlife habitat	More is better
Resource efficiency	-Non-renewable resource consumption in the production and use of vehicles and transport facilities	Less is better

In order to effectively address the issues presented in Tables 8.2 through 8.4, local communities need to develop and implement potential solutions. The potential solutions to these comprehensive sustainable transportation issues are shown in Table 8.5.

The focus of the solutions is related to ecological integrity, human health, economic welfare, social equity, and social welfare. In order to address the diversity of stakeholders, the local community needs to focus on how transportation can improve at embracing sustainable ideals. By perceiving transportation issues as integrated, the interdependence of the actions can address these transportation issues by addressing multiple needs from multiple stakeholders. The goal would be to move toward improved travel choices, road design incentives, efficient travel choices, land use patterns, the ability to reduce the need to travel, and support of alternative transportation modes.[13]

Corporate sustainability and government

Governments play two keys roles in corporate sustainability by providing the context for corporate sustainability and by acting to shape corporate sustainability through policies and allocation of resources. Governments provide an overall legal context by developing a legal framework for civil society development and participation. In addition, governments provide a broad context of the rule and potential monitoring mechanism for the corporate sustainability actions of the firm. Governments can also fill governance gaps of firms through legislation. The impact of a government on a firm's corporate sustainability commitment is based on the development of programs that reflect the political and economic institutions, traditions, and policies of the firm's home country.

Table 8.5 Proposed solutions to comprehensive sustainable transportation issues[12]

Sustainability	Sustainability	Transportation	Transportation solution
Ecological integrity	Reduce climate change	Reduce climate change emissions	Corporate average fuel efficiency standards, emission taxes, alternative fuels, travel demand management
	Preserve wildlife habitat	Reduce impervious surface	Reduce parking and road capacity standards, parking management, road design to minimize habitat impacts, travel demand management
	Reduce pollution	Reduce harmful vehicle air and water emissions	Emission standards, vehicle emissions inspection and maintenance (I/M) programs, travel demand management
Human health	Reduce pollution exposure	Criteria emission controls	Emission standards, I/M programs, alternative fuels, travel demand management
	Increase exercise	Increase active transport	Improve walking and cycling conditions, traffic calming, encourage non-motorized transport, travel demand management
Economic welfare	Consumer's mobility	Insure adequate transport services, provide mobility choices, reduce traffic congestion and barriers	Adequate road capacity, transit services, travel demand management, walking and cycling improvement, desirable communities, delivery services
	Business productivity	Freight mobility and affordability	Adequate road/rail/air freight capacity, efficient land use, freight priority, travel demand management
Social equity	Horizontal equity	User pay principle	Cost-based pricing
	Vertical equity	Progressive pricing	Low prices/taxes for basic driving, transit
		Mobility for non-drivers	Provide adequate walking, cycling, rideshare, transit services
Social welfare	Community cohesion and	Improve mobility within neighborhoods	Smart street planning, traffic calming, pedestrian/cycle planning, mixed land use
		Enhance the public realm through street improvements	Traffic calming, pedestrian planning, livable community design features

There are four types of government policy that can encourage corporate sustainability: endorsement, facilitation, partnering, and mandate.

Endorse

This type of government policy supports corporate sustainability through general information campaigns and websites, political rhetoric, and awards. Endorsement actions by the government can raise awareness for corporate sustainability and promote good practices.

Facilitate

Governments can facilitate corporate sustainability by providing incentives for firms to adopt programs using subsidies, tax incentives, and public procurement. Some examples of government policies which facilitate corporate sustainability issues include providing subsidies and tax expenditures for contributions to charities, the adoption of clean technologies, and the employment of disadvantaged workers in public procurement policies.

Partner

Government organizations can form collaborations with firms to develop standards and guidelines usually at the industry-wide level. Partnership approaches by the government can assist in disseminating knowledge about corporate sustainability issues.

Mandate

Governments can set regulations for minimum standards for firm performance of corporate sustainability issues such as human rights, labor rights, discrimination, bribery, and environmental standards.

Through partnerships with government organizations and industry-specific organizations, the government has the opportunity to use all four types of government policies. It is through the shared vision between the public and private partners that a holistic approach can be used to present solutions to industry-specific problems. An example of this type of partnership occurs in addressing corporate sustainability issues in the garment industry in Bangladesh.

Using both government and private partnerships to address corporate sustainability issues in the Bangladesh garment industry

The working conditions in garment factories has traditionally been dangerous. The women working in the factories must deal with crowded factory conditions, making it difficult to move around and leave quickly if there is a fire. The factories also traditionally have had poor ventilation systems which expose the workers to toxic dust floating in the air. Many of the factories traditionally did not have a fire exit or a fire alarm to warn the employees to evacuate the building.

Garment factories in Bangladesh have had a long and horrific history of disasters due to negligence by the factory operators. From 2005 to 2013, there have been seven major disasters where either fires or collapsing buildings killed workers who were trapped inside the building. The turning point occurred on April 24, 2013 when 1,129 people were killed after the Rana Plaza building caught fire and a garment factory collapsed. The cause of the collapse was due to building violations and structural flaws, including a substandard foundation.[14]

This "final straw" created outrage in not only Bangladesh but also internationally with global stakeholders demanding that initiatives be developed and executed to ensure these tragedies do not continue to occur in the future. The result was the establishment of regulatory solutions which included both mandatory governmental programs and voluntary private sector programs. The four regulatory initiatives are presented in Table 8.6.

As a result of the Rana Plaza disaster, two monitoring mechanisms were established related to fire, electrical, and building safety for Bangladesh garment factories. The first mechanism developed was called the Alliance, which was

Table 8.6 Regulatory initiatives for the Bangladesh garment industry[15]

Imitative	Examples	Scope	Membership	Decision-making	Requirements
Business only – no government role	Alliance for Bangladeshi Worker Safety	Establish a standard for fire and safety	North American garment companies, retailers, brands (Gap, Walmart)	Business-only initiative	Not legally binding
Private regulation of international corporate sustainability	Accord on Fire and Building Safety in Bangladesh	Establish a fire and building safety program	200+ garment companies from 20 countries, two global unions, Bangladeshi Unions, International Labor Organization	Multi-Stakeholder Initiatives (MSI)	Legally binding
Government regulation of international corporate sustainability	US trade agreement with Bangladesh	US trade access dependent on labor standards in Bangladesh	US government, Bangladeshi government	Bilateral trade	Legally binding
Government regulation of international corporate sustainability	EU trade agreement with Bangladesh	Everything but Arms	EU27 countries and Bangladeshi government	Bilateral trade	Legally binding

a US-based partnership with firms and the second was the multi-stakeholder-oriented program called the Accord, which was led by European Union (EU) stakeholders. It was the pressure from union organizers and anti-sweatshop activists that forced global European brands such as H&M to sign the Accord and to take accountability for monitoring safety conditions and allow access to trade unionists. The brands that agreed to sign the Accord represented production in over 1,500 factories that employed more than 50 percent of the garment workers in Bangladesh. Approximately 200 garment corporations have agreed to sign the Accord from two countries in Europe, North America, Asia, and Australia.

The US retailers and brands would not sign the EU-based Accord due to fears of legal liability. As an alternative, a group of North American garment companies, retailers, and brands, including Gap and Walmart, founded the Alliance for Bangladesh Worker Safety. In addition, the EU and US governments used trade policy to implement changes in the working conditions and safety measures in the garment industry factories. The EU policies are agreements on behalf of all the EU member states. The EU promotes its trade policy of non-conditional trade access through its motto "Everything but Arms" program for Bangladesh. This trade access is based on a duty-free, quota-free access program.

Therefore, using government and private initiatives, industries can adjust the expectations and performance of the firms within that industry related to corporate sustainability. The use of top-down, hierarchal trade regulations imposed by foreign governments can promote better labor standards for the workers. Alternatively, a bottom-up approach of the establishment of private regulations in the form of multi-stakeholder initiatives and the formation of firm collaboration in alliances also forces the industry to change its focus toward corporate sustainability issues.[16]

Corporate sustainability and NGOs

The origin of the term "non-governmental organization" is from the Charter of the United Nations created in 1945. The definition of an NGO is any type of organization which is independent from government influence and operates as a not-for-profit. The impact of NGOs worldwide is significant. There are an estimated 10 million NGOs globally focusing on the diversity of corporate sustainability issues. There are more than 1.4 million NGOs in the United States that have approximately 11.4 million employees.[17]

Top ten NGOs in the world

NGO Advisor does an annual ranking of the top NGOs globally. The top five NGOs for 2019 are: BRAC, Doctors Without Borders, Danish Refugee Council, Open Society Foundations, and Mercy Corps.

BRAC

Originally named Building Resources Across Communities, BRAC was founded in Bangladesh in 1972 to receive foreign donations for the newly sovereign country. It now focuses on improving the quality of life of people not only in Bangladesh but also in other parts of the world. The organization focuses on numerous corporate sustainability issues such as: children and youth, community building, economic empowerment, education, emergency crisis, gender issues, health, law and justice, micro finance, refuges, shelter, sanitation, and water. BRAC has dramatically helped reduce the mortality rates of children under five years old. It has also enrolled hundreds of thousands of children in primary schools and has focused on gender equality issues. One of BRAC's goals for 2020 is to reach an additional 2.7 million girls through education and empowerment programs. BRAC currently addresses the needs of 138 million people and is striving to empower an additional 20 million women and men who are underserved and disenfranchised in areas related to resources, decisions for their communities, and actions for social transformation.[18]

Médecins Sans Frontières (Doctors Without Borders)

Doctors Without Borders was founded in 1971 in Paris by a group of journalists and doctors because of the war and famine in Biafra, Nigeria. The goal of Doctors Without Borders was to establish an NGO which would focus on delivering emergency medical aid that was quick and effective. The vision of Doctors Without Borders is based on the belief that all people should have access to healthcare regardless of gender, race, religion, creed, or political affiliation. This healthcare should be given regardless of the national boundaries of countries globally. In 2019, there were more than 67,000 people who were involved with the NGO.[19] Doctors Without Borders provides healthcare in over 60 countries and focuses on catastrophic events such as armed conflict, epidemics, malnutrition, and natural disasters, which can overwhelm local health systems. Doctors Without Borders also helps people who are discriminated against or are neglected based on the current policies of their local healthcare system.[20]

Danish Refugee Council

In November 1956, the Danish Ministry for Foreign Affairs asked various Danish organizations to come together to give aid to 1,000 Hungarian refugees who were displaced due to the Hungarian Uprising. As a result, what was started as an ad hoc temporary organization became a permanent NGO to address the needs of refugees globally. From those humble beginnings, the Danish Refugee Council has developed programs for counselling and language training as they welcome new refugees into Danish society. In addition, the

Danish Refugee Council has collected donations to help the world's refugees. The Danish Refugee Council began its international operations in the early 1990s when it sent Danish drivers to Bosnia and Kosovo during the civil war in Yugoslavia. In 1997, the Danish Demining Group was founded through a partnership with other organizations to clear unexploded mines and other devices in war zone areas. By 2005, Danish Refugee Council had operated in 23 countries and by 2010, the number had grown to 29 countries. In 2019, Danish Refugee Council had operations in 40 countries and had 8,300 employees and 8,000 volunteers.[21]

Open Society Foundations

Open Society Foundations was founded by George Soros and is the largest private funder of independent groups working on justice, democratic governance, and human rights in the world. Open Society Foundations funds groups and projects in more than 120 countries. The mission of the NGO is based on the belief that the solutions to the national, regional, and global challenges are based on the free exchange of ideas and thought, and that everyone should have a voice in the polices that can impact them. Since its inception, Open Society Foundations has spent over $15 billion to support these causes. Open Society Foundations gives over 2,500 grants annually to groups and individuals that focus on the promotion of tolerance, transparency, and open debate. In addition, it also funds human rights litigation and engages directly with governments and policy-making groups to develop policies that advance positive change.[22,23]

Mercy Corps

Mercy Corps was originally founded in 1979 as Save the Refugees Fund in response to helping Cambodian refugees fleeing their country due to famine, war, and genocide. In 1982, Mercy Corps was formed, which shifted focus from just providing relief assistance to incorporating long-term solutions to hunger and poverty as its revised mission. By 2019, Mercy Corps was involved in over 122 countries and had delivered over $3.7 billion in lifesaving assistance. This assistance included: food, shelter, health care, agriculture, water, sanitation, education, and small business loans. Mercy Corps helps over 28 million people annually and includes using relief and development programs to strengthen the civil society in local communities.[24]

The benefits of a partnership between an NGO and a firm

There are several reasons why a firm might engage with NGOs. Having a partnership with an NGO may allow the firm to enter or strengthen its position in global markets. The NGO's credibility with the public related to stakeholder issues can be beneficial if the firm must address those same type of issues. The sharing of information and knowledge between the partners can help the firm in its strategic focus, which could lead to greater efficiencies in resource allocation. The partnership with an NGO will also aid the firm in minimizing negative public confrontation as well as expanding opportunities to engage with its stakeholders.

Alternatively, there are many reasons why a firm would dissolve a partnership with an NGO. One concern the firm may have is sharing confidential and proprietary information with the NGO. Another problem can occur if the firm believes that it has difficulties in addressing a broadening agenda of a sustainability-focused NGO. The firm may also be concerned with the short-term financial impact of its partnerships with an NGO, reducing the perceived value of the partnership.

From the NGO's perspective, there are several benefits in having a partnership with a firm. One reason is if the NGO does not believe that the government is able to provide solutions to the issues of concern to the

Table 8.7 Types of firm–NGO relationships[25]

Type of Relationship	Activities	Company participation Level	Target stakeholders
Challenge	Media campaigns, boycotts	Reactive response	Customers, shareholders
Sparring partner	Periodic exchanges, "healthy conflict"	Reactive or proactive response, formal or informal communication mechanism	NGOs, regulators
Support	Charitable giving, sponsorship, gifts in kind	Primarily financial contribution to support project	Customers, public
Product endorsement	Endorsement by NGO, eco-labelling	Initial audit/assessment of operations/practices ongoing information exchange/verification	Customers, NGOs
Company endorsement	Ratings, certification	Initial audit of operations, practices, reporting, ongoing information exchange/verification	Shareholders, NGOs
Site or project	Environmental mediation, environmental impact assessment	Formal communication process, joint agenda-development	Communities, NGOs
Strategy dialogue	Discussions over business issues	Joint agenda-development research, formal communication process and results dissemination	NGOs, regulators
Project joint venture	Formal partnership for duration of project	Project planning and development, financial support	Communities, NGOs
Strategic joint venture	Formal partnership or public alliance	Full business participation, jointly developed principles or strategy	NGOs, public

NGO. Another benefit is that the NGO may get access to additional resources in the form of funding or technical and managerial expertise. The NGO may enhance its credibility with its stakeholders if it has a strong positive relationship with a firm. The NGO may also get access to supply chains that have been developed by the firm.

As is the case with the firm, there can be situations in which the NGO no longer wants to remain in a partnership with a firm. One reason is if the NGO believes that the firm's true motives are to create a positive public relations image to its stakeholders and is not truly committed to the goals of the NGO. Another reason is if the NGO believes that the firm is not transparent with its actions and those actions are perceived to be hypocritical. The NGO will also potentially dissolve the partnership if the members of the NGO no longer agree with the beliefs and philosophy of the firm.

As a result, the relationship between firms and NGOs is complex and complicated. With diversity in objectives and vision, these relationships create different levels of comprehensiveness. A listing of the types of relationships in shown in Table 8.7.

The typology of NGOs

The types of relationship between firms and NGOs cover a large spectrum from short-term confirmations to long-term commitments. Firms that want to have a relationship with an NGO must determine which NGOs to partner with and the type of relationship wanted with the NGO. These two critical decisions are the basis of a typology of NGO relationships.

Integrator versus polariser

The first trait that separates the focus of NGOs is the extent to which the NGO will seek to integrate the role of businesses and public interest groups in achieving corporate sustainability goals. At one end of the spectrum is the integrator NGO. An integrator is an NGO which places a high priority on developing productive relationships with businesses. The goal of this type of NGO is to identify and implement non-confrontational "win-win" strategies. As a result, integrator NGO are business friendly and seek out productive relationship with firms. Integrators prefer having collaborative relationships with firms.

At the other end of the spectrum is a polarizer NGO. A polarizer NGO is one which focuses not on developing close working relationships with businesses, but on developing the role of a stakeholder watchdog. As a result, the polarizer is business–unfriendly. This type of NGO avoids alliances with companies and prefers confrontation to collaboration.

Discriminator versus non-discriminator

The second dimension of an NGO is whether the NGO discriminates between firms within a specific industry based on a firm's real or perceived commitment to corporate sustainability. Discriminator NGOs focus on a specific industry and monitor the progress made by each firm within the industry as compared with the industry benchmarks of corporate sustainability commitments.

At the other end of the spectrum is the non-discriminating NGO. The focus is not how individual firms are advancing its corporate sustainability commitment but on the industry as a whole. Therefore, a non-discriminating NGO focuses on the big picture by monitoring corporate sustainability from an industry-wide perspective.

The typology of NGOs is presented in Table 8.8. Using the analogy of sea animals, the types of NGOs are orca, dolphin, shark, and sea lion.

NGO orca

An NGO which focuses on firm performance and is classified as business-unfriendly is an orca. Orca NGOs focus on firms which have a strong stakeholder reputation and enjoy high levels of stakeholder trust. Since they are discriminators, they are well versed on the issues related to corporate sustainability within the specific industry and can evaluate the firm's progress as compared with the industry's best practices. Since they are business-unfriendly, they will purposely be unpredictable when responding to firm

Table 8.8 Typology of NGOs[26]

NGO characteristics	Polarizer	Integrator
	Business-unfriendly	Business-friendly
Discriminator	Orca	Dolphin
Scrutinizes firm performance	– Highly intelligent strategy – Can adapt behavior and strategy, but prefers to use fear to succeed in its goals – Fierce in appearance – Uncertain in behavior	– Intelligent, creative – Adapts behavior and strategies to context, but strategic in approach – Popular spectacle
Non-discriminator	Shark	Sea lion
Ignores firm performance	– Relatively low intelligence – Tactical – Acutely responsive to distress signals – Undiscriminating in terms of targets	– Moderate intelligence – Tactical – Popular spectacle – Friendly

crises to keep the firm unbalanced. Any benefits for the firm with its partnership with an Orca are incidental instead of preplanned.

NGO *dolphin*

An NGO which focuses on firm performance and is business friendly is a dolphin. A dolphin strategy for an NGO is one of the hardest strategies for an NGO to develop and sustain. The business-friendly, intelligent approach of a dolphin creates an ideal partnership with a firm that is serious about corporate sustainability and serious about engaging the firm's stakeholders. Since they are willing to integrate their actions with the firm, dolphins bring the needed partnership skills to develop a strong foundation of trust, openness, and the willingness to understand the firm's perspective. Since this type of NGO is a discriminator, the NGO brings credibility to the project. In a crisis, the role of the NGO will be based on the amount of accumulated respect the NGO has for the firm in the partnership.

NGO *shark*

An NGO which focuses on the whole industry and is business-unfriendly is a shark. An NGO shark focuses on industries that are easy targets due to historical lack of commitment to corporate sustainability. For environmental issues, sharks focus on industries which traditionally have been the heaviest polluters. Because of its inherent lack of trust for firms in the industries which it focuses upon, an NGO shark will not likely form any long-term relationship with any firms since the shark will not likely be loyal to the firm when crisis circumstances arise.

NGO *sea lion*

An NGO which focuses on the whole industry and is business-friendly is considered to be a sea lion. Environmental conservation organizations are examples of sea lions. The partnership between the sea lion and the firm will be extremely safe and cordial. The type of partnerships that work well with a sea lion are firms that include marketing or public relations activities. Because they are not discriminating, sea lions will work with most firms regardless of their current corporate sustainability commitment. This lack of discrimination can potentially negatively impact the credibility and effectiveness of the sea lion in representing itself as a positive impact on corporate sustainability.[27]

Bill and Melinda Gates Foundation

It all started with a single article appearing in *The New York Times* in 1997. The headline for the article written by Nickolas Kristof was "For Third

World, Water Is Still a Deadly Drink." In the article, Kristof describes how a family in rural India had to continuously address the challenge of having water that was safe to drink. The Bhagwani family had to use water that came from a pipe that ran into the slum where the family lived. The contaminated water they had gotten from the pipe had killed two of the children in the family, both under the age of 15 months. While the mother, Usha Bhagwani, knew that it was unsafe to drink the water without boiling it, there were few options available to the family. She stated that "I try to boil the water ... But the boys sometimes insist on drinking right away because they're thirsty." In addition, it was costly to boil water. It would cost approximately $4 a month in kerosene to boil water, which was almost one-third of Mrs. Bhagwani's earnings.

The underlying problem related to contaminated water is human waste. The water in the pipe the Bhagwani's used was contaminated with feces. There are numerous diseases and parasites that infect people globally due to fecal contamination. Contamination can occur in water, in food, or in the preparation of the food.[28]

It is from this article that Bill and Melinda Gates would eventually develop a non-profit foundation that spends billions of dollars annually to address corporate sustainability issues globally. In 2018, the Foundation spent over $5 billion in global programs related to development, health, growth and opportunity, and policy and advocacy.

For global development, the Foundation focuses on programs related to emergency response; global libraries; funding of their African and Indian Offices; maternal, newborn, and child health; family planning; and polio and vaccine delivery. Polio and vaccine delivery are the two largest expenditures accounting for 29 percent and 25 percent respectively. The Bill and Melinda Gates Foundation spent $1.817 billion on global development in 2018.

For global health, the Foundation spent $1.345 billion on social issues such as: life science partnerships; enteric and diarrheal diseases; vaccine development; neglected tropical diseases; pneumonia; tuberculosis; material newborn and child health discovery and tools; malaria; and HIV. Of these issues, the largest percentage of resources spent were for HIV at 16 percent and malaria at 15 percent.

For global growth and opportunity, the Foundation spent $646 million on areas such as: gender equality; water, sanitation and hygiene; financial services for the poor; and agricultural development. The largest expenditure was in agricultural development, which accounted for 61 percent of expenditures in this category.

For global policy and advocacy, the Foundation spent $501 million on social issues such as: philanthropic partnerships; tobacco control; development policy and finance; donor government relations; U.S. program advocacy and communications; global program advocacy and communications; and global fund core contributions. Global fund core contributions had the highest level of expenditures at 46 percent in this category.

The overall mission of the Bill and Melinda Gates Foundations is to make investments so that people around the world can live healthy, productive lives. The umbrella focus of the Foundation is to ensure that more children and young people survive and thrive; to be able to empower the poorest, especially women and girls, to transform their lives; to be able to combat infectious diseases that particularly affect the poorest in the world; and inspire people to take action to change the world.[29]

Questions for thought

1. IKEA has a very comprehensive strategy related to corporate sustainability and its suppliers. Do you think this type of relationship is common in Fortune 500 firms? Why or why not?
2. Do you think most people think about corporate sustainability issues related to supply chain and transportation? Why or why not?
3. What role should government play in encouraging firms to be proactive toward corporate sustainability?
4. Should taxpayer money be used to support corporate sustainability initiatives?
5. Why didn't major retailers such as the Gap, Walmart, and H&M demand better working conditions in Bangladesh before the Rana Plaza collapsed occurred?
6. Do you think it would take a major event like the Rana Plaza collapse for this type of government private partnership to take place in other countries which also have poor working conditions in factories?

Notes

1 Mette Andersen and Tage Skjoett-Larsen. 2009. Corporate Social Responsibility in Global Supply Chains. *Supply Chain Management: An International Journal.* 14(2):75–86.
2 www.ikea.com/ms/en_CA/about_ikea/pdf/IWAY_purchasing_home_furnishing_ products.pdf
3 Mette Andersen and Tage Skjoett-Larsen. 2009. Corporate Social Responsibility in Global Supply Chains. *Supply Chain Management: An International Journal.* 14(2): 79.
4 Mette Andersen and Tage Skjoett-Larsen. 2009. Corporate Social Responsibility in Global Supply Chains. *Supply Chain Management: An International Journal.* 14(2):75–86.
5 Mette Andersen and Tage Skjoett-Larsen. 2009. Corporate Social Responsibility in Global Supply Chains. *Supply Chain Management: An International Journal.* 14(2):75–86.
6 Mette Andersen and Tage Skjoett-Larsen. 2009. Corporate Social Responsibility in Global Supply Chains. *Supply Chain Management: An International Journal.* 14(2):75–86.
7 Constantin Blome and Anthony Paulraj. 2013. Ethical Climate and Purchasing Social Responsibility: A Benevolence Focus. *Journal of Business Ethics.* 116: 572.
8 Constantin Blome and Antony Paulraj. 2013. Ethical Climate and Purchasing Social Responsibility: A Benevolence Focus. *Journal of Business Ethics.* 116: 567–585.
9 Todd Litman and David Burwell. 2006. Issues in Sustainable Transportation. *International Journal of Global Environmental Issues.* 6(4): 337.
10 Todd Litman and David Burwell. 2006. Issues in Sustainable Transportation. *International Journal of Global Environmental Issues.* 6(4): 338.

11 Todd Litman and David Burwell. 2006. Issues in Sustainable Transportation. *International Journal of Global Environmental Issues*. 6(4): 338.
12 Todd Litman and David Burwell. 2006. Issues in Sustainable Transportation. *International Journal of Global Environmental Issues*. 6(4): 343.
13 Todd Litman and David Burwell. 2006. Issues in Sustainable Transportation. *International Journal of Global Environmental Issues*. 6(4): 331–347.
14 Peter Stanwick and Sarah Stanwick. 2015. The Garment Industry in Bangladesh: A Human Rights Challenge. *Journal of Business & Economic Policy*. 2(4): 40–44.
15 Jette Steen Knudsen. 2017. Government as a Regulator of CSR: Beyond Voluntarism. In eds. Andreas Rasche, Mette Morsing and Jeremy Moon. *Corporate Social Responsibility: Strategy, Communication, Governance*. Cambridge University Press: Cambridge, United Kingdom. 262.
16 Jette Steen Knudsen. 2017. Government as a Regulator of CSR: Beyond Voluntarism. In eds. Andreas Rasche, Mette Morsing and Jeremy Moon. *Corporate Social Responsibility: Strategy, Communication, Governance*. 246–271.
17 http://techreport.ngo/previous/2017/facts-and-stats-about-ngos-worldwide.html
18 www.ngoadvisor.net/ong/brac
19 www.msf.org/who-we-are
20 www.ngoadvisor.net/ong/msf
21 www.ngoadvisor.net/ong/danish-refugee-council
22 www.opensocietyfoundations.org/who-we-are
23 www.opensocietyfoundations.org/how-we-work
24 www.ngoadvisor.net/ong/mercy-corps
25 John Elkington and Shelly Fennell. 1998. Partners for Sustainability. *Greener Management International*. 24 Winter: 53.
26 John Elkington and Shelly Fennell. 1998. Partners for Sustainability. *Greener Management International*. 24 Winter: 56.
27 John Elkington and Shelly Fennell. 1998. Partners for Sustainability. *Greener Management International*. 24 Winter: 48–60.
28 Nicholas D. Kristof. 1997. For Third World, Water Is Still a Deadly Drink. *The New York Times*. January 9.
29 www.gatesfoundation.org/Who-We-Are/Resources-and-Media/Annual-Reports/Annual-Report-2018

9 Corporate sustainability communications and consumers

Introduction

All firms must be able to effectively manage the needs and expectations of their stakeholders. One of the primary methods used by firms is the development and maintenance of a comprehensive communication process with their stakeholders. This chapter highlights how firms can capture information, interpret and make decisions based on the information and then disseminate information to stakeholders. In addition, this chapter focuses on the interaction of the firm and its customers. It is critical that firms not only understand what the expectations are for their customers, but they must understand how to adjust their actions if those expectations are not being properly met. Concepts that are presented in this chapter include: the corporate sustainability communication process; communication styles; the phases in the development of corporate sustainability communication; communication in a corporate sustainability crisis; data privacy and consumers; social media influencers and corporate sustainability; consumer boycotts; and product recalls. The chapter opens with a description of the recall of Tylenol by Johnson & Johnson. The chapter concludes with a description of how MARS communicates its corporate sustainability strategy to its stakeholders.

The gold standard of product recalls: Johnson & Johnson and Tylenol

In 1982, reports surfaced that seven people had died in the Chicago area after taking Extra-Strength Tylenol capsules. The capsules were contaminated with cyanide. Even though Johnson & Johnson did not believe the company was at fault, it recalled all Tylenol capsules across the United States. The capsules were not contaminated during the manufacturing process but were altered at various retail stores in Chicago. The cyanide poison was injected into the capsules. The cost of the recall to Johnson & Johnson was approximately $100 million even though Johnson & Johnson was not at fault. Johnson & Johnson took responsibility for the illegal actions of others when it recalled its product. Furthermore, Johnson & Johnson recalled Tylenol even though it knew it did not have product recall coverage in its insurance policy. That information was confirmed when a federal judge in 1986 ruled that Johnson & Johnson and not its insurance company was responsible for the $100 million spent on recalling the Tylenol.[1]

As a communication process with its stakeholders, Johnson & Johnson set the standard for other firms to follow. Johnson & Johnson was able to react quickly to a crisis which it was not able to anticipate. Through its actions, Johnson & Johnson was able to demonstrate that it was willing to put the safety of its consumers ahead of any decisions related to legal liability. Johnson & Johnson blanketed different news sources to inform all its stakeholders of its actions. It created advertising for newspapers and television explaining its crisis response. It set up toll-free hotlines for consumers to ask questions about the recall and the safety of Tylenol. It also sent over 450,000 email messages to various concerned stakeholders about its crisis management strategy and the implementation of the strategy. Johnson & Johnson used its credo, which is similar to a code of ethics, to help guide the process to ensure the needs of the stakeholders were addressed.[2]

James Burke, CEO of Johnson & Johnson at the time, went on *60 Minutes* and *The Phil Donahue Show* to explain to the audience what Johnson & Johnson was doing to resolve the crisis. He was candid and compassionate while informing Johnson & Johnson stakeholders that they were implementing a course of action which would reinsure the consumer's faith in Tylenol and Johnson & Johnson products. Johnson & Johnson repackaged Tylenol to include a tamper-proof top. By the spring of 1983, the company had recaptured most of its lost market share.[3]

The corporate sustainability communications process

There are five steps in the corporate sustainability communication process: scanning and monitoring; conducting formative research; creating the corporate sustainability initiative; communicating the corporate sustainability initiative; and evaluating and providing feedback. The continuous loop of this process is shown in Figure 9.1.

Scanning and monitoring

Scanning and monitoring requires the firm to search its external environment in order to identify emerging social and environmental corporate sustainability concerns that can impact stakeholder relationships. The scanning and monitoring process also involves the identification and capturing of the vested interests of critical stakeholders.

The scanning process for corporate sustainability issues can include many forums. The firm must understand what current social issues are considered the highest importance for its stakeholders. As it scans and collects information from the external environment, the sources of information may include

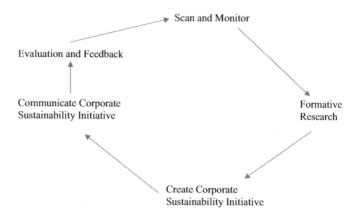

Figure 9.1 The corporate sustainability communications process[4]

activist discussions, potential government actions, reputation evaluations, and polling data results of government actions. The firm also needs to scan its internal environment to understand the current issues related to its own employees.

When scanning the external environment, the managers must be cognitive of the types of corporate sustainability issues which have a high priority for stakeholders. The managers must look at two critical factors: likelihood and impact of a corporate sustainability issue arising for its stakeholders. Likelihood refers to the potential that a specific corporate sustainability concern will attract enough interest from a variety of stakeholders. Impact refers to the effect that the corporate sustainability issue will have on society and the firm. Stakeholders expect and demand that firms address corporate sustainability concerns that have a potential future impact on society. These issues may also have a significant negative impact on the firm.

While environmental scanning focuses on identifying emerging corporate sustainability issues, monitoring involves doing an evaluation of the reaction by stakeholders to the firm's current corporate sustainability initiatives. This evaluation links the corporate sustainability initiative with the determination of whether its stakeholders are satisfied with the results of the initiative. Firms need to understand that past satisfaction of its initiatives does not guarantee future success. The factors that drive corporate sustainability expectations for stakeholders in the present may be very different than the expectations in the not too distant past.

Furthermore, any type of crisis can quickly change the level of stakeholder satisfaction. For example, BP's Deepwater Horizon disaster immediately changed how stakeholders perceived BP's operations. From previously being a pioneer in alternative energy, BP became the classic example of a company

Table 9.1 Ten critical questions for scanning and monitoring corporate sustainability issues[5]

1. What sources should be scanned for possible corporate sustainability concerns?
2. What sources should be monitored for possible corporate sustainability concerns?
3. Which stakeholder should be engaged in the scanning process?
4. Which stakeholders should be engaged in the monitoring process?
5. How will the engagement process for scanning be structured?
6. How will the engagement process for monitoring be structured?
7. Do stakeholders still consider the existing corporate sustainability initiatives to be relevant?
8. How are stakeholders reacting to current corporate sustainability initiatives?
9. Have any events occurred that suggest the need to modify expectations or efforts?
10. What criteria should be used for the preliminary identification and assessment of corporate sustainability concerns?

only focusing on its shareholders instead of its other critical stakeholders as thousands upon thousands of barrels of crude oil were being released into the Gulf of Mexico.

Both scanning and monitoring are considered continuous activities since "real-time" information is needed to interpret real-time concerns, resulting in real-time solutions. Scanning and monitoring are complementary activities since scanning identifies potentially new corporate sustainability concerns and monitoring accesses current corporate sustainability concerns. A list of critical questions that should be addressed by the firm related to scanning and monitoring activities in shown in Table 9.1.

Formative research

Formative research focuses on the potential opportunities to benefit society and the firm as well as to identify problems that may have a negative impact on society and the potential reputation of the firm. In this step, the information is collected and evaluated in order to convert corporate sustainability concerns into corporate sustainability initiatives. The collection and evaluation of the information is a valuable tool in order to begin the process of creating and maintaining critical stakeholder engagement at each step of the communication process. It is through this stakeholder engagement that the firm can understand the expectations of the stakeholders and then is able to identify any gaps between what the company is currently doing and what the stakeholders expect the firm should be doing. This information is a foundational resource in creating an active dialogue with stakeholders.

From the information that is collected about each corporate sustainability concern, the concerns are evaluated based on potential problems and opportunities. For the opportunities, the focus of the corporate sustainability issue is the potential benefit of an initiative for the firm and society. For the problem component of the concern, an examination focuses on the potential negative effects on the

Table 9.2 Corporate sustainability issues and their critical stakeholders[6]

Stakeholder	Issue					
	Climate change and environment	*Customer service*	*Health, safety, and security*	*Human rights*	*Supply chain responsibility*	*Diversity and inclusion*
Charities and NGOs	X	X	X	X	X	X
Customers	X	X	X	X		
Employees	X	X	X	X	X	X
Government	X	X	X	X		X
Investors	X	X	X	X		
Communities	X	X	X			X
Regulators	X	X	X			
Suppliers	X		X	X	X	X
Trade unions				X	X	X

firm and society. For each specific corporate sustainability issue, the firm must identify the critical stakeholders that can be fundamentally impacted by the actions of the firm when addressing or ignoring the issue. An example of the identification of issues and stakeholders in presented in Table 9.2.

The firm can use numerous research methods to identify stakeholder engagement, including archival research, interviews, real-time media analysis, surveys, panels, and focus groups. Based on the accumulation and interpretation of the data collected through these sources, the firm will determine whether or not to pursue an action on the corporate sustainability concern. One of the objectives in deciding whether to act on the corporate sustainability concern is to determine whether there is an expectations gap.

An expectations gap occurs when the firm has not been proactive in identifying stakeholder concerns and the stakeholders confront the firm. The firm must respond in a reactive manner. There are three major causes for a firm having an expectations gap with its stakeholders: organic, expose, and villain.

Organic gap

An organic gap appears when shifts occur in a corporate sustainability issue over time and the firm has not been able to continuously adjust its corporate sustainability commitment. For example, climate change has become more of a dominant discussion point for numerous stakeholders, yet some firms have not been able to implement corporate sustainability initiatives to keep up with the escalating expectations of the stakeholders. The proper course of action for the firm is to implement continuous alignments so that a gap does not grow between the firm and its stakeholders.

Expose gap

An expose gap occurs when one or more of the firm's stakeholders reveal information that was not transparently presented to the stakeholders. The release of this information usually reveals how a firm's claim of its corporate sustainability commitment is either exaggerated or is untrue. Exposes are dangerous for a firm because the firm is "ambushed" by this revealed information without any preparation. The expose will also have a significant negative impact on the firm since it can erode the trust the firm has with the stakeholders and raise doubt about the overall credibility of the information released by the firm. This weakening of credibility and trust could result in a direct threat to the firm's reputation from all of its stakeholders.

Villain gap

A firm is portrayed as a villain when activist stakeholders, usually NGOs, target a firm in a series of attacks. This confrontation is ongoing with each side refuting the attacks of the other side while demonstrating why their actions are correct and valid. An example would be the NGO, People for the Ethical Treatment of Animals (PETA), continuously attacking firms that use animal testing as part of the research and development process.

A more desirable action by the firm is to decide on the relevance of the corporate sustainability concern based on alignment. In this proactive stance, the firm anticipates future concerns and makes adjustments before the stakeholders demand that the firm take action. Therefore, it is critical to ask the correct questions in order to ensure a firm relies on alignment instead of adjustment of the expectation gap. A list of relevant questions to ask are shown in Table 9.3.

Table 9.3 Critical questions for formative research[7]

---

1. What sources of information should be utilized in the formative research?
2. Which stakeholders should be engaged in the formative research?
3. How will the engagement process for formative research be structured?
4. Do the stakeholders perceive the engagement process as just?
5. Which stakeholders could be positively affected by the corporate sustainability concern?
6. Which stakeholders could be negatively affected by the corporate sustainably concern?
7. How salient is the corporate sustainability concern to stakeholders?
8. Are there expectation gaps?
9. How should each gap be addressed?
10. Is there a possibility to use the alignment approach – is a social concern emerging?
11. Is there a chance for the firm to become an industry leader on an emerging corporate sustainability concern?
12. How might the firm utilize an alignment approach beyond being an industry leader?

Creating the corporate sustainability initiative

The creation of the corporate sustainability initiative converts the corporate sustainability concern into practice. The information collected in the formative research process is used in order to plan the concrete actions involving the firm and its stakeholders. Since different stakeholders have different corporate sustainability priorities, it is challenging to present an initiative that will satisfy all relevant stakeholder expectations.

Stakeholder engagement is critical at this step since the stakeholders need to be involved in the discussion of the proposed initiatives and objectives. The more vested the stakeholders are with the initiative, the more they will take ownership of the successful implementation of the initiative and its objectives.

A critical factor in the development of a corporate sustainability initiative is the firm's determination as to what role the stakeholders play in the decision-making process of stakeholder engagement. Stakeholder engagement requires collaborative decision making in order to get a satisfactory result. However, collaborative decision making requires the firm to share some of its power with its stakeholders. Stakeholder participation can range from simple involvement to collaboration to empowerment.

Involvement occurs when the firm wants to understand the stakeholders' concerns and desires and asks the stakeholder to contribute that information. The feedback received is used as part of the decision-making process in the development of the initiative. The stakeholders do not have a direct voice in the decision, but their input can be used to address the stakeholders' concerns.

Table 9.4 Critical questions for creating the corporate sustainability initiatives[8]

---

1. Which stakeholders should be engaged in creating the corporate sustainability initiative?
2. How does the firm assess stakeholder power, legitimacy, and urgency?
3. How will the engagement process for creating the corporate sustainability initiative be structured?
4. What level of collaborative decision making will be utilized in the engagement process?
5. What type of decision-making approach will be used?
6. What are the stated stakeholder objectives for the corporate sustainability initiative?
7. What are the measureable benefits of the initiative for stakeholders?
8. Which stakeholder will benefit from the initiative and how will they benefit?
9. Which stakeholders may be upset by the initiative, and why?
10. How consistent is the corporate sustainability concern with the firm's current business strategy?
11. How well does the corporate sustainability concern fit with the firm's industry?
12. What are the potential costs and benefits of the corporate sustainability concern to the firm?
13. Where can the firm make the most difference related to corporate sustainability initiatives?

If the firm embraces collaboration with its stakeholders, the firm is allowing the stakeholders to have a say in both the development of the corporate sustainability initiatives as well as the selection of the initiatives that will be implemented by the firm. Collaboration is an effective tool used by the firm when the issue is contentious, and the firm needs the support of the stakeholders in accepting the initiative.

The third and least likely option available for the firm to engage with its stakeholders is empowerment. It is the rarest option since firms do not want to give up the power and control to determine the initiative. Through empowerment, the firm is allowing the stakeholders to make the final decision on what the corporate sustainability initiative should be to address the concerns of the stakeholders. A list of the relevant questions related to creating corporate sustainability initiatives is shown in Table 9.4.

Communicating the corporate sustainability initiative

The communication of the corporate sustainability initiative involves facilitating the learning process for both the internal and external stakeholders about the initiative. The responsibilities of the firm include ensuring that the content of the initiative is conveyed effectively to those stakeholders who will be potentially impacted by the initiative.

One of the underlying challenges for any firm when it describes its corporate sustainability initiatives is the potential backlash from stakeholders. This backlash is the basis of the promotional communication dilemma where stakeholders become cynical and skeptical based on the perception that the firm has excessively promoted itself with its link to corporate sustainability.

The ability to communicate its corporate sustainability commitment can be a double-edged sword by wanting to inform its stakeholders of its action but not in a narcissistic manner. Stakeholders can become skeptical if it appears that the firm is trying "too hard" to show what a wonderful firm it is through its corporate sustainability commitment. One communication method which stakeholders may not like is the firm's message tone. Message

Table 9.5 Critical questions for communicating the corporate sustainability initiative[9]

1. Which internal and external stakeholders should be targeted?
2. How should the corporate sustainability message be communicated to internal and external stakeholders?
3. Which communication channels should be used to reach internal and external stakeholders?
4. What steps can be taken to prevent a backlash from overpromotion?
5. What potential exists for using social media to communicate the corporate sustainability concern?
6. What potential exist for third-party endorsements?

tone occurs when the firm repeats the same message multiple times and the message is too prominent in the communication pattern. Stakeholders prefer a low-key approach where the firm focuses on the facts of its initiatives rather than focusing on the promotion of the firm's involvement in the initiatives.

Stakeholders also look for third-party endorsements of the firm's actions in communications to stakeholders. This type of endorsement helps legitimize the message sent to the stakeholders since an external source is supporting the actions of the firm. The relevant questions related to communicating the corporate sustainability initiatives are shown in Table 9.5.

Evaluation and feedback

Evaluation and feedback allow the firm to be able to determine if the corporate sustainability process and the objectives of the initiative are met. The evaluation process includes gauging the impact the initiative has on society, stakeholders, and the firm itself. The firm must be transparent in the information provided to stakeholders and needs to solicit feedback from stakeholders related to the process and the outcomes of the corporate sustainability initiatives. The evaluation and feedback phase provides the foundation for the next reiteration of the scanning and monitoring phase of the communication process. The communication process is a closed circle in which communication with the firm's stakeholders is continuously updated, monitored, and evaluated in its quest to be proactive related to corporate sustainability.

There should be a formal process to capture the feedback from the stakeholders as well as the evaluation of the effectiveness of the corporate sustainability initiative. Some critical questions that the firm needs to answer related to evaluation and feedback are shown in Table 9.6.[10]

Table 9.6 Critical questions for evaluation and feedback[11]

---

1. What evidence is there to support that the corporate sustainability initiative met the stakeholders' and firm's objectives?
2. Is there a need for third-party verification of the corporate sustainability evaluation?
3. Which stakeholders should be involved in the evaluation process?
4. What role do stakeholders play in the evaluation process?
5. Do stakeholders feel that the corporate sustainability initiative has sufficiently addressed the corporate sustainably concern?
6. Do stakeholders feel the initiative is effective?
7. What might be done to improve the initiative?
8. Do stakeholders feel the overall corporate sustainability process was just?
9. Is a corporate sustainability audit warranted?
10. Were there any unintended consequences from the corporate sustainability initiative?

Communication style and corporate sustainability

In order to effectively communicate to its stakeholders, the firm must ensure that there is a clear link between its actions and the contributions those actions have with society. The firm must be seen as a positive contributor to both local and global communities with corporate sustainability initiatives. The second dimension is that the communication needs to be perceived as sincere. The managers of firms must present corporate sustainability initiatives in not only strategic, technical, and rational terms but also show their own personal and emotional commitment to the initiatives. The third dimension is transparency. By being open and willing to engage in a dialogue with stakeholders, the firm must present the perspective that it is not hiding any relevant information that stakeholders may use to evaluate the firm's corporate sustainability commitment. Transparency includes not only actions by the firm but also any non-actions.

In order to effectively communicate the firm's message to its stakeholders, the firm must decide on its corporate sustainability communication strategies. There are three types of strategies: stakeholder information, stakeholder response, and stakeholder involvement strategy. A summary of these three strategies is shown in Table 9.7.

Stakeholder information strategy

For the stakeholder information strategy, the communication is perceived as a vehicle for telling the stakeholders instead of merely listening to them. Since the communication occurs in only one direction from the firm to the stakeholders, the purpose of the communication is to disseminate information that informs its external stakeholders about the actions of the firm related to corporate sustainability. The description of the firm's actions is linked to how these actions benefit society. In this communication strategy, the managers believe

Table 9.7 Corporate sustainability communication strategies[12]

Corporate sustainability communication ideal	Stakeholder information strategy	Stakeholder response strategy	Stakeholder involvement strategy
Direction of communication	One-way	Two-way asymmetric	Two-way symmetric
Corporate communication task	Design appealing corporate sustainability concept message	Identify relevant stakeholders	Build relationships on issues of shared concerns
Managerial communication task	Inform about favorable corporate sustainability action	Demonstrate integration of corporate sustainability concern	Establish proactive dialogue with stakeholders
Engagement of stakeholders	Unnecessary	Considered in surveys, rankings, and opinion polls	Central involvement in development of corporate sustainability

that the actions of the firm are valid and credible in supporting the firm's corporate sustainability commitment The purpose of the communication is to tell the stakeholders the firm's "story" on how it is helping society so the firm does not need any input from its stakeholders.

Stakeholder response strategy

For the stakeholder response strategy, the communication is two way and asymmetrical. The firm engages in a dialogue and listens to its stakeholders in order to understand the stakeholders' concerns. Based on the information from the stakeholders, the firm designs the corporate sustainability messages that will hopefully be endorsed by the stakeholders. This communication strategy is commandingly used in corporate sustainability reports and the firm's response to surveys, rankings, and opinion polls based on public assessment and critique.

Stakeholder involvement strategy

The stakeholder involvement strategy is based on a two-way symmetric communication between the firm and its stakeholders. The interaction and exchange of information is based on an ongoing dialogue between the firm and its stakeholders. In this strategic focus, both the firm and the stakeholders seek to influence the decisions of each other related to the firm's commitment to corporate sustainability. Both the stakeholders and the firm should be willing to make changes in their beliefs based on the dialogue. The stakeholder involvement occurs when firms engage in multi-stakeholder initiatives and partnerships with NGOs.

Three phases in the development of corporate sustainability communication

There are three phases in the development of corporate sustainability communication. The three phases are: instrumental, political, and network. A summary of three phases is shown in Table 9.8.

Instrumental phase of corporate sustainability communication

The instrumental phase of corporate sustainability communication is based on the underlying philosophy that the mission of any firm is to maximize its level of profitability. The role of communication is to inform the firm's stakeholders about the firm's activities. The corporate sustainability communication focuses on the positive activities of the firm as a method to influence the perceptions of the firm. A common medium used in an instrumental phase is to release a corporate sustainability report highlighting how the firm is helping society. This report would include information which is integrated with the firm's marketing strategy, its branding strategy, and its public relations strategy. This communication strategy is viewed as a method of improving the firm's image and reputation.

Table 9.8 Three phases in the development of corporate sustainability communication[13]

	Instrumental	Political	Network
Institutional characteristics			
Central actor	Firm	Firm with its stakeholders	Networks
Company-social relations	Market mechanism: consumption	Societal development: deliberative processes	Networks: fluid, non-hierarchical relations
Corporate sustainability communication focus			
Corporate focus on corporate sustainability communication	Control-orientation	Consensus-orientation	Conflicting-orientation
Corporate sustainability communication is a:	... means to build favorable reputation	... means to enhance deliberate dialogue to improve action	... communicative action that mobilizes new communicative actions
Manager communication rule	To inform commercially important stakeholders	To engage with politically influential stakeholders and build consensus	To engage and contribute to critical debate in socially alert networks

Political phase of corporate sustainability communication

The political phase of corporate sustainability communication is based on the premise that firms are able to exert a significant level of influence on society. This influence is based not only on its economic importance but also its ability to influence the norms and values that are incorporated in the overall development of society. Since firms are engaging in social and environmental issues of public concern, the firms can influence not only its customers but also the agendas of policymakers, NGOs, and civil society. The communication focus of the firm becomes an activity in which norms and values are adjusted based on the political boundaries allowed for firms. One of the challenges with this approach is that the firm may become embedded in a highly complex political issue in which the firm is seen as a political actor supporting a specific side of a political debate.

Network phase of corporate sustainability communication

The network phase of corporate sustainability communication is based on the premise that firms are embedded in society and are one point in a societal-based network. The underlying belief is that corporate sustainability communication is not a simple mechanism that is employed by firms to convey messages, but is a continuous process in which different actors in society interact to construct, negotiate, and modify the norms and values of society.

The network phase incorporates the view that managers are not the only ones who have legitimate ideas and interests for what constitutes a firm's corporate sustainability commitment. The challenge for managers in this phase is the ability to engage in ongoing communication processes from the firm's stakeholders while the firm's own social responsibilities are being challenged, defined, and redefined. The explosion of social media has allowed those who previously did not have a voice on a firm's corporate sustainability commitment to be able to be heard globally. This type of social networking makes it difficult for firms to ignore the organic power of the global network. While in the past, firms have been able to have strict control on the type and quality of information released to the public, advances in technology no longer give firms the luxury to be opaque.[14]

Communication in a corporate sustainability crisis

One of the most challenging tests for a firm is how it handles a crisis. The challenge is not only what actions are needed and implemented to resolve the crisis but also how the firm is able to communicate its actions to its stakeholders. As part of its strategic emergency disaster plans, the firm must have a coordinated effort in the release of information which satisfies the expectations of its stakeholders.

An organization crisis can be defined as an extraordinary condition that is disruptive and potentially damaging to the firm's operations. The crisis of a firm can be categorized on two major dimensions. The first dimension is whether the crisis is internal or external in nature. The second dimension is whether the crisis is normal or abnormal. The determination of the frequency can significantly impact the actions of the firm and the communication content and medium of the interaction with its stakeholders. A 2×2 matrix summarizing the interaction of the two dimensions is shown in Table 9.9.[15]

Internal–normal crisis

These are the most predictable crises for a firm with respect to timing and magnitude. The impact of this type of crisis is limited to the firm and its stakeholders. Due to its predictability, the firm should have a crisis response plan in place which includes how the firm disseminates information to the relevant stakeholders. Some examples of internal-normal crises are BP's Deepwater Horizon oil rig releasing thousands of barrels of oil into the Gulf of Mexico and NASA's Challenger Shuttle disaster. Since the crisis occurs within the firm and there is a relatively high level of predictability that over time a crisis can occur, the firm is able to develop protocols addressing these types of crises. Incorporated within those protocols should be a procedure describing how the firm should communicate with its stakeholders. The protocol would determine what mediums to use for communicating, what type of information should be disclosed, how the stakeholders can be

Table 9.9 Typology of crisis responses by the firm[16]

	Normal	Abnormal
Internal	– Crisis occurs within the firm and is relatively predictable – Crisis is firm-specific – One firm suffers – Crisis can be anticipated and prepared for *Examples:* – Physical crisis (industrial accident, product failure/recall) – Personnel crisis (strike, key employees leaving, workplace violence, vandalism, sexual harassment)	– Crisis occurs within the firm and is unpredictable – Crisis should be loosely expected – Crisis is firm-specific *Examples:* – Criminal crisis (executive hostage situation, corporate scandal) – Information crisis (information theft, copyright infringement, data tampering) – Other (product/brand boycott, firm-specific cyberattacks)
External	– Crisis occurs outside the firm – Crisis is relatively predictable – Crisis should be loosely expected – Crisis can affect multiple firms – All relevant firms suffer *Examples:* – Economic crisis (depression, hostile takeover, currency markets collapse) – Industry crisis (supplier failure, technology, obsolescence, industrial espionage, product) – Other (industry-wide cyberattacks)	– All relevant firms suffer – Crisis originates outside the firm – Crisis usually impossible to anticipate – Flexibility enables adequate response – No finalized response until crisis ceases *Examples:* – Political crisis (terrorism, war, expropriation) – Industry deregulation (legal changes, privatization) – Reputation crisis (malicious rumors, slander, logo tampering) – Natural disasters (earthquake, tsunami)

involved in the communication process, and the timing of the release of information to the public.

External-normal crisis

This type of crisis is also predictable; however, it impacts multiple firms. For example, when there is an economic slowdown in the economy, all industries related to tourism may be affected since people will not travel if they have lost their jobs or are worried about losing their jobs. When there is an external industry crisis such as the failure of a major supplier, all the firms that use that supplier will be negatively impacted. This type of crisis may impact only selected stakeholders. In an economic downturn, the employees of the firm will be the most critical stakeholder since this could result in them losing their jobs. For an external crisis like a supplier failure, the shareholders will be concerned about the impact this crisis would have on the level of profitability of the firm.

Since these types of crises can be expected over time, the firm must have a communication plan to address the concerns of the stakeholders that are directly impacted by the crisis. The firm needs to tailor the information and the information flow to its stakeholders. During an economic downturn, the firm must be transparent to its employees of the financial condition of the firm and what actions must be taken by the firm. The firm must also ensure that there is a channel of communication for the employees so they can ask managers for specific details relevant to the actions of the firm.

Internal-abnormal crisis

An internal-abnormal crisis originates within the firm and is considered to be rare and unpredictable with respect to its magnitude and consequences. Since the crisis is unpredictable, it is difficult for the firm to have a crisis plan in effect before the crisis occurs. An example of this type of crisis is when the firm's CEO suddenly leaves or dies. Based on how dynamic the competitive environment is for the firm, the firm may need to find an immediate replacement, yet that type of replacement may not be the optimal course of action. Another example of this type of crisis occurs when financial fraud has been committed by the top-level executives of the firm. This type of ethical scandal needs to be resolved quickly to restore the trust the stakeholders have with the firm. However, the firm may not have a preplanned course of action developed in this rare case within the firm.

From the stakeholders' perspective, there can be great concern about the viability and sustainability of a firm which must address an internal-abnormal crisis. For the relevant stakeholders, the firms must first identify the uniqueness of this event so that they are not "blamed" for failing to plan ahead for this crisis. The firm must also be transparent in communicating how it is resolving the crisis. Since the resolution is being developed in real time, the firm must be careful not to release information before it can be confirmed and supported by the firm. In addition, the firm must ensure that there is the establishment of a communication channel for the relevant stakeholders to develop a dialogue on how the resolution of the crisis will impact them.

External–abnormal crisis

Since the crisis is outside the firm and is not common, this type of crisis is idiosyncratic and almost impossible to anticipate. The net effect is that multiple firms are impacted by the crisis. The terrorist attacks on the United States on September 11, 2001 had significant impact on multiple industries including the tourist industry. Directly after the attacks, many people were afraid to fly on airplanes and, therefore, cancelled their trips, which not only impacted the airline industry but also the hotel industry. Natural disasters such as Hurricane Katrina in 2005 impacted numerous businesses across the Gulf Coast of the United States, including some businesses located in Louisiana and Mississippi.

Consumers and corporate sustainability

Data privacy

The internet has allowed firms to collect, store, and analyze data on every consumer who interacts with a firm. This type of data collection can result in numerous corporate sustainability issues related to privacy rights of the consumers. Through the use of its information technology systems, managers are able to have unlimited access to information on individuals which would be considered private and personal. The firms are also able to capture information at great speeds and can permanently store and have access to private personal information from critical stakeholders including customers, employees, suppliers, and even special interest groups. Firms also have the ability to have access to the information history of any person for which data has been collected by the firm.[17]

Data brokers

The collection of data is so valuable that there are firms called data brokers who collect information about consumers and then sell the data to other firms including other data brokers. Data brokers do not have a direct relationship with the individuals they have collected data from, so customers are not aware of these firms and they are not aware that their information is bought and sold to various firms without their knowledge or consent.

Data brokers collect data from public records such as property records, court records, drivers' licenses, and motor vehicle records. They can also obtain data from census data, birth certificates, marriage licenses, divorce records, state, professional and recreational license records, voter registration information, and bankruptcy records. Data brokers can also obtain data through collection or purchase from commercial sources that have consumer purchasing histories. Information can also be collected from social media sites, web browsing activities, apps, media reports, websites, and other publicly available sources.

Even when consumers are aware of both data brokers and the type of information that is collected on them, there is still no easy method for the consumer to control the information. Furthermore, some data brokers store all of their data indefinitely even if corrections had been made to the inaccurate data.

There are three categories of data brokers. The first category consists of search sites where a user can input a piece of data such as a person's name and the search result will display all the related personal information of the search person. Some of the more popular websites for people searches are Spokeo, PeekYou, and PeopleSmart.

The second category of data brokers are those that focus on marketing. Divisions of Experian and Equifax has this feature in which the firm develops a dossier of everyone based on the data collected and that information is used to target customized marketing to that person. These data brokers will categorize consumers based on age, ethnicity, education level, income, number of children, and hobbies. The marketers would use these profiles to develop personally tailored marketing promotions such as discounts and coupons.

The third type of data brokers use ID Analytics that can verify identities and help detect fraud. The problem for the consumer is if you have the same name as a person who is suspected of fraud, based on the results of the ID Analytics, the person who did not commit fraud may have their credit history incorrectly frozen. A related concern is using information from a data broker to steal a person's identify or use their credit history.[18]

Social media influencers and corporate sustainability

Social media has become the dominant method for millions of people to communicate with one another, to receive their local and global news, and to be able to purchase goods from anywhere in the world. Embedded in social media are influencers. Social media influencers describe things they do and products they like. Then, the followers are influenced into following the advice of the influencer.

Social media influencers have become a global marketing tool of firms who want to target specific customer groups which correspond with the followers of the influencers. However, the influencers must identify any products for which they were given financial compensation to endorse. The corporate sustainability issue is misleading the followers when the influencers fail to report the endorsement. Without the "#ad, #spon, or #partner" identification with a product, the followers are led to believe that the influencer actually uses the product because he or she likes the product. The Federal Trade Commission (FTC) has regulations that require these endorsements be identified by the influencer if the influencer has received financial compensation for the endorsement. The FTC defines financial compensation as not only money but also includes free products and other items with financial value.

A 2018 study of influencers conducted by eMarketer found that only 41 percent of the influencers who responded to the study labelled their endorsements with FTC mandated hashtags when they were explicitly asked to label the content, and 7 percent of the respondents admitted that they never label any of their sponsored content.

Because of the potential lack of trust and credibility, consumers are becoming savvier in questioning the endorsements of influencers. For example, a 2018 study by Bazaarvoice found that 47 percent of customers were tired of influencer content that appears to be unauthentic, and 62 percent of customers in the survey believe that influencer endorsements take advantage of impressionable audiences.

A related social issue is the authenticity of the followers of an influencer. Influencers can purchase followers or have a high number of automated bots which can make up a significant number of followers. In a 2019 study conducted by Hit Search, the results showed that 98 percent of the respondents had spotted an influencer's Instagram follower count rise in an unnaturally high manner usually over a very short time period. This could have been caused by the influencer using bots to grow quickly or having bought a large number of fake account followers.[19]

Consumer boycotts and corporate sustainability

The origin of the term boycott comes from Charles C. Boycott who was an English estate manager for wealthy landowners in Ireland. In 1880, the farmers who were working on the land managed by Boycott had a poor harvest. The farmers asked Boycott to reduce the land rent and Boycott refused. The farmers refused to work the land and people in the local community led peaceful protests to complain about the unfair treatment they were given by Boycott. Boycott became isolated and ostracized in the local community and the term boycott was created.

A consumer boycott can be defined as an attempt by one or more parties to achieve certain specific objectives related to a firm or firms by urging consumers to refuse to do business with the firm(s). Traditionally, boycotts are started by special interest groups or NGOs that disagree with the actions of the firm related to one of the causes of the NGOs. The primary goals of a boycott are twofold. The first is to increase awareness to the general public of the perceived inappropriate actions of the firm. The second goal is to punish the firm financially be reducing its sales and profits with a decrease of purchases by the consumers. The solution for consumer boycotts is for the firm to understand the issues presented by the group or group protesting and adjust its decision-making processes to incorporate these social issues that are being protested by this select group of people.

Boycotts can result in fundamental changes in society. The bus boycott in Montgomery, Alabama in 1955 created the start of the Civil Rights movement. The emergence of Mahatma Gandhi in India was based on a boycott of British sales of cloth. The increasing pressure of global boycotts of products and services facilitated the dismantling of apartheid in South Africa.

Boycotts are usually triggered by one or more events which become the "final straw" for the special interest groups or NGOs. This event creates a negative perception toward the firm and consumers through information obtained by the interest groups who evaluate whether they want to do business with the firm.

The determination of whether a consumer will boycott a firm is based on four factors: the desire to make a difference; the scope of self-enhancement; counterarguments that inhibit boycotting; and the cost to the boycotter of constrained consumption.

The desire to make a difference

The underlying belief of an individual's desire to make a difference is that a firm will change its behavior if the individual participates in a boycott. The message that the individual wants to convey to the firm and other firms in the industry is that the actions of the firms are unacceptable, and the boycott will continue until the firm's behavior changes. The individual's belief is based on perceived efficacy. Perceived efficacy is the belief that the individual along with others has the power to achieve the collective goal of changing the behavior of the firm.

The scope of self-enhancement

The scope of self-enhancement refers to the intrinsic benefits of the individual when he or she participates in a boycott. The individual has an internal good feeling about him/herself by participating in the boycott because they are actively doing something to create change. There is also a utilitarian belief that by participating the individual is helping others, which also enhances the high level of satisfaction in the actions of the individual. The individuals can increase both social and personal self-esteem by supporting a cause in which the goal is to correct the unjust actions of a firm.

Counterarguments that inhibit boycotting

The third factor is the evaluation by the individual to determine what would be possible negative outcomes by participating in the boycott. A counterargument for boycotting sweatshop conditions for factory workers in different parts of the world would be that this may be the only avenue available for these workers to earn a wage. Furthermore, a boycott may lead to the closing of the factory, which would displace all of the workers. Another counterargument is that individually a person does not have the power to change how a firm makes decisions. Therefore, it is considered a "waste of time" to join a boycott because no change will occur.

Cost to the boycotter of constrained consumption

A direct cost for an individual who boycotts the firm's product is that the individual no longer has access to those products. If the individual is a heavy user of the firm's products, there will be a significant negative impact on the individual's way of living. For the individual to commit to the boycott, the "cause" must be more important than the loss of the firm's products.

Product recalls and corporate sustainability

There are several reasons for a firm to recall a product. Some examples are a design flaw, a production defect, new scientific information linking a health danger to the product, or the contamination of the product during the manufacturing process.

The steps of a product recall

There are four primary steps in a firm's recall of a product: policy and planning; product development; communications and logistics; and information systems.

Policy and planning

Top-level managers of the firm need to set the tone for the procedures of the recall process. The process begins with the firm having a crisis management plan already established in case of a recall. Since the firm needs to resolve the crisis as soon as possible, the firm does not have the flexibility of spending time making decisions on what the procedure should be. Those decisions need to be made before the crisis occurs. The procedures should include the development of instruction manuals and the assignment of specific responsibilities to employees during the recall process which correspond with the development of a response team.

Product development

The firm should have in place safeguards to make sure the product is safe and therefore a recall is not needed. These safeguards could include total quality management techniques, as well as evaluation of its current products to verify that the products meet the quality and safety standards that have been established. Once a recall has occurred, an evaluation of the product is needed to make any necessary adjustments to the design and composition of the product to reduce the probability that a recall will occur in the future.

Communications

Before a recall takes place, the firm must identify the critical stakeholders that will be affected by a recall. The recall procedure should be included in the corporate crisis communications plan. Once a recall has been announced, the firm must act quickly to communicate what the product issues are and what the course of action will be to resolve the crisis. It is critical for the firm to present a clear, honest, and transparent message to all critical stakeholders. The firm also needs to present to the stakeholder a timeline spanning from when the recall was announced to the crisis resolution is expected to occur.

Logistics and information systems

Before a recall occurs, the firm must establish a traceability system for the product as well as provide a mechanism to ensure that managers are quickly notified of product defects throughout the firm. Once the recall has been announced, the firm needs to trace the product and develop a recall-management information and logistics systems. After the recall has taken place, the firm must continue to maintain recall logistics after the recall deadline in case some of the recall products continue to come back to the company after the deadline.[20]

MARS: using corporate sustainability to communicate to its stakeholders

Probably best known for its chocolate bars, MARS is a global player in not only confectionary but also other divisions, which are: MARS Petcare, MARS Food such as Uncle Ben's rice, and MARS Edge which focuses on improving human health through targeted nutrition.[21]

Founded over 100 years ago, MARS has over 125,000 employees working in 80 countries. The five principles guiding MARS's vision is quality, responsibility, mutually, efficiency, and freedom. MARS embraces quality of not only its products but also its contribution to society. Embracing responsibility of both the individual and the firm to act now helps to solve social issues. MARS makes its decisions based on mutuality of the benefits to its stakeholders. MARS uses efficiency to maximize the use of its resources and has the financial freedom to be able to make its own decisions.[22]

This type of comprehensive commitment to its stakeholders is fostered by its strong communication links with them. MARS asks its stakeholders to actively participate in activities that address corporate sustainability issues. This active participation is based on an agreement in the form of a planet pledge. Individuals can share their pledge on Facebook, Twitter, and Instagram. The pledge includes agreeing to drive less since road transport accounts for 17 percent of global greenhouse gas emissions. The stakeholders also agree to buy local produce since it not only reduces the individual carbon footprint but can reduce the amount of food that is lost, wasted, or spoiled.

The MARS Earth Pledge also includes using reusable products since up to 5 trillion single-use plastic bags are annually polluting global oceans. The pledge asks stakeholders to say yes to five-minute showers to reduce the amount of wasted water. Saying yes to unplugging electronics is also part of the pledge since households use approximately 30 percent of all global energy. In addition, the pledge encourages recycling since it is estimated that by 2025, there could be up to 250 million tons of mismanaged waste ending up in landfills.

Saying yes to renewable energy to power individual houses is part of the pledge since renewable energy can be cost effective and reduce greenhouse gas emissions. The pledge also includes saying yes to repurposing old clothing since it not only saves space in landfills, but it takes 10,000 liters of water to produce one pair of jeans. The final component of the pledge is to refill and reuse plastic bottles since one million plastic bottles are purchased every minute and then discarded. Discarded plastic bottles generate over 300 million tons of plastic waste annually.[23]

Questions for thought

1. How likely do you think it is that a Fortune 500 company would spend $100 million on a recall which was not the company's fault?
2. How effective do you think firms are in communicating with stakeholders about corporate sustainability issues?
3. Does the perceived severity of a corporate sustainability crisis depend on its location in the world and type of industry? Why or why not?
4. Do you worry about having a lack of control over your personal data on the internet?
5. Do you follow social media influencers? If you do, do you buy products that they recommend?
6. Have you ever had to return a product because of a company recall? If you did, how easy was the process?

Notes

1 Peter A. Stanwick and Sarah D. Stanwick. 2016. *Understanding Business Ethics.* Third Edition. Sage Publications: Thousand Oaks, CA.
2 Peter Snyder, Molly Hall, Joline Robertson, Tomasz Jasinski and Janice S. Miller. 2006. Ethical Rationality: A Strategic Approach to Organizational Crisis. *Journal of Business Ethics.* 63: 371–383.
3 Andrew Caesar-Gordon. 2015. The Perfect Crisis Response? *PRWeek.* October 28.
4 W. Timothy Coombs and Sherry J. Holladay. 2012. *Managing Corporate Social Responsibility: A Communication Approach.* First Edition. Wiley-Blackwell: Malden, MA. 47.
5 W. Timothy Coombs and Sherry J. Holladay. 2012. *Managing Corporate Social Responsibility: A Communication Approach.* First Edition. Wiley-Blackwell: Malden, MA. 61.
6 W. Timothy Coombs and Sherry J. Holladay. 2012. *Managing Corporate Social Responsibility: A Communication Approach.* First Edition. Wiley-Blackwell: Malden, MA. 64.
7 W. Timothy Coombs and Sherry J. Holladay. 2012. *Managing Corporate Social Responsibility: A Communication Approach.* First Edition. Wiley-Blackwell: Malden, MA. 86.
8 W. Timothy Coombs and Sherry J. Holladay. 2012. *Managing Corporate Social Responsibility: A Communication Approach.* First Edition. Wiley-Blackwell: Malden, MA. 107.
9 W. Timothy Coombs and Sherry J. Holladay. 2012. *Managing Corporate Social Responsibility: A Communication Approach.* First Edition. Wiley-Blackwell: Malden, MA. 134.
10 W. Timothy Coombs and Sherry J. Holladay. 2012. Managing Corporate Social Responsibility: A Communication Approach. First Edition. Wiley-Blackwell: Malden, MA.
11 W. Timothy Coombs and Sherry J. Holladay. 2012. *Managing Corporate Social Responsibility: A Communication Approach.* First Edition. Wiley-Blackwell: Malden, MA. 149.
12 Mette Morsing. 2017. CSR Communication: What Is It? Why Is It Important? In eds. Andreas Rasche, Mette Morsing and Jeremy Moon. *Corporate Social Responsibility: Strategy, Communication, Governance.* Cambridge University Press: New York. 292.
13 Mette Morsing. 2017. CSR Communication: What Is It? Why Is It Important? In eds. Andreas Rasche, Mette Morsing and Jeremy Moon. *Corporate Social Responsibility: Strategy, Communication, Governance.* Cambridge University Press: New York. 294.
14 Mette Morsing. 2017. CSR Communication: What Is It? Why Is It Important? In eds. Andreas Rasche, Mette Morsing and Jeremy Moon. *Corporate Social Responsibility: Strategy, Communication, Governance.* Cambridge University Press: New York. 281–306.
15 Peter Snyder, Molly Hall, Joline Robertson, Tomasz Jasinski and Janice S. Miller. 2006. Ethical Rationality: A Strategic Approach to Organizational Crisis. *Journal of Business Ethics.* 63: 371–383.
16 Peter Snyder, Molly Hall, Joline Robertson, Tomasz Jasinski and Janice S. Miller. 2006. Ethical Rationality: A Strategic Approach to Organizational Crisis. *Journal of Business Ethics.* 63: 374.
17 Peter A. Stanwick and Sarah D. Stanwick. 2016. *Understanding Business Ethics.* Third Edition. Sage Publications: Thousand Oaks, CA.

18 Yael Grauer. 2018. What Are 'Data Brokers,' and Why Are They Scooping Up Information About You? *Vice.com*. March 27.
19 Olivia Iurillo. 2019. 6 dangers of Influencer Marketing. *Social Media Today*. July 11.
20 Peter A. Stanwick and Sarah D. Stanwick. 2016. *Understanding Business Ethics*. Third Edition. Sage Publications: Thousand Oaks, CA.
21 www.mars.com/made-by-mars
22 www.mars.com/about/five-principles
23 www.mars.com/pledgeforplanet?gclid=EAIaIQobChMIrqulhaG95gIVl5OzCh0M pwmMEAMYASAAEgIXmvD_BwE#header-content-main

10 Corporate sustainability and the natural environment

Only when the last tree has been cut down, the last fish been caught, and the last stream poisoned, will we realize we cannot eat money.

Cree Indian Prophecy[1]

Introduction

As Mahatma Gandhi once said, "Earth provides enough to satisfy every man's needs, but not every man's greed."[2] This chapter can be considered the most important in any textbook regarding the discussion of firms and the long-term survival of the planet. The natural environment impacts every living organism every day around the world. The focus of this chapter is for the reader to get a better understanding of some of the daunting issues the managers of firms must acknowledge and address in the decision-making process. While there are a number of environmental challenges facing firms and their stakeholders, this chapter identifies new technologies and new mind-sets to help resolve these complex issues. Some of the concepts discussed in this chapter include: the natural environment as a stakeholder; the role of NGOs in the natural environment; how the circular economy can improve environmental conditions; environmental management systems; greenwashing; environmental justice; environmental sustainability; environmental audits; impacts of climate change; and carbon footprints. The chapter begins with a discussion on how a social enterprise in the Philippines recycles the previously unrecyclable plastic sachets and concludes with a discussion of the new discovery by IBM to produce a battery from seawater.

Turning plastic sachets into building blocks: Green Antz Builders

Customers in emerging economies need the same necessities as all global citizens but can only afford to purchase small quantities at a time. Plastic sachets are used to contain single use packets of toiletries and food. These small single use packages allow the global poor to be able to afford these necessities.

The alternative is to buy larger, typically multi-ounce packaged bottles and containers which in most cases are not affordable.

Plastic sachets allow global multinationals such as Unilever and Procter & Gamble to acquire market share in these developing countries by repackaging products to serve the needs of these customers. The net result is a flood of single use plastic sachets that end up in the water ways and landfills throughout the region. The plastic sachet is more complicated than a traditional plastic bag given in retail stores to recycle. It is composed of a thin film of plastic and aluminum in a laminated plastic form.

Due to its lack of recyclability, there is no economic value put on the used plastic sachets resulting in them being scattered indiscriminately after use. These discarded sachets can increase the level of flooding in local communities due to clogging the municipal drains. Another problem is that the residue of the consumable within the sachet, like toothpaste, makes it difficult for people to even consider recycling the sachets.

Pradeep Banerjee, the head of Unilever's Indian subsidiary supply chain, states the paradox of plastic sachets:

> Sachets are the most visible face of litter in any developing market ... But they are (a) very efficient means to get items of everyday use to remote areas of the country ... if you have to transport one liter of a fluid, a plastic bottle would give 10 times the carbon footprint of a lighter sachet. It's not going to be an easy nut to crack.

In 2014, it was estimated that the Philippines would need to build 200 new large landfills by 2020 to dispose of the plastic sachets at the current usage rate. In the Philippines, a social enterprise called Green Antz Building has addressed this environmental issue by converting the plastic material in the sachets into dark grey eco-bricks that can be used for building schools and homes.

Green Antz Builders was founded by Rommel Benig, the former Industrial Services Head for Nestlé, Philippines. Following the corporate sustainability lead from Nestlé, Benig adopted the creating shared value business model. It is through this model that negative corporate sustainability issues that impact a community are converted into a positive impact.

Green Antz focuses on not just construction using eco-bricks but also other opportunities of developing and promoting practices and technologies that help protect the environment. Green Antz views residual wastes as a valuable resource that can be converted into green products to be utilized by local communities as the foundation of the circular economy.

This circular approach creates a closed loop of the same plastic being recycled over and over again. The challenge with plastic sachets is that they are made up of a laminated film of plastic and aluminum in order to create the necessary sturdy container. The recycling process separates the plastics from the other materials in the sachet. Without this recycling process, the plastic cannot be recycled and the sachets are thrown away. As a result, billions of sachets are thrown away annually due to the lack of recyclability options. Using the same amount of energy, the recycling process for plastic sachets can recover six times the amount of plastic that is produced from using new materials. The eco-bricks are solid and not hollow like traditional building bricks.[3]

The eco-bricks produced by Green Antz are composed of wet cement and shredded plastic from the sachets. The plastic material in the eco-brick increases the level of thermal insulation of the brick, which is beneficial in reducing the heating and cooling costs of the building. Green Antz has also designed a Pervious Paver Eco-Brick for roads and parking lots which can absorb one liter of flood water within 8–10 seconds, helping to reduce the threat of flooding.

In November 2018, Nestlé Philippines and Green Antz Builders announced a partnership to expand its eco-brick program. Nestlé and Green Antz invited local governmental units (LGUs), NGOs, private businesses, and schools to work together to set up eco-brick hubs in local communities. The hubs would not only develop more bricks but would add jobs in areas with high unemployment rates. People in the local communities collect the plastic sachets and exchange them for eco-bricks for free. Green Antz also provides local communities with the equipment to produce the eco-bricks to allow them to create their own bricks.[4,5,6,7]

Natural environment as a stakeholder

While the natural environment does not have a physical voice as a stakeholder, its needs and expectations must be identified and addressed by firms. NGOs such as Greenpeace and the Sierra Club are proxy voices for the natural environment to ensure that the needs of the natural environment are met. Whether it relates to air and water pollution or the reduction of greenhouse gases (GHGs), the natural ecosystem depends on these special interest groups to serve as agents in protecting the natural environment from harm and permanent damage.

This perspective reconfigures the traditional viewpoint that a stakeholder needs to be a human being. However, if a more inclusive definition of a stakeholder is presented, the natural environment can be a stakeholder. If a stakeholder is viewed as any entity that can have an impact on the decisions made and the consequences of those decisions by the firm, the natural environment would qualify as a stakeholder.

NGOs as environmental stakeholder

As was mentioned previously, NGOs represent the voice and the monitoring mechanism for the environmental activities of the firm. The modern environmental movement in the United States started in 1962 with the publishing of the *Silent Spring* by Rachel Carson.[8] In her book, Carson warns of the permanent devastation to the environment if farmers and others continue to use pesticides and other chemical toxins to eliminate insects and weeds.

The next milestone was the publication of Garret Hardin's *The Tragedy of the Commons* in 1968.[9] The author warns the readers that people will misuse common goods such as the air and water if there are no consequences for their misuse. This increased focus on the natural environment entrenched the importance of environmental-based NGOs to continue the cause of warning the global stakeholders of the negative consequences if the traditional corporate view of the natural environment continues. The three largest and most widely known environmental NGOs are Greenpeace, Sierra Club, and the Environmental Defense Fund.[10]

Greenpeace

Started in 1971, the mission of Greenpeace is a global independent campaigning organization that uses peaceful protests and other types of communication to identify global environmental problems and promote sustainable environmental solutions. Greenpeace has offices in over 50 countries and focuses on fundamental environmental issues such as global warming, the destruction of ancient forests, the deterioration of the oceans, and the threat of nuclear disasters. Greenpeace has 250,000 members in the United States and 2.8 million members globally with virtually all of its funding received through individual contributions.[11]

Sierra Club

In 1892, John Muir and his friends created the Sierra Club to protect the natural environmental beauty of California. The mission of the Sierra Club became to ensure that natural and human environments are protected regardless of the location. The major initiatives of the Sierra Club are climate change and energy usage; the protection of lands, air, water, and wildlife; and environmental justice. The Sierra Club has over 3.5 million members and has held 4,500 rallies and events to focus on environmental issues. Over 7,500 Sierra Club volunteers lead over 15,000 trips annually around the globe that highlight environmental issues.[12,13,14]

Environmental Defense Fund

The Environmental Defense Fund is one of the world's largest environmental NGOs with more than 2.5 million members and 700 employees who are scientists, economists, policy experts, and other professionals. The underlying philosophy of the Environmental Defense Fund is the belief that prosperity and environmental stewardship can be integrated together. Its mission is to find long-term sustainable solutions related to climate by moving toward a 100 percent clean economy; by expanding sustainable fishing in the oceans; increasing resilience of the ecosystems and reducing exposure to pollutants; and improving health globally based on science and economics. Its core values are based on results, respect, innovation, optimism, and integrity.[15,16,17]

Circular economy

The circular economy is a closed looped approach to resources and sustainability. The underlying premise is that financial growth of the firm does not necessarily mean that the consumption of resources will occur at the same growth rate. This decoupling of financial growth and use of resources is based, in part, on making existing resources as productive as possible for as long as possible. A significant benefit to the firm for embracing the circular economy is the firm's focus on re-evaluating its process related to product design, procurement, and waste management. The strategy related to a circular economy has three dimensions: recycling more efficiently and effectively through closed-loop recycling; renting goods instead of selling them; and lengthening the longevity of products.

Closed-looped recycling

There are two types of recycling: open and closed loop. Open-loop recycling occurs when the materials that are being recycled deteriorate over time. This reduction in quality of the material makes them less viable to be recycled continuously. Closed-looped recycling involves reusing materials that can be recycled, including plastic, glass, steel, and aluminum, in a continuous manner.

Companies like Dell are evaluating the materials they use to convert them from open-loop to closed-looped recyclable systems. Dell has formed partnerships with other companies such as Wistron Greentech in order to make the plastics it uses more durable. Plastics will have some of its properties weakened with consistent recycling. Dell has developed a new way to prevent the plastics from deteriorating so the plastic can be recycled numerous times. The net result is that this process not only saves Dell money, but it also reduces carbon emissions by 11 percent when compared with using virgin plastic.

Rent instead of sell

Instead of selling its products and having its customers take ownership, firms can just provide the product's service instead of selling the product, called "servitization." The firms retain ownership of their products for the full life of the products. This life cycle approach allows the firm to control the final "retirement" of the product.[18]

An example of this approach is MUD Jeans. MUD Jeans uses a subscription model for its customers. MUD Jeans gives the option for customers to "lease" the jeans, offers free repairs, and the customer can swap their old pair for a new pair. MUD Jeans recycles the denim from the old jeans and includes it in the manufacturing process. Forty percent of its jeans are composed of recycled content. The customers are given the option to lease the MUD Jeans for 7.5 euros per month. After one year, the customer has three options. They can exchange their old jeans for a new pair and continue leasing for another year, keep the jeans and wear them as long as they like, or return the jeans and end the lease by receiving a voucher for a new purchase.[19]

Offer ways to lengthen and wide the use of products

Instead of melting the materials of a used product for the commodity content of the materials, an alternative process would be the remanufacturing of the product to extend its usefulness. An example would be Apple, who buys its old phones and refurbishes them to be sold at the lower price. These refurbished phones can help satisfy the global demand for smartphone use regardless of the country.

Caterpillar has been remanufacturing its heavy machinery since 1973. It is extremely beneficial for Caterpillar to use this strategy since 65 percent of the company's manufacturing costs involve the materials in the products. There are significant cost savings when Caterpillar can salvage materials for remanufacturing since it is cheaper to restore old existing parts than producing new ones. For example, the remanufacturing of a cylinder head in an engine instead of producing a new head results in a 61 percent reduction in greenhouse gasses, a 93 percent reduction in the use of water, and an 86 percent reduction in energy.

European Union projects that encourage a circular economy

Under the Horizon 2020 program, the European Union (EU) has funded the development of numerous projects across Europe that capture existing resources to be converted to new applications. Here are some examples of how the EU is inspiring the circular economy in Europe:

- In Slovenia, a biotech firm is converting waste whey into protein-rich biomass. Whey is the liquid byproduct after milk has been curdled and strained. Whey is used as a main ingredient in a microbial fermentation process that will create sustainable high-value products such as vitamin B12. The B12 is incorporated into a protein-rich biomass that can be used as animal feed and completes the closed loop.
- In Europe approximately 3.4 million tons of old tires are discarded and end up in landfills. The Rubberised Concrete Noise Barriers (RUCONBAR) project is sponsored by the EU under its Competitiveness and

Innovation Framework Programme. The used tires are shredded and used as noise protection panels near urban roads and railway lines. The result of this program is that it not only reduces the noise levels for the neighborhoods around roads and railroad tracks, but it captures a new use for the tires which would otherwise be dumped or sent to a landfill.

- The SLAG-REC project, which is co-funded by the EU's Eco-innovation programme, converts steelmaking waste into roads. In the steelmaking process, there is a generation of a byproduct called slag. Slag is the residue from the ores that are used to make the metals in the steel manufacturing process. The slag is used in road construction and replaces nonrenewable natural resources such as sand and gravel.[20]

Voluntary environmental compliance

Voluntary environmental compliance is a useful tool for firms to demonstrate corporate sustainability commitment to the issues related to the natural environment. Voluntary environmental compliance is usually governed by an environmental code of the ethics that have been created by the top-level managers of the firm. A summary of the firm's activities related to voluntary environmental compliance are usually released in its corporate sustainability report or as a separate environmental report. In order to address the needs of stakeholders, there should be a number of components that are presented in the firm's summary of voluntary environmental compliance activities, including: the firm's environmental policy; specific measurable environmental performance metrics; description of environmental training for its employees; its environmental decisions related to supply chains; its strategy related to fossil fuel; and toxic chemical reduction in its operations.[21]

Environmental management systems

An operational mechanism that reinforces the firm's commitment to the environment and in many industries serves as an example of a voluntary environmental compliance is the establishment of environmental management systems. Even though it is considered voluntary, external pressure by stakeholders can be effective in coercing a firm to adopt formalized environmental management systems. It is the underlying pressure of the firm's stakeholders that will move a firm to adopt an environmental management system that is beyond mere government and legal compliance. These pressures not only impact the parent firm but also the operations of the firm's facilities. This allows NGOs to use two pressure points on the firm if the NGO believes that the firm is not fulfilling its environmental commitment. The two pressure points are the corporate firm and the firm's plants. From a corporate sustainability perspective, this dual approach to present the needs of the stakeholders to the firm allows two avenues to pursue both environmental and social concerns that the stakeholders have concerning the operations of

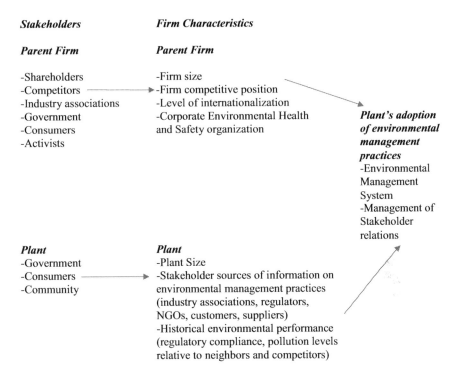

Stakeholders

Parent Firm

-Shareholders
-Competitors
-Industry associations
-Government
-Consumers
-Activists

Firm Characteristics

Parent Firm

-Firm size
-Firm competitive position
-Level of internationalization
-Corporate Environmental Health
and Safety organization

***Plant's adoption
of environmental
management
practices***
-Environmental
Management
System
-Management of
Stakeholder
relations

Plant
-Government
-Consumers
-Community

Plant
-Plant Size
-Stakeholder sources of information on
environmental management practices
(industry associations, regulators,
NGOs, customers, suppliers)
-Historical environmental performance
(regulatory compliance, pollution levels
relative to neighbors and competitors)

Figure 10.1 The firm's adoption of the environmental management system[22]

the firm. A framework demonstrating the firm's adoption of an environmental management system is shown in Figure 10.1

Figure 10.1 shows that for the parent firm and the firm's plant perspective, there are external pressures from the stakeholders to develop and support an environmental management system.

Government pressures

Government pressures can be one of the most dominant pressures facing the stakeholders since they have the power to demand that a firm adjust its behavior and follow rules and regulations that may be incorporated into the environmental management system. This type of coercive power can strongly recommend making changes even if it is not required by law. An example of this power is the adoption of ISO 14001. ISO 14001 is a voluntary environmental management system established by the International Organization of Standardization. A firm can become ISO 14001 certified if it can verify that it is following the formal procedures required by ISO 14001. The certification process focuses on the improvement of the firm's environmental performance through more efficient methods of using resources, reducing waste, and establishing a strong relationship with stakeholders. Governments can strongly encourage firms to become ISO 14001 certified by promoting those firms that are certified. Governments may also encourage adoption by providing technical assistance to potential adopters.

Customer and competitive pressures

A firm can be pressured into adopting an environmental management system based on the demands of its customers and the environmental strategy of its competitors. If the industry leaders are using an environmental management system as a method to enhance their competitive advantage, other firms will follow suit in order to negate this competitive action. In Asia and other parts of the world, firms demand that suppliers be required to either have an ISO 14001 certification or some other validation process for their environmental management systems. This requirement forces firms to adopt an environmental management system in order to sell its products to current and potential future customers.

Community and environmental interest group pressures

Local communities can also impose a coercive type pressure on firms to adopt an environmental management system. Communities and NGOs want to make sure that firms are accountable for their impact on the environment and will monitor firms to do due diligence on the firm's environmental impacts on its local and global operations. By having an environmental management system in place, the firm establishes not only creditability and transparency with stakeholders but also has facts and figures to support its claims of environmental performance.

Industry pressure

Industry associations can also motivate firms in adopting environmental management systems. Membership in the industry association may be contingent on the firm having a comprehensive environmental management system. The concentration of market share within an industry may also play a role in the firm's adoption. If there are a small number of firms that each have a relatively high level of market share, those firms can greatly influence the adoptability of the management system by all firms in the industry. The size and power of the firms make it a necessity to copy each other's practices including not only adopting the environmental management system but demanding its suppliers also have a formalized environmental management system.

Firm characteristics

Within a given industry the stakeholder pressure for firms to adopt an environmental management system can vary among firms. If the firm in the industry is a multinational firm, it is usually held to higher environmental and social standards than national firms. This higher standard is usually due to both increased awareness and exposure of these firms as well as increased pressure by NGOs who investigate the global operations of the firm. Firms that are market leaders in the industry are also under more intense scrutiny because of their strong global recognition and brand names. The third factor is that firms that have had a history of poor environmental performance will also be targeted by stakeholders since they do not necessarily have the credibility and trust as compared with firms that have a strong, long-standing, positive environmental commitment.

The types of stakeholder pressures can vary whether the focus is on the parent headquarters or the firm's plant. Community pressures will focus on plants that are located near the community, while shareholders will focus on the management at the corporate headquarters. Firms will also view the pressure differently based on the functional area within the firm. The firm's legal department will focus on potential risks and liabilities, the public relations department of the firm will focus on corporate reputation, the department responsible for environmental issues will focus on potential ecosystem damage and regulatory compliance, and the sales department will focus on the potential loss of revenue.

The firm's response to stakeholder pressures

The firm has multiple options to respond to the pressures of its stakeholders in demanding that the firm has an environmental management system. The firm can adopt a strategy which does not include a management system. This "basic" strategy would ensure that the firm complies with government regulations and standard industry practices.

The more "comprehensive" strategy would be to move beyond compliance and focus on developing voluntary environmental strategies which will reduce the environmental impacts of operations in a proactive nature. This would include not only developing an environmental management system but also developing an environmental policy and a formal training program for its employees. The firm could also have a voluntary environmental audit performed on its operations. The firm can emphasize the importance of its environmental commitment by including an employee's environmental performance as part of his/her annual performance evaluation. This proactive environmental commitment can lead to the firm being able to develop improved relations with government regulators and could result in participation in various voluntary governmental environmental initiatives.[23]

Greenwashing

Greenwashing occurs when the firm provides misleading information to its stakeholders pertaining to its environmental practices. There are two types of greenwashing, which are firm level and product level. Firm level provides misleading information about the firm's overall environmental commitment. Firms can also develop a product-level greenwashing strategy where the firm misleads stakeholders on the environmental benefits of a product or service.

The overall effect of greenwashing is that stakeholders become skeptical about the actual performance of any firm that has a strong, positive environmental message. Greenwashing can result in a significant negative effect on consumer confidence in green products, which weakens the demand for these products. This lack of confidence by consumers is based on firms being guilty of one or more of the seven sins of greenwashing.

Seven sins of greenwashing

1. Hidden trade-off

For this sin, firms label products as being environmentally "friendly" even though it is based on a small set of attributes. For example, a firm can state that its product is made from 20 percent recycled material. The firm does not discuss where the other 80 percent of the materials come from, neither does it calculate the negative impact such as the carbon footprint of the product, which could more than offset the 20 percent use of recycled material.

2. No proof

For this sin, the firm makes an environmental claim without providing its stakeholders with any evidence of the claim. A light bulb manufacturer may claim that its bulbs are the most energy efficient in the industry and not provide any evidence to support that claim.

3. Vagueness

For this sin, the firm makes vague claims that cannot be easily defined. Terms such as "organic," "all-natural," and environmentally friendly may be presented as purposely vague so that the firm does not have any accountability for these claims. An example would be an "all-natural" cleaner which still could contain harmful chemicals that are found in nature.

4. Irrelevance

For this sin, the firm makes a claim which is technically true but is not a factor in the decision process of the customer when the customer is looking for eco-friendly products. An example would be to make a claim that the product is CFC (Chlorofluorocarbon) free, which is irrelevant since the use of CFCs in products has been banned since 1996.

5. Lesser of the two evils

For this sin, the firm makes a claim that its products are more eco-friendly when the category of products is considered to be environmentally unfriendly. An example would be a cigarette firm claiming that its cigarettes are organic and environmentally friendly when the product contains numerous carcinogens.

6. False claim

For this sin, the firm lies about the claim since it is not true. An example of this type of sin is when a firm claims the product is made from recycled material when it is not.

7. Worshiping false labels

For this sin, the firm claims to have an endorsement or certification related to the environment when it does not have the endorsement or certification. Firms that use these marketing ploys would create a false certification label to put on products.

A 2010 study of environmental claims made by products sold in the United States found that 95 percent of the products were guilty of some form of greenwashing with the two greatest sins being no proof and vagueness in products.[24]

Typology of greenwashing firms

The perception of greenwashing occurs for stakeholders when a firm has poor environmental performance yet has positive communication about its environmental performance. This greening strategy can vary among firms based on these two dimensions, as shown in Table 10.1.

Table 10.1 Typology of firms related to greenwashing[25]

		Environmental performance	
		Bad	Good
Communication about environmental performance	*Positive communication*	Greenwashing firms	Vocal green firms
	No communication	Silent brown firms	Silent green firms

Firms which have a poor environmental performance are classified as brown firms while those firms with a positive environmental performance are called green firms. Brown firms that communicate misleading positive messages to stakeholders are greenwashing firms and those that do not are called silent brown firms. For green firms, those who communicate their environmental commitment are vocal green firms and those that do not communicate their environmental commitment are silent green firms.

Drivers of greenwashing

There are a number of internal and external factors that can influence a firm to develop a greenwashing strategy. There are four major sets of drivers which are: non-market external; market external; organizational; and individual psychological. Figure 10.2 shows the relationship among these drivers.

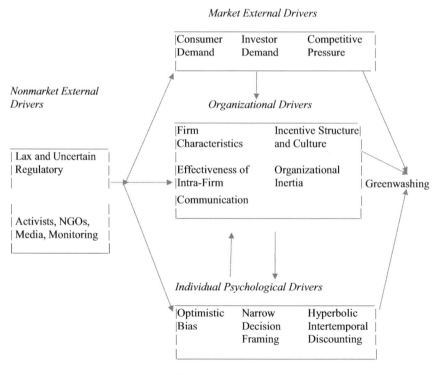

Figure 10.2 Drivers of greenwashing[26]

Non-market external drivers

Lax and uncertain regulatory environment

In the United States, regulations related to greenwashing are very limited and enforcement of violations to the regulations are rare. The Federal Trade Commission (FTC) can file a complaint related to a violation if it perceives that the firm is providing unfair or deceptive marketing practices.

Activists, NGOs and media pressure

Since government enforcement of greenwashing practices is limited, the burden of exposing greenwashing is left to environmental activists and NGOs. These stakeholders, along with the media, have become the watchdogs for monitoring the environmental claims made by firms. Greenpeace has a "stopgreenwash" monitoring website to expose firms falsely claiming environmental achievements. Activists can present a convincing story they can demonstrate to the firm's stakeholders when the firm is being hypocritical related to its environmental commitment.

Market external drivers

External market drivers may force reluctant firms to increase environmental performance to match environmental claims communicated to stakeholders. Alternatively, brown environmental firms must address pressure from both consumers and investors and will greenwash environmental messages if they do not have the true environmental record to match their claims. If competitors are making comprehensive environmental claims, brown firms will view this strategy as a tool for their competitors to enhance competitive position. Brown firms will greenwash their responses to try to negate competitor strategies. This greenwashing marketing strategy, if exposed, will have a significant negative impact on the firm's consumers who cannot trust the firm. An exposed greenwashing strategy will also create panic from investors who would be concerned about how this information will negatively impact the firm's reputation and result in a subsequent decrease in the firm's stock price.

Organizational-level drivers

Firm characteristics

The characteristics of the firm, including its size, the industry it competes in, the level of its profitability, resources, and core competencies, include the firm's overall strategic focus. Based on these characteristics, there are actions that "fit" with the firm's strategy which the firm can "afford" to implement.

These limitations can hamper the firm's ability to develop and implement a comprehensive environmental commitment. For firms that can afford to have strong comprehensive environmental commitments, the benefits of communicating those environmental virtues result in the ability to capture the interests of future green consumers and investors.

Incentive structure and ethical culture

Incentives for marketing employees and departments to reach quotas for communications and customer recognitions for messages that put the firm in a positive environmental spotlight would increase the incentive for a brown firm to use greenwashing. If the culture of the firm does not have a strong positive commitment to ethics, decision makers may use unethical shortcuts to promote misleading environmental claims by the firm and its products.

Organizational inertia

Organization inertia refers to the strong persistence of the firm supporting the existing systems and the employees creating a strong resistance to change. Organizational inertia could explain why some firms are slow to react to shifts in the external landscape on how to address environmental issues. This could also explain, in part, a temporary greenwashing in which the firm has plans for being environmentally proactive, yet those plans have not yet been executed. This type of disconnect can occur when there is a change in the top-level managers and the implementation of the firm's strategy needs to catch up with the actions of the new top-level managers.

Effectiveness of intra-firm communication

The ability to internally transfer knowledge within a firm can be difficult to achieve, which could lead to less developed innovations due to a sub-optimal transfer of information. This sub-optimal communication channel can lead to a disconnect between what marketing and public relations are claiming to be true and the actual actions related to the firm's environmental product development, production process, and packaging process. The public relations department can exaggerate the environmental claims because they have not received all the critical information from the relevant departments within the firm.

Individual-level psychological drivers

Optimistic bias

Optimistic bias occurs when an individual tends to over-estimate the likelihood of positive outcomes and under-estimate the likelihood of negative outcomes, resulting in greenwashing. Optimistic bias is the result of forecasting future events that are anchored on plans and scenarios of success instead of past failures.

There are three types of optimistic biases, which are: unrealistically positive self-evaluation; unrealistic optimism about future events and plans; and illusion of control. Unrealistically positive self-evaluation is based on the perception that the individual has the skills and knowledge to get the task accomplished even though objectively that belief is not true. Unrealistic optimism is rejecting any information that does not support the planned course of action and embrace any information that does support the planned course of action. Illusion of control refers to the perception that the decision maker has more control of external events that can impact the implementation of an environmental strategy than is true.

Narrow decision framing

Narrow decision framing, also called narrowing bracketing, refers to the tendency by individuals to make decisions in isolation. Decision makers in the firm may decide to establish an environmentally based communication strategy without adequately considering what the requirements to implement that strategy are in the future, eventually leading to greenwashing.

Hyperbolic intertemporal discounting

Hyperbolic intertemporal discounting refers to the tendency to emphasize short-term behaviors and ignore the disconnect that behavior has on the individual's long-term goals. From a firm's perspective, hyperbolic intertemporal discounting refers to focusing on the short-term communication about environmental issues and discounting the potential long-term impact. This behavior can lead to greenwashing since the firm can claim several environmental initiatives currently that have not been implemented with an intention to eventually bear the costs to implement the firm's promised future green practices.[27]

A classic example of greenwashing is the Volkswagen case in this textbook. Volkswagen manipulated the emissions levels of its diesel vehicles in order to pass government regulations related to emissions as well as market its vehicles as environmentally friendly.

Environmental justice

Environmental justice can be defined as the allocation of environmental benefits and burdens in a systematic, equal manner. The evolution of the idea of environmental justice is based on the traditional allocation of activities which create an environmental burden. In the past, areas with lower income levels or a high level of minority ethnic groups would have received a disproportionate amount of environmental burdens. Environmental burdens can include being in close proximately to toxic dump sites or heavy manufacturing plants. In addition, these areas would not have the opportunity for environmental benefits such as parks, walking trails, and hiking paths close to their neighborhoods.

A related concept to environmental justice is Not In MY Back Yard (NIMBY). NIMBY is the neighborhood belief that local communities do not want any type of environmental burdens. Every community wants the benefits of the environment but no communities want to absorb the burdens of issues related to the environment. The environmental burdens are not only eye sores to the community, but they can create a number of health issues such as higher cancer risks and higher rates of breathing disorders by being within close proximity of toxins in the air, ground, and water.

Environmental sustainability

From a firm's perspective, environmental sustainability can be defined as the ability of the firm to protect the use of needed future resources, implementing an environmental strategy that is designed to maintain and develop these resources in the future. There are three major components of sustainability. They are: the development of a system that ensures the sustainable management of all stakeholders of the earth's natural resources; the development of both social and institutional structures that support and protect through sustainable management of the world's natural resources; and changes in the global economic system to support sustainable management of the earth's natural resources.[28]

From a corporate sustainability perspective, different parts of the world view sustainability and the issues related to sustainability very differently. There are three major classifications of economies based on the country's stage of economic development. The three types of economies are survival, emerging, and developed.

Survival economies are at the lowest level of economic development globally. Since the people in this type of economy focus on means of sustainable survival, the major challenges to sustainability are related to the depletion of natural resources and the contamination of water, land, and air in their communities.

Emerging economies are those including India and China, which were survival economies in the past and are now transforming to developed economies. The third type of economy is the developed economy, which is based on economically developed countries. The major issues of these three types of economies related to pollution, depletion, and poverty are shown in Table 10.2.[29]

Table 10.2 Major challenges to sustainability[30]

	Pollution	Depletion	Poverty
Developed economies	– Greenhouse gas – Release of toxins	– Scarcity of raw materials – Insufficient reuse and recycling	Urban and minority unemployment
Emerging economies	– Industrial emissions – Contaminated water – Lack of sewage treatment	– Overexploitation of renewable resources – Overuse of water for irrigation	– Migration to cities – Lack of skilled workers – Income equality
Survival economies	– Dung and wood – Lack of sanitation – Ecosystem	– Deforestation – Overgrazing – Soil loss	– Population growth – Low status of women dislocation

Environmental audits

In order to have a strong positive relationship with its stakeholders, firms may disseminate accurate and transparent environmental information pertaining to all of its operations. In order to safeguard that trust related to environmental issues, the firm should do an environmental audit.

Even though this audit is voluntary, there are a number of benefits for the firm to do an environmental audit in addition to providing information to its stakeholders. An environmental audit will ensure compliance with government regulations, identify areas which could reduce environmental impacts, identify cost savings based on the reduction of waste, water, and energy usage, and coincide with the firm's environmental management system.

The audit can be done internally or the firm can hire an external firm to perform the audit. Typically, an environmental audit will cover areas such as energy, CO_2 and other GHG emissions, waste, water, transport, biodiversity, and procurement.[31] An audit plan needs to be developed to provide both the structure and the requirements of the audit.

Steps in the environmental audit process

There are six steps in the traditional environmental audit process: reviewing documentation; reviewing policies and procedures; giving staff a questionnaire; interviewing the managers; conducting site visits; and reviewing the results of the audit.

Reviewing documentation

There are a number of areas in which documentation needs to be reviewed as part of the environmental audit. From a macro level, an overall review of the firm's operational activities and processes must take place. A review of the firm's environmental management system policies, procedures, and programs must occur. The audit team must review all relevant records related to environmental issues.

The review of the relevant records is the micro stage of reviewing the documentation of the firm's environmental impact. There are several areas in which detailed documentation is required for a comprehensive environmental audit. For example. the firm's fuel and water consumption amounts are needed as a benchmark for future progress. The records of transportation and staff business travel are needed for carbon emissions calculations. The waste collection invoices give information to the audit team about not only the cost of disposing of waste but also the potential cost savings of recycling. Procurement records are needed for direct and indirect impacts on the carbon footprint and other environmentally related issues. The floor plans of the manufacturing facilities are needed to understand the current layout and determine if there are opportunities to increase employee efficiencies. Documentation on the details of the construction of the facilities including how the walls and roof were constructed, type of insulation, and when the facilities were built are needed. Documentation on services within the facilities including ventilation and air conditioning systems are also needed.

Review of policies and procedures

A comprehensive review of the policies and procedures must take place on an annual basis. This review is imperative since government regulations and stakeholder demands can change over time. It is during this step in the process that the audit team needs to scan the external environment to see if there are potential changes that will impact the environmental policies and procedures in the near future.

Employee questionnaire

An employee questionnaire should serve two functions. The first function is to ensure that the employee is aware of the current environmental policies and procedures of the firm. The employee can be asked questions on what their response would be if certain environmental issues were to arise during work. The areas to be included in this section of the questionnaire include policies and procedures related to overall environmental management, procurement, energy management, materials management, water and wastewater management, waste management, noise monitoring, air quality monitoring, and emergency response.

The second function is to obtain information related to the staff's use of office equipment, business travel, commuting, water use, employee awareness and training, health and safety concerns related to environmental issues, and response to public enquiries and complaints.

Interviews with managers

Managers whose decisions have a direct impact on the environmental performance of the firm should be interviewed by the audit team. The relevant questions managers should be asked concern such areas as the overall activities of any facilities the firm operates, organizational structure, heating and cooling systems, procurement policies, IT policies, waste and recycling procedures, and any areas of environmental concern of the managers.

Site visit

For each site, the audit team needs to meet the officer in charge and explain the purpose of the environmental audit. At the site, the audit team needs to determine whether the background information related to the site is accurate and up to date. The audit team should focus on whether the site is in compliance with relevant government regulations and internal environmental policies, procedures, and guidelines. The audit team should also determine the status of current environmental practices and determine the employees' level of awareness of internal environmental policies, procedures, and guidelines. The auditors would identify and request any additional information, if necessary. After the audit of the site is completed, the audit team would send a follow up to the site manager with a listing of the preliminary audit impressions.

Results of the audit

After the audit has been completed, it is the responsibly of the audit team to generate a written evaluation of the current environmental performance of the firm. In addition, the written report would also include any recommendations for changes needed by the firm before the next audit takes place. The audit team would also generate a package of background information and provide the results of the employee questionnaires and the audit checklists.[32,33]

Impacts of climate change

There is a global consensus among the scientific community that the earth is warming and the warming is caused by the ever increasing release of GHGs. The earth's temperature has increased by 2 degrees Fahrenheit since the beginning of the Industrial Revolution in 1880 to 2015. The atmospheric concentrations of CO_2 has increased from 290 ppm (parts per million) to 430 ppm during that same time period. The primary source of this increase of GHGs is due to the burning of fossil fuels (coal, oil, gas), agricultural practices, and deforestation. Higher GHG emissions in the atmosphere increases the amount of radiative energy that is caught leaving from the earth. This energy is redirected back towards the earth's surface.

Rising sea levels

As the earth's temperature increases, sea levels will rise for two reasons. The first reason is that ice from glaciers and other frozen parts of the world will melt and cause the volume of water in the ocean to increase. The second reason is that as the ocean water warms, it expands in volume.

The immediate danger of rising sea levels is that two-thirds of the world's largest cities are in low-lying areas which could ultimately be submerged by the ocean. This danger is also critical for low-lying islands around the world because they could become completely submerged in the future.

Changing weather patterns and extreme weather

Rising temperatures on earth lead to the atmosphere being able to hold more water vapor, which can lead to more frequent, intense rainstorms in certain areas of the world. In addition, increased drought conditions in other areas due to changing weather patterns could also occur.

Pressure on water and food

Food production is intertwined with weather conditions. These unpredictable patterns can lead to certain crops no longer being viable in some areas while the introduction of previously unsuitable crops are now possible due to climate change. Furthermore, warmer weather leads to insects, weeds, and parasites thriving in new areas causing possible destruction of farmland, crops, and livestock.

Political and security risks

Climate change can lead to political insecurity through shortages of food and the lack of water. This political insecurity can lead to political protests. Countries with an unstable political climate are more susceptible to potential overthrows of the government by the country's citizens demanding immediate change, which also could lead to heightened security risks.

Human health costs

Higher temperatures also have a human cost due to heat-related injuries and potential death. Human health is also impacted due to the higher levels of GHGs emissions in the atmosphere as well as health issues related to the introduction of new species of insects which previously could not survive in that area of the world.

Impact on wildlife and ecosystems

Climate change can impact all living species. The natural habitat of many species are at high risk to be extinct, which will result in those species needing to find other places to survive. Higher temperatures can also impact the survival rate of wildlife due to lack of food and water, resulting in lower reproductive rates for those species.[34]

Carbon footprint

A carbon footprint refers to the amount of carbon that is released in GHG emissions in the atmosphere. The carbon footprint is based on the impact the release of carbon has on the earth. While a footprint eventually disappears on the ground, a carbon footprint does not disappear. As with a regular footprint, the larger the footprint, the larger the impact of a carbon footprint on the earth's climate. The total impact of a firm's carbon footprint is based on the total annual GHG emissions that directly result from the firm's operations. Carbon emissions can be released through the burning of fossil fuels, chemical reactions during the manufacturing process, as well as GHG emissions related to electricity bought by the firm. The firm's carbon footprint is based on both its organizational and product footprint. There are three categories or scopes of carbon emission that can be generated by the firm.

Carbon footprint scopes

Scope 1

Scope 1 emissions are direct emissions generated by the firm through sources that are either owned or controlled by the firm. The first type of source is stationary combustion. Stationary combustion emissions occur from the production of electricity, steam, heat, or power from stationary equipment. The second type of scope 1 emissions result from mobile combustion. Mobile combustion includes transportation and construction sources such as automobiles, trucks, tractors, and airplanes. The third source for scope 1 emissions is the release of emissions due to physical and chemical processes, including the manufacture of cement and aluminum. The fourth source includes accidental sources such as unintentional leaks and evaporation.

Scope 2

Scope 2 emissions are indirect emissions related to the firm's operations and are the result of activities of the firm but have occurred in another firm's operations. Some examples of scope 2 emissions are energy purchased by the firm from another firm which supplies electricity.

Scope 3

Scope 3 emissions are other indirect emissions that have been created from sources that were not identified in scope 1 or 2. Some examples of scope 3 emissions include employee travel, the extraction and processing of raw materials, and the shipment of the firm's products to distribution centers, retailers, and customers.

The overall framework on the carbon footprint for the organization is shown in Figure 10.3.

Calculating the product's carbon footprint

An additional measure of the carbon footprint related to the firm is its products. The calculation of the GHG emissions related to the product's carbon footprint includes extraction, production, and transportation of raw materials, manufacturing, distribution, product use, and disposal or recycling.

The total carbon footprint for products can be much higher than the carbon emissions generated by the firm. An example is a smartphone. The carbon footprint for the distribution and use of a smartphone can far exceed the footprint of the firm. The continuous charging of the smartphone generates a large carbon footprint based on the product's use of energy. Another

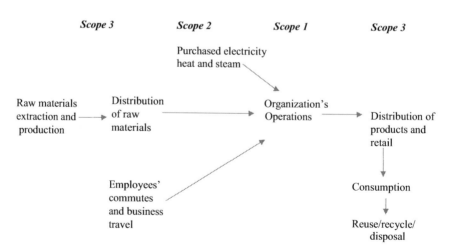

Figure 10.3 Organizational and product carbon footprint[35]

example is automobiles. Approximately 90 percent of the GHG emissions that are associated with an automobile over its lifespan come from gasoline consumption. Calculations of product use are typically included in the calculation the firm's product carbon footprint.

An example of a company that has attempted to calculate the total carbon footprint of its products is the UK retailer Tesco. The basis of Tesco's calculation is shown in Figure 10.4.[36] Tesco has identified numerous components of the calculation included in the goods its sells to the public.

IBM's better corporate sustainable battery

On December 18, 2019 IBM announced a major breakthrough for one of the most complex corporate sustainability issues, a battery design without any heavy metals. Through a partnership with Daimler AG's Mercedes-Benz, battery electrolyte supplier Central Glass and battery manufacturer Sidus, IBM announced a new battery design which uses saltwater.

As is discussed in the case in this textbook about cobalt mining in Congo, there are numerous inherent risks of using heavy metals in battery manufacturing. Not only are these metals relatively scarce, but numerous communities in areas of Africa have been negatively impacted by the mining of precious metals such as cobalt. The extraction process of nickel, which is highlighted in the Ambatovy project case in Madagascar, demonstrates that if battery

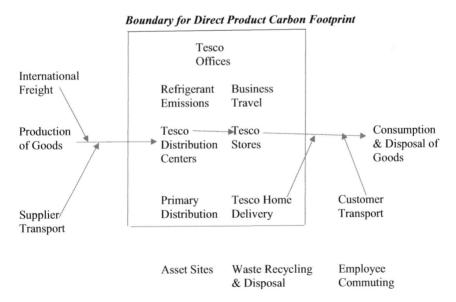

Figure 10.4 Calculation of Tesco products' carbon footprint[37]

production does not require heavy metals, the net result would lead to significant global social and environmental benefits.

The new battery design by IBM is based on the chemical discovery that does not require the use of heavy metals. The materials of the battery are extracted from seawater, which is not only a less invasive sourcing technique but also the use of an abundant global resource.

The battery has also been tested with the result that it surpasses the capabilities of lithium-ion batteries in a number of attributes including lower cost, faster charging time, higher power and energy density, strong energy efficiency, and low flammability. These attributes are very attractive in the electric vehicle industry where battery concerns include flammability, cost, and charging time. The battery is designed to reach an 80 percent charge in five minutes. The lower cost is due to not having metals in the battery.[38,39]

Questions for thought

1. What role should firms have in being accountable for the recycling of their products and packaging globally?
2. How effective are environmentally based NGOs in changing the behavior of firms?
3. Do you think the circular economy is a current fad or a long-term strategic focus of firms?
4. Do you think the benefits outweigh the costs of voluntary environmental compliance of firms globally?
5. What is your view on greenwashing? Do you think it is common for the majority of firms that release information pertaining to its environmental commitment?
6. Why wouldn't a firm perform an environmental audit on its operations?
7. Do you believe climate change exists? Why or why not?
8. Have you ever thought about the carbon footprint related to anything you have purchased?

Notes

1 www.goodreads.com/quotes/755798-only-when-the-last-tree-has-been-cut-down-the
2 www.goodreads.com/quotes/30431-earth-provides-enough-to-satisfy-every-man-s-needs-but-not
3 https://businessmirror.com.ph/2018/11/19/nestle-green-antz-help-address-waste-plastic-laminates-as-corporations-lgus-join-up/
4 https://resource.co/article/unilever-unveils-new-plastic-sachet-recycling-technology-11840
5 https://tagpuanph.wixsite.com/creatingsharedvalue/copy-of-why-creating-shared-value

6 Leila Abboud. 2019. Can We Overcome the Curse of the Single-Use Sachet? *Financial Times*. December 4.
7 Dennis Posadas. 2014. Sachets Help Low-Income Communities But Are a Waste Nightmare. *The Guardian*. May 22.
8 Rachel Carson 1962. Silent Spring. Houghton Mifflin: New York.
9 Garrett Hardin. 1968. The Tragedy of the Commons. Science. 162:3859. 1243–1248.
10 Peter A. Stanwick and Sarah D. Stanwick. 2016. *Understanding Business Ethics*. Third Edition. Sage Publications: Thousand Oaks, CA.
11 www.greenpeace.org/usa/about/
12 www.sierraclub.org/about-sierra-club
13 www.sierraclub.org/explore-issues
14 www.sierraclub.org/about-sierra-club
15 www.edf.org/about
16 www.edf.org/our-mission-and-values
17 www.edf.org/our-work
18 Terence Tee, Mark Esposito and Khaled Soufani. 2016. How Businesses Can Support a Circular Economy. *Harvard Business Review*. February 1.
19 www.ellenmacarthurfoundation.org/case-studies/pioneering-a-lease-model-for-organic-cotton-jeans
20 https://ec.europa.eu/easme/en/news/closing-loop-ground-10-eu-projects-working-towards-circular-economy
21 Peter A. Stanwick and Sarah D. Stanwick. 2016. *Understanding Business Ethics*. Third Edition. Sage Publications: Thousand Oaks, CA.
22 Magali Delmas and Michael W. Toffel. 2004. Stakeholders and Environmental Management Practices: An Institutional Framework. *Business Strategy and the Environment*. 13: 212.
23 Magali Delmas and Michael W. Toffel. 2004. Stakeholders and Environmental Management Practices: An Institutional Framework. *Business Strategy and the Environment*. 13: 209–222.
24 www.ecowatch.com/7-sins-of-greenwashing-and-5-ways-to-keep-it-out-of-your-life-1881898598.html
25 Magali A. Delmas and Vanessa Cuerel Burbano. 2011. The Drivers of Greenwashing. *California Management Review*. 54(1): 67.
26 Magali A. Delmas and Vanessa Cuerel Burbano. 2011. The Drivers of Greenwashing. *California Management Review*. 54(1): 68.
27 Magali A. Delmas and Vanessa Cuerel Burbano. 2011. The Drivers of Greenwashing. *California Management Review*. 54(1): 64–87.
28 Peter A. Stanwick and Sarah D. Stanwick. 2016. *Understanding Business Ethics*. Third Edition. Sage Publications: Thousand Oaks, CA.
29 Stuart L. Hart. 1997. Beyond Greening: Strategies for a Sustainable World. *Harvard Business Review* 75: 66–76.
30 Stuart L. Hart. 1997. Beyond Greening: Strategies for a Sustainable World. *Harvard Business Review*. 75: 70.
31 www.greenconsultancy.com/environmental-solutions/environmental-audits
32 www.greenconsultancy.com/environmental-solutions/environmental-audit-process
33 https://3+ENVIRONMENTAL+AUDIT+CONDUCTING+AN.pdf
34 Rebecca M. Henderson, Sophus A. Reinert, Polina Dekhtyar and Amram Migdal. 2018. *Climate Change in 2018: Implications for Business*. Harvard Business Publishing. January 30.
35 Michael W. Toffel and Stephanie Van Sice. 2013. *Carbon Footprints: Methods and Calculations*. Harvard Business School Publishing. 3.

36 Michael W. Toffel and Stephanie Van Sice. 2013. *Carbon Footprints: Methods and Calculations*. Harvard Business School Publishing. 1–16.
37 Michael W. Toffel and Stephanie Van Sice. 2013. *Carbon Footprints: Methods and Calculations*. Harvard Business School Publishing. 15.
38 www.ibm.com/blogs/research/2019/12/heavy-metal-free-battery/
39 www.cnbc.com/2019/12/18/tesla-and-gm-want-to-deliver-on-the-hype-over-self-driving-and-electric-vehicles.html

Case studies on corporate sustainability

OwlTing and blockchain technology in Taiwan

Toxic chemicals in food additives

In May 2011, it was disclosed that the Yu Shen Chemical Company was using a potentially cancer-causing plasticizer, Di(2-ethylhexyl) phthalate (DEHP), instead of palm oil as a clouding agent in its foods and drinks. The chemical is designed for industrial use only and is added to the manufacture of shoes and other products in order to make them more flexible.

An edible clouding agent, such as palm oil, is used as a food additive in order to make beverages primarily look cloudier. This is a desired look by some manufacturers who want cloudy beverages so they can look more "natural" and appealing. DEHP also yields a cloudy appearance in beverages and is cheaper than palm oil. In addition, beverages which used DEHP could be preserved for up to six months longer than beverages which used palm oil. Furthermore, while DEHP was a pure white substance which would not impact the color of the beverages, palm oil has a yellow tinge which could impact the coloring. In addition, palm oil is less stable than DEHP and over time will give off a bad odor, which limits its shelf life. It was also disclosed that the use of DEHP as a clouding agent began in the early 1990s in Taiwan.[1]

In June 2011, it was announced that Yu-Shen Chemical Company was also selling DEHP instead of palm oil to bakeries and other food manufacturers. The DEHP was used in sports drinks, juices, tea drinks, dietary supplements, jams, and fruit fillings. The Taipei, Taiwan City government withdrew Yu-Shen's business licenses and factory registration and fined Yu-Shen $5,220 for selling toxic food products.[2] On June 14, 2011, the owner of Yu-Shen Chemical, Lai Chun-chieh, was charged with violations of the Act Governing Food Sanitation, and also with fraud. Government prosecutors had requested a 25-year sentence and a fine of $300,000. The owner's wife, Chien Ling-yuan, was also charged and the prosecutors requested a sentence of 20 years and a fine of $210,000. On December 10, 2011, Lai Chen-chieh was sentenced to 18 years and his wife Chien Ling-yuan was sentenced to 16 years in prison. The court had ruled that Lai and Chien both knew that DEHP was toxic and committed a serious crime by mixing them in food additives and selling them to clients that were not aware that DEHP was included in the additives.[3]

In December 2013, Yu-Shen Chemical was ordered to pay $4.4 million to the largest food producer in Taiwan, Uni-President Enterprises, for selling DEHP as a clouding agent for Uni-President food products. Uni-President Enterprises was not aware that they were buying DEHP from Yu-Chen Chemical. It was estimated that over 460,000 of DEHP tainted beverages were removed from shelves. In addition, 28,000 kilos of fruit juices, jams, and syrups were removed from retail stores. It was estimated that Yu-Shen had used five tons of DEHP monthly to manufacture the clouding agent to be distributed throughout Taiwan.[4]

Tainted cooking oil

In September 2014, customers in Taiwan were told that a Taiwanese cooking oil suppler, Chang Guann Co., had made substandard cooking oil by mixing lard oil with restaurant and slaughterhouse waste. The altered cooking oil was used by hundreds of bakeries and eateries in Taiwan. The chairman of Chang Guann stated in a press conference that the company was also a victim because it had been misled by its own suppliers in the manufacturing process.

Within one week after the announcement had been made about the altered cooling oil, over 200 tons of tainted products, which were primarily baked and processed goods, were removed from store shelves and restaurants in Taiwan. It was determined that some of the tainted products had been certified as being safe. In order for food products to be certified, the Taiwanese government industrial development bureau uses outsourced labs to test food and give ad hoc investigations on food manufacturing facilities.

At the time of the scandal, the Taiwanese government had 500 food safety workers who made inspections of approximately 300,000 food and beverage manufacturers. The test results from the labs are then sent to the Taiwan Food Good Manufacturing Practice Development Association, which is an industry-controlled organization that certifies the quality of the food products. Under the certification process, a quality certificate can be issued only when one of the manufacturer's products passes the relevant tests. As a result, products can be certified without passing the tests under the umbrella certification that one product does pass the tests. The head of the association, Bonnie Sun Pan, stated that, "We need to do more to improve the certification process and regain public trust."[5]

The Taiwanese company, Chang Guann, bought and reprocessed 782 tons of tainted oil. Of the 782 tons that were sold throughout Taiwan, only 236 tons were recovered. Authorities were not able to calculate how many tons of the tainted oil had been consumed by customers. In addition to the sanitation issues associated with illegally recycling oil, the reused oil used in a cooking process may contain carcinogens such as benzopyrene and afatoxin.[6]

On July 28, 2015, Yeh Wen-hsiang, the chairman of Chang Guann Company, was sentenced to 20 years in prison and ordered to pay a fine of $1.6 million for selling tainted oil that was used by food manufacturers in Taiwan and Hong Kong. The company's vice-president, Tsai Chi-chuan, was sentenced to 20 years in prison for food safety violations. The tainted or "gutter oil" was collected from cookers, fryers, grease traps, and recycled grease from leather processing plants. Hundreds of tons of cakes, breads, instant noodles, cookies, steamed buns, and dumplings had to be recalled after news of the tainted oil was released to the public. It was estimated that over 1,000 restaurants, bakeries, and food manufacturers had used the tainted oil. The scandal led to the resignation of Taiwan's health minister, Chui Wen-ta, in October 2014.

In September 2014, Yeh Wen-hsiang made a public apology and drank a cup of the company's cooling oil to prove that it was safe to consume.[7] Three years later, in September 2017, Yeh Wen-hsiang drank detergent in an apparent suicide attempt after the Taiwan Supreme Court rejected his appeal.[8] In 2016, Yeh Wen-hsiang appealed the prison sentence to the Taiwan High Court, who not only rejected the appeal but added two years to his prison sentence.

OwlTing and food safety

In 2009, Darren Wang, CEO and co-founder of OwlTing, moved back to Taiwan after working at Google in the United States. Wang saw an opportunity of using technology in order to create a location-based system for firms. In 2011, Taiwan was facing a food safety crisis which involved tainted milk imported from China. As a father of two young children at the time, Wang wanted to develop a solution to any opaque food supply system which killed dozens of children and made several hundred more ill. In addition, as was discussed in the previous section, Taiwan consumers could not rely on the quality and safety of its food sources.

Wang and his CIO and co-founder John Hsieh developed a solution to the tainted milk program by establishing a trusted network of high-quality dairy farmers. After vetting the farmers and their processes, OwlTing developed a "farm to the table" e-commerce platform to help the farmers sell their milk online. The customers were reassured about the quality of the milk since they were acquiring the milk directly from the original source. This idea of linking the original source with the end user became the starting point of developing a blockchain system. In 2014, Wang started to personally invest in various blockchain ventures to get a better understanding of how blockchain can be used to guarantee food safety.

By 2016, OwlTing was focusing on using blockchain technology to fundamentally change food safety and build a trusting relationship between the end user and the firms that were part of the food supply chain. In 2017, OwlTing announced the launching of OwlChain (food safety) and OwlNest (hotel booking) focusing on building blockchain solutions.[9]

OwlTing's e-commerce platform has developed a blockchain on the food supply in Taiwan to track every step in the food distribution process. The online platform connects consumers directly with producers of food products in Taiwan. Its product, OwlChain, which was introduced in 2017, establishes a new benchmark in food supply transparency and ensures integrity and an immutable state in the food distribution channel. OwlChain creates a tamper-resistant food provenance system. Food provenance refers to the ability to know the original origin of the food as well as being able to identify which companies are responsible for the production, transportation, and delivery of the food. For example, any client that uses OwlChain to buy fish can specifically track the fish through each step of the supply chain to the fisher who caught the fish.

For companies who promise its consumers that its fish have been caught in a sustainable way, OwlChain can guarantee that claim. One of OwlTing's clients, Upwelling Ocean, is able to make that claim with its fish products. The founder of Upwelling Ocean, Steven Shyu, stated that:

> Blockchain technology is unique as it cannot be altered, it is traceable, and it will bring higher credibility to our marine environment protection label. Not only will it facilitate sustainable use of ocean resources in Taiwan, we can share this concept with fishing industries in other regions in the world that rely on local productions and distributions.[10]

An example of blockchain food safety

An example of how OwlChain is used to guarantee transparency in milk is based on a four-stage process. The vetted farmers document how their cows are raised in stage one. The data from the farmers is stored in a distributed blockchain network and then validated that the cows are truly free range and organic.[11] Data that would be included in the database would be animal births, vaccinations, and feeding routines.[12] In the second stage, the logistic provider (trucking firm) proves that the milk is being transported safely using the correct food handling procedures. The third stage occurs at the processing and bottling plant where the supplier proves that the milk is pasteurized safely and provides details which the end users (customers) can see. At the fourth stage, the customers can track and trace every bottle of milk sold in the grocery store back to the farmer. The benefits for the firm selling the milk to consumers is that OwlChain builds trust and engagement with the customer resulting in increased loyalty to the brand. The firm also is confident when it states that the milk is organic and complies with all health regulations and, therefore, can be a source of competitive advantage for the firm.[13]

On May 28, 2019, OwlTing announced the launching of OwlTing Block-chain Services, which consolidates its OwlChain, OwlNest (blockchain based hotel management service which eliminates double-booking of hotel rooms), and OwlCheck (blockchain anti–counterfeiting system) services that target multiple industries with exclusive blockchain applications. Darren Wang, the founder and CEO of OwlTing, states that:

> Blockchain is the fundamental structure in the future internet, and OwlTing is working hard to change the world in the next decade. We hope to build customized blockchain applications and services for every industry to explore the infinite possibilities of blockchain technology.[14]

From blockchain to climate change

Rice farmers in Taiwan rely on the rain from the typhoons in the late summer and early autumn to give the crops much needed water for the early growth phase. In 2018, the tropical storms that usually hit Taiwan moved north to hit Japan instead. As a result, as the climate changes, so are the resources needed to monitor the crops for the rice farmers. One farmer, Chen Cheng-hung, stated that, "The changes in climate is something we can't predict. Many farmers rely on the traditional farming calendar, but in fact the climate no longer follows that calendar." In a pilot project, OwlTing has equipped one organic rice field with a set of sensors which monitor the rain, temperature, and chemicals in the soil. The farmers can monitor the growth of their rice and relay that information to the confirmed buyers of the rice. The collection of data will be used to allow the farmers to optimize their production cycle.

The net result of this data collection is that farmers in Taiwan will be more willing to produce under contract at a set price based on the analysis of previous production schedules. The entity that controls the data, whether it be an insurance company, financial institution, or a technology company, will have input into determining what crops are grown, when they are grown, and how they are grown.

In addition, farmers of organic rice can use the data to more effectively market their crops. As is the case with OwlTing's other blockchain applications, the farmers can provide complete transparency as to who grew the rice and the exact location where the rice was grown. For example, rice that is grown in areas without heavy industry in Taiwan are grown in cleaner air, water, and soil, which allows farmers to charge a premium for their rice. The use of data collection also becomes the learning tool for the next generation of farmers in Taiwan. As the children of farmers migrate to the large cities in Taiwan, the collection of data will become the "collective memory" for how to grow crops in the future.[15]

Questions for thought

1. Why do you think there have been so many problems in the past with food safety in Taiwan?
2. Do you think the prison sentences were appropriate for the executives who sold chemicals and tainted oil to food producers? Why or why not?
3. Do you think blockchain is a useful technology in any industry? Any country? Explain.
4. What other applications are there for blockchain based on the shifting conditions of climate change?
5. Are there ways in which a firm can "tamper" with the blockchain tracking system?

Notes

1 Juan Yi-yu, Wei Yi-chia and Hung Su-ching. 2011. Food Scare Widens: Tainted Additives Used for Two Decades: Manufacturer. *Taiwan News*. May 29.
2 Chen Ching-fang, Sunrise Huang and Elizabeth Hsu. 2011. Toxic Additives Tracked to Bakeries as Scandal Escalates. *Focus Taiwan News Channel*. June 4.
3 www.asiaone.com/print/News/AsiaOne%2BNews/Crime/Story/A1Story20111210-315461.html
4 Anonymous. 2013. Yu Shen sentenced to compensate Uni-President for Plasticizer. *Taiwan News*. December 4.
5 Fanny Liu and Aries Poon. 2014. After Tainted Oil Scandal, Taiwan Pledges to Clean Up Food Safety. *The Wall Street Journal*. September 11.
6 Austin Ramzy. 2014. Taiwan Reels from Gutter Oil Scandal. *The New York Times*. September 8.
7 Agence France-Presse. 2015. Taiwan Food Company Boss Jailed for 20 Years Over 'Gutter Oil' Scandal. *South China Morning Post*. July 28.
8 Fang Chih-hsien, Hung Chen-hung and Jonathan Chin. 2017. Chang Guann Boss Yeh Hospitalized after Suicide Bid. *Taipei Times*. September 15.
9 www.owltingusa.com/owlting-is-building-trust-in-food-supply-chains-using-blockchain-tech/
10 Samburaj Das. 2017. Taiwan's OwlTing Launches Ethereum-Based Blockchain for Food Safety. *CCN*. May 30.
11 www.owltingusa.com/product/
12 Cindy Wang. 2018. Ex-Googler Wants to Upend Pigs and Hotels With the Blockchain. *Bloomberg*. March 22.
13 www.owltingusa.com/product/
14 www.prnewswire.com/news-releases/taiwan-blockchain-startup-owlting-launches-obs-platform-providing-commercial-solutions-with-blockchain-technology-in-biotech-logistics-automobiles-smart-agriculture-and-food-industries-300857226.html
15 Kathrin Hille. 2018. Taiwan's Rice Farmers Use Big Data to Cope with Climate change. *The Financial Times*. December 9.

Sumitomo and Ambatovy project in Madagascar

Madagascar

Off the east coast of the continent of Africa, the island of Madagascar is the world's fourth largest island. Despite its proximity to Africa, the strong ocean currents have historically isolated the island, which has affected both its natural environment and its economy. It is estimated that approximately 90 percent of the flora and fauna in Madagascar cannot be found anywhere else in the world. The French colonized Madagascar in 1896 and the country regained its independence on June 26, 1960.

The 2018 population of Madagascar was approximately 25.6 million people. The nationality of the citizens is called Malagasy. Madagascar has two official languages: French and Malagasy, while English is also spoken on the island and is extensively used in commerce and tourism.

Madagascar has a number of valuable natural resources including nickel, graphite, cobalt, gems, chromite, coal, bauxite, and rare earth elements. Despite its abundant natural resources, Madagascar is one of the poorest countries in the world. In 2018, the poverty rate reached 75 percent of the population living on less than $1.90 per day. Eighty percent of the working population participates in agriculture-related businesses.

The World Bank ranks Madagascar 140th out of 157 nations based on its Human Capital Index (HCI). The HCI measures the amount of human capital a child born in Madagascar can expect to attain by the time the child reaches adulthood at 18 years of age. A child in Madagascar will be 37 percent as productive as a child who has access to full education and access to full health care. In Madagascar, the average length of schooling is 7.5 years. For global harmonized test scores, the average global student scores 351 on a scale where 625 represents advanced attainment and 300 represents minimum attainment.

Madagascar has numerous environmental issues including erosion and soil degradation due to deforestation, overgrazing, desertification, and agricultural fires. Much of Madagascar's surface water is contaminated with raw sewage and other organic waste. Of the total population, only approximately 13 percent has access to electricity. The country has the world's fourth highest rate of chronic malnutrition with 50 percent of the children under the age of two having stunted growth due to the lack of proper nutrients.

Madagascar has a largely unregulated economy, which the government and global firms exploit for its natural resources. In addition, there are no capital markets for investment development; a weak judicial system with weak enforcement of contracts; and rampant government corruption. Madagascar had economic support from the World Bank and the International Monetary Fund (IMF) from the mid-1990s to 2009 to improve the economic conditions of the country. In 2009, many nations, including the United States, withdrew their economic support when a military coup d'état occurred which overthrew the government. An elected government was reinstated in 2013, resulting in foreign aid returning to the island.[1,2,3]

Based on the challenging components of current conditions in Madagascar, foreign-based companies have formed partnerships to develop both Madagascar's natural resources and its standards of living. In 1960, the Malagasy Geologic Services mapped out significant nickel and cobalt reserves in central Madagascar.

The Ambatovy project in Madagascar

The Ambatovy development in Madagascar is one of the largest lateritic nickel mining operations in the world. It is the largest-ever foreign investment in Madagascar and one of the largest foreign investments ever in sub-Saharan Africa and the Indian Ocean region.[4]

The Ambatovy project yields three commercially viable products: nickel, cobalt, and ammonium sulphate. Nickel is a silver metal whose properties include resistance to corrosion and oxidation and the ability to withstand high temperatures without being compromised. While nickel is used in hundreds of products, its primary use is in the production of stainless steel.

Cobalt is a shiny gray metal which is usually incorporated into copper and nickel ore. Originally used to add blue color to glass and pottery, cobalt is now used in hundreds of commercial industrial applications including the manufacture of super alloys, electronics, and rechargeable batteries.

Ammonium sulphate is created as a byproduct of the mining process used by Ambatovy. Ammonium sulphate is an agricultural fertilizer used to lower the pH level in the soil and provides plants with nitrogen and sulfur as nutrients.[5]

In March 2015, the 90/90 production test was completed, which refers to achieving 90 percent capacity for a 90-day time period. When the project is fully operational, Ambatovy will generate 60,000 tons of refined nickel, 5,600 tons of refined cobalt, and 210,000 tons of ammonium sulphate fertilizer each year for at least 29 years. When full operations occur, nickel will become Madagascar's top global export.

The ore is extracted from the mining site and mixed with water, which becomes a light mud-like substance called slurry. The slurry is transported by pipeline 220 kilometers to the plant site on the east coast of Madagascar. Almost 22,000 pieces of 60-cm-wide pipe were welded together to construct the pipeline, which has the capacity to transport 826 tons of slurry ore hourly. Due to the 1,000-meter high elevation of the mining site, the slurry moves through the pipeline primarily via gravity. At the plant site, the ore is processed and refined.[6]

Stakeholder impacts of the Ambatovy project

In January 2006, as the operator of the mine, Dynatec issued a comprehensive external environmental report highlighting the stakeholder impacts of the Ambatovy project.

The report proposed the development of an open pit mine to extract nickel and cobalt that would last at least 27 years. The mine would give an opportunity to greatly enhance the employment and economic benefits for the Malagasy people. The mine was expected to have a workforce of 390, of which 360 were to be Malagasy.

The total population around the mine site was approximately 80,000 people in 2003. There were several cultural sites near the project area which needed to be addressed with great sensitivity. These sites included ancestral burial areas and cemeteries, ceremonial sites for family, and communal altars for prayer, areas that are considered "nefarious," sacred waterfalls, and other cultural symbols.

Environmentally, the mine site was covered with natural forest and includes 127 flora species. Of the 127 different flora, 53 species were identified in the Convention on International Trade in Endangered Species of Wild Fauna and Flora (CITES) listing. The site also included five amphibian and reptile species unique to Madagascar. Sixteen bird species and nine lemur species located in the mining area were also listed by CITES. An overall total of 104 species listed by CITES were located in the mining site.

Some of the major concerns with the opening of the mine included the resettling of people living where the mined tailings would be located; the health and safety effects on people in the region including HIV/AIDS that could be linked with migrant workers; the reduction in water quantity and quality downstream from the mine and tailings area which could impact the natural environment including people and agriculture; and the negative impact on biodiversity and forest areas.[7]

Ambatovy and its stakeholders

In 2017, the Ambatovy project employed approximately 3,350 direct and 5,560 contractor employees of which 93 percent of the direct employees were Malagasy. It had purchases of $240 million goods from local merchants and financially supported over 240 children with their education. The project provided over 156,000 hours of training and discovered and preserved over 800 cultural artifacts.

Ambatovy has identified its critical stakeholders as national, regional, and local government authorities; local communities and People Affected by the Project (PAPs); the general public; the international community; civil society organizations and local NGOs; the press and media; the private sector/business community; employees; and shareholders.

Several issues have been raised by its stakeholders which they want Ambatovy to address with its actions. These issues include the development of the livelihoods of the people connected to the project; the access to resources; royalties for the metals extracted; employment opportunities; business opportunities; the impact the project has related to the environment, human health, the economy, and society; compliance with national and international standards; strong corporate governance, safety, and security issues; and the ability to present grievances.

Ambatovy works with the Malagasy government on a wide range of issues including its commitment to its Social Investment Fund (SIF) as well as its other environmental and social commitments. Ambatovy regularly offers informational visits and tours to regional and local authorities. In 2012, Ambatovy created the SIF, which had an allocation of $25 million to be used for social and infrastructure projects that benefited local communities. Projects that have been funded by the SIF include the rehabilitation of a marketplace in the port town of Toamasina, the establishment of an integrated poultry farm, the purchase of two generators producing electricity for Toamasina, the donation of two fire trucks, and the rehabilitation of the Technical and Vocational High School in Toamasina. In addition to its commitment to its SIF, in 2017 Ambatovy also provided relief efforts when Cyclone Enawo hit the island and when there was a plague outbreak which occurred from August to November 2017.

Ambatovy meets with regional authorities every two months through its Dialogue Structure for the Region and Ambatovy program. For the local communities and PAPs, Ambatovy includes continuous dialogue with local authorities and native leaders. In 2017, Ambatovy provided 100 desks for the Antanambao Public Primary School as well as provided help to local farmers with training and farming supplies. For the Malagasy general public, Ambatovy has an "info van" which provides information to the local communities through presentations and face-to-face interactions. In addition, Ambatovy participates in numerous national and regional fairs, celebrations, and World Day events including World AIDS Day, World Environment Day, and World Lemur Day.[8]

One of the many challenges of the Ambatovy project was having the necessary infrastructure needed for the operational functions of the project. When construction started at Ambatovy, there were virtually no supporting roads or utilities, resulting in Ambatovy being considered one of the largest "greenfield" mining projects globally. In order to effectively move commodities between the port and the mining site, a new 12-kilometer railway line was built that was parallel to an existing railroad which could not hold the necessary capacity. An ammonia storage facility was built between the port and the plant site where the ammonia is transported via an underground pipeline.[9]

Additional infrastructure support projects that need to be developed include a coal-fired steam and electricity generating plant; plants to produce oxygen, hydrogen, sulfuric acid, and hydrogen sulfide; a water treatment plant; residential and recreational facilities for the workers; and a medical clinic. Ambatovy also built a vocational training center and a primary school. A road 11 kilometers in length was also built from the mining site to the port, which resulted in the reduction of traffic congestion in the port city of Toamasina. Ambatovy also constructed and upgraded approximately 100 kilometers of public access roads. Some of the public roads had not been opened to the public since 1969 for safety reasons, and the upgrading of these roads allowed bus services for 11 rural communities for the first time.[10]

In its 2017 annual report, Sherrill stated that the Ambatovy site was planned to be mined for 18 years and would continue for an additional 11 years with the reclamation of low-grade ore that has been stockpiled after the initial mining had been completed.[11]

The partners of the Ambatovy project

Sumitomo Corporation

Headquartered in Japan, Sumitomo Corporation started as a land development firm and has evolved into six business groups: (1) metal products such as steel sheets, tubular products, and aluminum; (2) transportation and construction systems such as ship and aircraft leasing; (3) infrastructure such as providing electricity, water, and railroad projects; (4) media and digital services such television and digital media productions; (5) retailing and real estate including supermarket and drugstore chains; and (6) mineral resources, energy, chemical, and electronics.[12]

Dynatec

Dynatec is a Canadian based mining company which has three major areas of investment, which include a minority interest in the Ambatovy Project, a 24.5 percent ownership interest in Canadian owned FNX mining, and a wholly owned coalbed methane lease agreement.[13] In 2003, Phelps Dodge Madagascar and Dynatec Corporation formed a joint venture called Dynatec Madagascar to develop the mine.

In 2004, Dynatec received a 53 percent interest in Ambatovy and subsequently obtained the other 47 percent from Phelps Dodge in 2005. In 2005, Sumitomo acquired 25 percent of the project, which left Dynatec with 75 percent ownership. In 2006, Dynatec was named as the project operator and Korea Resources (27.5 percent) and SNC-Lavin Group (5 percent) acquired minority interests in the project. As a result, Dynatec has 40 percent ownership, Sumitomo has 27.5 percent, Korea Resources Corporation (KORES) has 27.5 percent, and SNC-Lavalin has 5 percent ownership.[14]

Sherritt buys Dynatec

Fifteen months after Dynatec released the stakeholder report of the Ambatovy project on April 20, 2007, it was acquired by Sherritt International Corporation. Sherritt is a diversified natural resource company whose operations include the production of coal, nickel, cobalt, oil, and electricity. Sherritt had acquired all of the issued and outstanding common shares of Dynatec for $1.6 billion. The President and CEO of Sherritt, Jowdat Waheed, stated that:

> This is an important step in the growth strategy of our Metals division, enabling us to become a premier, globally diversified lateritic nickel producer based in Canada. The Ambatovy nickel project enhances our already strong metals operating platform, from which we will be able to meet demand in a growing market.[15]

In 2015, SNC-Lavalin sold its 5 percent ownership to Sumitomo Corporation.

Current issues related to the Ambatovy project

Cyclone Ava

In January 2018, cyclone Ava made landfall for two days on Madagascar and killed at least 29 people and impacted at least 83,000 people. The cyclone hit the eastern part of Madagascar and flooded roads and towns. Buildings also collapsed and communication systems were knocked out. Unfortunately, cyclones are a common occurrence on Madagascar. In 2017, tropical cyclone Enawo hit the northeastern part of Madagascar.[16]

In the initial aftermath of cyclone Ava, both Sumitomo and Sherritt issued short statements that only referred to the safety of its employees and that production at the mine would be shut down for a month. There was no information released about any potential environmental issues related to the cyclone hitting Ambatovy. Four months after Ava hit Madagascar, an Ambatovy spokesperson confirmed that the cyclone had caused "extensive damage to facilities and equipment." Members of the local community were concerned about potential chemical leaks from the mine's holding ponds and the impact the cyclone had on its open-air stockpile of sulfur, which is used to manufacture its fertilizer.

After the cyclone, local taxi driver Dada Niry stated:

> I can't find words to denounce the negative effects on public health of the pollution caused by Ambatovy. This factory lets out some unbearable smells and since the last cyclone, we are all scared ... We are hearing that the storage of chemicals, such as sulfur, has been affected by the cyclone. The danger becomes more and more alarming.[17]

Introduction of Asian common toads

The Asian common toad was introduced into the ecosystem in Madagascar. The Asian common toad is not an indigenous species to Madagascar. They are bigger and tougher than toads native to Madagascar and the Asian common toad quickly became the dominant species. The Asian toads were first spotted around 2008 with a commonly held belief among local people of the island that they were accidentally shipped inside a container from Vietnam and were unloaded at the Toamasina port and opened at the Ambatovy processing plant.

The toads do not have brightly colored markings that would warn native predators such as snakes and birds that their secretions are poisonous. While toads native to Madagascar may lay as few as ten eggs at a time, the Asian common toad can lay between 10,000 and 40,000 eggs. Therefore, the Asian common toad is an extreme threat to Madagascar's ecosystem since invasive species are second only to habitat loss as the biggest cause of extinction. An Ambatovy spokesperson commented that:

> During the timeframe that the toad is speculated to have arrived in Madagascar, Ambatovy accounted for less than 5 percent of the Port of Toamasina's total traffic – and that percentage is even lower for shipments coming from the toad's zone of origin, according to our records and those we obtained from Madagascar's customs office. Research has not found evidence of the real carrier of this invasive species in Madagascar ... We recognize that the spread of invasive toads can have a serious impact on local flora and fauna. Ambatovy has joined the government's national committee, which is comprised of several stakeholders, to mitigate the impacts of the Asian toad. We continue to bring our contribution in its eradication that we hope will lead to lasting results.[18]

Investment stake by the partner changes

On May 1, 2017, it was announced that the partnership percentages of the Ambatovy project had changed. Sherritt reduced its ownership percentage from 40 percent to 12 percent in exchange for the elimination of $1.02 billion of debt that it owed the other two partners, Sumitomo and Korea Resources Corporation (KORES).

Sherritt's CEO, David Pathe, stated that this ownership revision "removes the largest area of uncertainty for both Ambatovy and Sherritt." The owner's share of Sumitomo would increase from 32.5 percent to 47.7 percent and KORES' ownership would increase from 27.5 percent to 40.3 percent. Under the terms of the agreement, Sherritt would remain the operator of Ambatovy until at least 2024. Sumitomo's total investment in Ambatovy is approximately $1.7 billion, which includes $600 million in loans to Sherritt.

Sherritt abandons Ambatovy?

Early in March 2019, it was announced that Ambatovy had problems fulfilling its short-term liquidity needs. As part of the partnership agreement,

Sherritt was required to supply a cash infusion of $45 million to the Ambatovy project. On March 6, 2019, Sherritt announced that it would not supply the required $45 million as it needed to preserve its liquidity and protect its balance sheet. As a result, Sherritt became a defaulted shareholder under the terms of the Ambatovy JV Shareholders Agreement. The consequences of this decision included: Sumitomo and KORES supplying the additional funding; Sherritt losing all voting rights related to Ambatovy and Sumitomo; and/or KORES can buy Sherritt's 12 percent interest at a lower price than market value.[19]

Two weeks later, on March 20, 2019, Sumitomo announced that there was a fire in February at the hydrogen plant in Ambatovy, which killed a worker. The fire was a result of a hydrogen leak when a valve was replaced during maintenance. The mine had to shut down for two weeks due to the fire. The shutdown affected both the production of nickel and cobalt at the mine.[20]

The performance of the Ambatovy project

Tables 1 and 2 highlight the output of the mine and the financial performance of Sherritt. While the estimated capacity of the Ambatovy project is an annual production of 60,000 tons of nickel and 5,600 tons of cobalt, the project has so far failed to come close to those production numbers. Table 1 highlights the struggles the owners of the mine are having to make this

Table 1 Ambatovy total production levels in tons[21,22,23,24,25]

	Nickel	*Cobalt*
2019 (Projection)	35,000 to 38,000	3,100 to 3,400
2018	33,185	2.825
2017	35,474	3,053
2016	42,105	3,272
2015	47,142	3,465
2014	37,052	2,915

Table 2 Sherritt financial performance at Ambatovy (in millions $)[26,27,28,29,30]

	Revenue	*Loss from operations*
2018	101.2	−40.8
2017	279.2	−109.5
2016	264.8	−150.9
2015	332.0	−1,934.1
2014	291.8	−158.4

project viable in the long term. While the peak of past production was 47,142 tons or 72.5 percent of the mine's capacity for nickel in 2015, in 2018 the production level had decreased to its lowest annual production level of 33,185 tons or 51 percent of capacity. Furthermore, the projections of nickel production for 2019 were lower that the production level in 2015 for nickel.

For its cobalt production, the peak production level was again 2015 with 3,465 tons or 61.8 percent of capacity. As is the case with its nickel production, its lowest annual cobalt production occurred in 2018 when the mine produced 2,825 tons of cobalt, which is 50.4 percent of the mine's capacity.

Table 2 shows why Sherritt may be eager to leave the Ambatovy project. Sherritt has endured losses in every year of the Ambatovy project's operations including an almost $2 billion loss in 2015. The 2015 loss was due to a lower adjustment in the overall value of the operation due to the lower forecast of nickel prices. The cumulative losses for Sherritt for 2014 through 2018 from the Ambatovy project were $2.393 billion.

Questions for thought

1. What are the pros and cons of investing in a mining operation in Madagascar?
2. Is it worth the risk for foreign mining companies to develop mining operations in Madagascar?
3. Do you think the owners of the Ambatovy project have addressed the needs of its stakeholders at a satisfactory level? Give one example supporting yes and one example supporting no.
4. There are a lot of species in Madagascar's eco-system that are unique to the island. Would not any mining operation result in permanent damage to the natural environment and threaten the long-term survival of its unique animal and plants? Explain.
5. Do you think Ambatovy did a good job persuading its stakeholders that it was not responsible for introducing the Asian toad into Madagascar?
6. Do you believe the Ambatovy project will ever be profitable? Explain your answer.
7. Do you believe that the Ambatovy project will ever reach 100 percent annual capacity?

Notes

1 www.cia.gov/library/publications/the-world-factbook/geos/ma.html
2 www.worldbank.org/en/country/madagascar/overview#1
3 https://databank.worldbank.org/data/download/hci/HCI_2pager_MDG.pdf
4 www.ambatovy.com/ambatovy-html/docs/index.html%3Fp=110.html
5 www.ambatovy.com/ambatovy-html/docs/index.html%3Fp=483.html
6 www.ambatovy.com/ambatovy-html/docs/index.html%3Fp=515.html

  7 *Environmental Assessment Ambatovy Project*. Dynatec Corporation of Canada January 2006.
  8 *2017 Ambatovy Sustainability Report.*
  9 www.ambatovy.com/ambatovy-html/docs/index.html%3Fp=515.html
 10 www.ambatovy.com/ambatovy-html/docs/index.html%3Fp=515.html
 11 https://s2.q4cdn.com/343762060/files/doc_financials/2017/WEB-2017-Sherritt-ENGLISH-Annual-Report.pdf
 12 www.sumitomocorp.com/en/jp/business
 13 www.sherritt.com/English/Investor-Relations/News-Releases/News-Release-Details/2007/Sherritt-to-Acquire-Dynatec/default.aspx
 14 www.ambatovy.com/ambatovy-html/docs/index.html%3Fp=166.html
 15 www.sherritt.com/English/Investor-Relations/News-Releases/News-Release-Details/2007/Sherritt-to-Acquire-Dynatec/default.aspx
 16 Yarno Ritzen. 2018. Cyclone Ava Kills at Least 29 in Madagascar. *Al Jazeera News*. January 9.
 17 Laurence Soustras and Riana Raymonde Randrianarisoa. 2018. Uncertainty around Madagascar Mine in Wake of Cyclone. *Mongabay*. June 27.
 18 Jonathan Watts. 2018. Toxic Toad Invasion Puts Ecology of Madagascar at Risk. *The Guardian*. February 24.
 19 Business Wire. 2019. Sherritt Provides Update on Ambatovy Joint Venture. *Financial Post*. March 6.
 20 Anonymous. 2019. Fire Shut Sumitomo's Ambatovy Nickel Plant for 2 Weeks in February. *Reuters*. March 20.
 21 https://s2.q4cdn.com/343762060/files/doc_financials/2017/WEB-2017-Sherritt-ENGLISH-Annual-Report.pdf
 22 www.mining.com/sherritts-year-end-2019-guidance/
 23 https://s2.q4cdn.com/343762060/files/doc_financials/Annual-Report/2016/2016-Financial-Report-FINAL.pdf
 24 https://s2.q4cdn.com/343762060/files/doc_financials/Annual-Report/2015/SHERRITT_ANNUAL_REPORT_2015_FINAL.pdf
 25 https://s2.q4cdn.com/343762060/files/doc_financials/Annual-Report/2018/2018-Financial-Results-2-20-Final.pdf
 26 https://s2.q4cdn.com/343762060/files/doc_financials/2017/WEB-2017-Sherritt-ENGLISH-Annual-Report.pdf
 27 www.mining.com/sherritts-year-end-2019-guidance/
 28 https://s2.q4cdn.com/343762060/files/doc_financials/Annual-Report/2016/2016-Financial-Report-FINAL.pdf
 29 https://s2.q4cdn.com/343762060/files/doc_financials/Annual-Report/2015/SHERRITT_ANNUAL_REPORT_2015_FINAL.pdf
 30 https://s2.q4cdn.com/343762060/files/doc_financials/Annual-Report/2018/2018-Financial-Results-2-20-Final.pdf

Bayer corporate sustainability initiatives in India

> We support the development of innovative solutions with impact on global social challenges.
>
> 2017–2018 Bayer India Corporate Societal Engagement Compendium

Introduction

Established over 150 years ago, Bayer is a life science company which competes in the healthcare and agriculture industries. With the philosophy of "Science for a better life," Bayer has four major business units, which are: pharmaceuticals, consumer health, crop science, and animal health. Bayer operates 420 companies in 90 countries and has almost 117,000 employees. In 2018, it had sales of 39.586 billion euros and net income of 1.695 billion euros.[1]

Bayer's view on sustainability

Bayer's philosophy towards sustainability relates to its long-term relationship with its stakeholders. Its association with its stakeholders is based on a commitment to long-term future viability which includes the integration of sustainability considerations when making decisions impacting everyday operations. A number of the products that Bayer offers relate to the improvement of short-term and long-term health and the reduction of hunger. Bayer allocates 50 million euros annually for global non-profit projects which focus on sustainable progress and societal innovation.

Sustainability objectives are integrated in the top-level decisions of the firm. The operational implementation of the decisions is supported through the development of non-financial targets and performance indicators. The insurance of the successful implementation of Bayer's sustainability initiatives is based on ongoing reviews of the outcomes of the initiatives as well as the verification through regular internal audits.

An integral part of Bayer's sustainability philosophy is responsible business practices. Bayer's responsible business practices are based on the identification and mitigation of risks in the early stage of the implementation process to ensure compliance in areas such as anti-corruption and responsible marketing, human resources policy, product stewardship, health and environmental protection, and supplier management.[2]

Bayer in India

In 1896, Bayer started its first wholly owned subsidiary of Bayer in Asia located in India. Farbenfariken Bayer and Co, Ltd was headquartered in Bombay, which is now called Mumbai. The Bayer Group in India includes the Crop Science, Pharmaceuticals, and Animal Health business units.

The Crop Science division is Bayer's largest business in India and includes seeds, crop protection, and pest control. It is organized into two operational units: Crop Protection/Seeds and Environmental Science. Crop Protection/Seeds' markets a comprehensive selection of high-value seeds as well as innovative chemical and biological pest management solutions. Environmental Science focuses on a broad range of services and products related to professional pest and vector control. In India Bayer is the market leader in Crop Protection.

The Animal Health business unit develops and markets products for the prevention and treatment of diseases for personal companion and farm animals. The Animal Health business unit is part of the Crop Science division for Bayer.

The Pharmaceutical division sells prescription products for medical areas such as cardiology, diabetes, women's health care, oncology, hematology, and ophthalmology. In addition, the radiology division, which includes diagnostic imaging, is part of the Pharmaceuticals division.

Corporate societal engagement (CSE)

Bayer's CSE programs have been implemented across 15 states of India and have helped approximately 9 million people. For example, Bayer's Child Care Program has moved children from working in seed production farms to receiving an education at school. The program also supports a number of educational, vocational training, and livelihood initiatives to open up new opportunities for the participants.

Bayer developed the CSE program in order to develop corporate sustainability initiatives for India. Bayer's CSE is based on four pillars: empowering women; fostering education; fostering rural development; and preventive health and sanitation.

Empowering women

Program for primary prevention of sexual violence

Bayer, along with various partners, has developed the Program for Primary Prevention of Sexual Violence. This program established primary preventive measures to protect women and children from sexual violence and the aftereffects of the violence. Bayer and its partners have developed a number of preventive measures including an online assessment tool used as a primary prevention of child sexual abuse through treatment. The program also has a smartphone app which is used as a mechanism for the primary prevention of sexual violence against women through deterrence. Bayer also sponsors research on child sexual abuse in India and has established an advisory council with various stakeholders to address the issues related to child sexual abuse and sexual violence.

Discovering hands

Breast cancer is the most common form of cancer for women in India, with 1.5 million women being diagnosed every year. The survival rate is low due to low levels of awareness and the failure of women having access to knowledge related to early detection and prevention. For many women in India, they will only visit a doctor after they have already observed other side effects of the cancer.

Because of this need, Bayer, along with its NGO partner NAB India Centre for Blind Women and Disability Studies, developed the Discovering Hands program, which develops awareness programs for breast cancer with the aid of visually impaired women. The program trains and deploys visually impaired women who have highly developed sensory skills of touch to detect the early signs of breast cancer. The Medical Tactile Examiners (MTEs) are trained to give physical breast examination in physicians' offices. The training takes nine months and includes training on how to use a standardized diagnostic method for examining the female breast. The MTEs are also trained in breast-specific psychology as well as effective communication skills. In 2018, there were eight visually impaired women who had been certified as MTEs and they are now working as interns in a hospital in Gurgaon, Haryana.

This program not only benefits the women in their detection of breast cancer, but it also benefits the MTEs. One MTE, Sakshi Dalmia, who lost her vision, feels empowered to be able to impact women who have breast cancer. She states that:

> I am thrilled at the opportunity to pursue my skills to improve the lives of others … Either I used to not interact with people due to [my] lack of vision and felt that there were not many career options available. After being associated with this project, I feel my communication skills and my overall personality have improved … This project has helped me learn braille and computers. I believe that this project could shape my future.

Samavesh

Samavesh is a preparatory course sponsored by Bayer whose goal is to improve the employability of underprivileged women in the agriculture and healthcare industries. The three-month program includes a designed curriculum in which Bayer experts provide hands-on training to the women. The curriculum includes areas such as sales, marketing, human resources, finance, and operations. The program also includes training on self-defense, safe driving, and being able to work safely in rural areas.

Fostering education

Bayer fellowship program in AgroScience

Being on the forefront for new development in agriculture in India requires programs that encourage innovation and sustainable mechanisms. Bayer grants Fellowships in AgroScience for Masters of Science and PhD students. These fellowships are in partnership with several universities in India, including those in Gujarat, Karnataka, Punjab, Tamil Nadu, Telangana, Uttarakhand, and West Bengal. As of December 2017, 114 Fellowships had been awarded.

Mini Science Centres (MSC)

Bayer has set up 20 MSCs that bring science knowledge to over 9,000 students in Nanded. The MSC program provides 65 tabletop models which allow the students to experience learning opportunities as well as enable effective learning on math- and science-related concepts.

Youth education program

The Youth Education Program in Vapi is enabling children to have a high quality education. Bayer funded a new school building with a smart class room and a science and computer lab at the Audhyogik Vasahat Primary School. This program will expand to other schools, which will include an upgrade and maintenance of the targeted schools, the creation of diagnostic health camps for children, and the distribution of notebooks, school uniforms, and sports gear.

Bayer Science Teens Program

The Bayer Science Teens Program is hosted by Bayer Science & Education Foundation and is partnered with the STEM Harmony Education Center at the University of Colorado. Students from India and around the world participate in the program, which includes doing research on science and medical health issues under professional conditions. The students exchange ideas with scientists and perform various experiments.

Vocation Training Center for Agriculture

Bayer, in partnering with the Ramanaidu Vignana Jyothi School of Agriculture, has developed a science program which focuses on scientific training and education, which is part of Bayer's overall philosophy related to sustainable agricultural practices. The program focuses on providing vocational training for underprivileged youth from rural areas in order to prepare them for entry-level jobs in agriculture. The program started in 2007 and the school enrolls 42 students per course with two six-month courses offered to the students every year. By 2018, 517 students had graduated from the program.

School nutrition project midday meal

Children critically need the daily allowance of nutrients and calories in food to be able to concentrate in class. Bayer has implemented the School Nutrition Project Mid-Day Meal program to address not only issues of hunger but also to help improve the literacy level of the children. This program provides midday meals to over 60,000 children in over 500 schools in various parts of India.

Making Science Make Sense

Bayer also sponsors the Making Science Make Sense which provides school students with the ability to learn about science and natural phenomena through experiments. Bayer employees go to the schools to teach the experiments and help the children carry out the experiments. From 2007 to 2017, over 75,000 students has benefited from the programs in cities such as Mumbai, Ankleshwar, Vapi, and Himatnager.[3]

Fostering rural development

Samagra Krishi

Bayer developed the Samagra Krishi-Agriculture Productivity & Livelihood Project to provide sustainable farming solutions to small and marginal farmers. Farmers were given mechanized tools such as wheat and potato planters and maize shellers along with field training on how to optimize mechanized farming. In addition, solar water pumps, which were subsidized by local governments, were introduced to the farmers to be used for irrigation as an alternative to conventional pumps. The farmers were also taught about the value of crop diversification including growing cash crops to meet the needs of the local region. Alternative revenue streams such as raising goats and chickens and planting kitchen gardens were also highlighted through the program supported through Bayer's Self-Help Groups (SHGs) of women. This program has directly and indirectly positively impacted over 10,000 people in 25 villages across India.

Water, Agriculture, Sanitation, and Hygiene (WASH)

Bayer's Water, Agriculture, Sanitation, and Hygiene (WASH) program improves the public health of people living in India through better sanitation conditions and the conservation of pure natural resources such as water. Through the WASH program, existing sanitation issues are addressed, as well as preventive training, so that these issues will not occur in the future. The training is based on providing the people in local villages with the knowledge needed to change their mind-set and their habits and convince the villagers to protect natural resources from pollutants.

Village Training Program (VTP)

The Village Training Program focuses on exposing young people in rural areas to the best practices and new technology developments related to raising goats and chickens, animal husbandry (which is the raising of animals for meat, milk, eggs, or other products), crop production tailoring, plumbing, and other trades. The goal of the program is to improve the livelihood of the villagers by increasing their current and future potential income opportunities.

Community Health Program

The Community Health Program focuses on knowledge transfer in rural areas related to health and hygiene issues. The program provides a high-quality holistic healthcare approach which includes health screenings, health education, and treatment of cases diagnosed during the screening process. In addition, special health camps provide women with healthcare and hygiene information.

Extension for Community Healthcare Outcomes (ECHO)

Working with its NGO partner Karuna Trust, Bayer developed the ECHO project as a collaborative model of medical education and care management. This program allows clinicians in India to provide better health care in local communities.[4]

The plight of children working in agriculture

It is common for children as young as 7 or 8 years of age to work in fields under extreme heat conditions. The children typically have no protection against fumes of poisonous pesticides, which they inhale during the spraying of the crops. The children can also be responsible for carrying heavy loads of fruits, vegetables, and other types of food on their heads.

For children who convert rice into puffed rice, they can suffer burns when they toss the rice into the ovens. The children's fingers go numb by shelling cashews, almonds, walnuts, and other shelled foods. The living conditions of the children can be horrendous and include living in cramped make-shift camps or cowsheds. As a result, these children do not have the opportunity to improve themselves by being able to go to school. Bayer has zero tolerance for child labor and will take action against any known cases of violations in any of its facilities.

Child Care Program

Bayer's Child Care Program is based on the philosophy that children should be at school instead of working on farms like the hybrid seed production fields. The program raises awareness among the farmers of the benefits of their children getting an education. The three main components of the program are: (1) having a supply chain that is completely free of child labor; (2) developing a comprehensive program for rehabilitating child laborers; and (3) building a consensus among the farming community and society against child labor. There is a six-step process Bayer uses in order to ensure child labor in not being used in its supply chain.

THE SIX-STEP PROCESS TO AVOID CHILD LABOR IN BAYER'S SUPPLY CHAIN

The first step is the establishment of the commitment from the producers to contractually agree that they will not employ child labor at any step of the crop production process. The second step is a commitment from the producers to agree to allow Bayer to monitor their fields. The Bayer teams come unannounced at least six times a year to verify that no children are working the fields. The third step is the use of sanctions, if necessary. For violations, the first incidence will result in a verbal warning, the second incidence will result in a written warning with the risk that the supplier's bonus might be cancelled, for the third incidence the farmer would not receive the bonus payment, the fourth incidence will result in a 10 percent reduction of the buying price of the supplier's goods, and the fifth incidence will result in the termination of the contract.

The fourth step is the use of internal monitoring and audits by Bayer. Bayer reviews each site visit and evaluates what course of action needs to be taken, if any. A summary of the audits is presented to the board members of Bayer through quarterly reports. The fifth step is external monitoring and audits. Bayer hires an external auditor to evaluate the results of the audits. The sixth step is giving incentives to those suppliers who have honored the contractual obligations regarding the use of child labor. The incentives include not only financial rewards but also Bayer-sponsored productivity improvement training programs.[5]

Role model project

Certain women healthcare issues in rural India are largely neglected including menstrual health and other hygiene issues. Bayer has partnered with other organizations in order to increase the level of awareness to women in rural villages on these topics, which are considered to be social taboos for women and adolescent girls. Bayer has also played a key role in the development and manufacturing of low-cost sanitary pads to be used by the women in rural villages. Entrepreneurial women have set up facilities to manufacture the sanitary pads and have improved the livelihood of the entrepreneurs and the other women in the villages. The project has been very successful in getting girls to embrace the use of sanitary pads.

Preventive health and sanitation

Disaster relief

This program focuses on providing targeted immediate assistance in the areas of health and hygiene such as providing disaster relief. When natural disasters occur in India, Bayer provides immediate assistance from both financial and medical donations. Bayer also provides financial support for the rebuilding of the infrastructure.

Special education of hearing impaired children

Bayer has developed a program which supports the rehabilitation efforts of children who have hearing impairments. Hearing loss affects over 24 million children in India. With one of the highest deaf populations in the world, approximately 6 percent of the population in India has suffered some degree of hearing loss. Bayer supports the education of 40 hearing impaired children as well as support providing speech therapy to 25 children studying at the Ashray Akrut School in Hyderabad.[6,7]

Smallholder Farming Initiative

Established in 2015 by Bayer, the Smallholder Farming Initiative supports small-scale farmers in emerging and developing countries including India. The initiative provides the farmers with access and knowledge related to the proper usage of farming inputs, irrigation, and access to credit and insurance. The goal of the program is to aid farmers in growing their farms into commercially viable and sustainable farming practices.

As part of the initiative, Bayer along with its partners, International Finance Corporation (IFC), Netafim, and Swiss Re Corporate Solutions, developed the Better Life Farming Alliance program, which supports small-scale farmers globally. This program is significant since out of the 2.5 billion people in developing countries who work in the food and agriculture section, 1.5 billion relate to small-scale farmers. Globally, the average farm size varies significantly in acres: Canada 820, United States 442, Brazil 156, India 3, China 1.5, and Vietnam 1.2.

The program's pilot stage started in India and Kenya. In India, there are 250 million Indian farmers operating on approximately 140 million farms, comprising 395 million acres.

These small-scale farmers do not have the resources to invest in modern crop protection products that increase the production yields of the farm. In addition, they often lack the necessary knowledge to use the most up-to-date farming techniques. Furthermore, a good harvest does not always guarantee that the farmer will generate a sufficient profit for long-term survival. These farmers do not have direct access to global markets and have to sell their produce to intermediaries at local markets. The Smallholder Farming Initiative gives these Indian farmers access to both the knowledge and resources needed to get a fair price for their produce. It allows the farmers to have the ability to sell their products directly to distributors for global distribution. By no longer relying on the pricing established by the intermediaries locally, the farmers have the ability to obtain higher prices for their full food production.

Indian farmers who suffer through poor harvests due to fungal and viral diseases were aided by the Bayer Better Life Alliance program that taught the farmers the latest technology in crop protection and seeds. The program also gave the farmers better information related to nutrient management and drip irrigation. The program also introduced the farmers to new food retailers in order to obtain higher prices for their produce. Indian farmer Pappu Singh stated that because of the Bayer program he "can pay for the education of my two daughters and expand my farmland. I want to buy two hectares of land and provide people from my village with new jobs." In general, the 20 farmers who initially participated in the program are able to double their yield and triple their income due to access to higher quality seed, better crop protection products, and the correct fertilizers. A field officer from Bayer visited the farmers every week to help implement the new practices. By 2017, the program included 250 farmers and Bayer brought in a new partner to buy the produce from the farms, which created competition with the intermediaries and increased the purchasing price of their produce. In 2018, the program had helped 1,500 farmers.[8]

A threat to Bayer's global commitment to sustainability?

In 2018, Bayer acquired the global US agrochemicals company Monsanto for $63 billion. While the merger was perceived as a method to increase market share and efficiency for Bayer, the consequences of the merger have been staggering. While Monsanto was the pioneer of genetically modified organisms (GMO), its most important legacy is as the manufacturer of the bestselling herbicide Roundup. Roundup has been linked to many cases of cancer for those who have applied the herbicide to kill weeds.

In 2015, the World Health Organization's International Agency for Research on Cancer identified that an ingredient in Roundup, glyphosate, was carcinogenic. Yet, Bayer's executive thought the enhanced value of the merger outweighed the risk of acquiring Roundup and with it the legal ramifications. Bayer also was not concerned that numerous countries globally have banned the selling of GMO seeds which it had acquired from the merger with Monsanto.[9]

There are over 18,000 legal cases in the United States seeking financial compensation for the negative health impacts of Roundup. Bayer is faced with the possibility of having to pay billions of dollars in compensation. From mid-2017 to August 2019, Bayer's stock price fell by over 50 percent, which resulted in a decrease of total market capitalization of 50 billion euros. In April 2019, the CEO of Bayer, Werner Baumann, lost a vote of no confidence at the Bayer annual shareholders' meeting. The shareholders were also upset that Bayer's merger with Monsanto was not presented to the shareholders before the deal was agreed upon by both parties. This raises the question as to whether Bayer will need to revisit the costs of its sustainability programs in both India and globally.

Questions for thought

1. Which of the Bayer's programs have the most impact on you personally?
2. How successful do you think Bayer will be in convincing farmers not to have their children working the fields?
3. What would you do to convince the farmers to send their children to school?
4. What changes are there in improving the sanitary conditions in India?
5. Do you think that Bayer will revisit its sustainability programs based on its acquisition of Monsanto?

Notes

1 www.bayer.com/en/profile-and-organization.aspx
2 2017–2018. *Bayer India Corporate Societal Engagement Compendium.*
3 www.bayer.in/development/corporate-social-responsibility/making-science-make-sense/
4 2017–2018. *Bayer India Corporate Societal Engagement Compendium.*
5 Vineeta Dutta Roy. 2013. Bayer CropScience, India: Building and Sustaining a Responsible Supply Chain. *South Asian Journal of Business and Management Cases.* 2(2): 207–216.
6 2017–2018. *Bayer India Corporate Societal Engagement Compendium.*
7 www.bayer.in/development/corporate-social-responsibility/
8 www.cropscience.bayer.com/en/stories/2018/smallholder-farming-in-india-small-farms-big-improvements
9 Ralph Atkins. 2019. Lex In Depth: Bayer's E50bn Blunder. *Financial Times.* August 6.

Aon and sustainability initiatives in South Africa

Introduction

Aon is a global professional services firm which offers its customers numerous options related to risk, retirement, and health solutions. Aon has approximately 50,000 employees in 120 countries. It uses proprietary data and analytics to develop industry-based insights that can reduce investment volatility and improve the financial performance of its customers.[1]

Aon and sustainability

As a global provider of insurance, Aon views sustainability as an area in which its clients should manage its risks. Aon describes sustainability as the process in which individuals or firms seek to integrate and produce balance among potentially competing objectives related to economic, environmental, and social goals. The risks associated with social and environmental factors can impact shareholder values as much as strategic and operational issues. By having a proactive sustainability strategic commitment, firms are able to gather information that can be used to develop new and better products and processes which increase the financial performance of the firm.

Aon describes several fundamental benefits from embracing sustainability throughout its activities globally. If the firm has a strong sustainability commitment, it will enhance its reputation and brand strength. Sustainability can also lead to innovative new products and services which can enhance its competitive advantage in the marketplace. Sustainability initiatives can improve the level of efficiency of the firm, which also increases the level of productivity of its employees leading to a higher financial performance. By embracing sustainability, the firm has been able to build trust with its stakeholders by providing truthful transparent information related to its activities which directly and indirectly impact its critical stakeholders. In addition, firms with a strong sustainability commitment are less likely to be subject to fines and penalties for violations of employee and/environmental regulations.

Aon proposes that adjustments need to be made regarding how firms perceive risk. A comparison of the traditional Enterprise Risk Management (ERM) and Aon's Business Sustainability Platform (BSP) are shown in Figure 1.

While traditional ERM examines factors such as economic, strategic, and operational risk, Aon proposed that a truly comprehensive risk management system should also include sustainability factors such social and environmental risk. This holistic approach ensures that firms are able to provide information and transparency related to achieving its sustainability objectives as well as having managers make more informed decisions related to the firm's operations.

Traditional Enterprise Risk Management Framework

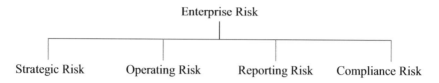

Aon's Business Sustainability Platform

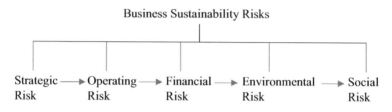

Figure 1 Traditional ERM and Aon's BSP[2]

Strategic risk

Strategic performance includes the selection and concentration of products that meet the current and future needs of a broad array of customers. It includes decisions such as: where manufacturing or other operations should be located; where products will be marketed; selection of suppliers; selection and training of employees; and corporate strategic vision. In Aon's model, sustainability issues related to these actions should be integrated into the decision-making process.

If sustainability issues are not included, the firm increases its strategic risk and the firm's subsequent strategic performance. Examples of strategic performance include: strategic planning, global expansion, potential mergers and acquisition, hiring and success planning for top-level managers, corporate governance, composition and strength of the board of directors, and the competitive advantage of its products and services.

Operating risk

The ability to incorporate efficiencies and effectiveness into the day-to-day operations is critical for a firm. Operational performance is based on the ability to develop systems which are able to monitor and measure the activities and outputs of the firm and give managers information on how to improve operations. From a sustainability perspective, operational risk is based on the ability of the firm to effectively communicate the information transparently to its stakeholders.

Therefore, it is critical for the firm to incorporate the needs and demands of its stakeholders in the design. The monitoring of its operations will endure a high level of operating risk. Examples of operational performance include manufacturing processes, control of operations, emergency response procedures, interdependency of operations, supply chain and review, employee retention and replacement programs, and ongoing monitoring and management.

Financial risk

Financial risk or economic performance risk includes prudent financial planning and the use of risk management systems that are customized to ensure that the firm is financially viable in the long term. The financial performance of a firm which embraces sustainability ensures that the needs of its stakeholders are incorporated into the risk management systems of the firm to meet its sustainability based financial obligations. Examples of objectives related to financial performance are profitability, cash flow, return on investment, asset value, credit rating, and capital expenditures.

Environmental risk

Environmental performance risk is based on the ability of the firm to develop processes and systems that are non-polluting, conserve energy and other natural resources, as well as use alternative energies rather than fossil fuels. The environmental goal of the firm is to establish a net zero ecological impact by being economically efficient, and provide a safe and healthy environment for its employees, consumers, local communities, and other critical stakeholders.

If the firm does not embrace a proactive environmental stance, it increases its vulnerability related to environmental risk. Examples of environmental performance risk are measurement of the firm's carbon footprint, energy source and consumption, recycling, use of hazardous material, waste generation, level of pollution, and raw material used in the manufacturing process.

Social risk

Social performance risk is based on the philosophy that managers need to understand the true value of human and natural capital and focus on the holistic experience of its stakeholders related to the activities of the firm. For example, employees, customers, local communities, and other stakeholders should be viewed not only on their interactions with the firm's goods and services but also through the value of social interactions. Examples of social performance risk are hiring of women and minorities, sexual harassment training, community outreach programs, family leave programs, safety of products, engagement with stakeholders, employee health and retirement plans, product quality and reliability, workplace violence responses, and charitable activities.[3]

Aon and sustainability in South Africa

Aon started operations in South Africa in 1996 and by 2017 had 700 employees in South Africa with operations in 8 local provinces.[4] Aon developed a Corporate Social Investment (CSI) program which is consistent with the firm's overall strategic focus and contributes to the overall mission and vision of Aon. Aon's CSI policy statement is based on the belief that Aon should be a responsible and contributing corporate citizen whose responsibilities include the equitable development of South Africa.

Objectives of Aon's CSI program in South Africa

There are seven strategic objectives of Aon's CSI program in South Africa:

1. The first objective is for Aon to make a positive sustainable and measurable impact in the local communities in which Aon has operations. The goal is targeting the improvement of the quality of life for the people living in these communities.
2. The second objective is for Aon to develop programs in which disadvantaged communities are able to improve their social, economic, and environmental commitments to yield long-term benefits for both the communities and South Africa.
3. The third objective is to enhance Aon's mutually beneficial relationships with its stakeholders.
4. The fourth objective is for Aon to further develop and enhance its reputation as a compassionate corporate citizen.
5. The fifth objective is for the CSI programs to facilitate loyalty and pride with its existing employees as well as be able to attract highly qualified potential employees who are committed to corporate sustainability.
6. The sixth objective is to enhance the relationship with Aon's employees by developing a strong bond of goodwill and loyalty based on the actions of the CSI programs.
7. The seventh objective is to support Aon's sustainability initiative of being a contributor in the development and strengthening of local disadvantaged communities.

The three primary focuses on Aon's CSI programs are: education, HIV/AIDS, and sports.

Education

Because of the educational inequalities that occurred during apartheid, less than one-third of the population of South Africa graduated from high school when measured on passing the national "end of school" final exam. The problems with educating students in disadvantaged communities include poverty, poor facilities, overcrowded classes, the lack of facilities, and resources and family problems.

In 2012, an estimated 3 million adults were illiterate, and another 8 million adults were functionally illiterate in South Africa. This lack of access to a quality education by students is an extreme burden for the nation. South Africa needs well-educated adults who are literate and have the skills necessary to improve the overall economy.

The legacy of apartheid

In 1948, the National Party gained power in South Africa and implemented policies to racially segregate the people of South Africa under a system called apartheid. Black South Africans were separated from white South Africans. This separation also included the type of schooling the white students would receive when compared with the black students. Schools located in black communities were neglected and did not receive the resources that schools received in white communities. After decades of pressure from the international community, apartheid was finally abolished in 1994. However, the challenges facing students in disadvantaged communities in South Africa continues more than 25 years after apartheid officially ended as the government policy.[5]

One of the legacies of apartheid was the implementation of the "Bantu" educational system. Under this system, black students were purposely given a poor education to ensure they would become subservient laborers to the whites in power. The prime minister at the time the Bantu system was implemented, Hendrik Verwoerd, wanted to ensure that Bantu educated students did not have an education in which the student would have access to "the green pastures of European society in which he was not allowed to graze."

The generational impact of the Bantu system can be seen in the education system today in which many of the teachers in South Africa schools located in disadvantaged communities received their education from the inferior Bantu system, which has negatively impacted their ability to teach their current students effectively. While these teachers are not tested on subject knowledge, in one study of the level of literacy of third grade teachers the majority of the teachers in the study scored less than 50 percent on a test for sixth grade students.

In 2009, half of the students in South Africa left school before they reached the 12th grade to graduate. In what some consider to be a "lost generation," many students that completed their education in rural and township (disadvantaged) schools are so poorly educated that they can only qualify for either menial labor or no job at all. An educational researcher at the Development Bank of Southern Africa, Graeme Block, stated that: .

> If you are in a township school, you don't have much chance ... That the hidden curriculum that inequality continues, that white kids do reasonably and black kids don't really stand a chance unless they can get into a formerly white school or the small number of black schools that work.

South African students consistently score at the bottom of internationally administered educational achievement tests, impacting the ability of South Africa to effectively compete in the global marketplace.[6]

Aon's education support in South Africa

As part of the CSI program, Aon has developed literacy projects and leadership guidance for primary school educators and students as well as developed programs for early development education. The objective of these programs is that through increasing the level of the education of the students in these disadvantaged communities, the students will increase their level of employability or be encouraged to become entrepreneurs when they have finished their schooling. Young people in South Africa in disadvantaged areas need to have corporate sponsored programs in which they can develop their business skills, are exposed to mentorship opportunities, and have access to leadership training. These programs are needed in order for the young people to be able to break away from the cycle of poverty and unemployment.[7,8]

HIV/AIDS in South Africa

South Africa has the largest epidemic of HIV/AIDS globally with 7.1 million people living with HIV in 2017. South Africa accounts for one-third of all new HIV/AIDS infections in southern Africa. A staggering 18.8 percent of the people aged 15 to 49 years of age have HIV/AIDS. There were 270,000 new HIV/AIDS infections annually in 2017. In addition, 110,000 South African died from AIDs-related illnesses in 2017.

In 2017, ninety percent of people who have HIV/AIDS are aware of their status, which is a significant increase from 66.2 percent in 2014. In addition, 61 percent of adults with AIDS are receiving antiretroviral treatment (ART) which virally suppresses AIDS while the percentage decreases to 58 percent for children receiving ART. An estimated 280,000 children aged 0 to 14 years old were living with HIV/AIDS in 2017 and the rate of annual new infections declined from 25,000 in 2010 to 13,000 in 2017. The reduction of new infections is primarily due to the success of the government's prevention of mother-to-child transmission programs with the infection percentage dropping from 3.6 percent in 2011 to 1.3 percent in 2017.

A subgroup of children, orphans, are at a high risk of contracting HIV/ AIDS. It is estimated that over 2 million children have been orphaned in South Africa by HIV/AIDS. Because of their inherent economic and social insecurities, orphans are more vulnerable to becoming infected with HIV/ AIDS because they can be forced into providing sexual acts in exchange for adult support and typically become sexually active at a younger age.

In 2015, the South African government spent over \$1.34 billion to fund its HIV programs. Due in large part to increased awareness and the ART programs, the life expectancy of people with HIV/AIDS had increased from 61.2 years in 2010 to 67.7 years by 2015.[9]

Aon's HIV/AIDS program

Despite the significant gains in awareness and treatment of HIV/AIDS in South Africa, it is evident that government funding is not enough to stop the spread of HIV/AIDS. Aon has developed community centers which take care of HIV/AIDS orphans and those who are infected by the disease. Aon also has financially supported safe centers for women who have been abused who may or may not be infected by HIV/AIDS.[10]

Sports and post-apartheid South Africa

As was mentioned previously with the legacy of apartheid in the educational system in South Africa, the same legacy is also very much present in sports in South Africa. While black South Africans have the political majority in South Africa, the white South Africans are still the economic majority. As a result, the white athletes have better sporting facilities, better coaches, better training, and better nutrition as compared with black athletes.

The impact of apartheid was significant throughout the history of South African sports. In 1958, the world governing organization of soccer, FIFA, recognized the white controlled Football Association of South Africa (FASA) was the governing body of soccer in the nation. After three years of international pressures, FIFA suspended FASA in 1961 and suspended South Africa from participating in FIFA events in 1964.

In 1964, South Africa allowed black athletes to compete in the Olympic Games. The South African Olympic Committee (SAOC) had separate Olympic trials for its black and white athletes. In addition, the black athletes were not allowed to fly in the same plane nor live in the same dorms as the white athletes. Because of these limitations and the refusal of the SAOC to condemn apartheid, the International Olympic Committee (IOC) withdrew the South African invitation to participate in the 1964 Olympic Games. The SAOC was expelled by the IOC in 1970.

In 1970, the International Cricket Council banned South Africa from participating in cricket matches because they did not allow black players on the national team. This ban was followed by the International Rugby Board banning South Africa from competing internationally in 1981.[11]

Segregation still occurs in sports in South Africa. A 2014 study highlighted that cricket and rugby still have predominately white players, while soccer has a majority of black players. The number of black players would have had to triple in rugby and cricket before it reached the South African government's goal of 50 percent representation. The cause of the under representation of black players is due to facilities and racism. Many of the top schools for rugby and cricket are not available to black players. In addition, Alec Moemi, who is a senior officer with the South African Sport and Recreation ministry, stated that, "There are still selectors (coaches) who are racist, who will not select a talented black player just because he is black."[12]

Aon and sports programs

Aon sponsors sports programs in disadvantaged communities for children to be exposed to the positive opportunities of playing sports. The positive values of sports participation include teamwork, discipline, strong work ethic, the desire to succeed, and the passion to play the game.

Aon's criteria for sustainability projects

Aon allocates a minimum of 1 percent net profit after tax to its sustainability initiatives. Aon has established a number of specific components which must be met before a project is accepted and funded by Aon. The criteria include:

- A comprehensive evaluation of what needs are being fulfilled and what is the estimated impact of the project.
- The creation of a formal contract which identifies the roles, rights, and benefits for each party involved in the project.
- An evaluation in order to ensure that the project is sustainable in the long term as well as the establishment of a measurable developmental impact.
- Identifying areas of employee involvement within the project.
- The assurance that the ultimate objective of the project is to improve the quality of life of people in disadvantaged communities within South Africa.
- The project should focus on disadvantaged communities in which Aon currently has operations.
- The ability to demonstrate strong internal controls and the vision to have the project incorporate long-term sustainability.
- The ability to partner with non-profit organizations in order to enhance the value of the project.
- The assurance that more than 5 percent of the people who benefit from the project are black.

Employee involvement in Aon's sustainability initiatives

Aon is committed to including its employees in its CSI projects since it will not only achieve Aon's sustainability goals but will also serve the holistic needs of its employees. Aon encourages its employees to volunteer on certain days during the year at numerous community development projects to receive one day's paid leave per year to volunteer.

The projects the employees can participate in include not only the programs that are based on Aon's CSI strategic focus but also other projects that may fall outside the identified CSI key focus areas. Employees can volunteer their support via time, financial contributions, and donations in kind.[13]

Questions for thought

1. Do you think other insurance companies have adjusted their risk models to include social and environmental risk?
2. Do you think South Africa will ever "fully" recover from apartheid?
3. What other type of sustainability initiatives should Aon implement in South Africa?
4. Is one annual paid day for the employees enough of a financial commitment by Aon for participation in its sustainability initiatives?
5. Do you think sports should be a top priority in Aon's sustainability initiative?

Notes

1 www.aon.com/getmedia/448f0bc2-e2ce-4630-82b8-653797eac2b8/Aon-plc-Fact-Sheet-2019-03-25.aspx
2 *Industry Update. Sustainability-Beyond Enterprise Risk Management.* Aon.
3 *Industry Update. Sustainability-Beyond Enterprise Risk Management.* Aon.
4 https://aon.co.za/assets/docs/general/aon_south_africa_brochure_2017_(electronic)_combined.pdf
5 www.history.com/topics/africa/apartheid
6 Celia W. Dugger. 2009. Eager Students Fall Prey to Apartheid's Legacy. *The New York Times.* September 19.
7 https://aon.co.za/csimarch.pdf
8 https://aon.co.za/corporatesocialresponsibility.aspx
9 www.avert.org/professionals/hiv-around-world/sub-saharan-africa/south-africa
10 https://aon.co.za/csimarch.pdf
11 https://globalsportmatters.com/culture/2019/04/16/south-africas-sports-lack-progress-in-the-post-apartheid-era/
12 David Smith. 2014. South African Sport Still a Racially Divided Field, Government Study Finds. *The Guardian.* May 2.
13 https://aon.co.za/csimarch.pdf

Dow Chemical corporate sustainability initiatives in Brazil

Dow Chemical and sustainability

Dow operates 178 manufacturing sites in 35 countries with 2017 sales of $55.5 billion.

On August 31, 2017, Dow Chemical merged with DuPont to form Dow-Dupont. The subsequent structure of the firm is to have three major divisions: Dow (which is the materials science division), DuPont (which is the specialty products division), and Corteva (which is the agricultural division of the new firm).[1]

Dow Chemical's Platform of Sustainability focuses on understanding its customers' sustainability needs and developing projects which help its customers to be more efficient and sustainable. The Platform helps identify opportunities for customers in the industries where Dow has expertise, including food, beverages, infrastructure, personal care, and home care.[2] Dow's sustainability initiatives for its customers include innovative methods to optimize the use of energy, reduce the customer's carbon footprint, save water, produce food, and capitalize on quality housing and health opportunities.

Dow Chemical's 2025 sustainability goals

In 2015, Dow Chemical announced its 2025 Sustainability Goals in which it would focus on developing collaborative partnerships in order to integrate public policy solutions, and science and technology innovations. The Dow 2025 Sustainability Goals are: leading the blueprint; advancing a circular economy; safe materials for a sustainable planet; world leading operations performance; delivering breakthrough innovations; valuing nature; and engaging for impact communities, employees, and customers.

Leading the blueprint

Leading the blueprint is based on the belief that the health of people, the planet, and businesses are linked and interdependent upon each other. Therefore, Dow wants to be a leader in developing public policy solutions that integrate scientific and technologically based programs to address these social issues. The Watershed Management project is a blueprint program which focuses on sustainable water management through collaboration from various stakeholders where Dow is a key player in offering technical and financial support in order to reduce water waste.

Advancing a circular economy

A circular economy is one in which waste and pollution are no longer byproducts of the production of new products and services. Methods to support the circular economy include: the development of innovative products that are more durable, designing and marketing products that are suitable for sharing, increasing the level of energy efficiency, and maximizing the utility of existing materials through recycling and reuse. Dow has collaborated in a European project which converts the material in mattresses to recycled material which can be sold as a raw material to new customers.

Dow has collaborated with local governments in Asian countries to convert plastic waste into long-lasting roads. Working with Indian cities such as Bangalore and Pune, Dow has helped convert 100 metric tons of plastic waste into 40 kilometers of roads. Volunteers pick up plastic waste, which is brought to local recyclers who ground the plastic into small pieces. The plastic pieces are sent to local asphalt plants and the plastic is added to the asphalt mixture with the resulting mixture applied on the roads. The plastic enriched asphalt lasts significantly longer than traditional roads. In Indonesia, Dow worked with the government and other stakeholders to convert 3.5 metric tons of plastic waste into 1.8 kilometers of plastic enhanced asphalt.

Safe materials for a sustainable planet

Dow's sustainability goals related to safe materials reflect the belief that in the future every material that Dow brings to the marketplace is sustainable for people and for the planet. Dow developed the LAUNCH competitive program which focuses on encouraging innovators and firms to submit proposals to make chemistry innovation easier by generating data, making data more accessible, analyzing the data, or applying the data to develop safer materials. A major focus on this initiative is to convert the use of toxic-based chemical materials into benign sustainable materials and connect with Dow's sustainability goal related to advancing a circular economy.

World-leading operations performance

Dow's goal related to operations performance is to "maintain world-leading operations performance in natural resource efficiency, environment, health and safety." The four key indicators for world-leading operations performance are: Unplanned Event Reduction, Total Worker Health Index, Environmental Stewardship Index, and Transportation Stewardship Index.

As part of the Total Worker Health Index, Dow measures and tracks seven health behaviors and risk factors for its employees: physical activity, healthy eating, tobacco use, blood pressure, glucose, total cholesterol, and body mass index. Dow also introduced telematics devices in all of its company owned or leased vehicles which monitor the driving patterns of the employees and banned all incoming and outgoing cellphone calls even if there is a hands-free system in the vehicle. Dow also is proactive in creating new technology innovations which remove employees from higher-hazard activities to achieve the goal of the elimination of fatalities, serious injury, and illness incidents from its global operations.

In 2017, Dow received the top rating of 100 in the Disability Equality Index and was voted one of the Best Places to Work for LGBT Equality by the Human Rights Campaign. Dow also was voted one of the 100 American Best Corporate Citizens and one of the Top 50 Employers by *Women Engineer Magazine* and *Minority Engineer Magazine*.

Dow with its partner the Erb Institute of the University of Michigan established the Sustainability Academy. The Sustainability Academy is a development-based program that gives Dow employees the skills and knowledge needed to incorporate sustainability ideas and innovations in their decision making as well as give them the opportunity to have hands-on experience on a sustainability related project.

Delivering breakthrough innovation

Dow's uses new breakthrough technical innovation to develop more sustainable chemistry-based innovations that help advance the well-being of humanity. Dow helps other firms in the design, manufacture, and use of more efficient, effective, safe, and more environmentally benign chemicals in order to increase the sustainability of the process.

Valuing nature

The valuing nature initiative focuses on Dow inspiring and educating employees on ways in which nature can be incorporated in the decision-making process. For example, a project in Brazil embraced the valuing nature initiative when an area of the Matarandiba Island had been excavated leaving 24-meter-high slopes. The slopes started eroding, which was causing safety issues. The Dow team did not use the traditional method of either removing the slopes or stabilizing the slopes using concrete, but instead used a sustainability support system which included steel mesh and natural fiber that was filled with rocks. The rocks were embedded with the native vegetation growing on the slope. This sustainability solution resulted in slopes not being removed, a lower carbon footprint for implementing the project, and a green living space.[3]

Dow's partnership with The Nature Conservancy

In 2011, Dow Chemical and The Nature Conservancy (TNC) established a partnership to demonstrate that the value of nature can be successfully integrated into the decision-making process of a global firm. The Collaboration team of representatives from Dow and TNC was created to visit Dow sites globally to conduct Nature Goal Workshops that resulted in the identification of potential projects that incorporated the natural environment in the decision-making process. The target for Dow is to develop $1 billion in business value from projects that add value to nature. The Collaboration team developed the Ecosystem Services Identification and Inventory (ESII) tool along with the Ecometrix Solutions Group in order to quantify the success of the projects. The ESII tool can measure the level of success of nature-based projects such as water provisioning, air quality control, climate regulation, erosion regulation, water quality control, water temperature regulation, water quantity control, and aesthetics.[4]

Engaging for impact

In 2017, Dow had over 3,000 Science, Technology, Engineering and Mathematics (STEM) Ambassadors who helped over 2,500 teachers with 700 science-based projects impacting over 380,000 students. Dow also funded a clean water initiative in Ethiopia, a flexible package recycling program in Ghana, a sustainability initiative focused on bringing clean water to schools in India, and the use of recycled plastic bricks for low-cost housing in Columbia. Furthermore, through its Leadership in Action and Global Health Corporate Champion programs, Dow deployed approximately 50 employees to work on ten projects with NGO partners on issues related to water quality and access, environmental cleanup, education, and career readiness. Dow also established the DowCorps Volunteer Portal, which is an online tool used by employees to find and track volunteer opportunities.[5]

Dow chemical sustainability in Brazil

Dow Chemical markets in Brazil are primarily energy, infrastructure, health, water, consumer goods, and agricultural sciences. In 2013, it had 22 manufacturing sites in Brazil and 5 research laboratories. Furthermore, in 2013 it received several awards and recognitions including: one of the best companies to work for in Brazil; one of the best companies to start a career; one of Brazil's most sustainable firms; and one of Brazil's most innovative companies.

Sustainability livestock production

Based on an initiative from the Union of Rural Producers of Paragominas and with partners Fundo Vale, Dow AgroSciences, and the State University of Sao Paulo, Brazil dairy farmers have access to new technology which increases productivity and sustainability of their cattle. Dow Chemical developed a type of plant used in pasture lands. The plant, brachiaria hybrid, along with herbicides, have increased the yield of the pasturelands for farmers of Brazil.

The major objective of the project is the development of new technology which improves the productivity of the milk production of the cattle in pasture areas. The net result of this project is that not only does the yield of milk for the cattle farmers increase, but the required amount of pastureland decreases. The technology used can increase up to four times the level of productivity of the cattle and decrease the demand of converting preserved or rainforest areas to pastures to increase the total amount of pastureland.

Sustainability with its stakeholders

Dow Chemical believes in the critical need to be transparent with its stakeholders. Daniella Souza Miranda, who is the Communications and Institutional Relations Director for Dow Chemical in Latin America, stated that, "To develop innovative product, more efficient processes and transforming social and environmental actions, transparency and proximity are essential for Dow's relationship with its main partners, and what moves us to make better and better, day after day."

Employees

The role of Dow Chemical is to embrace and engage its employees by providing them with the necessary skills and resources to not only develop their careers but also to be able to integrate sustainability opportunities as part of their decision-making process. The partnership the employees have with their supervisors as well as their interactions with other stakeholders are used to develop customized strategies and establish viable and specific goals incorporated in Dow's evaluation of the employees' opportunities for career advancement. Dow's Brazilian operations also have a pension plan called Previdow in which 86 percent of its employees participated at the end of 2013.

Dow Chemical also supports a diverse workplace. Its Brazilian operations have been certified with Sao Paulo's Diversity and Inclusion Seal and have diversity and inclusion programs such as the Disability Employee Network (DEN), Gays, Lesbian & Allies at Dow (GLAD), the Women Innovation Network (WIN), and mentoring and coaching programs for women. All the Brazilian employees have had training sessions related to anticorruption and human rights policies.

Suppliers and sustainability

Dow Chemical has been training suppliers on sustainability issues since 2012. The training includes on-site workshops, educational guidance, and practices such as diagnostics and action plans. In 2013, 34 suppliers participated in the program. Dow also established the Dow Go! Award for its suppliers in 2001. The criteria for winning the award includes not only safety related issues but also the establishment of strong positive relationships with Dow.

Public sector

Dow partners with the Rio de Janeiro city Department of Education in improving the educational opportunities for students. The focus of the partnership is to: emphasize Dow's investment commitment to education; emphasize Dow's commitment to Rio de Janeiro; make stakeholders aware of Dow's commitment to innovation and science; and encourage students' interest in primarily chemistry, but also other branches of science.

Based on these objectives, Dow has established the Educopedia program, which is an educational content platform which includes interactive modules to help facilitate learning and support for teachers. The modules of the program focus on the four primary science topics of physical states of matter; the evolution of the atomic models; the periodical properties of chemical elements; and atoms, molecules, and simple and compound substances.

Communities

Dow has developed the Ecosmar program, which focuses on the development of jobs related to human development through social, cultural, economic, and environmental initiatives. The initial target of the Ecosmar program is to focus on disadvantaged areas which have access to microcredit programs that can finance entrepreneurial ideas.

Dow, in partnership with the United States Embassy and the National Institute of Research of Amazonia, have developed science camps for girls to help support their interest in studying science. Dow has also developed a project with Brazilian and US companies to give access to English courses for 100,000 students through a digital platform and provide 10,000 students who speak English with the technological infrastructure needed to prepare them for the TOEFL certification.

Dow's AgroSciences Arginho program provides resources and support for public schools in Brazil that focus on topics such as citizenship, hygiene, health, and work. The goal of the program is to improve the quality of life for people who live in rural areas as well as enhancing the resources of the teachers who teach the children in rural areas.

Environmental sustainability projects

Dow has developed the Lime S project in Brazil, which converts solid waste into raw materials to make cement. This project is beneficial since it not only develops a sustainable use for the solid waste but also reduces the amount of waste material in landfills. Dow also has an alternative clean energy project which uses eucalyptus biomass as an energy source to supply energy to Dow's largest manufacturing unit in Brazil.[6]

2016 Olympic Games

Dow AgroSciences worked with Brazilian farmers in order to implement more sustainable agricultural practices as a way to counter the direct carbon footprint being generated by the Olympic Games. Dow in Brazil became the

Official Carbon Partner of the Rio 2016 Organizing Committee to examine opportunities to reduce the country's carbon footprint.

Through third party-verified emissions reductions, Dow was able to mitigate 500,000 tons of CO_2 equivalents. Areas in which Dow focused on CO_2 reductions were food packaging, agriculture, industrial processes, and building and construction. Dow's Rio 2016 Abraca (Embrace) Sustainability program focused not only on the short-term benefits during the Olympic Games but also developed a positive social legacy for Rio and Brazil. The technology innovations used at the Olympic Games can be dispersed throughout Brazil with the goal of exploiting environmental sustainability initiatives nationwide. For example, Dow along with its partner Farmers Edge, introduced new irrigation management technology for farmers in the Mato Grosso regions considered to be one of Brazil's main "breadbaskets."

The technology used in the Olympic Games will result in not only minimizing environmental impact but also optimizing the farmer's productivity in growing corn and soybean crops through higher yields, more varieties, and higher pest resistance. The technology requires the farmer to use less synthetic fertilizer, which results in the reduction of N_2O gas. N_2O is a greenhouse gas which is released into the atmosphere when fertilizer decomposes. Farmers that participate in the project also have access to technologies such as satellite imagery, precision harvest maps, intensive soil sampling, laboratory analysis, weather monitoring, and a review of their crop plans and goals.[7,8]

Dow and the nature conservancy in Brazil

In 2011, Dow announced a joint venture with Mitsui & Co to turn sugar cane into ethanol and plastic, which has a high level of sustainability as compared with using the traditional raw material of petroleum. In its focus to consider nature in its decision-making process, Dow stated that the purpose of this joint venture was to supply green alternatives to their customers.[9]

The Dow-Mitsui joint venture sought out Santa Vitoria Acucar e Alcool (SVAA) who has sugar cane located in Santa Vitoria, Brazil as a partner to grow the sugar cane. Santa Vitoria is located on the border of two critically endangered biomes, which are the Cerrado and the Atlantic Forest. It is located in the heartland of Brazil's agricultural region. In this region, less than 20 percent of the natural vegetation has survived and the vegetation is highly fragmented and poorly protected. SVAA wanted to expand its sugar cane fields to existing pasture fields while obeying Brazil's Forest Code.

The Code states that a minimum proportion of natural vegetation must be preserved on privately owned ground. The Dow-TNC Collaboration focused on the identification of methods which SVAA could use to expand agricultural production while adhering to Brazil's environmental regulations. The Collaboration developed protocol of SVAA to comply with environmental regulations related not only to vegetation but also to the protection of bird and mammal species and ensuring high surface water quality.[10]

Questions for thought

1. Dow Chemical's sustainability initiatives focus on science-based projects. Should that be the primary focus of a firm's sustainability strategy?
2. Evaluate Dow's 2025 Sustainability Goals. How many of these are unique to Dow?
3. Make a recommendation about how employees could be encouraged to participate in Dow's sustainability initiatives.
4. Can all of the sustainability initiatives for Dow in Brazil be transferred and implemented in other countries? Why or why not?

Notes

1 Dow 2017 Sustainability Report.
2 Dow 2013 Sustainability Report: Brazil.
3 Dow 2017 Sustainability Report.
4 *Working Together to Value Nature, 2017 Summary Report. A Collaboration of the Nature Conversancy & Dow Chemical Company.*
5 Dow 2017 Sustainability Report.
6 Dow 2013 Sustainability Report: Brazil.
7 https://corporate.dow.com/en-us/news/press-releases/rio-2016-and-dow-partner-to-implement-the-most-comprehensive-carbon-program-in-olympic-games-history
8 https://corporate.dow.com/en-us/news/press-releases/dow-implements-sustainable-agriculture-in-brazil-as-part-of-carbon-mitigation
9 Ernest Scheyder. 2011. Dow Chemical, Mitsui in Brazil Sugar Cane Venture. *Reuters.* July 19.
10 www.conservationgateway.org/ConservationPractices/EcosystemServices/tnc_dow_collaboration/brazil/Pages/default.aspx

Lydian International and gold mining in Armenia

Introduction

Lydian International is a gold developer listed on the Toronto Stock Exchange that has 100 percent ownership in the Amulsar Gold Project, located in Armenia. The Amulsar site had an estimated gold reserve in 2018 of 4.8 million ounces. Its estimated annual production of the mine is 225,000 ounces of gold; however, the mine site construction has not been completed. The mine is also projected to yield 25.1 million ounces of silver. The estimated production life of the mine is ten years and the estimated cost of capturing the gold is $579 per ounce.[1]

Minerals and metals account for approximately 50 percent of Armenia's exports. Mining operations in the country accounted for 3 percent of Armenia's economic output in 2017.

The Amulsar gold mine is surrounded by three rivers and two artificial lakes and includes the Kechut reservoir. The Kechut reservoir is connected by a Soviet-made underground tunnel leading to Armenia's largest reservoir, Lake Sevan. Lake Sevan is the Caucasus region's largest body of water.[2]

The local rural population near the Amulsar project is approximately 6,600 people. There has been a migration out of rural areas in Armenia in search of employment opportunities. A potential impact of hiring local people for the mining operations is the shifting away from traditional livelihoods, which can impact the cultural identity of the surrounding areas. However, employment opportunities may encourage people into the area, which will increase the size of the local communities.[3]

Once Amulsar is operational, the project will consist of three open pits, crushing and screening facilities which are housed in an enclosed purpose-built building, a covered conveyor transporting ores from the processing area to the heap leach facility, a heap leach pad for extraction of the gold, a recovery plant, and a barren rock storage facility.[4]

The beginning of the project

In the middle of 2006, Lydian International had identified the Amulsar region in central Armenia as a significant opportunity to mine gold. The estimated gold deposit was calculated to be 3.5 kilometers in length and 500 meters in width.[5] In November 2011, Lydian announced that the prospect drilling resulted in a projected total gold recovery of 2.5 million ounces that can be relatively easily extracted from the gold ore.[6] Based on this announcement by Lydian, its stock price had increased from a low of 11 cents (CDN) in October 24, 2008 to a high of $3.00 (CDN) on December 9, 2011.[7]

Lydian International started construction of its mining operation in Armenia in 2016 and by the end of 2017 had invested approximately $225 million and is estimated to have invested $400 million when the project is completed.

Ninety percent of the employees who work in the mining operations are expected to be Armenian.

Lydian's approach to sustainability

Lydian's values include: being honest and ethical in all activities; providing a workplace culture where the employees are treated with respect and dignity and are free from discrimination, harassment, and violence; fully complying with all applicable laws, rules, and regulations; avoiding all potential conflicts of interest; providing transparent transfer of information to stakeholders; and maintaining mutual respect and understanding in partnering for sustainable development.

Lydian's identification of stakeholders

The Amulsar project is one of the most significant financial investments in Armenia and there are numerous stakeholders who are impacted by the project. Those stakeholders include the local communities within Armenia, which are Jermuk, Gndevaz, Gorayk, Kechut, Saralanj, Saravan, and Ughedzor, as well as local herders and areas where the villagers' livelihoods might be impacted by its operations. Other critical stakeholders include local and national government agencies, Lydian's employees, shareholders, suppliers, contractors, NGOS, business associations, trade unions, and the media.

Lydian has organized numerous visits to the mining site in order to show community members, business groups, and government officials the operations occurring at the mine. Lydian has had problems with its contractors who were not following the international best practice standards related to safety, the environment, and local employment. The explanation of these actions is based on Lydian's belief that these standards have not been embedded in Armenian businesses, so the contractors were not well informed about the required standards of operations.[8]

Lydian's international practices and certifications

Lydian participates in a number of voluntary international practices and certifications. Lydian is a member of the Armenian Multi-Stakeholder Group, which follows the guidelines of the Extractive Industries Transparency Initiative (EITI). The EITI is a global country standard related to corporate governance in the oil, gas, and mineral resource industries.

The EITI principles

The EITI principles are:

1. The belief that prudent use of natural resources will create sustainable economic growth that contributes to sustainable development and poverty reduction but will have negative impacts if it is not managed properly.
2. The belief that the management of natural resource wealth benefits the citizens of the country and is in the domain of sovereign governments for their interests in national development.
3. The revenue streams for natural resources occur over many years and can have significant price variations.
4. The government revenues from natural resources will allow for appropriate and realistic options for sustainable development.
5. Transparency by both the government and mining operators is critical in enhancing public financial management and accountability.
6. Transparency is also critical in the context of respect for contracts and laws.
7. Financial transparency also will encourage more domestic and foreign direct investment in the country where the natural resources are located.
8. Government needs to be accountable to all citizens for the stewardship of the revenue streams and public expenditures.
9. High levels of transparency and accountability are needed in public life, government operations and in business operations.
10. There should be a broadly consistent and workable approach to the disclosure of payments and revenues.
11. Payment disclosures in a country should include all mining companies operating in the country.
12. Critical stakeholders have important and relevant contributions and include: government, mining companies, service companies, financial organizations, investors and non-governmental organizations.[9]

Lydian also participates in the International Cyanide Management Code. The Cyanide Code was developed under the guidance of the United Nations Environmental Program and the International Council on Metals and the Environment. The Cyanide Code is a voluntary program for companies that participate in gold and silver mining. The Code ensures that there is safe management of cyanide and cyanide tailings as part of the mining process. Cyanide is a toxic chemical which can be used in the mining process. Cyanide can easily be combined with many metals including gold. As a result, a sodium cyanide solution is exposed to the gold ore in order to separate the gold from the ore. This separation or "leaching" process can occur in two forms: heap leaching and tank leaching. In heap leaching, the sodium cyanide is sprayed over large heaps of crushed gold ore which have collection pads underneath to collect the gold. The cyanide dissolves the gold from the ore and the gold-based solution trickles down to the collection pads. The gold is separated from the solution and the solution is collected and reapplied on the heap again. The tank leaching of the gold occurs when the gold ore is mixed with the cyanide solution in large tanks. After the gold has been separated, the remaining ore waste called tailings is stored in tailings dams. These tailings are tainted with the cyanide solution. It is estimated that 20 tons of mine waste are generated in order to produce enough gold to make a typical 18 carat, 0.333 ounce gold ring.[10,11]

Lydian will be using a cyanide solution to separate the gold and silver from the ore. The cyanide will be purchased in solid briquettes, which are safer to transport than a liquid. The briquettes will be mixed with water to form the cyanide solution. The cyanide will be either destroyed or recycled after use through a close circuit without any discharge. Lydian states that gold mining produces up to 200 parts per million (ppm) released in the atmosphere while road salt can release up to 350 ppm and cigarette smoke can release up to 1,600 ppm.[12]

Lydian also participates in The Voluntary Principles on Security and Human Rights. These principles were established in 2000 and are designed to guide firms in the mining industry to maintain safety and security of their operations to protect the human rights of their stakeholders. The principles focus on risk assessment, relations with public security, and relations with private security. This risk assessment is based on the evaluation of the firm's engagement with public and private security providers to ensure that the human rights are protected both within the company facilities and on the company premises. An additional benefit is the access to information from other firms including mutual learning, joint problem solving, and building the best global practices related to addressing both security and human rights challenges.

The framework is based on initially conducting a comprehensive assessment of human rights risks associated with security. The second step is to engage with public and private security service providers in surrounding communities. The third step involves instituting a human rights screening process and training for public and private security forces. The fourth step is developing systems to report and investigate allegations of human rights abuses.[13] In its 2017 Sustainability Report, Lydian stated that it had made significant progress in implementing the principles in 2017 with the goal to be fully implemented by 2018.

Environmental compliance

Lydian developed the Environmental Social Impact Assessment (ESIA) and the Environmental Impact Assessment (EIA) management systems for the Amular project. The ESIA is the first environmental system completed for a project in Armenia and the EIA is the required system for a country issuing permits for mining.

The ESIA was developed based on the Equator Principles, which is a credit risk management framework for determining, assessing, and managing the environmental and social risk. The ESIA for the Amular project covers:

the applicable framework to ensure that national and international policies related to environmental assessment are implemented; the identification of presenting information about the project description including geographical, ecological, environmental, and social influences and effects; the establishment and analysis of baseline data which includes environmental, biodiversity, socio-economic, and human interest impacts of the project; review of alternative sites for various project facilities which take into account environmental, biodiversity, cultural heritage, social and community health and safety issues; the prediction and evaluation of the potential environmental and social impacts associated with project construction, operation, mining closure, and reclamation; development of key component management plans in the creation of the overall Environmental and Social Management Plan for the project; development of a preliminary Mine Closure Plan; and measurements for post-mining management.[14]

Lydian's ESIA assessment had concluded that the Amular project could have a number of adverse impacts on the physical, biological, and social environments. However, Lydian believed that these impacts would be adequately mitigated with the implementation of industry-standard, good-practice management measures. Since some of the local communities depend directly on the water sources near the mine site, Lydian stated that particular care would be given to ensure that the availability and quality of surface water and groundwater in the area would not be affected by the project.

It was estimated that no resettlement of villagers was necessary as a result of the project. For those landowners that need to have Lydian acquire their land for the project, Lydian was going to use good practice compensation methods.[15]

Current issues related to Lydian

In April 2018, there were mass protests by the people of Armenia accusing the government of corruption and cronyism. The result was a peaceful revolution in which Nikol Pashinyan was elected as Prime Minister of Armenia in December 2018.

Due to the demands of the public for transparency and full compliance of mining projects with environmental standards, the government of Armenia commissioned a new independent assessment of the Amulsar mining project. On June 22, 2018, protesters who were worried about the potential environmental damage of the Amulsar operations blocked access to the mining site, which stopped the completion of the mining project. In June 2019, with the blockade still in effect, Lydian announced that it would have to fire over 1,000 employees. The company lost more than $60 million since the blockade began. A group of local residents set up makeshift checkpoints on the unpaved roads that led to the extraction and treatment facilities built on the summit slopes of the Amulsar mountain where the mining site was located.

Due to its proximately to major bodies of water in Armenia, opponents of the mine were concerned that the release of toxins from the gold extraction process could contaminate the water used for drinking and irrigation, both locally and in the major food production region of Armenia, the Ararat valley. Lydian stated that they would implement the necessary procedures to prevent cyanide from entering the water sources.

There was also concern that the mine would deter tourists from visiting the local town of Jermuk, which is famous for its hot water springs and spas. One hotel owner in Jermuk, Tigran Margaryan, stated that, "People who want to recover their health will not come to a place where there are industries with heavy chemical elements involved … This town will become a miners' town." The philosophy of one protestor was that it was the moral duty of the local people to stop the Alumsar project. "This is a paradise land that we received from our ancestors … and we are obliged to leave it to our future generations at least in the current conditions." By June 2019, Lydian stated that it had invested over $3 million in social projects supporting local businesses and infrastructure and was planning to invest more money in developing a natural park.

The managing director of Lydian Armenia, Hayk Aloyan, stated, "Imagine your biggest investment project is blockaded illegally … It is a huge reputational damage. We are too small a country to have the luxury of damaging our reputation." Lydian said that at least 30 percent of the 700 permanent employees of the mine would be hired locally, but that most of the approximately 1,400 people hired for the construction of the mine had to be fired due to the protests.[16]

On December 10, 2018, Lydian stated that it had filed a lawsuit appealing a directive issued by the head of the Republic of Armenia's Environmental and Mining Inspection Body for Lydian to refrain from any mining-related activities at the Amulsar project. The Court accepted the lawsuit, which had resulted in an automatic suspension of the directive until the appeal was heard and a decision was made. The directive was based on new ecological factors that had come to light through the sightings of newly found rare plants and animal species.[17]

On March 11, 2019, due to ongoing blockades at that time, Lydian notified the Government of the Republic of Armenia that it had filed a complaint under the Bilateral Investment Protection Treaties. The filing made by its UK subsidiary and Canadian operations asked for relief based on the bilateral agreements between Armenia and the governments of Canada and the UK.

Under the UK bilateral agreement, Lydian UK was allowed to submit the dispute to international arbitration three months after the formal notification to the Armenian government. For Lydian Canada, the wait was six months after formal notification. Lydian also stated in the press release that the Government of Armenia had the opportunity to continue amicable discussions with the goal of settling the disputes. The possibility of Lydian UK or Lydian

Canada starting arbitration proceeding is dependent on the conduct of the Government of Armenia.[18]

On January 29, 2019, Lydian was notified by the Investigative Committee of the Republic of Armenia that a criminal investigation had taken place investigating whether employees of the Ministry of Environmental Protection had withheld information related to the Alumar project. Therefore, the Armenian government had selected the international consultancy group Earth, Link and Advanced Resources Development (ELARD) to perform an environmental audit on Lydian's operations.[19]

On March 19, 2019, Lydian announced that the Government of Armenia was going to start a third-party assessment by ELARD for the Amulsar project's environmental impact on water resources, geology, biodiversity, and water quality. The scope of the audit would include a review of Lydian's ESIA and its EIA. Lydian has disputed the need for a new audit since Lydian's EIA had been approved previously by Armenian authorities in accordance with Armenian law before construction started on the Amular site.

Lydian CEO Joao Carrelo stated that:

> We have cooperated fully with the two previous government ordered audits since inception of the blockages in June 2018 and we will collaborate with ELARD (assessment firm) in what we have been told by the government will be the final audit … No other company in Armenia has been subjected to three audits since June 2018 and been unable to continue its operations.

Lydian stated that it did not accept the need or legal basis for the third audit since the Armenian government had already approved the project and Lydian relied on the government's approval when investing millions of dollars into the project.[20]

On April 10, 2019, the Administrative Court of the Republic of Armenia ruled in favor of Lydian by ordering the Armenian Police to remove trespassers and their property from the Amulsar site.[21] On April 19, 2019, the Criminal Court of Appeal of the Republic of Armenia ruled that the police were required to start a criminal investigation against the protestors. The appeal was based on the initial complaint filed by Lydian on July 24, 2018, which asked the Jermuk Unit of the Vayots Dzor Police Department to initiate an investigation and file criminal charges against the protestors who had set up illegal blockades. The police had denied the request.

Lydain President and CEO at the time of the appeal stated that:

> Lydian has suffered unlawful actions and inactions that have been in breach of both Armenian and international law. The recent rulings of the courts in Armenia support Lydian's position with respect to the illegal road blockades that have deprived Lydian of its legal right to operate … We strongly believe that the restoration of the rule of law is in

the best interest not only of Lydian, its shareholders, lenders, employees and the surrounding communities, but also serves the interests of Armenia as a whole.[22]

On May 15, 2019, in a press release, Lydian stated that the Government of Armenia is not enforcing the rule of law to remove illegal blockades and has failed to prosecute other illegal acts carried out against Lydian. The government's actions and inactions has substantially restricted Lydian's access to capital and has had a critical negative impact on Lydian's resources. The failure to complete the construction of the site has created conditions that are considered to be events in which the financial lenders of Lydian can claim that Lydian is in default of the conditions of the agreement. The result of these conditions was that Lydian had to agree to amended financial agreements with its lenders. In the same press release, Lydian warned that its ability to continue as a going concern was dependent upon the Government of Armenia's resolution of the disputes the government had with Lydian and enforcing the rule of law to protect Lydian's investment.[23]

On June 17, 2019, Lydian posted a press release that stated that trespassers are still on the mining site despite a court order to have them removed. The police informed Lydian that they believe it has complied with the court rule by relocating some of the trespassers' trailers that had blocked access to the Amulsar site to alternative locations. Lydian had argued that full access to the site had not been restored.[24] From a high of $3.00 (CDN) per share on December 9, 2011, Lydian International's stock price had dropped to 12 cents per share by August 16, 2019.[25]

Questions for thought

1. Identify Lydian's four most critical stakeholders.
2. How effective has Lydian been in addressing the needs of these four critical stakeholders?
3. Do you think the mine will ever become operational?
4. Why didn't Lydian anticipate the problems it has had to address in the Amulsar mining project?
5. Why does it appear that the Armenian government changed its mind about the viability of the Amulsar mining project?

Notes

1 www.lydianinternational.co.uk/images/factsheet/2018/Lydian_Fact_Sheet_FINAL_20180712.pdf
2 Umberto Bacchi. 2019. Gold of Contention: Armenia Land Dispute in Spotlight as Government Steps in. *Reuters*. June 5.
3 www.lydianarmenia.am/files/ce6438e396d45ede6ea75.pdf
4 www.lydianarmenia.am/files/415f0c1aff1e0a46a5721.pdf

5   www.lydianinternational.co.uk/news/2008-news/57-lydian-prepares-for-20-000-metre-drilling-programme-at-its-amulsar-gold-discovery-in-armenia

6   www.lydianinternational.co.uk/news/2011-news/130-lydian-reports-further-metallurgical-results-for-amulsar

7   www.google.com/search?q=TSX%3ALYD&oq=TSX%3ALYD&aqs=chrome…69i57j69i58.1596j0j8&sourceid=chrome&ie=UTF-8

8   2017 Sustainability Report. Lydian Armenia.

9   The EITI Standard 2016. EITI International Secretariat. May 24.

10 www.cyanidecode.org/about-cyanide-code

11 https://earthworks.org/issues/cyanide/

12 www.lydianarmenia.am/files/f13e9a2106737c3cd4571.pdf

13 https://docs.wixstatic.com/ugd/f623ce_32362edd5ae345fb9956dd01f16bce75.pdf

14 www.lydianinternational.co.uk/reponsibility/esia

15 www.lydianarmenia.am/files/f98af3cfa515c5989d662.pdf

16 Umberto Bacchi. 2019. Gold of Contention: Armenia Land Dispute in Spotlight as Government Steps in. *Reuters*. June 5.

17 www.lydianinternational.co.uk/news/2018-news/448

18 www.lydianinternational.co.uk/news/2019-news/452-

19 www.lydianinternational.co.uk/news/2019-news/451-

20 www.lydianinternational.co.uk/news/2019-news/455-

21 www.lydianinternational.co.uk/news/2019-news/459-

22 www.lydianinternational.co.uk/news/2019-news/457-

23 www.lydianinternational.co.uk/news/2019-news/459-

24 www.lydianinternational.co.uk/news/2019-news/464-

25 www.google.com/search?q=lydian+international+stock+price&oq=lydian+international+stoc&aqs=chrome.2.0j69i57j0l4.6401j1j8&sourceid=chrome&ie=UTF-8

Shell and oil production in Nigeria

Introduction

Shell has had a presence in Nigeria since 1937 and was a pioneer in the development of onshore, shallow, and deep-water oil exploration and production in the country. Nigeria depends on revenues from the oil and gas industry to generate 90 percent of its export income and 75 percent of the total revenue for the government of Nigeria.

Shell Petroleum Development Company of Nigeria

The Shell Petroleum Development Company of Nigeria Limited (SPDC) is the largest Shell company in Nigeria and discovered the first commercial oil field at Oloibiri Bayelsa State as part of Shell-BP and produced Nigeria's first commercial oil exports in 1958.[1] SPDC is the operator of a joint venture between the government-owned Nigerian National Petroleum Corporation (NNPC) with 55 percent ownership share, SPDC 30 percent, Total E&P Nigeria Ltd 10 percent, and Agip Oil Company 5 percent. The primary focus of the joint venture is oil exploration and production in the Niger Delta. The SPDC joint venture's assets include approximately 500 productive oil fields, approximately 5,000 kilometers of oil and gas pipelines and flow lines, five gas plants, and major oil export terminals in Bonny and Forcados, Nigeria.

SPDC owns the largest amount of land in Nigeria and produces 39 percent of the total oil in the country. SPDC employs over 4,500 people of whom 95 percent are from Nigeria. Sixty-six percent of the Shell staff employees are from the Niger Delta. An additional 20,000 people are employed indirectly through a network of companies including suppliers and those providing services to SPDC.[2,3]

Shell Nigeria Exploration and Production Company

Shell Nigeria Exploration and Production Company (SNEPCo) was established in 1993 and is responsible for Shell offshore oil projects. SNEPCo has operations in the Bonga field, which is the site of the first deep-water oil discovery in Nigeria. The field was named after the Bonga fish whose habitat is along the coast of Nigeria and West Africa.

When the Bonga field started yielding oil in 2005, it increased Nigeria's total oil production capacity by 10 percent. From 2005 to 2018, the Bonga field produced over 819 million barrels of oil. The Bonga field is operated by SNEPCo with Esso Exploration and Production Nigeria (Deepwater) Limited, Tot E&P Nigeria Limited, and Nigerian Agis Exploration as partners. The partnership is under a Production Sharing Contract with the Nigerian National Petroleum Corporation.

Shell estimates that the Bonga facility has the capacity to produce more than 225,000 barrels of oil daily and 170 million standard cubic feet of gas daily. In 2018, SNEPCo accounted for 37 percent of Nigeria's deep-water production and 15 percent of Nigeria's total oil production. Ninety-six percent of the offshore staff of SNEPCo are Nigerians. SNEPCo has offshore operations in Bonga, Bolia, Zabazaba, and Doro fields. Shell's deep-water production has supported the Nigerian economy by creating a demand for goods and services including offshore vessels and platforms, materials, floating hotels, helicopters, and manpower along with creating training programs and the need for maintenance services.[4,5]

Shell Nigeria Gas (SNG) is the only global oil and gas company to have set up a gas distribution market in Nigeria to supply industry customers. SNG's gas transmission and distribution network is 115 kilometers in length in Nigeria. SNG's customers include a range of businesses from medium-scale to large corporations and includes markets such as glass making, food and beverages, packaging, pharmaceuticals, and chemicals. The natural gas can be used for power generation, industrial manufacturing uses, chemical feedstock for fertilizer, and methanol production, and for transportation in the form of compressed natural gas for natural gas vehicles.[6,7]

Shell's relationship with Ogoni People of Nigeria

In 1990, environmental rights activist Ken Saro-Wiwa created the Movement for the Survival of the Ogoni People (MOSOP) and started to campaign for more of the wealth from Shell's production to go to the Ogoni people. The Ogoni people live near the oil fields and their villages have been significantly impacted by environmental damage caused by oil production by Shell. In January 1993, MOSOP organized 300,000 Ogoni people to protest the pollution generated by Shell's operations.[8] This protest occurred after MOSOP demanded $10 billion in oil royalties and environmental compensation from Shell and the Nigerian government in December 1992.[9]

Environmental complaints made by MOSOP about Shell include having leaky oil pipes crisscrossing the Ogoni land and contaminating the farm land. There were also complaints about frequent oil spills which destroy crops and pollute the water sources where the Ogoni fish live. In the response to the environmental concerns about Shell's operations in Nigeria, Shell regional coordinator for Africa, Dick van den Brock, stated, "It's a question of priorities ... Nigeria is a poor country. How much should it spend on environmental protection." Shell also points out that the Nigerian government is a majority partner in Shell's operations and, therefore, must pay 55 percent of all environmental spending and Shell does not want to sacrifice profits to pay more for environmental protection.[10]

The military ruler, Sani Abacha, overthrew the Nigerian government in 1993. While promising democracy, he banned political activity, controlled the press, assembled a personal security force of 3,000, and eliminated any dissenting voices in Nigeria.[11]

With these protests, Shell asked the military government of Nigeria for protection of its operations from recurring vandalism. Shell withdrew from the Ogoni region in early 1993 but asked the government to continue to protect its operations that were left behind by Shell. The violence continued after Shell left with one pumping station being destroyed and four other stations in Ogoniland being damaged. Shell declared that is was unwilling to produce oil under conditions of civil unrest and military oppression and would only return when the local community was on Shell's side.

The Nigerian government sent its brutal "mobile police" to crush the unrest by the Ogoni people, which resulted in the destruction of whole Ogoni villages. Shell had specifically asked the Nigeria government to send in the mobile police who were known as the "kill-and-go mob." Shell not only requested the mobile police, but they also paid for the transportation and salary bonuses for some of the members who may have been oilfield guards who committed the abuses on the Ogoni tribe.

Shell stated that they did nothing wrong in trying to protect personnel and equipment and that they had no control over the actions of the Nigerian security services. Shell also stated that is not unusual for companies seeking protection of assets to pay transportation costs and salary supplements for troops that live outside the Shell compound. During the time of the confrontation, Shell was producing half of Nigeria's oil and producing 900,000 barrels daily in which Shell took 257,000 barrels and gave the rest to the Nigeria government. Shell's profits in Nigeria during that time frame were between $170 million to $190 million, which was 10 percent of Shell's total exploration and production profits.[12]

The government, in its official account, blamed vigilantes with ties to Saro-Wiwa for attacking the Shell installations and murdering 40 Ogoni opponents. The brother of Saro-Wiwa refuted that claim by stating that the vandalism was carried out by soldiers who stole generators and corrugated iron sheets to sell for a 100 percent profit.[13]

Shell response to its Ogoniland operations

From the 1950s to the 1990s, Shell was part of the SPDC joint venture and carried out exploration and production operations in Ogoniland. Production ceased in 1993 due to the rise of violent threats to its employees and facilities. However, one of Shell's major pipelines in the Niger Delta goes through Ogoniland. In addition, Shell has five non-producing fields and a network of 100 wells and associated infrastructure in Ogoniland.

In 2006, the Nigerian government commissioned the United Nations Environment Programme (UNEP) to develop an environmental assessment of Ogoniland. Shell funded the report and provided the necessary data. In 2011, the report highlighted several significant negative environmental impacts from oil pollution in Ogoniland. The UNEP called for Shell, the government, communities, and other oil and gas operation to implement a comprehensive clean-up of Ogoniland and to take coordinated action to end illegal oil bunkering, crude theft, and artisanal refining of crude oil which Shell claimed was causing the oil contamination in Ogoniland. Shell stated that they "welcomed" the report and were committed to implementing the recommendations.[14]

Illegal oil bunkering

A common method of theft is illegal bunkering where the "vandals" create a breach in the pipeline and siphon off the crude oil. The stolen oil is then sold to local refiners who refine it into diesel and kerosene to be sold at the local Nigerian markets as well as shipped to international ports for sale. The skill set of these vandals can range from technically sophisticated operators who had once been trained by oil companies, to local villagers who use simple tools to siphon off crude oil or liquefied gas. In Nigeria, it is estimated that illegal "bunkerers" can earn between $8 million to $20 million daily by stealing between 50,000 and 300,000 barrels of oil.[15]

Shell estimates that approximately 90 percent of the spills of more than 100 kilograms occurring in the Niger Delta are caused by illegal refining and third-party interference. In 2018, Shell estimated that 11,000 barrels of oil daily were stolen from its Niger Delta based facilities. From 2012 to 2018, Shell had removed more than 1,160 illegal theft points where oil was stolen.

In 2018, Shell had 111 sabotage-related spills of more than 100 kilograms, which was an increase from 62 in 2017. The increase was due, in part, from access to Shell's production facilities after the repair of a major export pipeline. In 2018, Shell reported 15 spills from its operations which were more than 100 kilograms, a 50 percent increase from the ten spills that occurred in 2017.[16]

Shell stated that from 2011 to 2014, it had completed a majority of the recommendations directed in the UNEP report. In 2015–16 Shell continued to develop initiatives in order to prevent and minimize the impact of theft and sabotage in Ogoniland. These initiatives included community-based pipeline surveillance, awareness campaigns, and alternative livelihood programs. From 2016–18, Shell actively supported the clean-up process as a member of the Governing Council and Board of Trustees of the Ogoni Trust Fund.[17]

In 1995, Sani Abacha, the President of Nigeria, ordered Saro-Wiwa and eight other MOSOP leaders to be executed on alleged murder charges.[18] Saro-Wiwa was found guilty of inciting a riot that led to the killing of four prominent government officials. The trial was considered to be a sham throughout the world.

MOSOP was able to persuade the Nigerian government to create an Oil and Minerals Producing Areas Development Commission to channel money into the oil production regions with, initially, 3 percent of Nigeria's annual oil income going to the region, which was later raised to 13 percent. Shell was being pressured by external stakeholders to use its influence to ask for clemency in order that Saro-Wiwa and the other leaders could live. Shell stated that "It is not for commercial organizations like Shell to interfere in the legal process of a sovereign state such as Nigeria."[19]

Mr. Saro-Wiwa had insisted that the MOSOP leaders had been framed because of their opposition to the oil industry destruction of the natural environment on their land. The purpose of the executions was to prevent the Ogoni from continuing to protest for improved environmental conditions and more money transfers from Shell to the tribe. The Nigerian government did not want the Ogoni to chase Shell away from the country. Shell's facilities in Ogoniland were sabotaged after the executions and the company was forced to temporarily stop production.[20]

In 2010, the United States Department of Justice found that Shell had paid up to $2 million in bribes in order to ease shipments of oil through Nigerian customs but did not prosecute because the Justice Department believed that Shell was strengthening its anticorruption safeguards. In 2011, Italian prosecutors alleged that Shell and the Italian-based partner in Nigeria, Eni SpA, paid more than $1 billion to win offshore licenses that went mostly for bribes.[21]

The social impacts of Shell in Nigeria

Local residents continue to siphon or sabotage the patchwork of pipes owned by Shell in the Niger Delta. The Delta, which is home to about 30 million people, has suffered oil spills for decades that have negatively impacted fishing and farming communities, fostered corruption, and have angered the native tribes in the area. In 2018, oil sales accounted for over 50 percent of the Nigerian government's federal revenue and Shell accounted for 7 percent of that total revenue. It is estimated that approximately 30 percent of the oil sent through the Shell pipelines in the Niger Delta is stolen.

In 2009, Shell agreed, without admitting wrongdoing, to pay $15.5 million to settle claims that it collaborated with the government executions of Ken Saro-Wiwa and the other eight leaders. After the executions, Shell and other oil companies offered local unemployed youth sit-at-home payments for financial support. When the payments stopped, the families became upset because they had become dependent on the financial support from Shell.

The frustration of the local villagers resulted in the young men arming themselves and intensifying the violence occurring near the Shell sites. The level of mistrust between Shell and the local people was evident when Shell developed a sustainability initiative to provide free medical care to the local communities and the people boycotted the offer based on principle.[22]

In April 2019, the Nigerian government filed a $1 billion lawsuit against Shell and ENI SpA of Italy for its alleged illegal payments of $1.1 billion in order to secure offshore drilling rights. The Nigerian government claimed that Shell and Eni knew that the money would trickle down to government officials and senior executives from both companies. Some of the Shell executives named in the lawsuit included former Shell Chief Executive Officer Peter Voser and the head of the natural gas business, Maarten Wetselaar.

The allegations are based on the purchase of the exploration rights of a tract of land in the Gulf of Guinea named Oil Prospecting License 245 (OPL 245). In the lawsuit, the Nigerian government claims that the acquisition of the drilling rights for OPL 245 was "part of a fraudulent and corrupt scheme, that involved the payment of bribes ... This scheme also involved (or at least intended) the payment of bribes to Shell and/or Eni executives."[23]

The Nigerian government also sued JPMorgan Chase & Co. for transferring payments for the deal. Both oil companies and some of the executives from those companies face a criminal trial in Milan, Italy. The Nigerian government is asking for $1 billion in damages as well as the right to revoke the drilling license from Shell and Eni for OPL 245. It is estimated the OPL 245 may have billions of barrels of oil that can be captured.[24]

OPL 245 was created in 1998 when the Nigerian petroleum minister, Dan Etete, established the boundaries for the site in order to award the licensing rights to his own company, Malabu Oil and Gas Ltd. Through the different government regimes in Nigeria, it was taken from him and given to Shell. The lawsuit alleged that former Nigerian government officials including President Goodluck Jonathan and Shell and Eni executives would receive personal payments from the $1 billion payment. It is alleged that Dan Etete received up to $400 million of the payment for himself.[25]

The environmental impacts of Shell in Nigeria

In 2011, it was disclosed that an oil spill from an offshore Shell oil well platform generated an oil slick that was approximately 350 miles in size and moving toward the southern Nigerian coast creating devastating environmental impact on wildlife and the Nigerian coast. Shell confirmed that a deep water spill did occur during a "routine transfer" of crude from a floating storage device in the Bonga oil fields 75 miles offshore to a tanker. The spill was caused by a leak in one of the transfer lines. Shell estimated that 40,000 barrels had been lost and that 50 percent of the oil had already evaporated into the air or had been dispersed through wave motion.

However, the head of Nigeria's National Oil Spill Detection and Response Agency estimated that the spill could be three times larger than 40,000 barrels.[26]

In 2018, Amnesty International released a report alleging that Shell and Eni has not done proper due diligence in cleaning up the pollution issues related to oil production in the Niger Delta. Amnesty International developed the Decoders network, which is an online platform to crowdsource human rights research. The Decoders network enlisted the efforts of thousands of supporters and activists to collect data about oil spills in the Niger Delta.

The results of the report showed that Shell and Eni were slow and taking weeks to respond to reports of spills and allegedly publishing information that was misleading about both the cause and severity of the spills. A Business and Human Rights researcher for Amnesty International, Mark Dummett, stated that:

> Shell and Eni claim they are doing everything they can to prevent oil spills but Decoders' research suggests otherwise. They found that the companies often ignore reports of oil spills for months on end – on one occasion Eni took more than a year to respond. The Niger Delta is one of the most polluted places on earth and it begs belief that the companies responsible are still displaying this level of negligence ... Adding insult to injury is the fact that Shell and Eni seem to be publishing unreliable information about the cause and extent of the spills. The people of the Niger Delta have paid the price for Shell and Eni's recklessness for too long.

Amnesty International has asked the Nigerian government to re-open investigations into 89 oil spills. An example of underreporting occurred when an oil spill occurred in the fishing town of Bodo between 2008 and 2009. Shell vastly understated the amount of oil and with the help of Amnesty International, the community of Bobo took legal action which resulted in Shell having to admit the true amount of the oil spill and pay the community £55 million in compensation.

There were a total of 3,545 people from 142 countries in the Decoders program that collected data regarding the oil spills in the Niger Delta. They worked the equivalent of 1,300 hours and answered 163,063 questions about reports and photographs. From 2011 to 2018, Shell has reported 1,010 spills with 110,535 barrels or 17.5 million liters that were lost in its network of pipelines and wells. From 2014, Eni reported 820 spills, with 26,286 barrels or 4.1 million liters lost. Both Shell and Eni claim that most of the oil spills are caused by theft and sabotage. This is not surprising since Shell and Eni do not have to compensate the local community if a third party (vandals or thieves) creates the spills. Data from the Decoders identified at least 46 spills from Shell and 43 from Eni where there was reasonable doubt that the spill had been caused by a third party. For example, the Decoders had photographs of spills where the cause appeared to be from the corrosion of the pipe rather than as a result of a third party.

The Nigerian government requires that for any oil spill, the parties responsible must visit the site within 24 hours of reporting the spill. However, Shell responded within 24 hours only 26 percent of the time for the incidents and Eni responded 76 percent of the time. For one spill, it took Shell 252 days to visit the site. For Eni, it took the company 430 days to respond to an oil spill in Bayelsa. Eni told Amnesty International that the delay was due to the local community refusing Eni permission to visit the site. When Eni finally visited the site, it estimated that the total amount of the oil spill was four barrels, which was based on the area in which the contamination was visible. Four barrels was not an accurate estimate since oil that spills into swampland and rivers quickly becomes invisible. The longer it takes a company to respond to an oil spill, the higher the risk that the oil will not be contained, resulting in the oil spreading into the food and water sources.

Therefore, Amnesty International concluded that Shell and Eni were deliberately reckless and were willfully negligent in their operations in Nigeria. Because Shell and Eni refused to operate within Nigerian law and best practices standards, the net result was a devastating negative impact on the human rights of the Niger Delta communities.[27]

In 2018, referring to its Nigerian operations, Shell stated that we "continue to engage with the government and non-governmental organizations, as well as local communities, to help promote human rights and a peaceful and safe operating environment. Our dialogue is underpinned by ongoing community development activities."[28]

Shell is trying to reduce its dependence on oil from Nigeria by shifting its oil and gas productions to other regions. The daily production of oil and gas globally for Shell in 2017 was: Asia Pacific 1.2 million barrels, Europe 687,000 barrels, North America 666,000 barrels, South America 413,000 barrels, Oceania 338,000 barrels, Sub-Saharan Africa 233,000 barrels, and Nigeria 159,000 barrels. The 159,000 barrels in 2017 was a significant drop from the almost 280,000 barrels of oil and gas that were produced daily in Nigeria in 2011. In order to reduce the conflicts with its onshore operations, Shell is shifting its focus to its offshore operations in the Gulf of Guinea off the coast of Nigeria.[29]

Questions for thought

1. Do you think Shell will ever completely shut down its Nigerian operations? Why or why not?
2. The alleged environmental violations against Shell have occurred for decades. Why hasn't there been global protests about Shell's environmental record in Nigeria?
3. Why didn't Shell more closely monitor the government's "mobile police" when they became involved with Shell's operations?
4. Why wasn't Shell more proactive in trying to save the lives of activist Ken Saro-Wiwa and the other leaders of MOSOP?
5. Is there any way in which Shell can limit or prevent the stealing of its oil from its pipelines in Nigeria? Explain.

Notes

1 www.shell.com.ng/about-us/who-we-are.html
2 www.shell.com.ng/about-us/who-we-are.html
3 www.shell.com.ng/about-us/what-we-do/spdc.html
4 www.shell.com.ng/about-us/who-we-are.html
5 www.shell.com.ng/media/nigeria-reports-and-publications-briefing-notes/poten tial-in-deep-water/_jcr_content/par/toptasks.stream/1554121804242/ e558970219b0e2c7571e7d6825386594c97b8026/unlocking-nigeria-potential-deep-water-2019.pdf

6 www.shell.com.ng/business-customers/natural-gas-supply.html
7 www.shell.com.ng/about-us/who-we-are.html
8 Ron Bousso. 2018. Timeline: Shell's Operations in Nigeria. *Reuters*. September 23.
9 Paul Lewis. 1996. Blood and Oil: A Special Report; After Nigeria Represses, Shell Defends Its Record. *The New York Times*. February 13.
10 Paul Lewis. 1996. Blood and Oil: A Special Report; After Nigeria Represses, Shell Defends Its Record. *The New York Times*. February 13.
11 www.britannica.com/biography/Sani-Abacha
12 Paul Lewis. 1996. Blood and Oil: A Special Report; After Nigeria Represses, Shell Defends Its Record. *The New York Times*. February 13.
13 Paul Lewis. 1996. Blood and Oil: A Special Report; After Nigeria Represses, Shell Defends Its Record. *The New York Times*. February 13.
14 www.shell.com.ng/media/nigeria-reports-and-publications-briefing-notes/ogoni land/_jcr_content/par/toptasks.stream/1554121806240/04a670487c5772cf45552 c604abb613035dd5515/ogoniland-2019.pdf
15 Will Connors. 2010. Vandals Disrupt Shell Pipeline in Nigeria. *The Wall Street Journal*. February 2.
16 www.shell.com.ng/media/nigeria-reports-and-publications-briefing-notes/secur ity-theft-and-sabotage/_jcr_content/par/toptasks_426262614.stream/ 1554121799010/f607e15fb5a85f30c73aaede68c66dcee23d42cb/security-theft-sabo tage-spills-2019.pdf
17 www.shell.com.ng/media/nigeria-reports-and-publications-briefing-notes/ogoni land/_jcr_content/par/toptasks.stream/1554121806240/04a670487c5772cf45552 c604abb613035dd5515/ogoniland-2019.pdf
18 http://news.bbc.co.uk/onthisday/hi/dates/stories/november/10/newsid_ 2539000/2539561.stm
19 Paul Lewis. 1996. Blood and Oil: A Special Report; After Nigeria Represses, Shell Defends Its Record. *The New York Times*. February 13.
20 http://news.bbc.co.uk/onthisday/hi/dates/stories/november/10/newsid_ 2539000/2539561.stm
21 Kelly Gilblom. 2018. Shell Tries to Come Clean on Its Dirty Past in Nigeria. *Bloomberg Businessweek*. September 27.
22 Kelly Gilblom. 2018. Shell Tries to Come Clean on Its Dirty Past in Nigeria. *Bloomberg Businessweek*. September 27.
23 Kelly Gilblom, Jonathan Browning and Chiara Albanese. 2019. Shell, Eni Officials Named in $1 Billion Nigeria Lawsuit. *Bloomberg Businessweek*. May 7.
24 Kelly Gilblom, Jonathan Browning and Chiara Albanese. 2019. Shell, Eni Officials Named in $1 Billion Nigeria Lawsuit. *Bloomberg Businessweek*. May 7.
25 Kelly Gilblom, Jonathan Browning and Chiara Albanese. 2019. Shell, Eni Officials Named in $1 Billion Nigeria Lawsuit. *Bloomberg Businessweek*. May 7.
26 Musikilu Mojeed and Leslie Kaufman. 2011. Oil Spill Moves toward Nigerian Coast. *The New York Times*. December 22.
27 www.amnesty.org/en/latest/news/2018/03/nigeria-amnesty-activists-uncover-ser ious-negligence-by-oil-giants-shell-and-eni/
28 www.shell.com.ng/media/nigeria-reports-and-publications-briefing-notes/secur ity-theft-and-sabotage/_jcr_content/par/toptasks_426262614.stream/ 1554121799010/f607e15fb5a85f30c73aaede68c66dcee23d42cb/security-theft-sabo tage-spills-2019.pdf
29 Kelly Gilblom. 2018. Shell Tries to Come Clean on Its Dirty Past in Nigeria. *Bloomberg Businessweek*. September 27.

Electronic products and cobalt mining in Congo

The Democratic Republic of Congo (DRC) is Africa's largest producer of copper and the world's largest source of cobalt. In 2017, the DRC produced 199.1 million pounds of cobalt. Despite these abundant natural resources, two-thirds of the total population of approximately 80 million people survive on less than $2 a day. The annual budget for the country has never been larger than $10 billion. The average life expectancy in the DRC is approximately 60 years of age. In 2015, the DRC ranked 176th out of 188 countries in the United Nations' Human Development Index. It is also ranked as having an extremely high level of corruption measure in a ranking done by the NGO, Transparency International.[1,2,3]

DRC is a country that has been inflicted with the "resource curse." The resource curse is based on the paradox of a country having an abundance of natural resources without improving the standard of living of its citizens. The common explanation for this phenomenon is that the revenue obtained from extracting the raw materials is mismanaged and/or embezzled by government officials. The focus on the revenue generating natural resource may crowd out domestic and foreign investments in other parts of the country, resulting in goods and services being more expensive. Furthermore, the country's fiscal and economic fate is based on the volatile pricing of the natural resources in the marketplace.[4]

Cobalt is a major component of lithium-ion rechargeable batteries. It is used in numerous devices like smartphones, laptop computers, and electric vehicles. In addition, new technology is being developed using super-sized rechargeable batteries to store electricity that is generated from solar and wind sources.[5]

Under current technology, each electric vehicle battery requires 18 pounds of cobalt, over 1,000 times more than the quarter ounce of cobalt needed in a smartphone. Therefore, as production and demand for electric vehicles increases rapidly, so does the demand for cobalt. From 2018 to 2025, the estimated demand for cobalt for just lithium-ion batteries is expected to triple and then double again by 2030. The 2030 estimated demand for cobalt for lithium-ion batteries is 357,000 tons annually, seven times the 2018 demand.[6]

Over 50 percent of the world's cobalt supply originates in the DRC, whose government estimates that 20 percent of the cobalt being exported comes from artisanal miners in the southern part of the country. Artisanal miners, called creuseurs, are small-scale miners who are not officially employed by a mining company. There are between 110,000 and 150,000 artisanal miners extracting cobalt in the DRC. The artisanal miners use basic tools and mine by hand to dig out rock from deep underground tunnels. Cobalt in the DRC is usually found in heterogenite ore but can be also found in other types of ore which contain copper.

The role of Amnesty International

Established in 1961, Amnesty International is a global NGO of over 7 million who seek countries where there are human rights violations. Amnesty International not only collects data related to alleged human rights violations, but it also lobbies government and companies trying to convince these organization to change their perspective regarding human rights.[7]

Amnesty International released a damning report on the cobalt mining industry in January 2016, titled *This Is What We Die For: Human Rights Abuses in The Democratic Republic of the Congo Power the Global Trade in Cobalt*. This report and the follow-up report, *Time to Recharge: Corporate Action and Inaction to Tackle Abuses in the Cobalt Supply Chain* in November 2017, exposed the horrendous human rights violations occurring in the cobalt mining industry in the DRC.

The human rights violations in cobalt mining in the DRC

The artisanal miners usually operate outside authorized mining zones and do not have the necessary protective or safety equipment like respirators, gloves, and protective shields for their faces. A major health issue due to the lack of safety equipment is that these miners are more likely to have chronic illnesses and serious and potentially fatal respiratory diseases due to the long-term exposure to toxic dust from metals found in the mining process.[8]

Chronic exposure to mining dust can result in "hard metal lung disease," which is a potentially fatal health condition. By inhaling cobalt dust, the miners may develop severe respiratory conditions such as respiratory sensitization, asthma, shortness of breath, and a reduction in the pulmonary function of their lungs. Cobalt dust can also cause skin irritation and dermatitis.

Artisanal mines dug by hand can extend for many meters underground without any structural support to prevent the tunnel from collapsing. In addition, the tunnels are poorly ventilated. The artisanal miners have many different methods of mining cobalt. At some mining sites the miners dig deep underground tunnels using chisels, mallets, and other hand tools. At other mining sites miners, including children, will dig for cobalt in discarded mine tailings from abandoned licensed mining operations.

The rocks containing the cobalt are collected without the owner's permission and then washed, sifted, and sorted in streams and lakes near the mine. Women and children are usually responsible for washing and sorting the rocks. Furthermore, women and children can be responsible for carrying extremely heavy sacks of cobalt, with the children carrying some sacks weighing up to 40 kilograms and the women carrying sacks up to 50 kilograms.[9]

Children mining and cobalt

Children as young as 7 years old are involved in mining cobalt in DRC. Children work alongside adult miners in tunnels and pick up mine tailings and sort and wash minerals before they are sold. Many of the children were forced into this hazardous work because their families could not afford to pay the fees needed to send them to school. Many families rely on the income from the children for the family's survival.

The DRC Child Protection Code of 2009 guarantees free and compulsory primary education for all children. However, the government of the DRC does not have the funding needed to offer free education. Therefore, schools must charge fees to the families to cover the costs of education. For example, the fees can be between $10 and $30 a month, which results in many parents not being able to afford to send their children to school.

There are allegations that the children have been beaten, extorted by security guards, and exploited by traders. The international standards for mining describe any mining by children under the age of 18 as the "worst form of child labor." Extortion occurs when an official demands illegal payment from both child and adult miners as a "tax" for each sack of ore that has been collected to get access to the mine sites. The children work up to 12 hours a day in the mines and would receive less than $2 a day for their intense manual labor. Children who went to school would also work in the mines on weekends and school holidays as well as before and after school. For those children who did not go to school, they would work at the mines all year round.[10]

In 2014, UNICEF estimated that approximately 40,000 boys and girls worked in the mines in the DRC with many of them working in cobalt mines. As with adults, the children do not have any protective gear when they are mining and work in very dangerous conditions in the mining process, including inhaling cobalt dust and working in extremely high temperatures.[11]

One former child miner stated that:

> It was a living hell ... As children we were exploited and worked in very dangerous situations. We saw things that no child should see. There was a culture of rape and violence. Girls often fell victim to rape, which as children we were powerless to prevent. Sometimes lives were lost for a few francs. No good can ever come from the mines and I'd like to see them all closed so no child has the same experience as me.[12]

Artisanal mining supply chain in the DRC

The traders will purchase the cobalt ore from the miners without asking any basic questions such as: Where did the ore come from? What are the conditions of the mine where the ore came from? Were children involved in the mining of this cobalt ore? The traders would then sell the cobalt ore to larger companies that supply the mineral smelters with cobalt, which is then processed and used in different industrial applications, including the manufacture of rechargeable batteries.[13] The majority of cobalt from DRC is shipped to China, where it is smelted, refined, and processed into chemical products used in the manufacture of rechargeable batteries.[14] The DRC supply chain for cobalt in shown in Figure 2.

Most of the cobalt reserves are found in the south-eastern provinces of the DRC. This part of the DRC is prone to violence because of government opposition groups and anti-governmental militia groups. These groups often approach mine managers to extort money from them in return for not attacking the mining operations. These "protection fees" are a valuable source of income for the groups in not only the mining operations but also the transportation routes to and from the mining operations. Once the cobalt has been mined, the cobalt moves through eastern and southern ports of Africa including Mozambique, South Africa, Zambia, and Zimbabwe.

Figure 2 The global supply chain for cobalt[15]

In 2016, 42 percent of the world's mined cobalt was used to make rechargeable batteries. Cobalt is extremely useful for rechargeable batteries since it has a higher energy density, allowing the batteries to last longer on a single charge. Because of its importance, the United States and the European Union have designated cobalt as a strategic metal. Both China and the United States have stockpiled an undisclosed amount of cobalt.[16] In 2018, the world's estimated future cobalt reserves are located in the DRC (49.3 percent), Australia (16.9 percent), Cuba (7.0 percent), Philippines (3.9 percent), Zambia (3.8 percent), and the rest of the world (19.1 percent).[17]

The DRC's new mining code

The DRC is one of the poorest countries in the world and has suffered through decades of civil wars. Many people in the DRC view mining as the best opportunity to make money for their livelihoods. The collapse of the largest state-owned mining company, Gécamines, in the 1990s created a chaotic marketplace of mining in the DRC. In addition, during the Second Congo War from 1998 to 2003, the president of the DRC encouraged ordinary people to start digging for themselves since the mining industry had collapsed in the country. As a result, the government established a mining code in 2002 to encourage foreign investment in the mining industry.[18]

The mining code encouraged foreign investments by offering a first come first served licensing system for mining exploration, a standardized tax system for the mining output, and a stabilization clause which guaranteed foreign investors that the current mining code provisions would apply for at least ten years after the permit had been granted by the government.

However, due to significant growth in mining since 2002, the DRC government decided it was time to make revisions to the code which would create more favorable conditions for the government.

In December 2017, mining companies in the DRC were urging the government not to implement the proposed new mining code for operations in the country. The mining companies wanted an opportunity to discuss the revisions with the government before being passed into law. The code required mining companies to pay royalties on copper, cobalt, and gold at 3.5 percent, a significant increase from the previous 2 percent. In addition, the DRC demanded that mining companies transfer 10 percent of their share of capital to the DRC for free. An additional 5 percent of the mining share capital must also be transferred to the DRC for free at each renewal of the mining permit. Every foreign-based mining company must have a local DRC partner who owns a minimum of 10 percent of the mining company's share capital. The stabilization clause was reduced from ten to five years, giving the government more flexibility in changing the conditions of mining in the DRC.

Any mining company must provide government authorities with a mitigation and rehabilitation plan which details the proposed measures taken to limit and correct any environmental damage caused by the mining process. Every company must also submit an environmental impact study and a draft environmental management plant which must include a description of the "greenfield" ecosystem and measures used to limit the negative environmental impact. Every company must also submit to government authorities a draft rehabilitation plan for the mining site after the operations have been completed.

In March 2018, the DRC adopted a new Mining Code replacing the previous code established in 2002. All the terms of the new mining code were immediately activated in the mining industry. After the mining code was passed, the DRC declared that cobalt was to be classified as a "strategic" mineral which has a royalty rate of 10 percent. The strategic designation is important for the DRC since cobalt revenue is seen as critical for supporting the economic, social, and industrial future of the DRC. Jean Nkunza, who is an advisor to the prime minister of DRC, stated that:

> We need to make enough money before we run out of these minerals so that is why they are strategic to the country … We have to make sure for the next 20 years we make money from these minerals because demand is going to be so high. It's going to continue to grow and we are not going to stop raising the royalties on these minerals.

The international mining companies warned that the new mining code will deter future foreign investments, but they have agreed to start negotiations with the DRC government over avenues available to implement the new requirements of the mining code.[19,20,21,22]

Will cobalt mining become the new blood diamonds?

There is an expectation that cobalt mining would become similar to conflict or blood diamonds. Change in the cobalt mining industry in the DRC will only occur if consumers and other stakeholders pressure the industry to change its operations. Tyler Gillard, a senior legal advisor to the Organization for Economic Cooperation and Development (OECD), stated that, "We have reached a tipping point where it's become more expensive not to abide by good standards … Companies see this as a major threat to brand value … Are consumers going to demand child-free, corruption-free electric vehicles? I think it is coming."

In response to the backlash related to cobalt mining in the DRC, Apple has identified every smelter providing cobalt to its supply chain. The smelters are audited by independent third parties. Apple announced that it would stop sourcing all cobalt from informal mines in the DRC, but it does not want to completely abandon using cobalt from the DRC. Apple stated that, "There are real challenges with artisanal mining of cobalt in the Democratic Republic of Congo ... But we believe deeply that walking away would do nothing to improve conditions for people or the environment."

Companies are also worried about future potential legal liabilities of using cobalt that could have been mined where there are human rights violations. In 2019, the London Metal Exchange (LME) implemented a new requirement for every company trading on the exchange that sources more than 25 percent of its metals from Congo's artisanal mines to have an independent audit done on its cobalt sources. Those companies that use sources that fail to meet human rights standards will be banned from trading on the LME.

Companies are also attempting to reduce their dependence on cobalt from the DRC by focusing on investing in new cobalt reserves in Australia, Papua New Guinea, Canada, and the United States. One danger is the dominance of China in processing cobalt. In 2018, it was estimated that China produced 80 percent of the world's production of cobalt sulfate, which is the compound used to make lithium-ion batteries. By 2020, China is projected to produce 56 percent of the world's lithium-ion batteries.

One option for companies is to decrease the amount of cobalt in its electric vehicle batteries from the current 10 percent to 5 percent or less. Companies such as Tesla and Volkswagen are investing in technologies that will produce cobalt-free batteries.[23]

Responsible Cobalt Initiative

Formed in November 2016, the Responsible Cobalt Initiative (RCI) is a partnership between the Chinese Chamber of Commerce for Metals, Minerals & Chemicals and the OECD. The voluntary initiative is designed to allow companies to undertake a collective action to address social and environmental risks in the cobalt supply chain. The companies who are members have agreed to work together with the coordination of the DRC government to ensure that there is agreement in aligning supply chain policies with the *OECD Due Diligence Guidance for Responsible Supply Chains of Minerals from Conflict-Affected and High-Risk Areas* and the *Chinese Due Diligence Guidelines for Responsible Mineral Supply Chains*. This agreement includes having transparency in the cobalt supply chain and improving supply chain governance. In addition, the initiative supports cooperation with various stakeholders including national and local governments and affected local communities. The group also strives to develop a common communication strategy to transfer information to its critical stakeholders. Original members of the RCI include Apple, Huawei, Samsung, and Sony. Additional companies that have joined the initiative include HP, Volvo, BMW, and Daimler.[24,25]

Questions for thought

1. Identify another country which has the resource curse. Explain the similarities and the differences in that country as compared to the DRC.

2. Do you think the DRC will be able to move beyond its resource curse?
3. Why is it not common knowledge for consumers to know that billions of electronic devices have cobalt in them?
4. What would be your idea to reduce the number of children working in the cobalt mines?
5. Who has the power in the cobalt mining industry in the DRC, the government or the mining companies? Explain your position.
6. Do you think it is a coincidence that the cobalt industry established the Responsible Cobalt Initiative (RCI) after the first Amnesty International report condemned its actions in the DRC?

Notes

1 William Clowes. 2017. Mining Companies Urge Top Congo Lawmakers to Block New Law. *Bloomberg BusinessWeek*. December 28.
2 https://eiti.org/democratic-republic-of-congo#-production
3 Vivienne Walt and Sebastian Meyer. 2018. Blood Sweat, and Batteries. *Fortune*. August 23.
4 Melissa Mittelman. 2017. The Resource Curse. *Bloomberg*. May 19.
5 www.amnesty.org/download/Documents/AFR6273952017ENGLISH.PDF
6 Vivienne Walt and Sebastian Meyer. 2018. Blood Sweat, and Batteries. *Fortune*. August 23.
7 www.amnesty.org/en/who-we-are/
8 www.amnesty.org/download/Documents/AFR6273952017ENGLISH.PDF
9 www.amnesty.org/download/Documents/AFR6231832016ENGLISH.PDF
10 www.amnesty.org/download/Documents/AFR6273952017ENGLISH.PDF
11 www.amnesty.org/download/Documents/AFR6231832016ENGLISH.PDF
12 James Gordon. 2019. Cobalt: The Dark Side of a Clean Future. *Raconteur*. June 4.
13 www.amnesty.org/download/Documents/AFR6273952017ENGLISH.PDF
14 www.amnesty.org/download/Documents/AFR6273952017ENGLISH.PDF
15 www.a2globalrisk.com/analysis/sub-saharan-africa/mapping-risks-cobalt-supply-chain/
16 www.a2globalrisk.com/analysis/sub-saharan-africa/mapping-risks-cobalt-supply-chain/
17 Vivienne Walt and Sebastian Meyer. 2018. Blood Sweat, and Batteries. *Fortune*. August 23.
18 www.amnesty.org/download/Documents/AFR6231832016ENGLISH.PDF
19 William Clowes. 2017. Mining Companies Urge Top Congo Lawmakers to Block New Law. *Bloomberg BusinessWeek*. December 28.
20 https://iclg.com/practice-areas/mining-laws-and-regulations/congo-d-r
21 https://politicsofpoverty.oxfamamerica.org/2018/04/understanding-drcs-new-mining-law-power-play-will-the-congolese-people-benefit/
22 Zandi Shabalala. 2018. Cobalt to be Declared a Strategic Mineral in Congo. *Reuters*. March 14.
23 Vivienne Walt and Sebastian Meyer. 2018. Blood Sweat, and Batteries. *Fortune*. August 23.
24 www.respect.international/responsible-cobalt-initiative-rci/
25 www.mining.com/web/chinese-battery-firms-join-responsible-cobalt-initiative/

Volkswagen emissions scandal

Introduction

In 2015, Volkswagen was the largest corporation in Germany with 600,000 employees globally and employed one out of every seven workers in Germany. Volkswagen started in 1945 when Adolf Hitler ordered the firm to develop the "people's car." Ferdinand Porsche, who later founded his own luxury sports car company of the same name, was commissioned by the Reich Association of the German Automobile Industry Commission to design the original Volkswagen Beetle.[1]

On September 18, 2015, the environmental watchdog agency of the US government, the Environmental Protection Agency (EPA), announced that Volkswagen allegedly illegally installed computer software into its diesel vehicles in order to manipulate the emission levels that were recorded to ensure the vehicles were not in violation of the Clean Air Act.

The EPA accused Volkswagen of designing software in which the full emissions control system would only be turned on when the vehicle was being tested for its level of emissions, which occurs when the vehicle is in a stationary position. If the vehicle is not in a stationary position, the full emissions control system would be turned off. It is beneficial for the full emissions control system to be turned off since it increased the power of the engine's attributes such as acceleration and torque. Therefore, Volkswagen was able to market the diesel vehicles as both environmentally friendly and powerful when the emissions control system was turned off.

When the full emissions control system was turned off, the EPA estimated that the vehicle could release up to 40 times the amount of N_2O that was allowed under the Clean Air Act. N_2O is an air pollutant that causes ozone and smog and has been connected with numerous respiratory problems in people who have been exposed to it. The announcement by the EPA was based on the initial investigation by the International Council of Clean Transportation (ICCT).[2]

The role of ICCT with the emissions scandal

ICCT is an NGO whose objective is to provide unbiased research, and technical and scientific analysis to environmental regulators. The ICCT's mission is to improve the environmental performance and energy efficiency of motorized vehicles used for roads, marine, and air transportation.[3]

The ICCT wanted to compare the emissions of vehicles sold in the United States with those sold in Europe since traditionally the EPA has more stringent air pollution standards then regulatory agencies in Europe. Therefore, the original objective of the experiment was to demonstrate that the United States had more stringent emission standards, which would result in pressuring the European regulators to increase their emissions standards. The ICCT had partnered with researchers from West Virginia University in testing the emissions of the vehicles. The ICCT also received support from the California Air Resources Board (CARB), which had a specially designed research facility that could measure the emissions of the vehicles.[4]

ICCT found emissions results that did not match what Volkswagen was claiming to be the total emissions released by their diesel vehicles. The ICCT tested three vehicles: Volkswagen Jetta and Passat, and the BMW X5. The Volkswagen Jetta exceeded the EPA N_2O emissions standards by 15 to 35 times and the Volkswagen Passat was 5 to 20 times higher than the EPA standards.

The BMW was generally at or below the standard with the only exception occurring during a rural uphill operating condition. The head of the ICCT program, John German stated that:

> The huge discrepancy in real-world performance among these vehicles makes it clear that without vigilant enforcement of air pollution laws, companies that comply with the standards will be placed at a competitive disadvantage. If left unchecked that could undermine the whole regulatory framework. That's why the actions by EPA and CARB are so important.[5]

The ICCT informed the EPA of the emissions test results on the Volkswagen vehicles. The EPA did additional tests and determined that there was software in the vehicles that would shut down the emissions control systems and ordered a recall of all four-cylinder Volkswagen and Audi vehicles from 2009 to 2015.

The crisis starts for Volkswagen

Two days after the announcement from the EPA, Volkswagen announced that it would stop all sales of its four-cylinder TDI diesel engine vehicles in the United States which had been marketed to consumers as being "clean diesel." It was revealed that the software did not only determine if the vehicles were in stationary positions but would also determine the position of the steering wheel and the speed of the vehicle since those variables are standardized when a vehicle is evaluated for its emissions. Based on these factors, the software emissions control system would be turned on to reduce the level of N_2O.

On September 21, 2015, the US Department of Justice announced that they had started a criminal investigation into Volkswagen's manipulating software. During the same day, it was disclosed that Volkswagen had lied to environmental regulators for over a year by claiming that the differences between previous emissions testing in a laboratory and the open road emission testing were due to technical errors. Volkswagen finally admitted to the tampering only after the EPA had threatened the company with withholding approval for its 2016 Volkswagen and Audi models.

The following day on September 22, 2015, Volkswagen admitted that up to 11 million vehicles globally had the illegal software installed to manipulate the emissions levels and it would allocate $7.27 billion in order to resolve the crisis. On September 23, 2015, Volkswagen's CEO Martin Winterkorn resigned and said that he would "accept responsibility ... [for the] ... irregularities that have been found in diesel engines ... I am shocked by the events of the past few days ... [and] ... Above all, I am stunned that misconduct on such a scale was possible in the Volkswagen Group." The executive board of Volkswagen stated that Winterkorn had "no knowledge of manipulation of the emissions data."[6]

Winterkorn had been instrumental in the rapid growth of Volkswagen in the United States. In 2008, he told executives of the Volkswagen US operations that he wanted the growth to triple in ten years and set a goal of selling 800,000 vehicles in the United States by 2018. Winterkorn had expected a large percent of that forecasted growth would be based on higher volumes of diesel engine vehicles.[7]

On September 25, 2015, Volkswagen announced that Matthias Muller, the head of Porsche, would take over as CEO. Despite replacing Winterkorn with a Volkswagen insider, Mr. Muller claimed that he would change Volkswagen's management structure and stated that, "The same thing must never happen again." Muller also proclaimed that decision making at Volkswagen would become more decentralized and that each individual brand would have more independence in developing and implementing its strategic focus.[8]

By October 5, 2015, the investigation of the emissions scandal focused on two top Volkswagen engineers, Ulrich Hackenberg, who was Audi's chief engineer, and Wolfgang Hatz, who developed Porsche's Formula One and Le Mans racing engines. The two engineers were in charge of research and development after Martin Winterkorn became Volkswagen's CEO in January 2007.[9]

It was reported that the emissions tampering started in 2008 due to the failure of Volkswagen to design an environmentally friendly diesel engine for the US market that met the EPA emissions standards. Volkswagen had spent several years developing a "cleaner" diesel engine named EA 189 for both the 1.6- and 2.0-liter versions, which was targeted to be used in not only the Volkswagen brand but also other vehicles in the Volkswagen group including Audi, Skoda, and SEAT. The EA 189 was going to be positioned as a clean diesel alternative in Volkswagen's marketing campaign globally.

Volkswagen was going to present this engine as an environmentally friendly alternative where consumers would also have high mileage per gallon and would not sacrifice the level of power of the engine. However, the EA 189 did not meet the EPA standards for pollution emissions. This was the second failed attempt by Volkswagen to produce an environmentally friendly diesel engine. Prior to the EA 189, Volkswagen had formed a partnership with Daimler who makes Mercedes-Benz to develop emissions reduction technology for its vehicles. This alternative technology was considered to be too expensive. Volkswagen abandoned the project in 2007 and decided to focus on developing its own proprietary "clean" diesel engine. Therefore, based on the two unsuccessful attempts of developing a diesel engine that would pass the EPA emissions regulations, Volkswagen decided to create an illegal shortcut by developing software to create the appearance of a clean diesel engine.[10]

By October 7, 2015, the emission scandal would entrap more top executives at Volkswagen. It was revealed that the head of Volkswagen's North American operations, Michael Horn, had been aware of the emissions problems since the spring of 2014. Horn had been told that there was a possible emissions noncompliance with the diesel vehicles sold in the United States. It was later revealed on the following day that Volkswagen had installed a second type of software in order to manipulate the emissions levels. When this disclosure was made to the public, the response from Volkswagen was that the additional software was both disclosed and approved by the EPA.

The justification of the installation for the second software by Volkswagen was based on EPA regulations which allowed automobile manufacturers to install auxiliary emissions control devices in their vehicles if they have informed and negotiated with the EPA when the vehicles have to climb steep hills or perform in very cold weather. Michael Jorn resigned from his position as the head of Volkswagen North American operations on March 9, 2016. Horn had admitted that he was aware of the emission manipulation in 2014.[11]

Realizing that it had to be proactive in addressing the emissions scandal, on October 13, 2015, Volkswagen announced that it would adopt the technology that it had partnered with Daimler and rejected in 2007. Volkswagen was committed to adopting the selective catalytic reduction (SCR) system which uses a urea-based liquid to neutralize the N_2O emissions. With this technology, a tank of fluid called AdBlue would be installed in the car and AdBlue would be added through the new emissions filtration system of the vehicle. The problems with the SCR system was that it increased the cost of the vehicle, it added more weight to the vehicle, and it took up more space than other emissions control systems. The problem with the amount of space needed was amplified in Volkswagen's smaller vehicles such as the Golf and Jetta, which were the largest selling vehicles in the United States. In addition, in the United States, vehicle owners are not allowed to refill the tank with AdBlue and, therefore, are required to take the vehicle to either the dealership or to a vehicle repair center.[12]

The results of Volkswagen's internal investigation

The results of an internal investigation made by Volkswagen concluded that the emissions scandal was the result a "chain of mistakes" based on

Volkswagen's aggressive growth goals for diesel vehicles in the United States and a "culture of tolerance" that allowed short cuts and rules' violations in order to accomplish those aggressive goals. Volkswagen admitted that the engineers did add the illegal software when it was determined that the diesel engines would not meet the EPA regulations on emissions due to the budget and time allocated to develop the new engine. The internal investigation also concluded that only a small group of employees were involved in the scandal and that members of the executive board or supervisory board were not involved in the emissions manipulation.[13]

The legal ramifications of the emissions scandal for Volkswagen

On September 22, 2015, Volkswagen announced that it would allocate $7.27 billion to resolve the legal issues of emissions manipulation for up to 11 million vehicles.

In March 2016, the Federal Trade Commission (FTC) filed a complaint against Volkswagen for misrepresenting its diesel vehicles as being more environmentally friendly than its competitors. In the complaint, the FTC stated that Volkswagen had claimed that its diesel vehicles had incorrectly reduced N_2O emissions by 90 percent. In fact, the diesel engines were generating N_2O levels that were up to 4,000 percent higher than the EPA standards.

Due to the increasing complexity and expanding legal issues, Volkswagen revised the amount reserved to resolve the scandal to $18 billion in April 2016. Part of this cost would be the result of Volkswagen either fixing or buying back all the tainted diesel vehicles sold in the United States, approximately 475,000 vehicles.

On June 27, 2016, Volkswagen announced that it had agreed to pay up to $14.7 billion in order to settle civil lawsuits related to the emissions scandal in the United States. Of the $14.7 billion, $10 billion was allocated to buy back the 475,000 vehicles sold to US customers. The other $4.7 billion would be given as cash compensation to the vehicle owners. Volkswagen also agreed to pay the EPA $2.7 billion to compensate for the negative environmental impact of the diesel vehicles and Volkswagen agreed to invest $2 billion in future technology projects related to cleaner vehicles.[14]

By September 8, 2018, the estimated costs of the emissions scandal had reached 30 billion euros ($35 billion). Over 4,000 shareholders were demanding Volkswagen pay them 9 billion euros in compensation since Volkswagen had failed to warn the shareholders of the scandal and the subsequent negative impact on Volkswagen's stock price.[15]

The legacy of the emissions scandal

On December 6, 2017, a former Volkswagen executive in Michigan, Oliver Schmidt, was sentenced to seven years in prison and fined $400,000 for his role in the diesel emissions scandal. Schmidt had pled guilty to conspiracy to defraud the US government and for violating the Clean Air Act. Schmidt was appointed the general manager of Volkswagen's engineering and environmental office in Auburn Hills, Michigan in 2013. Schmidt's responsibilities included being Volkswagen's representative for the federal and California regulatory agencies related to environmental issues, including emissions. A German citizen, Schmidt had been transferred back to Germany and came to the United States for a vacation and was arrested while waiting for his flight back to Germany at the Miami airport.[16] This was fortunate for US prosecutors since Germany does not extradite its citizens for criminal prosecution in another country.[17]

In May 2018, the US Department of Justice indicted former Volkswagen CEO Martin Winterkorn and several other Volkswagen executives with conspiracy to manipulate the emissions levels to evade compliance with federal pollution standards.

In March 2019, the US Securities and Exchange Commission (SEC) sued Volkswagen for defrauding US investors since Martin Winterkorn had been aware of the emissions fraud since November 2007.

Martin Winterkorn was charged with fraud by German prosecutors on April 15, 2019. Winterkorn along with four other Volkswagen managers were linked to the starting point of the emissions scandal in 2006. At this point, Volkswagen had paid $33 billion in fines and settlements, but it was still facing additional legal issues and investigations from authorities in both Germany and the United States.

The specific charges against the five employees included breach of trust, tax evasion, and false certification. Winterkorn could serve up to ten years in prison if he is convicted of the charges. Winterkorn is alleged to have concealed the emissions fraud even after Volkswagen knew that external parties were investigating Volkswagen's false emissions claims. Winterkorn is also accused of approving a software update at a cost of 23 million euros ($26 billion) which he knew was useless in eliminating the emissions problem. In the indictment of Winterkorn, it was identified that over 9 million cars were subjected to the emissions manipulation software licensed in Europe and the United States. German prosecutors are also demanding that Winterkorn return nearly $12 million in salary and bonuses.[18,19]

On July 31, 2019, the former CEO of Volkswagen's Audi division, Rupert Stadler, was charged with fraud for his role in the diesel emissions scandal. Stadler along with three other executives were accused of developing the illegal emissions software that was used by Volkswagen, Audi, and Porsche. The four executives were charged with falsifying certificates and providing illegal advertising for the diesel vehicles. German prosecutors had alleged that Stadler had known about the emissions manipulation at least since September 2015 and continued to allow the cars to be sold with the illegal software.[20]

Questions for thought

1. How does a company like Volkswagen commit such unethical and illegal acts?
2. Do you think there is permanent reputational damage to Volkswagen because of this scandal?
3. Why do you think Volkswagen thought they would never be caught manipulating the emissions tests?
4. How widespread do you think the knowledge of this manipulation was within Volkswagen?
5. If you think it was widespread, why didn't someone within Volkswagen become a whistleblower and inform the EPA and the media?
6. Evaluate how this scandal has impacted Volkswagen's five most critical stakeholders.

Notes

1 William Boston. 2015. Volkswagen CEO Resigns as Car Maker Race to Stem Emissions Scandal. *The Wall Street Journal*. September 23.
2 Peter Stanwick and Sarah Stanwick. 2017. Volkswagen Emissions Scandal: The Perils of Installing Illegal Software. *International Review of Management and Business Research*. 6(1): 18–24.
3 https://theicct.org/mission-history
4 Peter Stanwick and Sarah Stanwick. 2017. Volkswagen Emissions Scandal: The Perils of Installing Illegal Software. *International Review of Management and Business Research*. 6(1): 18–24.
5 https://theicct.org/news/epas-notice-violation-clean-air-act-volkswagen-press-statement
6 William Boston. 2015. Volkswagen CEO Resigns as Car Maker Race to Stem Emissions Scandal. *The Wall Street Journal*. September 23.
7 William Boston 2015. Volkswagen Emissions Investigation Zeroes In on Two Engineers. *The Wall Street Journal*. October 5.
8 Jack Ewing and Bill Vlasic. 2015. Volkswagen Names Matthias Muller, and Insider, as Chief Executive. *The New York Times*. September 25.
9 William Boston 2015. Volkswagen Emissions Investigation Zeroes In on Two Engineers. *The Wall Street Journal*. October 5.
10 Peter Stanwick and Sarah Stanwick. 2017. Volkswagen Emissions Scandal: The Perils of Installing Illegal Software. *International Review of Management and Business Research*. 6(1): 18–24.
11 Peter Stanwick and Sarah Stanwick. 2017. Volkswagen Emissions Scandal: The Perils of Installing Illegal Software. *International Review of Management and Business Research*. 6(1): 18–24.
12 Peter Stanwick and Sarah Stanwick. 2017. Volkswagen Emissions Scandal: The Perils of Installing Illegal Software. *International Review of Management and Business Research*. 6(1): 18–24.
13 William Boston, Hendrik Varnholt and Sarah Sloat. 2015. Volkswagen Blames 'Chain of Mistakes' for Emissions Scandal. *The Wall Street Journal*. December 10.
14 Peter Stanwick and Sarah Stanwick. 2017. Volkswagen Emissions Scandal: The Perils of Installing Illegal Software. *International Review of Management and Business Research*. 6(1): 18–24.

15 Bloomberg. 2018. VW Fights Investors as Diesel-Scandal Cost Could Top $35 Billion. *Fortune.* September 8.

16 Bill Vlasic. 2017. Volkswagen Official Gets 7-Year Term in Diesel-Emissions Cheating. *The New York Times.* December 6.

17 William Boston. 2019. Volkswagen Ex-CEO Faces Fresh Fraud Charges Over Emissions Scandal. *The Wall Street Journal.* April 15.

18 Christopher F. Schuetze. 2019. Former VW C.E.O. Martin Winterkorn Is Charged by Germany in Diesel Scheme. *The New York Times.* April 15.

19 William Boston. 2019. Volkswagen Ex-CEO Faces Fresh Fraud Charges Over Emissions Scandal. *The Wall Street Journal.* April 15.

20 Melissa Eddy. 2019. Rupert Stadler, Ex-Audi Chief, Is Charged With Fraud in Diesel Scandal. *The New York Times.* July 31.

Global outsourcing of Nike

When Nike was founded in 1964, 4 percent of footwear sold in the United States was imported. By 2014, that percentage had jumped to 98 percent with Nike being a major adopter of an outsourcing strategy related to manufacturing footwear.[1]

The underlying philosophy for Nike's founder, Philip Knight, was to change the supply chain to reduce costs and increase efficiencies. Knight, who was both a track enthusiast and accountant, had observed the success of Japanese camera manufacturers gaining market share at the expense of higher priced German-made cameras. Knight realized that this type of shifting of manufacturing location to a lower labor cost country could also be very beneficial in the footwear industry where the major competitors were the German brands of Adidas and Puma.

The manufacturing of athletic shoes has a high level of labor intensity in which rubber, leather, and plastic are used to make the shoes. The rubber of the shoes is initially mixed with chemicals and color pigments based on the shoe's design. The rubber is then rolled and pressed into flat sheets, which are cut into the outer sole of the shoes. The middle sole on which the foot rests is composed of polyurethane or ethylene-vinyl acetate and mixed with different chemicals and color pigments. It is then pressed into sheets and cut into the form of the shoe. Once the outer and mid soles have been cut, they are glued together to form a complete sole unit. The upper sole is composed of different parts of leather or plastic and are sewn together. The upper sole is then joined to the sole unit using glue and air pressure, which results in the formation of a complete shoe. A majority of the manufacturing process is done manually with very low levels of automation.

Nike had operated small manufacturing plants in New Hampshire and Maine but started outsourcing its production to factories in Taiwan and South Korea. To ensure high quality, Nike developed good relationships with the factory owners in Asia and posted technicians at the factory sites to be able to collaborate with local managers. This gave Nike the ability to check the quality of the shoes before they were shipped from the factories to be sold globally.

Nike's initial promise for its outsourced workers

In 1992, Nike released a memorandum of understanding with its outsourced suppliers. There are seven points to the memorandum. The first point is *Government Regulation and Business*. Nike demands certification from all suppliers that they are in compliance with all applicable local labor government regulations including: minimum wage, amount and payment of overtime, ensuring child labor is not used, provisions for pregnancy, allowing the workers to not work during vacations and holidays, and mandatory retirement benefits.

The second point refers to employee *Safety and Health*. The supplier certifies that it is in compliance with all applicable laws and regulations regarding occupational health and safety. The third point refers to *Worker Insurance*. Nike requires the supplier to certify compliance with all applicable laws and regulations related to providing health insurance, life insurance, and workers' compensations. The fourth point refers to the use of *Forced Labor*. The supplier is required to certify that the supplier and its suppliers do not use any form of forced labor.

The fifth point refers to the suppliers' commitment to the *Environment*. The supplier certifies that it is in compliance with all applicable laws and regulations and adheres to the environmental practices at Nike, including the prohibition on the use of chloro-fluoro carbons (CFCs). The sixth point refers to *Equal Opportunity*. The supplier certifies that it does not discriminate against any individual in hiring, salary, benefits, career advancement, firing, or retirement based on gender, race, religion, age, sexual orientation, or ethnic origin. The seventh and final point refers to supplier *Documentation and Inspection*. The supplier agrees to create and maintain any documentation needed to verify compliance with the previous six points and agrees to supply the documents to Nike upon request.[2]

The lack of compliance with the Nike promise

An internal inspection investigation by Ernst & Young in 1997 found numerous worker violations in one of Nike's outsourced factories in Vietnam. The factory employed 9,200 workers and produced 400,000 pairs of athletic shoes monthly. The report highlighted that workers in a factory near Ho Chi Minh city were in a working environment where the exposure to carcinogens exceeded the local legal standards by 177 times in certain sections of the plant. In addition, 77 percent of the workers in the factory had experienced respiratory problems.

The workers were also forced to work 65 hours a week, which is higher than is allowed in Vietnam, and the workers were only paid $10 a week. The young female workers, most younger than 25, worked 10½ hours daily six days a week. The workers who had skin or breathing problems from absorbing the chemicals in the air were not transferred to areas of the factory which did not have chemicals. In addition, the employees who worked with dangerous chemicals did not wear protective masks or gloves. Furthermore, the dust level in the mixing room was 11 times the local health and safety standard.

When the information from the investigation was released to the public by *The New York Times*, Nike spokesman Vada Manger commented that, "We believe that we look after the interests of our workers ... There's a growing body of documentation that indicates that Nike workers earn superior wages and manufacture products under superior conditions."[3]

Despite the lofty points of the Memorandum and the results of the factory investigation by Ernst & Young, Phil Knight admitted in 1998 that Nike's suppliers were not following the certified actions that Nike had demanded of them for them to continue as suppliers. Nike was facing a backlash from various stakeholders for not monitoring the actions of its suppliers and promised that suppliers would not use underage workers in the future, neither would the suppliers be allowed to deviate from the health and safety standards required by Nike.

Phil Knight also announced that stakeholders from labor and human rights groups would be allowed to join independent auditors who inspected the Asian factories. These stakeholders would also be allowed to interview the workers and be able to assess the working conditions of the workers. Knight announced that the minimum age for hiring new workers at the shoe factories would be 18 and the minimum age of new workers at other factories would be 16. It is common practice for factory owners to hire children as young as 14 to work in textile plants that do not produce shoes. The distinction is based on footwear factories being inherently more dangerous due to the use of heavy machinery and the use of dangerous raw materials, including chemicals and solvents which can release toxins into the air. Knight announced that the factories must face the same air-quality standards as have been established by the US Occupational Safety and Health Administration (OSHA).

In a speech to the National Press Club, Knight stated that, "We believe that these are practices which the conscientious, good companies will follow in the twenty-first century ... These moves do more than just set industry standards, they reflect who we are as a company." However, Knight did not mention any new policy related to the wage rate paid to the workers. In 1998, Nike's suppliers paid Chinese and Vietnamese workers less than $2 a day while the rate was less than $1 a day in Indonesia. It is estimated that these workers needed to be paid at least $3 a day to be able to have sustainable living conditions. Nike's response was that the factories in Indonesia and Vietnam were paying the legal minimum wage rate for that country.

However, Knight did acknowledge that Nike's reputation and image have been damaged by its past relationship with its Asian supplier. "The Nike product has become synonymous with slave wages, forced overtime and arbitrary abuse ... I truly believe that the American consumer does not want to buy products made in abusive conditions."

In order to try to ensure that these conditions do not occur in the future, Knight said that Nike would become more diligent with the monitoring system in evaluating the working conditions of the factories:

> Independent monitoring is a critical element of an overall system of improving labor practices ... Nike's goal is to reach a point where labor practices can be tested and verified in much the same manner that

financial audits determine a company's compliance with generally accepted accounting principles.[4]

The strategic shift of Nike's outsourcing strategy

The traditional relationship between Nike and its suppliers has been transactional in nature. The supplier's performance is based solely on the supplier's performance on price, quality, and delivery. As a result, the supplier's commitment to corporate sustainability issues was not relevant in the decision-making process for which suppliers would be selected by Nike. The suppliers were forced to use a global low-cost strategy in which they would be willing to match other suppliers based on pricing. Therefore, suppliers would be encouraged to "cheat" on adopting strong corporate sustainability initiatives since price was driving the contract agreements. The initial relationship between Nike and its suppliers is shown in Figure 3.

Under Nike's traditional outsourcing process, there are three types of independently owned and operated factories, which are: developed partners, volume producers, and developing sources.

Developed partners

Nike has the most sophisticated relationship with its developed partners. These suppliers have advanced levels of technology and the factories produce the newest and the most expensive "statement" products which are the primary focus of Nike's marketing campaigns. These products are the most desirable by the consumers and Nike is able to generate high profit margins

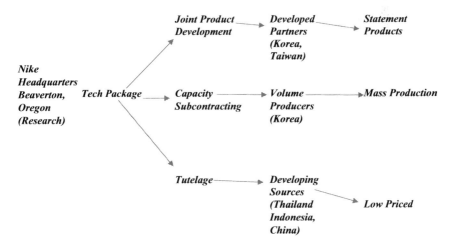

Figure 3 Nike's traditional relationship with its suppliers[5]

due to the premium price of these products. While technology information is sent from Nike's headquarters, developed partners are also actively involved in the joint development of these new products. Developed partners either have an exclusive relationship with Nike or limit its production to a few buyers.

Volume producers

Volume producers focus on the mass production of Nike products. These products are not the newest but are the stable line of products in which demand is consistent from year to year. The factories for the volume producers are large in size with capacity between 70,000 and 85,000 pairs of shoes daily. This production level is five times the level of products produced by developed partners' factories. Most of the volume producers are owned by Korean firms and they can engage in capacity subcontracting. Capacity subcontracting occurs when the production level of the developed partners is at 100 percent and the developed partners will contract out the excess production demand to the volume producers to satisfy the overall demand for the product. Volume producers do not have an exclusive agreement with Nike and can have as many as ten buyers.

Developed sources

Suppliers who are developed sources are usually located in Thailand, Indonesia, and China. These factories have only rudimentary manufacturing skills and Nike helps the factory owners in improving their operations through Nike's guidance or tutelage. It is through this assistance that Nike hopes that the developed sources would be able to become developed partners in the future.

This system gave Nike absolute power in controlling the pricing of the manufacturing of its products by having factories compete against each other to gain Nike as a buyer. Nike would look at what the firm could offer based on product performance and price standards only. This arm's length transactional relationship ensured the failure of the supplier complying with all the terms of the Code of Conduct since the supplier was not rewarded for compliance with corporate sustainability but was rewarded for financial performance metrics. Therefore, consistent downward pressure on pricing also forced the factory owners to ignore the impact this pressure had on its employees.

The limitations of this production model were highlighted in the late 1990s when various stakeholders identified the poor working conditions in the factories producing Nike products.

It is through this external pressure from Nike's stakeholders, including labor groups and the media, that Phil Knight responded in 1998 with the fundamental change on how Nike would view corporate sustainability and its relationship with its suppliers.

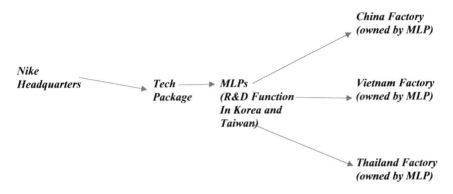

Figure 4 Nike's corporate sustainability embedded relationship with suppliers[6]

Nike realized that for suppliers to embrace its Code of Conduct, the suppliers must be viewed as partners that are incentivized and rewarded for the relationship. The new future relationship between Nike and its suppliers is shown in Figure 4.

In this model, the suppliers are not viewed as a transactional relationship, but are viewed as Manufacturing Leadership Partners (MLPs). This is a fundamentally different relationship since collaboration instead of price competitiveness is the criteria for the selection of Nike's suppliers. This collaboration fosters a high level of interdependence based on goodwill and trust. The interdependence and trust are evident since in this model the MLPs are involved in not only the R&D with Nike but also have ownership in the manufacturing factories.

The synergy created with this relationship includes having one MLP develop a more efficient step in the manufacturing process and sharing that information with the other MLPs. This sharing of information is not possible under the traditional model where there is no interconnectedness among the manufacturing facilities.

Therefore, since the relationship between Nike and the suppliers has become highly independent and long term in focus, Nike is able to demand and expect the suppliers to be completely in compliance with its Code of Conduct. What was potentially considered an afterthought in the traditional model, now became a main component of the criteria used to select and maintain suppliers for Nike.[7]

Still some challenges with suppliers' commitment to Nike's Code of Conduct

In 2016, the Worker Rights Consortium (WRC) released a summary of its investigation of a Nike factory in Hansae, Vietnam. This NGO found that the factory was in flagrant violation of the standards that Nike had established in 1992 and reconfirmed in 1998. WRC found that there were reckless management practices which resulted in endangering the health of the workers.

These practices including enforcing extremely high production quotas, relentless pressure on the employees to work faster, insufficient rest breaks, and excessive heat in the factory building. The excessive heat resulted in a significant number of workers fainting from heat exhaustion at their workstations. WRC also found that the factory managers would verbally harass the workers through yelling, swearing, and insults, as well as physical harassment. The factory managers also restricted the workers' access to the toilets. The factory managers denied legally guaranteed sick leave, forced overtime, and fired pregnant workers.

There were also examples of the factory owners not paying the workers the full amount of money owed based on hours worked. The factory owners charged the worker an illegal recruitment fee and actively extorted money from the workers. The factory owners would also appoint the factory managers to oversee the factory's labor union.[8,9]

Due to the stakeholder pressure of having this information, the Korean parent company of the factory owner signed a memorandum of understanding with the WRC agreeing to address the labor rights violations highlighted in the investigation. The agreement included the reinstatement of all women workers who were fired because they were pregnant; the reinstatement of other workers who were wrongly dismissed; an agreement to reduce the temperature in the factory to acceptable standards; the payment of $750,000 to the workers for underpaying and not paying the required amount for overtime; and the removal of factory managers as heads of the factory union.[10]

Nike's current outsourcing performance

As of February 2019, Nike has over 1,086,000 contract factory workers globally manufacturing its finished goods. Nike has suppliers in 41 countries and 525 factories that make Nike products. Nike also has suppliers for its raw materials in 11 countries and 76 facilities.[11]

Nike, along with the Fair Labor Association (FLA) and Better Work, which is a joint program of the International Labour Organization (ILO) and the International Finance Corporation (IFC), performed 471 audits of its supplier factories and found zero violations of the use of child labor. Nike increased the number of unannounced audits and the use of third-party auditors in 2018 from the previous levels in 2017.

Nike's 2018 Code of Conduct for its outsourced suppliers is much more detailed than its original memorandum of understanding from 1992. Nike's philosophy is based on not having a finish line for its standards with its suppliers, but only a clear starting line. The Code of Conduct puts forth the minimum acceptable standards for each factory Nike uses globally. Nike focuses on codes which support the unique vulnerabilities and needs of employees such as women, migrants, and temporary workers, and the factories need to strive to improve the welfare of the workers and the communities. Nike seeks and maintains relationships with factories that can demonstrate leadership in corporate responsibility and sustainability and who have developed agile and resilient management systems that foster a strong positive culture of support to the workers.[12] Nike breaks down the Code of Conduct into four major categories: respected, fair, safe, and sustainable.

Respected

Nike believes that employment is voluntary. The supplier must not use forced labor, which includes prison labor, indentured labor, bonded labor, or any other forms of forced labor. The employees must be at least 16 years of age and have completed compulsory education, or be above the legal working age in the country where the factory is located. Employees who are under the age of 18 are not allowed to be employed in hazardous conditions.

Nike forbids any type of discrimination of its workers including hiring, compensation, promotion, or discipline based on the worker's gender, race, religion, age disability, sexual orientation, pregnancy, marital status, nationality, political opinion, trade union affiliation, social or ethnic origin. In addition, women and men workers should receive equal pay for work of equal value. Nike also requires the suppliers to recognize and respect the worker's right of freedom of association and collective bargaining.

Fair

The workers should not be subject to physical, sexual, psychological, or verbal harassment or abuse. In addition, the working hours for the employees should not be excessive. The suppliers are not allowed to require the workers to work more than the regular and overtime hours allowed by the government's laws and regulations in the country of the factory location. The regular working week cannot be more than 48 hours and the suppliers must allow the workers at least 24 consecutive hours of rest in every seven-day period. The factory owners must receive consent from the workers for any overtime hours and suppliers cannot request overtime on an ongoing regular basis. All overtime must be paid at a premium rate to the worker and the combination of regular and overtime hours in a week must not exceed 60 hours unless there are extraordinary circumstances.

Safe

The factory owners must provide a safe work environment for workers and take a proactive stance to prevent accidents and injuries on the job. The supplier must also have monitoring systems in place to detect, avoid, and respond to potential risks to the safety of all its employees. All facilities operated by the suppliers including residential, dining, and childcare must be safe, hygienic, and healthy. All the facilities must abide by all government rules and regulations or the appropriate Nike standards for building construction and health and safety. The suppliers must also have safety management systems in order to reduce or eliminate safety and health risks. The supplier's building and load-bearing structures must be built in accordance with the government laws and regulations of the manufacturing country.

The suppliers must have fire prevention and emergency action plans to effectively protect workers during normal working operations and in emergency situations. The suppliers must also install alarm systems to notify workers of emergencies along with safe shelters and exit routes. In addition, the suppliers need to ensure that potential occupational health and hygiene hazards should be anticipated, recognized, and evaluated before the hazards impact the workers. This includes ensuring that the workers are not exposed to physical, chemical, or biological hazards that are above the occupational exposure limits.

Sustainable

Suppliers must appreciate the value of water by minimizing freshwater withdrawals and wastewater discharges in compliance with government rules and regulations, and Nike standards. The supplier must be a good steward of the water and strive to maximize the efficient use of water. The supplier must also minimize waste and handle all waste properly. The supplier is responsible for properly segregating, managing, transporting, and disposing of all solid and hazardous waste in compliance with government regulations and Nike standards. The supplier must also measure and continuously improve material efficiency and value added recycling. The suppliers are also responsible for finding cost-effective ways to improve energy efficiency and reduce the level of GHG emissions and increase the level of renewable energy sources.

The suppliers are also responsible for minimizing the impact on air emissions of volatile organic chemicals, aerosols, corrosives, particles, ozone depleting chemicals, and combustion based byproducts. The suppliers are also responsible for properly managing all chemicals in the manufacturing process through a comprehensive chemical management system. The system must be able to properly identify and mitigate chemical risks to workers, the environment, and consumers through proper handling, storage, procurement, and disposal of the chemicals.[13]

Nike classifies the performance of its suppliers based on color. If the factory is a global leader based on the conditions of Nike's Code of Conduct, it is considered to be a gold supplier. If the supplier exceeds the conditions of the Code of Conduct, it is classified as a silver supplier. If the supplier meets the baseline compliance with the Code of Conduct, it is classified as a bronze supplier. Suppliers that are inconsistent with their compliance with the Code of Conduct are classified as yellow suppliers and suppliers who fail to meet the conditions of the Code of Conduct are classified as red suppliers. Nike has set the goal for 100 percent of its suppliers to be classified as bronze or higher by 2020.

In a 2018 evaluation of the performance of its outsourced suppliers, Nike found that seven footwear factories (1 percent of all factories) exceeded the conditions of its Code of Conduct and were silver suppliers. Nike found that 92 percent of the suppliers were at a baseline compliance with its Code of Conduct and were classified as bronze suppliers. This included a total of 499 factories of which 113 factories were for footwear, 305 factories were for apparel, and 81 factories manufactured equipment. There were 12 inconsistent (2 percent) yellow suppliers, which consisted of 11 apparel manufacturers and 8 equipment manufacturers. Nike also found 23 unsuccessful (4 percent) or red suppliers. This included 4 footwear factories, 11 apparel factories, and 8 equipment factories.

The six highest areas of noncompliance by the suppliers based on the audits were: working hours (39 percent), wages and benefits (34 percent), regular employment (7 percent), forced labor risks (5 percent), harassment and abuse (3 percent), and discrimination (3 percent).

For those suppliers that are either yellow or red, any critical issues must be corrected immediately. The factory is also put on probation and if the factory continues to fail its compliance with the Code of Conduct, Nike will no longer do business with the factory. If Nike does exit the relationship with the suppliers, Nike will give early notice of the termination of the relationship and present the supplier with a ramp-down schedule.[14]

Questions for thought

1. Outsourcing of manufacturing is a common method for a global firm to use to reduce costs. Why is there controversy when a firm outsources its products?
2. Tariffs are used to increase the price of products produced in one country and sold in another country. Do you think tariffs are effective in reducing the level of outsourcing by global firms?
3. Why do you think Nike's suppliers continued to violate the working conditions after they agreed to Nike's memorandum of understanding in 1992?
4. Identify three critical stakeholders who were effective in putting pressure on Nike to change its philosophy related to outsourcing.
5. Why do you think Nike's suppliers had so few violations in 2018?

Notes

1 Hayley Peterson. 2014. One Stunning Stat That Shows How Nike Changed the Shoe Industry Forever. *Business Insider*. April 22.
2 Philip Rosenzweig. 1994. International Sourcing in Athletic Footwear: Nike and Reebok. *Harvard Business Publishing*. July 14.

3 Steven Greenhouse. 1997. Nike Shoe Plant in Vietnam Is Called Unsafe for Workers. *The New York Times*. November 8.
4 John H. Cushman Jr. 1998. Nike Pledges to End Child Labor and Apply U.S. Rules Abroad. *The New York Times*. May 13.
5 Suk-Jun Lim. 2007. Embedding CSR Values: The Global Footwear Industry's Evolving Governance Structure. *Journal of Business Ethics*. 81: 145.
6 Suk-Jun Lim. 2007. Embedding CSR Values: The Global Footwear Industry's Evolving Governance Structure. *Journal of Business Ethics*. 81: 148.
7 Suk-Jun Lim. 2007. Embedding CSR Values: The Global Footwear Industry's Evolving Governance Structure. *Journal of Business Ethics*. 81: 143–156.
8 www.workersrights.org/wp-content/uploads/2016/02/WRC-Assessment-of-Hansae-Vietnam-Nike.html
9 www.workersrights.org/wp-content/uploads/2016/02/New-WRC-Report-on-Hansae-Vietnam-Nike.html
10 www.workersrights.org/communications-to-affiliates/new-remediation-commitments-at-hansae-vietnam/
11 https://purpose.nike.com/sourcing-manufacturing-standards
12 *FY18 Nike Impact Report*.
13 Nike 2017 Code of Conduct.
14 *FY18 Nike Impact Report*.

Index